Standard Real Estate

Appraising Manual

Standard
Real Estate
Appraising Manual

Samuel T. Barash

Prentice-Hall, Inc.

Englewood Cliffs, New Jersey

Prentice-Hall International, Inc., *London*
Prentice-Hall of Australia, Pty., Ltd., *Sydney*
Prentice-Hall of Canada, Ltd., *Toronto*
Prentice-Hall of India Private Ltd., *New Delhi*
Prentice-Hall of Japan, Inc., *Tokyo*
Prentice-Hall of Southeast Asia, Pte., Ltd., *Singapore*
Whitehall Books, Ltd., *Wellington, New Zealand*

Library of Congress Cataloging in Publication Data

Barash, Samuel T
   Standard real estate appraising manual.

   Bibliography: p.
   Includes index.
   1. Real property--Valuation--Handbooks, manuals, etc.
I. Title.
HD1387.B374   333.3'32   78-12984
ISBN 0-13-842401-2

DEDICATION

Dedicated to the memory of Daniel Barash whose
parting words were, "Always have hope in the future."

Samuel T. Barash

Samuel T. Barash has been active in the real estate field since 1947. He served for 15 years with the New York office of the Veteran's Administration as a supervisory appraiser covering all of New York state except the Buffalo region. For seven years he was Chief appraiser for the Newark, New Jersey Loan Guarantee Office of the Veteran's Administration responsible for the entire state of New Jersey.

As a supervising appraiser Mr. Barash appraised personally and supervised the appraisals of more than 300 fee and staff appraisers averaging more than 12,000 appraisals per year to values in excess of 250 million dollars each year.

Mr. Barash has lectured on appraising techniques at colleges and government seminars and has been qualified as an expert witness in many courts. He is also the author of How to Reduce Your Real Estate Taxes, *Arco Publishing Company, Inc.*

Mr. Barash is a licensed real estate broker and conducts his appraising office in Monroe, N.Y. He holds a B.S.S. degree from the College of the City of New York and has done graduate work at New York University and Columbia University in real estate and allied studies.

How this book can help you

This real estate appraising manual includes everything you need to appraise quickly, correctly and professionally. It is a complete, modern manual based on decades of practical appraising experience. These standard, comprehensive appraisal techniques and procedures can be relied on to save valuable time and to help you accurately appraise dozens of different types of real estate.

During the past three decades, tens of millions of Americans have left our cities creating our present-day suburban-urban United States. Many new shelter types reflecting new ways of living have arrived on the American scene during these decades.

Unique suburban dwellings such as the Bi-level and Split-level detached homes, as well as "singles" and "Senior Citizens" apartments, have been added by the millions to the stock of urban apartments and rowhouses we lived in previously.

Not only have our shelter types changed but for many our life style itself has been dramatically altered by this shift. For many millions, it is now house to car-to school-to car-to shopping center-to car-to work in suburban offices and industrial "parks" in the "shelter and service" communities now surrounding most of our urban areas.

This manual addresses itself to the new and contemporary scene, to the effect the developments of the past three decades have had on real estate values and, most importantly, *on the methods used to determine those values*.

As the real estate scene has changed during these past decades, as life styles and shelter styles have evolved, so also has the real estate appraisal process itself changed in order to continue to reflect and properly value all types of property.

Various traditional appraisal approaches to value—such as the use of the Gross-Rent Multiplier for one-family dwellings and the Income approach for three- and four-family dwellings—are mentioned here, mainly for historical-background purposes. They, like other hoary appraisal concepts, have not stood the test of time and the numerous recent changes in the real estate scene. The more substantive Cost approach to value, and especially the use of costs to adjust to comparables in the Market approach, are detailed in this up-to-date manual.

Even here, appraisal experience has taught us that there are many times when the Cost approach is not applicable. The value marketplace is harsh and quickly rejects pure mathematics. For example, during tight mortgage money periods when construction building costs and construction itself are way down, you could theoretically build a new house cheaper than you could buy a used home (if you could borrow money to build). According to the traditional appraisal rule, you should not buy when you can build cheaper, and vice-versa. Yet, during these "tight money" periods, many real estate people continue to do arithmetic gymnastics to force the Cost approach somehow to act as an upper limit of values. This simply is not accurate.

The one appraisal method which has withstood the test of these three dynamic decades is the *Market approach to value*. Therefore, I have stressed and amplified this approach in this standard appraising manual. Our marketplace, the only objective taskmaster, will give us value *if we observe and record properly*. Various modern day concepts such as the "Best Comparable" technique are emphasized here rather than the older methods of (heaven forbid!) "averaging" of comparable sales or "bracketing" the subject with comparable sales. Appraisal today involves modern market analysis techniques which real estate professionals must understand in order to cope intelligently, profitably and safely in the cyclical real estate and construction industry.

During these three decades, I have been a federal construction cost analyst, cost estimator, inspector, supervisory appraiser and chief appraiser. In my daily work then and in my independent appraising since retirement from government service, I've appraised and supervised the appraisal of many types of real estate. The purpose of this handbook is to record this practical experience and to show you how you too can complete appraisals accurately and quickly in your everyday real estate work.

The practical purpose of this standard real estate appraising manual is to provide time and quality benefits. Time in real estate is fleeting and costly. This up-to-date standard appraising manual is organized to help you save time and prepare complete, accurate appraisal reports. The introductory chapters of this book present valuation theory and general how-to-do-it tools for appraising specific types of property. Whether you are out in the field or in your office, you can look at your subject property, flip to the appropriate handbook section and find all the information you need.

There are chapters on more than 100 specific types of real estate, showing in detail how to appraise each type. For example, all types of one-family dwellings, including the many forms of Bi-levels and Split-levels, are discussed in detail. In addition, you'll find practical information on multi-family structures, including specially designed and funded housing for senior citizens and specially oriented apartment-recreational complexes for singles. The burgeoning "fast foods" and "convenience" commercial properties springing up everywhere, as well as typical smaller commercial-industrial properties, are also discussed along how-to-do-it lines and model appraisals are provided for guidance.

The sample appraisals in clear step-by-step style, from data gathering to analysis to conclusion are presented in report form so that you can see exactly how an actual appraisal of each type of property looks on paper. You can use these models to help gather your data and complete your own appraisal assignment in written form.

I believe deeply that if you work, invest or act as an agent for others in real estate you must know how to value and how to recognize *acceptable quality* for the specific product, be it a lot, home, apartment house, store, shopping center, factory or industrial park. To the broker, lender or developer, mistakes in value or failure to report unacceptable construction or quality of improvements can be *fatal* to his or the client's economic life. Therefore, to value a property you must know how it is put together and also be able to recognize when it is not built properly. This standard appraising manual presents you with construction guides and construction checklists, so that on the way to arriving at your value estimate you do not fall into unreported jerry-built construction holes without reporting them and taking them into account in determining final value.

I also discuss the practical aspects of important present day concerns such as inner-city "redlining" and "urban disinvestment." The countervailing movement of many people from the suburbs back to the cities, noted recently, makes it very probable that mortgages will eventually become available again in many areas denied financing previously. Those of us working in real estate in these inner city areas must be aware of previous practices, alert to the changes now portended by legislation and by the movement of people.

Since you open your real estate door daily to such a variegated business, I have included practical guidance on comparatively recent real estate phenomena such as condominiums, Planned Unit Developments and Property Owners Associations, as well as chapters and sections on construction cost estimating, real property assessment appeals, condemnation appraisals and utility right-of-way appraisals (including the evaluation of the ultra-high tension lines beginning to criss-cross our country). Farm appraisals, quarry appraisals and other subsurface appraisals are covered, as well as especially important chapters on appraisal ethics, photographs, expert testimony, the appraiser's equipment, a glossary of appraisal-construction terminology and finally, of course, appraisal fees.

Caution, please. You have here all the key appraisal data and tools you need in your real estate work. To be and earn your best, you must continue to learn, to experience sensitively, to observe, to measure, to apply these handbook precepts with skill and judgment and to record clearly our dynamic real estate marketplace.

Samuel T. Barash

ACKNOWLEDGMENTS

No book writes itself. It is not possible to mention all who have encouraged and helped. Particular acknowledgment is given to Robert Coon, Harris B. Fish, Thomas J. MacCarthy, Robert Lipsyte, Richard Keppler, Dexter B. MacBride, Morris Paladino, Mal Davidson, Esq., Al Lucas, Steven Molnar, Frank Giustiniani, Nancy Greenman, Frank Fini, Herman Leimzider and Andrew LoConti. Special thanks, with love, to Julia Barash, Esq. and Kit Barash, helpmate.

S. T. B.

Illustrations

Contents

3. How to Estimate Building Costs (cont.)

4. How to Conduct Building and Site Inspections: Procedures and Checklists 53

5. How to Appraise Land 73

6. Techniques and Procedures for Appraising New Construction 89

Contents

Contents

22. How to Prepare Reports and Use Terminology Correctly (cont.)

Chapter 1

Real estate appraising today—
a changing scene

The appraisal process is intimately involved in every phase of the real estate and mortgaging business you work in today.

This important first chapter spells out this critical relationship so that you can use it in your daily real estate work. Our way of life, where we live and what we live in, have changed enormously since WWII. As a result of all these changes, the appraisal process has also changed dramatically.

The real estate appraisal process by its very nature reflects society. As a result, the techniques used in the first half of this century have led to advanced, yet essentially simpler, methods of appraisal to cope with modern living and work environments. The "holy trinity" of Market, Cost and Income approaches is now no longer as sacred as it once was. Gross rent multipliers for one-family dwellings are also discussed here. However, the real estate market creates and destroys values daily. Because of this fact, we must look to the market itself to find values. Therefore, I have emphasized the Market approach and the comparatively new "Best Comparable" Market approach throughout this book.

THE GROWING IMPORTANCE OF THE APPRAISAL PROCESS

The appraisal process is involved in, reflects and reports on every phase of real estate and mortgaging. The real estate business is such a varied industry. Any day, your real estate door as a broker, say, can open not only to listing appraisals but also to a request for a residential appraisal or a commercial or an

25

industrial or perhaps a farm appraisal. The farm appraisal may later become a subdivision appraisal, or perhaps 35 individual lot appraisals. Landowners and takers continually need condemnation appraisals. Dissatisfied land and homeowners need appraisals to appeal unfair and unequal real property tax assessments.

Lenders need appraisals to value security for their loans. Government agencies need appraisals to guaranty, insure or subsidize these loans or improvements. Developers and real estate investors need appraisals to hedge their land and building bets. Builders and subcontractors need appraisal cost estimating techniques to get their contracts and their financing.

All these needs for appraisals have multiplied during our nation's growth since the forties. Continued and even expanded involvement of the appraisal process throughout real estate can be anticipated.

THE IMPACT OF SUBURBANIZATION
ON VALUE CONCEPTS

Architectural and planning critics have bemoaned the "spread city" pattern which has developed open land on the outskirts of our cities. The modern offices, hotels, shopping centers and concentric rings of suburban and exurban residential development have all been decried. Convenient parking is criticized for its blacktopping of acreage as far as one can see. The point has even been made that suburbanization, although apparently profitable and what so many in our society want, is architecturally and aesthetically banal.

Yet, this is where we are. The action in real estate is now not only concentrated in the cities. It has spread outwards to these suburban-exurban metropolises that have resulted from decades of expansion. It is a changed, expanded market we appraise in today.

But the fact is that many appraisal techniques originated in and were well-suited to "city" appraising. Now, appraisal techniques themselves have evolved with this transformation in order to be able to reflect values in our modern suburbanized society. Before suburbanization, people lived mainly in cities and in small towns along railroads. Today, the suburbs have changed our way of life and what and how we appraise. Years ago, appraisers used rent multipliers because there were ample house rentals. Now, millions of homes are sold regularly, but comparatively few are rented. Also, tens of millions of new homes have been built in the suburbs, mainly from model types. We now have massive comparable sales of similar homes similarly situated. As a result, the Market approach has become the best approach. Also, the "Best Comparable" approach has evolved as even a more refined and accurate market analysis technique, since there are so many nearly similar comparable properties sold daily in most areas.

WHY THE "HOLY TRINITY" OF APPRAISAL APPROACHES IS NO LONGER SACRED

The current specifications of the U.S. General Services Administration, GSA Form As41A, Specifications for the GSA Analytical Narrative Report, is quoted in part below. It is a very good description of the "classical" appraisal process as we know it today and as we see it changing to meet changing modern conditions:

". . . . . General—In the preparation of this report, the contractor shall follow current professional appraisal practices giving consideration to three approaches to value, namely, the Cost Less Depreciation, Income and Comparative (or Market) approaches, unless otherwise specified in the contract. . . . .

13. "Value Estimate by Cost Approach—This section shall be in the form of computative data arranged in sequence, beginning with reproduction or replacement cost, and shall state the source (book and page if a national service) of all figures used. The dollar amounts of physical deterioration and functional economic obsolescence, or the omission of same, shall be explained in narrative form. . . . .

14. "Value Estimate by Income Approach—This shall include adequate factual data to support each figure and factor used and shall be arranged in detail form to show at least (a) estimated gross economic rent or income; (b) allowance for vacancy and credit losses; (c) an itemized estimate of total expenses including reserves for replacements. Capitalization of net income shall be at the rate prevailing for this type of property and location. The capitalization technique, method and rate used shall be explained in narrative form supported by a statement of sources of rates and factors.

15. "Value Estimate by Comparative (Market) Approach—All sales used shall be confirmed by the buyer, seller, broker or other person having knowledge of the price, terms and conditions of sale. Each comparable shall be weighed and explained in relation to the subject property to indicate the reasoning behind the appraiser's final estimate from this approach.

16. "Interpretation and Correlation of Estimates." The appraiser shall interpret the foregoing estimates and shall state his reasons why one or more of the conclusions reached in items (13), (14) and (15) are indicative of the market value of the property. . . . ."

Not only academicians but also many practicing appraisers are questioning the continuing worth of this balanced three-part appraisal process on *all* appraisal assignments. It appears that it is past time for doing away with the hoary practice of "correlation" of the three separate approaches to value on every appraisal.

It is clear that the Cost approach with its built-in subjective margins of error should be utilized in modern day appraising only in those appraisals where no other approach is feasible. For example, if the home being appraised is in an area with no sales of similar properties, then you will have to depend on the Cost approach. The Income approach should be used where appropriate, such as in most commercial properties which are bought mainly to secure return on investment. Yet, even here you also analyze sales prices and net incomes of similar properties to determine that you are using proper capitalization rates. Pragmatically, you work for your client in the manner he directs. And, of course, you should know and use classic correlation if the GSA or similar assignment instructions so direct. However, in most cases you depend mainly on your market data analyses for your value conclusions.

Value has been argued only on a Market approach basis whenever I have appeared as an expert witness in court. The appraisal assignment instructions and forms of corporate transfer firms also generally require market data sales and analysis *only*. These are but a few examples of the trend in the courts, in the marketplace and in appraisal practice towards a mainly one-approach appraisal process.

Individual approaches to value and how they are applied are also constantly being modified to meet changing times. For example, in the thirties when few properties were being bought or sold, the "economic approach" for one- to four-family dwellings was an excellent tool because there were millions of rented houses. It was practical and proper to use the Income approach, to capitalize the rents, project the economic life and come up with an estimate of value. However, WWII and the post-war decades of suburbanization and market expansion then occurred. Appraisers tried to cope with this situation by coining terms like "amenity" income and "fair rental" factors to substitute for the lack of an actual rental market. But the Income approach for one- to four-family homes has now become extinct.

Similarly, according to the theory of substitution, one should never buy when one can build a similar improved property for less. Under this theory, much arithmetic has been expended in the Cost approach to arrive at opinions of value. Assuming all this arithmetic to have been free of error, what did the appraiser do during the many "tight money" periods we've experienced during these decades of growth? In those periods, prices of existing improved properties went up because, without available financing, new construction could not be built to act as a "substitution" upper limit cost control. In spite of all this, valiant efforts were made to continue the balanced interplay of the "holy trinity," Market, Cost and Income approaches on each appraisal.

The Market approach using the same good theory of substitution—that no one should buy an improved property if a similar one can be found for less—is the approach to value which has withstood best the impact of recessions, of tight money and of changes in the way we live.

The Federal Housing Administration Underwriting Manual states, for example, "A buyer in any case is not warranted in paying any more than substitute properties would cost to acquire. This basic theory applies to any means of securing a substitute property whether by outright purchase or by assembling a duplicate." The FHA, an institution venerable in its appraisal work since the thirties, still uses cost, not depreciated cost, as an upper limit to value. The FHA also still capitalizes income as another upper limit to value in its appraisals. However, the Market approach for all practical purposes is what this agency appears to rely upon. So do the V.A. and most other federal agencies. Later chapters will detail how government agencies make and review appraisals, the forms they use and the controls they impose. Suffice to say here that the Market approach is what is used in most of their appraisal work as the main indicator of value.

THE GROSS RENT MULTIPLIER

Even today, with most one-family homes sold rather than rented, a number of these same federal agencies still require that the Gross Rent Multiplier approach be used.

We present this approach here so that when you do appraisals for these agencies or for other clients who require this approach on their appraisal reports, you will know how to use it. Again, terminology has come to the rescue of an appraisal technique threatened with extinction by the evolution of our society. There is no real one-family rental market extant, so appraisers have coined the word "fair" rent. Thus, it is left up to the appraiser to estimate what the house would rent for, if it were rented. Then the appraiser locates comparable sales, divides their estimated "fair" monthly rent into the sales prices and comes up, lo, with a Gross Rent Multiplier. This is how the Gross Rent Multiplier, a simpler extension of the Income approach, has been used in recent years. Know it, understand it, use it when it is required. But don't count on it as your main approach to value, or you do injustice to your client.

KEY FACTORS IN USING THE MARKET APPROACH

Since the Market approach should be stressed on most appraisals as the best indicator of value, it is important that certain practices and techniques be emphasized. It is important that your valuation thinking and analysis be presented in a clear and orderly manner. When your client reads your report, there can be no question in his mind as to how *your* mind worked on his assignment.

Try to keep your comparable sales of similar properties as close to the subject geographically, in price, in date of sale, in similar improvements and amenities as your diligent research can reveal. Match split level apples to split level apples. Avoid using two-story oranges for one-story, ranch apples. Better a similar bi-level in the next similar town than a 1½-story "cape cod" comparable adjacent to the bi-level subject. Don't "bracket" your comparables around the subject, then show your client an *average* of sales prices of your comparables to arrive at your opinion of value. Avoid statistical medians and means. Such techniques may impress statisticians. They do not give you a "Best Comparable" (discussed in detail later) and they may mystify your client.

You do not need different comparables for each appraisal. It is better to know intimately and use good "benchmark" comparables for a number of similar appraisal assignments in your area than to jump about for three to five new comparables on each appraisal assignment. There may not be time to learn thoroughly all the conditions and details of each comparable property sale each time. It is also better to use these "benchmark" comparables until they are no longer current than to submit hosts of semi-verified new comparables on each appraisal.

Beware of time adjustments. The less we intrude our subjective opinions of how much value time has added or subtracted, the better our estimate. The marketplace is full of information if we seek it diligently. No matter how experienced, guess-timating time adjustments should be avoided. Leg work and research are still vital no matter how learned we become. The market is too dynamic for subjective time guesses. Get recent comparables instead.

HOW TO USE THE
"BEST COMPARABLE" TECHNIQUE

Your appraisal, no matter how well-presented, is only as good as your market data. Real estate people who are engaged daily in buying, selling, developing, building and closing on real estate properties are in the best position to know their area, their market and comparable sales data.

Modern computerized aids are being used today to assist the appraiser. Printouts of sales data, analyzed by computers, are available to appraisers seeking comparables. Realtor organizations provide data books of sales activity in their regions to their members which are valuable sources for comparables. Assessors' records are public and available and include invaluable descriptive and sales data. Records of sales of active brokers, real estate attorneys, lenders and mortgage title companies are often available to local appraisers who deal with them. And last, and certainly the most informed, is the owner of the comparable property.

The owner is the one best qualified to confirm the details and conditions of sale of the comparable. As a reviewing VA appraiser spot-checking the work of fee appraisers, I have many times checked out a subject property appraisal in the field, found it to be in a development subdivision surrounded by many similar properties, knocked on a few doors and found much better comparables on the same block than those in the report.

Always seek the "Best Comparable." Particularly in the developments, concentrate on getting the best comparable property, one which is most similar in location, date of sale, improvements and amenities. Computer printouts are impressive, modern and sophisticated. Yet, there is no substitute for experience, knowledge and personal field analysis and verification of each comparable. Your quest for your best opinion of value has to be found on complete, personally explored market data and wherever possible, on a "Best Comparable," chosen from and buttressed by your list of sales.

In sum, the real estate appraisal process as we know it today has been changed by the suburbanizing forces that have also changed our life style. The various historical, economic and legal bases for real estate values have endured but our appraisal techniques are constantly in change, mainly to emphasize the Market approach to value. Later chapters will demonstrate by specific how-to-do-it instruction and by actual appraisal models what was presented in theory here.

Some years ago, Hans, a venerable appraiser-inspector who worked for me when I was a VA Chief Appraiser, called one day to say he could not work for a while. "I broke my leg," he said.

"How, Hans?"

"I was checking out this veteran's complaint on this house I had inspected and I fell through the attic ceiling."

"What was the complaint, Hans?"

"No attic catwalk, as required by the plans."

When you appraise today, you give the best of your experience, your judgment, your leg work to make certain you too don't "miss the catwalk." Since the Market approach has become so important today, you always have to be personally inquisitive in your market research and systematic in your presentation to the client.

Chapter 2

Defining real estate value: contemporary factors

Real estate value is created, maintained and changed by the interaction of a complex of factors in a dynamic process.

This chapter spells out for you these many dynamic factors so that you can observe, measure and record this interaction and accurately determine real estate value. There is change from day to day in every property you appraise. Timeliness on your appraisal assignment is so important because value, by definition, is fleeting. The very value you set may, for different purposes and different clients, have a different "face," in fact, possibly a different value. Yet, you will also see here, how even though value may have different names (sometimes even different amounts for the same property), the solid basis for appraisals of practically all properties remains market value.

Our land has become urbanized, suburbanized and even regionalized into the "sunbelt" and the older, Eastern and Midwest areas. Our federal and local governments have increased their impact on real estate values. Modern, sophisticated "no-growth" and "slow-growth" zoning laws are now being used by more and more local communities. Environmental concerns and controls are also mounting. All these modern factors are increasingly affecting real estate development and values.

Although value may be made in the marketplace, it is confirmed in law. This chapter also lays out for you how the courts have ruled to define value. Finally, contemporary factors which make value are described here. Subsequent chapters, of course, will spell out the how-to-do-it details of appraisal.

HOW "THE MARKET" MAKES VALUE

From time immemorial men have bartered their possessions, exchanging what each owned after settling on what each wanted. Now we exchange money for property and we call the medium of this exchange, value. Sophisticated definitions involving market value have been developed, mainly based on value meanings our laws have given us. For example, "market value" is "the present worth of rights to future benefits arising from the ownership of the property." However, value continues to be made in our society by the free interaction of many factors affecting the desires and needs of buyers and sellers of property.

All factors interact. Yet, in any given property appraisal, one factor (such as zoning) may practically overwhelm the operation of most other influences including even the highest and best use of the property. The factors and influences which follow in this chapter are all part of the environment of each and every property you appraise.

WHY LOCATION IS PARAMOUNT

The geographical location of the property in its urban, suburban, exurban, rural area is of paramount importance. The vitality of the city, the suburb and exurb, the strength or weakness of the area's economic base must be analyzed. The neighborhood surrounding the property, its immediate block, are equally critical to value. The real estate adage that the three factors which make value are location, location and location, cannot be over-emphasized. This paramount value factor of location is stressed here and throughout this book.

THE IMPORTANCE OF A FREE MARKET
OF COMPARABLE SALES DATA

Reasonably informed buyers and sellers, all at "arm's length," make for a free market and for valid comparable sales data. Sales to relatives, foreclosures sales, speculator sales involving little or no down payments backed by government-guaranteed or insured mortgages, "forced" sales because of buyers' or sellers' needs to move right away, condemnation sales, "impatient" sales where sellers reduced drastically without offering for sale for a reasonable period—all are examples of transfers which should not be used for comparable sales data.

THE CRITICAL IMPACT OF PERMISSIVE ZONING

This is critical to real estate value. Zoning must permit the existing or proposed usage for which you are appraising. It can give this permission in the written zoning ordinance by right or by exception or by permitted non-conformance. Whenever a zoning ordinance is in force in the area you are appraising, you first check whether the zoning does permit the subject usage. Only then can you proceed to the next steps of appraising all the other physical influences and amenity factors in the property.

THE EFFECT OF FINANCING AVAILABILITY

Real estate values are seriously affected whenever financing is not available in specific areas. For example, when the FHA did not insure loans in many parts of many cities, real estate values were seriously affected. Wherever ''Redlining'' exists (discussed in later chapters), real estate values are usually seriously affected. After WWII, many white people moved to the suburbs and many black people and other minority groups took their place in the cities. Dynamic value changes occurred, sometimes spurred by alleged ''blockbusting'' speculators. In our sophisticated society which has evolved from barter to cash and now to computerized credit, financing must be available for a real estate market to exist.

DETERMINING HIGHEST AND BEST USE
AND OTHER FACTORS

Highest and best use, always legally and actually important, must also be ascertained. In addition, the topography, the access to the property, the utilities, the quality, the structural integrity, the sanitation, the protection from the elements, the functional utility, the habitability of the building improvements all have to be considered.

For example, real estate values in Orange County, New York where I live and work, have been affected by all of the value factors discussed here. This county is on the outer exurban rim of the New York City metropolis about 60 miles from the George Washington Bridge. In 1959, its economy was changing slowly from mainly agricultural dairy farming and summer recreational hotel and bungalow improvements. Scattered commuter residential development had begun. Four years later, a number of large developments were under construction. The typical 140-acre dairy farm was starting to sell for twice its $400-per-acre agricultural value—$800 to $1,000 an acre. Investors and developers were purchasing the land, speculating on its potential highest and best use as residential building subdivisions for New York City commuters rather than for resident cows.

Later, in the sixties, the Interstate Highway system thrust Route 84 West across the county opening up arterial access to most parts of the county and increasing land values to about $1,500 an acre. Commercial-industrial values at highway interchanges rose to $15,000 an acre and more for specialty commercial usages. But in 1967 financing became "tight" and the escalating land values halted their upward march.

By 1970, with money available again, development and wholesale land speculation were again rife. Land values for farms were now up to $2,000 per acre. In 1972, a national appraisal concern was hired by the county to appraise all properties at 100% market value, as New York State assessment law now requires. Most large tracts were appraised for $2,000 per acre, reflecting the prior several years of comparable market sales activity which had reached as high as $3,300 per acre for prime farm tracts. As a result real estate taxes tripled in most cases.

In 1973, we had the gas shortage. Commuters began to fear the 60-mile, one-way ride to New York City employment. The demand for land, homes and associated commercial-industrial development ceased. By 1975-1976, with this complex of interacting factors putting mounting downward pressure on value, the county itself owned hundreds of large farms through non-payment of mortgages. There was no discernible real estate land market in the area. Meanwhile, real estate taxes on an average 140-acre tract amounted to over $10,000 per year (still assessed at that average $2,000 per acre). By 1976, practically no buyers could be found for $500 an acre, almost the same price the property sold for 13 years earlier! However, hope springs eternal in real estate. A scattering of comparable sales have recently been noted (at the lower average $500 figure). Perhaps this value history of rising and falling values will begin to repeat itself.

This example is but one of thousands of such illustrations of the constant dynamic interplay of factors on values in local areas, involving supply-demand, "cheap" land, new access routes, reactive zoning, financing, taxation and all the other factors.

THE CRITICAL IMPORTANCE OF TIMELINESS

Always vital for proper appraisal, timeliness is critical when you peg your opinion of value for the property you are appraising in its time frame. It is important, of course, that you meet the client's deadline for delivery of the report so that it meets his particular needs and gives current value by the deadline requested. It is equally important that you be given the correct date by the client for which you must ascertain value.

On one assignment, working under written instructions from a client's attorney to appraise as of a certain date regarding a condemnation taking of a land tract for highway purposes, I studied the market and ascribed $2,000 per acre. This was based on a good spectrum of recent sales comparables including a "Best Comparable" nearby. Later, testifying in court on the witness stand from my written report, I was asked by my client's new attorney and the opposing counsel to give an opinion as to market value nine months after the date in my report. In that short nine-month period, comparable sales and values had plummeted. The land was worth less than $1,500 an acre, a 25% drop!

THE DIFFERENT "FACES" OF VALUE

For many years, jurists, economists, government administrators and appraisers have been attempting to define value by ascribing "different faces" to value for different purposes. The history of all these valiant attempts by professionals, dedicated to their craft, shows an ever increasing awareness that in the end, no matter how it is dissected, the definition of value is what the market, not us, says it is.

All manner of terms have evolved: fair value, exchange value, assemblage value, loss value, present value, scrap value, speculative value, replacement value, loan value, insurance value and others. In the end, however, no matter what we call it, it basically remains market value.

If you study all of the above terms, one constant emerges. Before you can determine whatever value you are seeking, you must first determine market value. Whether it be for real estate tax assessment, for condemnation, for assemblage, for speculation, for loan value or for almost any other purpose, you find out first what other properties similarly located with similar amenities and improvements have sold for recently. You try to find a "Best Comparable" if you can. You then adjust the subject property to the market data and deduce your opinion of current market value. Only then can you seek and ascertain and report on any of the other "faces" of value involved in your appraisal assignment.

On income-producing property, you generally capitalize the income flow to arrive at your value opinion. Even here, you are basically using only another technique to measure what the market says a property is worth. Often there are similar commercial comparable sales which are better indicators of value than capitalization of the rents involved in the property.

This pertains also to appraisals for insurance replacement purposes. The present market value of the property should be determined first to keep the whole value picture in proper perspective. For example, during today's rocketing construction costs, to avoid becoming "insurance poor," your client might have to consider becoming a co-insurer himself. Thus, if his property is worth much less than replacement cost, he might decide to take out less insurance than full coverage. Certainly, he should know current market value in order to make an informed decision.

GOVERNMENTAL IMPACT ON VALUE

Since the depression when the government entered the sales market with its first subsidy and guaranty agencies, our governmental infrastructure has had a far reaching affect on building development, real estate values and sales. The FHA, the VA, the SBA, the FNMA, the FmHa, HUD, the Federal Reserve or other federal and state agencies have all helped to build our nation and define our real estate values. During depression, recession, inflation and "tight money" times, governmental impact on real estate is direct and influential. Drive throughout our land and you see FHA-VA land planned developments with curvilinear road layouts ringing the cities. The very suburbs and exurbs they are in were created by the Federal Interstate Highway system. Many of the commercial-industrial complexes at highway interchanges and in these suburbs were constructed with funds from lending institutions and from government agencies. Like the everyday reviews of the Federal Reserve, which controls credit in this country and the availability of financing, this governmental impact on real estate values is dynamic and constantly changing.

GOVERNMENT DEFINITIONS OF VALUE

The government has also helped to define real estate value. Many years ago, the FHA's Underwriting Manual originally stated that, "value . . . is a price which a purchaser is warranted in paying for a property, rather than the price at which the property may be sold, and is defined as: The price which typical buyers would be warranted in paying for the property for long term use or investment, if they were well informed, acting voluntarily and without necessity."

The Veterans Administration has since the mid-forties been involved in guaranty of bank loans to veterans who buy homes. Its definition of value is: "Reasonable Value . . . is that figure which represents the amount a reputable and qualified appraiser, unaffected by personal interest, bias or prejudice, would recommend to a prospective purchaser at a proper price or cost in the light of prevailing conditions."

An impersonal, objective appraiser, according to these still prevailing government definitions of value, observes and reports in a free market to establish market value.

"NO AND SLOW GROWTH" ZONING

The enlarged towns, the denser suburbs, the newer exurbs, appear to be calling a halt to further rapid growth. Many communities are limiting and even stopping this almost half-century of explosive growth through "no growth," large lot, low-density zoning and other local community controls.

Plans like the "Ramapo Plan," which originated in the early 1970's in Rockland County, New York, are being extended in different forms everywhere. These plans severely limit residential, commercial and industrial development to areas which have the utilities and facilities to handle and absorb the development. For example, an owner of land beyond the sewer and water lines would be denied permission to subdivide or improve his land. However, he or others who might buy the land from him, might be permitted to use certain "credits" he has in his non-developable land to apply these "credits" to another tract within a developable area. Some call this "confiscation without proper compensation," but courts have generally upheld such plans as being a proper function of local community control.

ENVIRONMENTAL IMPACT ON VALUES

As local communities throughout our country have reacted to uncontrolled or only partly controlled growth, so also have environmental concerns and controls further limited development. The "energy crunch" was dramatized by the Arabs turning off the oil spigot. The coldest winter in 100 years in 1976-1977 made many areas east of the Rockies barely habitable for months, causing value depreciation in under-insulated houses. Houses heated by electricity became almost unmarketable. Heating cost of buildings fueled by gas increased dramatically. Environmental Impact studies are now required by law before practically any proposed development can take place. This adds further to the inflation of building values. Farmers have been striking and laying their tractors across the right-of-ways to try to bar the ultra-high-voltage electric transmission lines beginning to criss-cross our country. Environmental laws and vigorous local environmental opposition have almost stopped the filling and development of lowland inland areas and tidal coastlands.

These examples reflect the mounting concern in our suburbanized, industrialized society that we cannot be profligate with our finite resources. When you appraise, you have to appreciate these environmental concerns and affects. You project these trends in your area and measure this environmental impact on your assignments. You reflect this environmental backdrop in your appraisal narrative "scenarios" in order to give complete value estimates to your client.

COURT RULINGS AND THEIR EFFECTS
ON VALUE DEFINITION

The many court rulings on value in our land of law are probably even more potent and certainly more binding than government value definitions.

Those who study precedent law as it is made in the many courts throughout our country can see how many of our present-day valuation meanings and appraisal techniques originated. There are tomes covering the entire American law in law libraries which give such fine-print court decision value defintions as:

- The word "valuation," the noun, is defined as meaning the setting or estimating of the value of anything.
- The primary meaning of "value" is worth, and the term is further defined generally as meaning estimated or assessed worth, marketable price, worth as estimated in terms of a currency.
- It is generally recognized that the word "value" has two different meanings and sometimes expresses the utility of an object and sometimes the power of purchasing other goods with it; the one may be called "value in use," the other "value in exchange." What a willing purchaser will give for the property under fair market conditions. The price a willing purchaser, not compelled to buy will pay a willing seller not compelled to sell.
- When the word "value" is applied to property of any description without qualification either by the context or by circumstances, it means the price it will command in the market, its equivalent amount in lawful money and usually it means market value. The word "value" means money value and not merely sentimental value, and it means a money value on some market and not a value only to a present owner.

THE IMPACT OF KEY COURT DECISIONS

On May 26, 1894, the U.S. Supreme Court in its famous "Brewer" decision, defined that value basically results from use. In this century, federal and state court decisions have continued to affect the way value is created and defined.

Particularly in recent years, critically important zoning decisions by our courts are reflecting and appear to be mainly supporting the trend of "no and slow" growth community controls.

On June 21, 1976, in Eastlake v. Forest City Enterprises, Inc., the U.S. Supreme Court ruled that this Eastlake, Ohio community, a suburb of Cleveland, could limit its rapid growth. It further stated that Eastlake citizens could exercise referendum veto powers over permissive changes in zoning law.

On January 11, 1977, the U.S. Supreme Court in a landmark case involving the village of Arlington Heights, a nearly all-white suburb of Chicago, ruled that it was not inherently unconstitutional for a suburb to refuse to change zoning restrictions whose practical effect is to block construction of racially intergrated housing. The court ruled in this case that there must also be an "intent" or "purpose" to discriminate.

On January 26, 1977, the New Jersey Supreme Court, involving Mount

Laurel Township, similarly held that it did not have the power to require cities to allow housing ''quotas'' for low and middle income families.

These decisions reflect an increasing trend towards limiting growth in our suburbs. These decisions are also reshaping patterns of development. Such decisions and trends have to be projected and interpreted in your appraisal work in your particular area.

There is a continuing thread in our appraisal work and value definitions, whether in our history of appraising or now. Thus, in V.S. Oertel Co. v. Glenn, 13 F. Supp. 651, 653 (W.D. Ky., 1936), the court ruled that ''to value'' is defined as meaning to measure the value or worth of . . . . . *to appraise*.

Chapter 3

How to estimate
building costs

This chapter provides specific instructions for estimating building costs.

Not only appraisers but our whole economy utilizes and observes trends of building costs. These trends are extremely sensitive reflections of inflation. This barometer effect will be discussed further in this chapter.

The building industry is probably one of the leading industries in our land. Yet, it is still peopled mainly by small, independent builder-businessmen. Instances of their cost work are exhibited in this chapter so that you can review and use in your appraisals the cost techniques developed by these many tens of thousands of builder-businessmen.

Appraisal theorists continue to dispute whether the cost approach must be used on all appraisals. However, there can be no argument with the fact that you must know cost work. You cannot use the Market approach properly and compare properties if you do not know costs in general and costs in your area specifically.

Various national cost manuals are available but many appraisers use their own control buildings to make certain that they are properly reflecting local costs in their area. You will see how this is done and how square foot costs are derived.

I've provided a list of available cost manuals in this chapter. You will also find guidance here on how to use these manuals as well as how to appreciate their limitations. So that you have an understanding of where these square foot (and cubic foot) costs come from, model builder subcontract component breakdowns are provided. "Quantity" material and labor cost breakdowns from plans and specifications on construction are also exhibited. Finally, you will also find here model cost estimates on a high-ranch dwelling and on an industrial warehouse building.

THE SENSITIVITY OF BUILDING COSTS AND TRENDS

Statistics track the annual upward thrust of inflation and of building costs. The building industry produces a large percentage of our nation's gross product. The industry is also extremely sensitive to pressures such as the availability of financing.

These statistics show generally an ever upward cost chart in our cyclical building industry. There are always countervailing pressures in areas such as the depressed Northeastern region as well as nationally whenever financing is not available. However, the broad decades-long sweep is up, mirroring inflation and putting constant upward pressure on real estate values.

THE MAKE-UP OF THE BUILDING INDUSTRY

There are practically no major industries left in this country which still are principally run by small businessmen. The building industry is the single exception. Small builders still mainly build most homes in this country.

Often, large corporations get into home building but usually find their corporate management structure is just not capable of managing the local problems, municipal delays and buyer complaints which local small builder-businessmen cope with daily.

The cycles in our building industry, so dependent on financing availability and on the vagaries of local zoning and other approvals, regularly drive out the large corporations which enter building as well as the small builder-businessman. The large corporation goes back to its other activities usually never to return. The small builder picks up his hammer and does alterations for a while until he or the next generation of small builders finds favorable conditions for a building project.

This multiplicity of small builder-businessmen and subcontractors causes competitive cost differences on a regional and local basis. When you appraise new or existing construction and adjust your comparable sales data to the subject property, you have to be aware of these current local cost differences caused mainly by this highly competitive nature of our building business.

HOW UNDERSTANDING COMPONENT COSTS
HELPS APPRAISERS COMPARE PROPERTIES

Some government agencies and other appraisal clients still require the three-part appraisal process (including market, cost and income approaches) on each appraisal. One-approach market data comparison appraisals are now done on many assignments. However even when this one-approach trend becomes universal, you will never outgrow your need for knowledge, understanding and usage of building costs.

You need to know costs to adjust your comparable data to your subject property for differences in size, equipment, condition and amenities. You must be familiar with costs and the way buildings depreciate in order to assess special purpose structures where similar comparable sales can be found locally or in similar locations.

You also need to know costs to estimate replacement cost for insurance purposes. You need to know costs in order to be able to estimate percentages of completion for bank mortgage loan payouts when you are assigned to inspect and appraise new construction.

HOW TO SET UP A TYPICAL "CONTROL" HOUSE FOR COSTS

You will see later in this chapter where to get and how to use standard material cost handbooks. These handbooks are invaluable to the appraiser. They also have limitations.

One serious limitation is the quarterly local multiplier index which these handbooks furnish in order to "adjust" regularly the costs in your local area. When I was chief of construction for the Veterans Administration in New York, our square foot costs on Long Island were usually 25% cheaper than national cost handbooks reported. Mass development, building plots with good sand and gravel subsoil and a large pool of experienced subcontractors caused this large cost difference. It is important to know local costs intimately.

If you regularly appraise many similar type structures, for instance, development-type new and existing homes in your local area, it may pay you to set up your own "control" house. Pick out a typical ranch or bi-level of say 1,200 square feet, if that is the norm in your area. If you have a building background, are associated with a builder in your real estate business or know a builder, get a stock set of plans and specifications for the typical house you pick.

Perhaps such a house has just been built and you can secure the "as built" costs on this house. If not, put the plans and specs out to bid. Then regularly, put the same house out to bid or secure the current building costs on it, say annually or semi-annually. This will be an effective control to make certain you are properly reflecting costs in your area. For example, if this six-room, one-bath, three-bedroom, living room, dining room, family room, one-car, built-in garage, frame construction, asbestos shingle, brick veneer front only, bi-level house of 1,200 square feet finished last month in your town cost $28,800, then your local construction cost for this type of house would be $24 per square foot instead of $26, say, by nationally adjusted handbook figures.

HOW TO DERIVE SQUARE FOOT COSTS

The foregoing control house would have given you a total cost of $28,800 for the 1,200 square foot house, without land value added but including financing and site improvements. The arithmetic steps are simple:

First step, divide 1,200 into $28,800. This equals $24 per square foot.

Second step, compare this figure to the square foot factor in your national cost handbook.

Third step, revise the handbook's local adjustment percentage factor using the data derived from your locally investigated "control" building.

For example, assume that the national cost handbook's local adjustment percentage factor for this type house in your area is 1.20. When you multiply 1.20 by the national book construction cost of $26,000 for this house, the resulting total handbook local cost becomes $31,200 or $26 per square foot. Since your "control house" indicates $24 per square foot or $28,800, you can then revise the adjustment figure of 1.20 downwards to 1.11. This enables you to use this locally refined adjustment factor to appraise more accurately in your area.

Industrial, commercial and multi-level apartment buildings which are sometimes appraised using cubic foot volume rather than square foot techniques can be controlled the same way locally. When appraising in suburbia, though, you deal mainly with square feet. Square or cube, knowing local current costs is vitally important.

HOW TO USE STANDARD COST BOOKS
IN APPRAISAL WORK

Many clients, particularly government agencies, require that you specify in your Cost approach your cost source. Some of the many are:

"Marshall Valuation Service"
Marshall and Swift Publication Company
1617 Beverly Boulevard
Los Angeles, Calif. 90026

"DODGE MANUAL"
McGraw Hill
P.O. Box 725
Garden City, N.Y. 11530

"Building Construction Cost Data"
R.S. Means Co., Inc.

509 Construction Plaza
Duxbury, Massachusetts 02332

"National Construction Estimator"
Craftsman Book Company
542 Stevens Ave., P.O. Box 109
Solana Beach, Calif. 92075

Generally, these handbooks give you a quick method of estimating current replacement costs. You'll find basic building descriptions, pictures of typical structures and a series of cost charts for each quality and type of structure.

A SEVEN-STEP APPROACH

First step, determine the type and quality of the dwelling you are appraising by comparing it with the handbook's basic description and pictures.

Second step, secure the appropriate square foot cost from the handbook table.

Third step, adjust the given basic cost for any important cost variations from the handbook's basic description.

Fourth step, multiply this adjusted basic square foot factor by the square feet of livable area in your subject house.

Fifth step, add for the cost of variations in your subject house from the handbook basic house specifications.

Sixth step, modify for locality difference, using the handbook local adjustment or preferably your own local control house costs described previously.

Final step, add landscaping cost and land value to secure total value for improved property.

For example, we can secure replacement cost using the _____ national cost handbook for a 1,500 square foot, one-story residence, two years old, of average quality and acceptable functional layout, slab, brick veneer, drywall, carpet over plywood, 1½ baths, gas range/oven, masonry fireplace, detached garage, as follows:

	Quan.	*Cost*	*Amount*
1,500 s.f. × basic cost handbook factor	1,500	$20.06	+$30,100
(Variations) carpet	1,000	1.21	+ 1,200
(Variations) ½ bath	(lump sum)		+ 500
(Variations) gas range/oven	(lump sum)		+ 400
(Variations) masonry fireplace	(lump sum)		+ 1,000
(Variations) detached garage	200	10.11	+ 2,000
Total			35,200
Current local cost multiplier.........	$35,200	1.11	39,100

No depreciation, two yrs old,
    modern layout, good location   0
Landscaping cost ....   (lump sum)   400
Land value............................   (by market data)   12,000
    TOTAL VALUE ....   (by Cost approach) $51,500

HOW TO DO COST BREAKDOWNS
BY BUILDING COMPONENTS

The day of the artisan builder who built the whole structure with his own small crew of craftsmen is just about over. Buildings are now built by highly specialized, efficient, competitive subcontractors such as rough carpenters, trim carpenters, siding applicators, roof installers, etc., supervised by the builder-general contractor. He carries as small an overhead as he can manage, perhaps a building superintendent and laborer.

You have to know how buildings are erected to understand how to get your square foot costs. Cost breakdown estimates can also be done by building components, or as many cost handbooks say, by segregated cost methods. To understand and work with square foot or segregated cost methods according to handbook guidance, you must first understand how builders estimate and "cost out" their structures.

HOW TO DO QUALITY COST BREAKDOWNS
FROM PLANS ON NEW CONSTRUCTION

Unless you also do cost estimating in connection with a building operation, you will rarely have occasion to do full quantity material and labor cost breakdowns from plans. You should know, though, how it is done so you can also appreciate how the square foot costs you use regularly are basically derived.

The average small homebuilder starts with a set of stock plans and a set of written architectural or government-type specifications. The drawings are generally to ¼″ scale and include plan, side, rear, section and detail views of all levels. The written specifications detail all proposed construction materials from excavation to foundation, to framing, to enclosure, to finish, to mechanical, to fenestration, to on-site and off-site improvements. The estimator carefully "takes off" all measurements, quantities and materials in a complete replacement cost estimate procedure and uses handbook current costs of material and labor to arrive at his total before ascribing contingency, profit and overhead percentages.

The following is a typical builder's cost sheet:

JOB ESTIMATE AND COST RECORD

Name _____ Location _____ Job No. _____

Item	Cost Esimate	Actual Cost	Item	Cost Estimate	Actual Cost
Land			Water Conn.		
Offsite Imp'vts.			Drywells		
Architect			Caulking		
Survey			Tile		
Permits			Hardware, Rgh.		
Insurance			Hardware, Fin.		
Excav. and			Vanity		
Backfl.			Med. Cabinets		
Fill			Shower Door		
Grading			Kit. Cabinets		
Foundation			Range		
Flat/Concrete			A/C		
Steel			Wr. Iron		
Damproofing			Cleaning		
Nails			Glazier		
Lumber			Floor Finish		
Sheetrock Matl.			Painting		
Sheetrock Labor			Lino., Carpet		
Trim Matl.			Labor		
Trim Labor			Drive		
Weatherstrip			Landscaping		
Carpentry, Fram-			Fuel		
ing and Shthg.			Electricity		
Roofing			Blinds, Shades		
Tape, Spackle			Mortgage Expense		
Leaders and			Title Fees		
Gutters			Legal		
Masonry			Accounting		
Insulation			Taxes		
Stairs			Interim Interest		
Windows and			Advertising		
Doors			Brokerage		
Flooring			Supervision		
Plumbing			Subtotal		
Heating					
Electric			Overhead, Profit		
Elect. Fixtures			and Contingency		
Sewer Conn.			Selling Price		

Figure 3.1

BUILDER'S COST SHEET

A MODEL COST ESTIMATE ON A ONE-FAMILY
HIGH-RANCH DWELLING

The following model cost estimate is a proposed development type dwelling set up on a building component basis as builders do it.

MODEL COST ESTIMATE

Address   *1 High St. Suburbia*   Appraiser   *Tom Jones*
Owner   *John Doe*   Type   *High-Ranch*   Date   _____

DESCRIPTION—Proposed detached frame dwelling on poured concrete, full basement foundation, asb. shingles and brick front, aluminum windows, interior drywall, oak floor, asph. title kitchen and rec. room, oil h.w., masonry chimney, 6″ insulation clg. 4″ walls, asph. sh. roof, built-in 2-car gar., 6 shrubs, front and side lawns—Liv. Rm., Din. Rm., Kit., 3 B.R.s, 1 Bath 1st floor, Recreation Rm, Utility Rm, 2-car gar, 1 Bath lower level—26 × 40 bldg.—Total sq. ft. livable—1,560.

Survey	$ 450		Tile Work	$ 400
Stock Plans	75		Med. Cab. and Showr. Dr.	140
Water Conn.	500		Stairs	200
Sewer Conn.	400		Floor	800
Permits	100		Linol. and Tile	500
Excavation and Grading	800		Garage Doors	300
P.C. Fdns. and Flatwork	2,700		Cabinets	600
Damp and Waterproofing	100		Paint	800
Lumber	3,300		Cleaning	150
Millwork	1,200		Glazing	50
Nails	100		Landscaping	350
Iron and Steel	200		Mortgage Exp.	1,000
Carpentry	2,400		Title and Legal	400
Roofing, Flashing,			Advertising, Brokerage	1,200
Gutters and Leaders	950		Insurance	200
Plumbing and Heating	3,700		Supervision	900
Electric Wire and Fixt.	1,250		Total	$29,200
Drywall	1,200		Profit and Overhead	7,300
Windows and Doors	700		(incl. contingency)	
Weatherstrip	70		Total	$36,500
Masonry	550			
Insulation	450		Sq. Ft. Cost—$23.40	

Figure 3.2

MODEL COST ESTIMATE ON A HIGH-RANCH

A MODEL COST ESTIMATE ON AN INDUSTRIAL WAREHOUSE BUILDING

The following model cost estimate is of a proposed industrial warehouse building and is set up on a builder's-type component cost basis:

MODEL COST ESTIMATE

Address *1 Low Street, Exurbia*   Appraisers *S. Barash*

Owner *John Roe*   Type *Beer Warehouse*   Date _____

DESCRIPTION—Proposed industrial building, concrete block walls, brick and alum. panel front facade, poured concrete reinforced foundation on spread footings, 24′ high structure, 900 sq. ft. finished office space, loading dock, 2 overhead doors, no sprinklers, individual well and septic system, 400-amp service, suspended heaters, paved, fenced parking area, building 100′ × 200′, 20,000 sq. ft.

Architect	$ 9,000	Office Finish	12,000
R.O.B. Fill	15,000	Electrical	14,000
Excavating, Grading	7,000	Painting	3,000
Septic System	4,000	Misc. Hardware	6,000
Well	3,000	Legal and Permits	4,000
Paving	18,000	Loan Interest	7,000
Fence	6,000	Insurance	1,000
Foundation	18,000	Subtotal	$286,000
Concrete Floor	24,000		
Masonry	55,000	Contingency and Job	
Front Facade	7,000	Overhead 5%	14,000
Roofing	22,000		
Plumbing	7,000	General Overhead and	
Doors	6,000	Profit 20%	57,000
Steel	38,000	Total	$357,000

Sq. Ft. Cost—$17.80

Figure 3.3

MODEL COST ESTIMATE ON AN INDUSTRIAL WAREHOUSE

Chapter 4

How to conduct building and site inspections: procedures and checklists

You will find several broad groupings in this inspection chapter. *First,* and most important as an office and field yardstick to help give your appraisals exactness, completeness and quality, is the section on *Characteristics of Habitable Properties*. This section is designed and structured as a Site and Building Code. "Characteristics" are set forth separately for each building and plot component, emphasized and underlined as good goals for properties acceptable to the market, with both good and bad practical illustrative examples detailed under each "Characteristics" component.

Second, and vital to your appraisal activities and particularly important for your field inspection and field appraisal data collection, is the *Inspection Checklist for Existing Buildings*, set up for you by building-space location. You can take this list with you to the property you are appraising and use it as a handy tool for inspection and reporting when you walk through each level, each room and about the property.

Finally, and most important for your appraisals of new construction and sites proposed for improvements, is the *third* section, *Inspection Checklist for New Construction*. Various pictorial illustrations from the Handbook, "Wood

Frame Building Construction,'' U.S. Department of Agriculture, are used in this section particularly and in the other sections also, to help you visualize these inspection procedures.

In appraising today, you must do more than merely value the property. You have to first ascertain the location, the topography, the acceptability, the drainage, the satisfactory utilities of the lot and the quality, the structural integrity, the sanitation, the protection from the elements, the functional utility, the very habitability of the building improvements.

If the property is unacceptable by normal market standards or requires upgrading to make it generally acceptable, you must so report to your client and consider these deficiencies in your valuation of the property.

It is truly amazing what can come to life in your reports to the client after you have walked and eyeballed your way through enough properties. The appraiser's building code, *Characteristics of Habitable Construction* and *Inspection Checklists for Existing* and for *New Construction* which follow will soon become like knee-jerk reflexes after you work with them a while. *With the help of these lists, the shoddy building built by a careless builder, the tired old house declining rapidly from years of neglect will not escape your informed scrutiny.*

You are not expected to nor can you certify a building structurally as a professional engineer (unless you are also an engineer), but you can be accountable to your client if you evaluate without reporting factually and completely what is basically wrong with the property. This chapter is here to help you make good inspections and write up complete appraisal reports.

SECTION I

CHARACTERISTICS OF HABITABLE PROPERTIES: A SITE AND BUILDING CODE CHECKLIST

The following ''Characteristics'' define by plot and building component what the market looks for in properties and what you must therefore ascertain to complete your appraisal reports accurately and professionally. Although they pertain mainly to existing properties, you can also use these ''Characteristics'' to check proposed site and building plans when you are appraising new construction. The examples which follow each set of component ''Characteristics'' in this Building Code for Appraisers are culled from a lifetime of appraisal and inspection activities. Both good and bad examples are set forth to detail and illustrate each set of ''Characteristics.'' As the appraiser-inspector, you must always keep the property in perspective, not picking inspection ''lint'' items for voluminous appraisal reports, but looking for and reporting on the quality and habitability of the whole property for your client.

CHARACTERISTICS OF GOOD PLOTS—WHAT TO LOOK FOR
DURING PLOT INSPECTIONS:

*The property should be free of hazards like subsidence, flood erosion and
other hazards which could affect the health and safety of the occupants or
the structural stability of the building or which could affect the customary
use by the inhabitants.*

- *Periodic Area Flooding*—Check for those low waterway areas,
  whether they be streams and watercourses that drain our inlands,
  or ocean tides and storms which periodically flood our ocean-front
  communities and properties. The Flood Disaster Protection Act of
  1973 (U.S. Pl 93-24) provides that no federal agency shall approve any financial assistance for any community that does not
  qualify for the National Flood Insurance program when notified of
  existence of flood-prone areas in the community. Flood hazard
  boundary maps for practically all communities are now available
  and can be secured from Department of Housing and Urban Development, Washington, DC or can be reviewed at your local
  building inspector or town engineer's office.
- *Storm Drainage Flooding*—As you observe or photograph the
  property you are appraising, look to see if there is a drainage
  catchbasin which sits at a low point on the street which when
  blocked with leaves or silt or lack of maintenance, has a history of
  overflowing into the property. Within the property lines, check if
  there is perhaps a catchbasin or a drainage pipe in an easement
  through the property which could have the same overflowing history. Look around. Ask around.
- *Periodic Property Flooding*—The site itself may be at a low point
  in the street. Observe whether there is silt or erosion evidence that
  street drainage during heavy runoff periods overflows the curb line
  for storm water relief *into* the subject plot. Check if the basement
  garage is sufficiently bermed or swaled at the street and at the
  garage apron to divert the storm water runnoff away from the
  garage. Built-in garages in so many of our split-levels, bi-levels
  and basement homes, so often adjoin expensively finished recreation rooms and other habitable rooms which become very uninhabitable when inundated with storm water.
- *Subsidence*—Be alert for evidence of unusual plot or building
  settlement. Watch out for storm or sanitary sewer mains which run
  too close to buildings and which may undermine footings and
  buildings. If you suspect improper building on fill or on unstable
  soils from observing foundation cracks or settlement or from your
  knowledge of the area, don't be afraid to cry, "Wolf!" Better a
  structural engineer testifying in court than you defending the
  omission in your appraisal report.

- *Inharmonious Uses*—Commercial or industrial usages of major portions of residential properties and vice-versa, must be fully reported and considered in value.
- *Heavy, Fast Traffic Exposure*—Residences on major arterial or on numbered highways should be carefully checked for *safety of access* and for *safe sight distances* for cars leaving the subject driveway. Commercial properties depend on traffic count from *both* sides of the fronting road which should be carefully monitored and researched for traffic flow. For example, check if the northbound car can cross the double line legally and safely into southbound traffic and into the subject property's driveway without having the potential customer's car go to a U-turn area past several competitors.
- *Zoning*—Business or industrial zoning of the residential property you are appraising could legally permit change of usage of the property or the neighbors' properties to non-residential use. Perhaps there is residential zoning on the commercial or industrial property you are appraising. Perhaps this non-conforming commercial or industrial property has been out of business just long enough under the zoning law to sink your client financially if he buys the property for business use.
- *Adverse Proximity*—Neighboring adverse uses for residences, such as junkyards, dumps, odoriferous factories, cannot be wished away. They can be reported and considered in value.
- *Airport Proximity*—Know your local airports. There are maps available at the U.S. Federal Aviation Agency (FAA) and at the larger airports which show runway, takeoff and landing height patterns. But trust your ears too. If you have to stop talking to the building occupant every 60 seconds or so and your ears hurt while 100 decibels or more roars from aloft, you might just check this section of the checklist.
- *Erosion*—From small rills come large washouts, including buildings sometimes too. Look at the land. See if there is ground cover on the steep grades. Check if the natural and manmade drainage swales are of sufficient width and gradient to contain the storm water runoff without erosion. Check for unmaintained erosion. Look particularly for threat to the building improvements. Add gravity to water and you have power to destroy. Observe and report this carefully.
- *Legal*—The plot should generally be a single real estate entity unless the property is separated but in such proximity as to still comprise a marketable real estate entity. If surveys, legal descriptions, correct lot dimensions, easements and encroachments are furnished or are available to you, these documents should be carefully reviewed to make certain that all of the improvements are

contained within the subject lot confines and that adjacent properties do not lie in yours. Measure the effect on value of such encroachments and report them. Your client may not know he will be unable to park his car in the common driveway.

CHARACTERISTICS OF GOOD UNIT FACILITIES—HOW TO CHECK FOR PRIVACY OF HABITABLE PROPERTIES:

Each living unit is a detached home, an attached "townhouse" or multi-family dwelling; each occupancy in a commercial or industrial building is to be used and maintained individually without trespass upon adjoining properties.

- *Narrow Sideyards*—Better a party wall between attached buildings than a 2-foot wide "cat-alley," for example, between "detached" older buildings on narrow plots which consequently cannot have their sidewalls painted or repaired.
- *No Maintenance Agreements*—Even wider appearing sideyards sometimes have most of the sideyard on the neighbor's property, there is no maintenance easement agreement and the neighbors don't talk to each other. One cannot set a ladder down with no land available in fee simple or by easement right.
- *Independent Facilities*—Air for heating, cooling or ventilating should be independent, and should not be circulated from one living unit or from one commercial or industrial occupancy to another.
- *Report and Value*—Observe, report and consider in value whenever you compare such diminution in privacy, function, usage or ability to maintain, to other properties which are not so afflicted.

CHARACTERISTICS OF GOOD UNIT UTILITIES—HOW TO CHECK FOR SEPARATE UTILITIES IN THE PROPERTY:

Each living unit or commercial-industrial occupancy should have independent utilities except that common services such as water, sewer, gas and electricity can be provided for multi-occupancy units. Separate utility service shut-offs for each unit should be available.

- *Common Wells*—Be alert to common wells where skimping builders installed one well on the boundary line between two parcels to serve both properties, usually inadequately. It is difficult to collect annual payments for maintenance and replacement regardless of what the deed covenants may or may not say and law suits are expensive.
- *Community Well and Sewers*—There are many small community well and sewer installations in rural and suburban areas which

never received local Health Department or State Public Utility supervision, and even if they did, are too small to be economically viable in terms of the continual maintenance which is needed. After a while, nobody pays and the sewage plant or large septic system overflows into the common water works. Also be alert for the common private sewer line or ''plumber's drain'' which may service a number of properties but unfortunately gets no maintenance until it reaches the public main. For example if the sewer pipe in the building you are appraising exits to a private common alley in the rear instead of to the public street in front, beware. A well in the dwelling, a shallow well, an inadequate yield well are unacceptable and make the property uninhabitable. Often this serious health problem affects much larger community water and sewer systems and there will be problems for your client if you do not report such situations. Look around, ask around. The long-suffering neighbor, the newspaper library ''morgue,'' the local health department should have much to tell you about such serious situations if you are not locally informed yourself.

CHARACTERISTICS OF GOOD ACCESS—HOW TO INSPECT FOR PROPER ACCESS:

Each property should be provided with access by an abutting public or private street. If the street is private, there must be a permanent easement to guaranty access. The width and construction of the street should enable cars, service and emergency vehicles, bicycles and people to get to the property safely at all times.

- *Private Streets*—If the street is private, there should be a deeded or recorded maintenance agreement among abutting landowners to share in maintenance costs. You should be aware that time and human nature perhaps and sometimes simmering neighbor one-on-one relations generally deteriorate the implementation of such legal arrangements. The proof of the agreement is generally what you see. If there is a private street and if there is a legal maintenance agreement and if there are many potholes and/or several feet of unremoved snow and ice, then let your eye guide your pen to save your client's pocketbook. Observe and report and consider in value. You might also be appraising a nice looking level lot with trees and a view for your client who has building plans in hand but who won't be able to get them approved for building. You see, there are many communities in this land which do not issue building permits for lots fronting on private roads.
- *Seasonal Building*—Access to seasonal properties should have access open during appropriate seasons.
- *Access to the Rear Yard*—Each dwelling unit and commercial-industrial occupancy should have access to its rear yard, if there is

one, without having to pass through any other living unit or occupancy.

- *Access to Each Living or Occupancy Unit*—A means of access should be provided to each unit without having to pass through any other unit. Be careful, for instance, of those cheap conversions where the former one-family center hall was not partitioned off properly when it was converted to a two-family and where all those who enter can watch what's on TV as they go by the downstairs apartment which has no privacy. Commercial-industrial occupancies as well as residential demand individual access and privacy for security purposes, and it is important that this access requirement be reported and valued.

CHARACTERISTICS OF GOOD BUILDING AND PLOT PLANNING—WHAT TO LOOK FOR IN PLANNING:

The building and plot should provide for a healthful environment and facilities arranged and equipped to assure suitable living and/or working conditions in line with the type and quality of the property being appraised. Design, like beauty, may be in the eyes of the beholder but basic criteria such as the following should be checked and evaluated against the yardstick of market acceptance:

- *Access and Circulation*—There should be convenient access and circulation around the building improvements.
- *Light and Ventilation*—There should be adequate light and ventilation of rooms and spaces.
- *Privacy*—There should be reasonable privacy for each living unit.
- *Outdoor Uses*—There should be reasonable utility of residential plots for such outdoor uses as laundry drying, gardening, landscaping and outdoor living when common to the area.
- *Individual Utilities*—If individual sewer systems or wells are involved, small plots like 50' × 100' should turn you off or make you look for sewage effluent or smelly tap water. Even if everything appears alright, this type of a potentially polluted environment should be considered in value.
- *Room Sizes*—Rooms too small to hold furniture. Doors, stairs and halls too narrow to get furniture in. Utility areas too small for equipment maintenance.
- *Storage*—Inadequate storage or kitchen cabinets are a problem for the cook-housekeeper and certainly a factor for you to consider in your appraisal report.
- *Garages* which are too small for cars can be given storage value only. Driveways which are too narrow for modern cars to get to the garage also depreciate the garage value to storage value only.

- *Bathrooms* without tubs make it hard to bathe in the washbasin and should be reported and valued.
- *Crawl Spaces* must be ventilated adequately to the exterior or to the basement area which itself must have openable windows. The crawl space should also have an access door for inspection and maintenance.
- *Ventilation* of structural spaces is critically necessary to prevent deterioration of the structures through condensation in winter and to reduce attic heat in the summer. Gable or soffit or hip vents and dormer windows of adequate size must be in place and not blocked off or sealed. (See Figures 4.1 and 4.2 for ventilation requirement illustrations.)
- *Electric Heat* is now very costly. Fortunately, our utility companies are no longer blowing their advertising horns on how economical and clean electric heat is to install and maintain. Unfortunately, during the decade before the energy crunch, millions of buildings were so equipped. Even then, wherever kilowatt hour costs were comparatively inexpensive, the electrically heated building had to be oriented, heavily insulated, with storm doors and windows in order to have reasonable operating cost. Many were not so carefully built and now that kilowatt hour costs are sky-high, it might be well for you to advise your client to get contracts for conversion to alternate energy heat systems or perhaps advise him to look elsewhere.
- *Insulation* is critical to help ward off today's rising utility bills. Six inches of insulation in the attic floor is better than 2 inches which was commonly installed during cheap energy times. Beware of blown insulation in the walls of existing houses, blown in after the house was built. The consequent lack of vapor barrier and ventilation will set up condensation, ice and rot conditions *inside* the walls. (See Figure 4.3 for insulation illustration.)
- *Privacy*—Privacy is an elemental need. Baths off kitchens and access to bathrooms through other bedrooms are for valuation depreciation when compared to comparable properties which have proper privacy for the occupants.
- *Stairs* need proper width and safety features. Narrow, steep interior stairs impede furniture movement. Loose treads, narrow treads, unequal treads, unequal risers, loose or missing handrails, low headroom clearance are all dangerous. Outside wood steps and platforms, supported on wood stringers embedded in dirt or concrete don't last very long.

CHARACTERISTICS OF GOOD MATERIALS—WHAT TO LOOK FOR IN BUILDING MATERIALS:

Building materials should be appropriate to the type of building and should provide adequate structural strength, resist weather and moisture and give reasonable durability and economy of maintenance.

- *Settlement*—Cracking, racking, the building no longer plumb nor level may indicate material failure as well as possible soil bearing problems or workmanship.
- *Exterior*—Windows, doors, obsolete roofings, flashings, chimneys which do not protect from the elements may signify material failure and may affect habitability and value significantly.

CHARACTERISTICS OF GOOD CONSTRUCTION—WHAT TO LOOK FOR IN CONSTRUCTION:

- *Wood members at grade* cause inevitable rot.
- *Clearance*—Crawl spaces should have 18-inch minimum clearance for ventilation and maintenance.
- *Wood posts buried* in concrete or in dirt floors rot.
- *Termites*—In most parts of this country, if you don't see evidence of termites, you should still recommend inspection by a recognized exterminator on all slab-frame buildings, split-levels, bi-levels, buildings low to the grade, buildings with finished basements, buildings with crawl spaces, buildings with attached garages, buildings with low wood sills or jambs in concrete or dirt, buildings in forested areas, buildings in sandy soil; in other words, most wood frame buildings in the United States.
- *Screw jack columns* in the basement may not only indicate understrength and over-stressed or failed floor framing but also will allow uninformed occupants to play with the jack mechanism to "level" floors and possibly bulge walls, rack roofs and generally jack up havoc. Screw jacks should be replaced with lally columns or welded so that the jack is inoperable.
- *Vacant properties*—Check if the building is drained, winterized, secure from vandalism.

CHARACTERISTICS OF EXTERIOR AND INTERIOR FINISHES— WHAT TO LOOK FOR IN FINISHES:

Finishes should provide protection against penetration of moisture, decay, corrosion, insect entry and other destructive elements. Reasonable durability, economical maintenance and an acceptable quality of workmanship is expected.

- *Exterior Paint*—A house needing exterior paint for aesthetic reasons certainly needs reporting and valuing. A house needing paint because the wood shows bare spots must be painted for it to continue to stand.
- *Interior Paint*—Flaking, peeling paint, particularly in older resi-

dential dwellings where it can be assumed lead-based paints were used in many layers, kills children. It must be scraped carefully and covered with lead-free paint or with panel materials.

CHARACTERISTICS OF GOOD MECHANICAL EQUIPMENT—WHAT TO LOOK FOR IN HEATING, PLUMBING AND ELECTRICAL:

Mechanical equipment designed to assure safety of operation, reasonable durability and economy, protection from elements and corrosion, adequate and appropriate capacity and quality for the intended use.

- *Heating*—Today, central heating in appropriate climes is elemental and expected by the market. Space heaters are dangerous.
- *Chimney connections*—Watch out for rotted or unsafe smoke pipe connections.
- *Electric Heat*—Check if the electrically heated dwelling has adequate insulation, storm sash. Check the utility bills if possible.
- *Plumbing*—Check area around the toilet bowl for spongy areas which signify a leaking seal. Turn on upper level faucets to check water pressure. Check if the water heater is a one-year guaranty job now on its tenth year. Check if the plumbing is a mixture of galvanized and copper piping without special insulated connections to prevent deteriorating galvanic reactions.
- *Electric*—Check the electrical service, for adequate size, for enough branches, for enough outlets. Make certain there is not an overloaded service and branches which will be dangerous when modern heavy demand appliances are installed.

SECTION II

INSPECTION CHECKLIST
FOR EXISTING BUILDINGS

This Inspection Checklist for Existing Buildings is designed for your use in the field. It is structured so that the plot, its environs, the building, its levels and rooms can be check-inspected as you ride up to and walk through the property. Location, condition, quality of improvements, safety of occupancy and all other criteria in the checklist are important for your valuation consideration and for the appraisal report you give to the client.

THE PLOT

___ Community facilities, transportation, schools
___ Area low, flood prone
___ Ponding on block, inadequate drainage

__ Ponding areas on lot
__ Is lot drained positively?
__ Does lot need fill?
__ Evidence of subsidence
__ Do gradients permit access and function?
__ Heavy, fast traffic
__ Inharmonious onsite or offsite usages
__ Zoning permits usage
__ Landscaping, setting
__ Usable yard areas
__ No septic effluent visible
__ Potable adequate yield (if well)
__ Erosion? Soils stable?
__ All improvements within lot—any encroachments?
__ Access to property safe, maintained?

BUILDING EXTERIOR

__ Worn, missing shingles on roof
__ Flashing serviceable?
__ Chimneys, fireplaces plumb, mortar okay, washcap alright
__ Any dry rot in wood exterior? Check near grade
__ Exterior paint hides all wood, well-caulked
__ All exterior openings maintained, serviceable
__ All grades drain water away from building
__ Berms at low built-in garage to divert water away from garage
__ No "swayback" roof ridge line
__ Splashblocks under downspouts
__ Adjustable vents for crawl spaces, louvers in attics
__ Paved areas functional, safe. No trip hazards
__ Exterior steps have uniform and proper riser-tread relationships
__ Stair railings sturdy, not rotted

BASEMENT (OR CRAWL SPACE)

__ Stair safe, handrails available
__ Light switch at head of stair
__ Basement floor serviceable, no settlement
__ Dry basement
__ If sump pump, where does it discharge? Does it recirculate back into basement?
__ Is there adequate electric service, branches?
__ Condition of heating equipment, flue pipes
__ Condition of domestic hot water supply
__ Condition of plumbing
__ Condition of walls, efflorescence, eroded mortar?

___ Was basement dug out after house was built? Are footings undermined?
___ All walls plumb; no structural thrust, failures
___ Termite tubes, damage
___ Dry rot in framing members
___ Spliced, sawn, cracked, deflected beams, girders
___ No floor insulation in electric-heated houses
___ Inadequate basement light and ventilation
___ Low ceiling height in basement
___ Less than 18-inch clearance in crawl space
___ Crawl floor reasonably smooth, has vapor barrier or concrete screed floor
___ Crawl space has vents, is insulated or has adequate heat pipes in space and is open fully to basement
___ Crawl space dry
___ Crawl space access openings adequate for inspection and maintenance.

BUILDING INTERIOR

___ Size of rooms adequate for furniture?
___ Width of doors, halls, stairs adequate for passage and furniture movement?
___ Number and depth of closets (bedroom, guest and storage)
___ Privacy of living, occupancy unit
___ Bathroom privacy
___ Adequate storage space for bulky, exterior storage items
___ Commensurate kitchen
___ Sufficient windows
___ Sufficient electrical outlets, switches operable
___ Fireplace works
___ Windows move freely
___ Plaster, drywall free of excessive cracks, "nailpops"
___ Locks work
___ Sufficient insulation in attic
___ Floor, wall finishes acceptable
___ Bath fixtures operable, pressure okay, toilet bowl seal not leaking
___ Paint not peeling, flaking (may brain-damage children)
___ Ceiling leaks (evidencing roof and or plumbing leaks)
___ If vacant, is building drained, secure?

MISCELLANEOUS CHECKLIST (FOR EXISTING BUILDINGS)

___ Is garage long enough for modern cars?
___ Garage door jambs clear of dirt grade, not embedded in concrete, not rotted nor infested
___ Plumbing pipes insulated in built-in garages
___ Is heating unit enclosed from garage?

___ Firewall on common wall of attached garage

___ Adequate insulation in built-in garage ceiling and in common wall of attached garage

___ Pool in a maintained state. All equipment available and apparently serviceable.

— Condition of common lands (if any) of condominium or homeowners association

___ Condition of buildings or improvements owned in common by condominium or association (if any)

SECTION III

INSPECTION CHECKLIST
FOR NEW CONSTRUCTION

This is a basic new construction checklist for appraisers who are requested to inspect buildings for, say, staged mortgage construction payouts by their lender-clients, and this checklist is so grouped by building payout stages. It is designed for typical frame house construction but the checklist's approach and framework is applicable as well to typical small commercial, industrial and residential improvements of other design and materials.

FIRST INSPECTION STAGE—Excavation complete and ready for footings and foundations. Forms, reinforcing (if required) in.

___ Soil virgin—no footings on fill

___ Excavation 6 inches into undisturbed soil

___ Soil appears to be in stable bearing condition

___ Ground water lower than proposed lowest floor elevation

___ Controlled fills engineered by soils engineer

___ Bottom of proposed footing is level

___ Footing side forms used where soil conditions warrant

___ Reinforcing installed when plans or soil conditions require or when footing projection excessive

___ Adequate edge insulation for slab construction

___ Footings measure per building plan

___ List all change orders from plans and specifications

___ List incomplete items for reinspection

SECOND INSPECTION STAGE—Foundation walls complete and ready for backfill. (Note that this second inspection stage may often be combined with the first inspection when no soil conditions nor ground water problems are known in area.) (See Figures 4.4 and 4.5 on pages 70 and 71 as examples of unit masonry foundation walls and second stage construction.

___ Footings installed per specification and plan and not less than 6 inch thickness. If plain concrete, thickness not less than 1½ times the footings's projection. Integral flared footings where soil and climate and plans permit

__ Foundation walls measure per plan and spec

__ Walls plumb, level, true

__ Walls solid capped if hollow masonry

__ Walls and piers minimum 8 inches above grade if supporting wood frame construction

__ Pilasters are integral with foundation and located under girders and wherever specified or shown on plans

__ Concrete block walls dampproofed and stuccoed as required

__ Concrete walls dampproofed properly per plan

__ No debris or organic matter in backfill area

__ Grade beams and pier bottoms below frost line

__ Mortar joints full, tooled average ½-inch maximum

__ Chases and recesses installed as wall built

__ No extensive honeycombing in poured concrete walls

__ Footing drains in place, have positive outfall

__ List change orders and incomplete items for reinspection

THIRD INSPECTION STAGE—Building erected, exterior enclosed, roofing installed, structural members still exposed on interior and roughing-in for heating, plumbing and electrical work in place. (See Figures 4.6, 4.7 and 4.8 on pages 71-73 for various illustrations of Third Inspection Stage construction.)

__ Building complies in size and layout with plans and specifications

__ List change orders to-plans and specifications

__ Foundation wood house sills have anchor bolts properly installed per plan

__ Floor wood girders are installed per plan, laminated properly, supported properly

__ Steel girders bear properly on steel or masonry supports

__ Columns are plumb with secure base and cap

__ Enough and proper size nails

__ Doubled joists under parallel partitions or specially supported

__ Floor framing cut for pipe runs properly reframed

__ Framing headers doubled were shown on plans or specs and as required

__ If attic accessible by stair, ceiling joists are sized larger for storage.

__ Roof rafters tied property to ceiling joists. Where cannot be tied, rafters properly supported by partitions or other positive support to prevent roof thrust.

__ In split-levels and other type balloon frame are these balloon walls fire-stopped?

__ Exterior walls have sheet sheathing, sheet siding or corner bracing to prevent wall racking.

__ All headers over openings rest *on* jamb studding.

__ Stair treads hardwood or covered with suitable finish material.

__ Plywood outerplies installed perpendicular to framing members.

__ Finish carpentry free of toolmarks and other objectionable defects.
__ Mechanical rough-ins acceptable and complete.
__ Roofing material per spec, nailed adequately and flashed properly.
__ Exterior openings flashed properly.
__ Exterior finish and trim material painted, protected from elements.
__ Brick veneer has good bearing, level, good joints, weepholes, flashed
    properly.
__ List incomplete items for reinspection.

INTERMEDIATE INSULATION INSPECTION STAGE—At client's option
because of its current critical importance, a special insulation inspection
can be done before the *Fourth Inspection* to check on thickness, vapor
barrier (to warm side) and installation workmanship. See Figure 4.3 for
insulation illustration.

FOURTH INSPECTION STAGE—All building construction, equipment,
utility connections, accessory buildings, grading, drainage, landscaping,
walks, drives, steps, retaining walls complete.

__ Building improvements comply with plans and specs
__ List change orders from plans and specs
__ Certificate of Occupancy Number
__ Underwriter's Certificate Number
__ Basement concrete floor level, finished properly
__ Electrical, heating, plumbing installed properly
__ Crawl space floor has screed coat or vapor barrier
__ Adequate ventilation of all structural spaces. (See Figures 4.1 and 4.2
    for ventilation illustrations.)

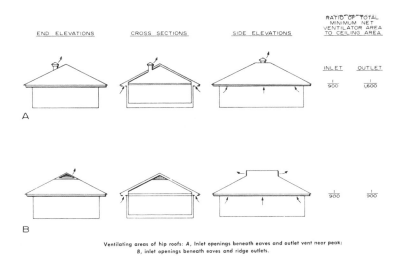

Ventilating areas of hip roofs: A, Inlet openings beneath eaves and outlet vent near peak;
B, inlet openings beneath eaves and ridge outlets.

Figure 4.1

VENTILATING AREAS OF HIP ROOFS

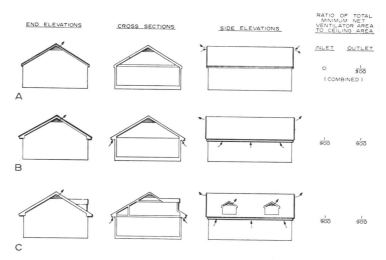

Ventilating areas of gable roofs: A, Louvers in end walls; B, louvers in end walls with additional openings in soffit area; C, louvers at end walls with additional openings at eaves and dormers. Cross section of C shows free opening for air movement between roof boards and ceiling insulation of attic room.

Figure 4.2
VENTILATING AREAS OF GABLE ROOFS

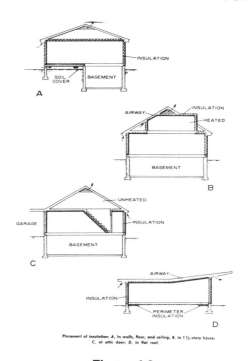

Placement of insulation: A, In walls, floor, and ceiling; B, in 1½-story house; C, at attic door; D, in flat roof.

Figure 4.3
PLACEMENT OF INSULATION IN HOUSES

___ All windows, doors operate freely
___ Water and all utilities on and operating
___ All lot improvements, drives, walks, steps, accessory buildings, land-
   scaping, topsoil per plan and specs, installed properly

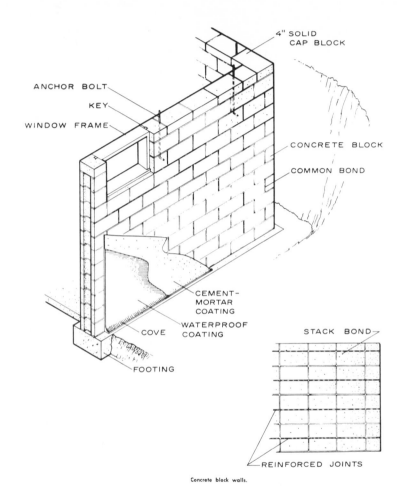

Concrete block walls.

Figure 4.4

UNIT MASONRY WALLS

___ All offsite improvements, streets, curbs, public walks, drainage in and
   paid for
___ List incomplete items for reinspection

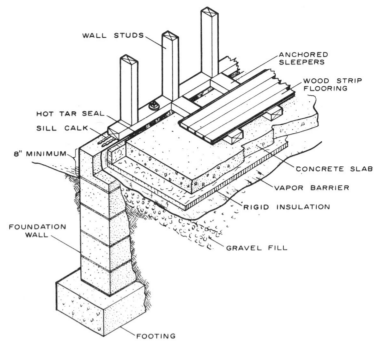

Independent concrete floor slab and wall. Concrete block is used over poured footing which is below frostline. Rigid insulation may also be located along the inside of the block wall.

Figure 4.5

FLOOR AND WALL CONSTRUCTION

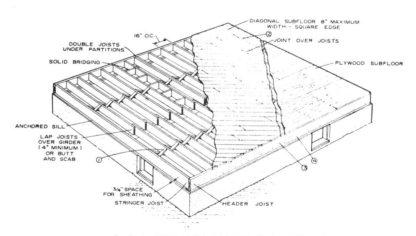

Floor framing: (1) Nailing bridging to joists; (2) nailing board subfloor to joists; (3) nailing header to joists; (4) toenailing header to sill.

Figure 4.6

FLOOR FRAMING

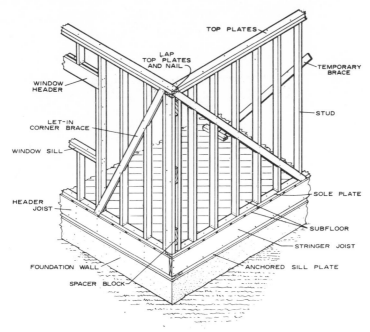

Wall framing used with platform construction.

Figure 4.7

WALL FRAMING, PLATFORM CONSTRUCTION

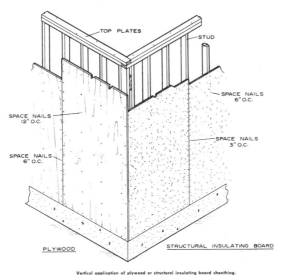

Vertical application of plywood or structural insulating board sheathing.

Figure 4.8

SHEATHING APPLICATION

Chapter 5

How to appraise land

Look to the land . . . Land is the basis for all value . . . Underlying all value is the land. . . .

These aphorisms are just a few of the many ways man has expressed the worth of land. You will find in this chapter explanations and practical examples of how this worth is measured and appraised.

Since we now live and work mainly in expanding suburban-exurban metropolitan regions, the first important section in this chapter deals with feasibility analyses for proposed residential land subdivisions. Current environmental concerns and land use controls are stressed here because of their mounting impact on land value.

In your day-to-day work you will also find helpful the sections on how to appraise land with subsurface resources, residential lots, commercial lots, lots with trees, leasehold lands.

Since feasibility studies and tract subdivision appraisal reports depend so much on each other, a Model Feasibility-Tract Subdivision Appraisal Report is presented. Also, since our nation appears to be on a "fast-food" binge, this is reflected here in a Model Commercial Lot Appraisal for a suburban "fast food" chain.

HOW TO DETERMINE FEASIBILITY FOR
PROPOSED RESIDENTIAL LAND SUBDIVISIONS

If you follow the old rule of thumb that land increases in value at 10% per year, you will surely direct your investor or speculator or developer clients into bankruptcy!

It is statistically true that on the whole, land throughout our country has been appreciating *in average value*, particularly since WWII. However, different areas and different regions have gone up and many have gone down to make this average. You cannot depend upon a regular upward sweep of land values to rescue your too optimistic projections in your area or for that matter in any area.

You have noted in the earlier definitions chapter how I appraised acreage in Orange County, New York in 1963 for about $500 an acre. You followed the escalation in multiples of $500 through 12 years of land sales to over $3,000 per acre. Fourteen years later, I appraised the same land tracts for $500 in this depressed region. A frightening saga. Land values fall dramatically as well as rise spectacularly in different areas for differing economic reasons, often during the same period.

Regionalization and localization are keys to land value. Economic recession in the Northeast and Midwest vs. growth in the "Sunbelt" causes differing regional rates of land value decline and appreciation. Many localized factors also affect each land tract including "no-and-slow growth" zoning, environmental concerns, coastal and wetland use controls, cost of gasoline and long-range fear of gasoline shortages affecting sale to commuters on metropolitan outer rings.

In addition, factors intrinsic to the tract such as its location, topography, subsurface conditions, drainage and access also remain critically important when you are determining whether a tract is feasible for proposed land subdivision.

Will buyers want to buy the plots and homes on this tract? How is the economy? Where will the buyers work? What's the development competition in the area? These local and area sales market questions must also be field-checked and analyzed for your tract feasibility report.

In the final analysis, even reviewing, understanding and reporting all national, regional, environmental, financial and intrinsic factors are not enough. Feasibility comes down finally to the simple question: Will it sell?

In tract subdivision valuation, risks can be forecast and exposed by careful field analysis and reporting. I have drawn from several decades of government and private experience in land tract feasibility reviews, the following feasibility field checklist for proposed residential land subdivisions. Take this checklist with you when you do your field inspection of the tract and your consultations with local authorities. It will help you cover the field data you need for your narrative feasibility and valuation report. (See also Model Proposed Subdivision Feasibility and Appraisal Report in later section.)

FEASIBILITY STUDY FOR PROPOSED LAND SUBDIVISIONS
A FIELD CHECKLIST

Subdivision _____ Acres _____ Date _____
Location _____ Owner _____

The Community	*Miles*
1. Schools	
2. Jobs	
3. Local shopping	
4. Major shopping	
5. Parks	
6. Churches	
7. Hospitals	
8. Nearest development	
9. Master plan	
10. Prelim. local approval?	

The Land	*Yes No*
11. Accessible	
12. Adverse views	
13. Adverse traffic	
14. Smoke or fumes	
15. Flooding	
16. Landslide	
17. Subsidence	

The Land	*Yes No*
18. Air traffic	
19. Existing fill	
20. Topog. acceptable	
21. Needs fill?	

The Utilities	*Yes No*
22. Public water	
23. Fire protection	
24. Electric	
25. Electric	
26. Phone	
27. Street lighting	
28. Garage removal	
29. Police protection	
30. Storm sewers	
31. Paved street to site	
32. Public transportation	
33. Zoning	
34. Further development of area	

35. List 3 comparable tracts and lot prices assigned to each:
_____ $ _____
_____ $ _____
_____ $ _____
36. Air Quality _____ 37. Water Quality _____
38. Environmental Criteria _____
39. Demand for Housing _____ 40. Typical Lot Price $ _____
41. Suitable for Development? __ 42. Typical Lot Size _____
43. Remarks (Use Above Nos.) _____
_____
_____

Figure 5.1

**FIELD CHECKLIST FOR FEASIBILITY
OF LAND SUBDIVISIONS**

HOW TO EVALUATE ENVIRONMENTAL REQUIREMENTS AND THEIR EFFECT ON LAND VALUES

Value is created through use. The buyer buys the right to use the land to its highest and best use and generally pays what others are paying for similar land, similarly situated.

This right to use, or "bundle of rights," as it is sometimes called, is diminished for practically all land to some degree. Zoning, local no-and-slow growth controls, easements, convenants and in the last decade particularly, environmental restrictions, continue to erode free use of all land to varying degrees. These land use controls are particularly effective insofar as use and market value of unimproved land is concerned. After all, land improved with an existing commercial structure can generally continue to be used on a non-conforming basis even though residential zoning is subsequently installed. An industrial building in lowland can continue to operate even though land use controls and environmental "wetlands" prohibitions would bar development of the adjoining tract.

The National Environmental Policy Act has had increasing effect on the use of coastal areas, wetlands, beaches, historical sites, archeological sites, watersheds, mineral land reclamation and housing. States like California have enforced strong state coastal laws. The National Flood Insurance Program requires that land use legislation be installed in all communities which have identifiable flood areas before any property in their communities can qualify for inexpensive government flood insurance. These all are but examples of the many national and state environmental restrictions which when added to local no growth and slow growth pressures bar or severely limit development of much of our vacant land.

Environmental restrictions have become a major modern concern, particularly in land development. For example, your most carefully researched and documented feasibility-appraisal report with value based on projected use for 300 building lots would count for nought if your client is later denied approval because wetlands, flood plain or historic location bars the development. Your feasibility and valuation report should include limiting conditions that full governmental (including environmental) approvals will ultimately be given. Pragmatically, the best advice to your client buying land for such major development should be to buy on option pending such approval.

The following Environmental Restrictions Checklist will help you to make site inspections and secure data from authorities.

ENVIRONMENTAL RESTRICTIONS CHECKLIST

	YES	NO
FLOODING		
Site Flooding?	———	———
Block Flooding?	———	———
Area Flooding?	———	———
Flood Insurance Available?	———	———
WETLANDS		
Local Land Use Plan Bars Filling?	———	———
COASTAL		
Federal, State Bars to Development?	———	———
Local Restrictions on Beach Development?	———	———
HISTORIC SITE		
Site Identified as Historic?	———	———
ARCHEOLOGIC SITE		
Site Identified as Archeological?	———	———
WATERSHED		
Site a Watershed for a Reservoir?	———	———
MINERALS (i.e., a sand and gravel pit)		
Land Reclamation Required?	———	———
AIRPORTS		
In Flight Pattern?	———	———
ENVIRONMENTAL PROTECTION REQUIREMENTS		
Impact Statement Needed on Air?	———	———
Impact Statement Needed on Water?	———	———
Impact Statement Needed on Solid Waste?	———	———
Impact Statement Needed on Sewage Discharge?	———	———
Impact Statement Needed on Noise?	———	———

Figure 5.2

ENVIRONMENTAL RESTRICTIONS CHECKLIST

HOW TO APPRAISE LAND WITH SUBSURFACE SAND AND GRAVEL, OIL, GAS OR OTHER MINERAL RESOURCES

The basic building material for suburban expansion has been the sand and gravel pit. Needed for roads, for concrete and masonry products and other improvements, these "borrow" pits have since WWII helped to pave and build our land.

In the process, borrow pits have increased in value, depending on location, grade of material, extent of and distance to construction in area and on available supply. In 15 years, I have seen bulk sand and gravel go in price in Orange County, New York from 25¢ a yard "run-of-the-bank," truck it yourself, to $3. Many of these pits contained a million yards or more. I have also seen pits abandoned and sold for taxes with front-end loaders rusted in place when construction fell off or ceased.

When land with subsurface oil, gas or other mineral deposits is appraised, it should be done only on the basis of specialized geologists' reports, including drilling reports. When you appraise land with sand and gravel, you should advise your client to secure drilling reports spotted throughout the acreage so that a subsurface contoured survey may be plotted for you together with the surveyor's estimate therefrom of the number of cubic yards of sand and gravel. Assuming the land is zoned for such mining and assuming that there is a ready market for the material, your appraisal can be completed on an economic approach capitalizing the projected net return on the minerals. The survey can be used subsequently by your client because simple surface surveys will easily measure material extracted.

Your appraisal must also take special account of the future cost of reclamation of the land during and after extraction which will surely be a condition of local approval under present environmental requirements.

HOW TO DO A RESIDENTIAL LOT APPRAISAL

How far does a rat run? When you appraise a lot for residential improvement purposes, you must check for adverse influences differently than if you were doing an industrially zoned lot for a proposed warehouse. For example, the residentially zoned lot near a garbage dump is affected by such proximity. In one neighborhood, it was determined that rats move regularly within a half-mile circle from a carelessly operated dump.

People don't like to live near garbage dumps and rats. Residential lot values reflect such adverse locations. Besides obvious adverse factors like garbage dumps your lot feasibility location checklist should include analysis of other adverse industrial-commercial or compatible residential usages in the neighborhood and on the block. Is the location convenient to schools, shopping, community facilities, transportation, employment? Is lot size adequate for improvement? Your field check should also include study and analysis of off-site road, sidewalk and utility improvements as well as on-site acceptable topography, subsoil conditions, positive drainage, ground cover and soil bearing information. If feasible to build, you should check your amenities, trees, views, neighboring usages, zoning, environmental controls, deed restrictions and covenants.

Highest and best use is defined as that use which can be appraised as most likely to give the largest net return over a period of time. This return can be in money or in the case of residential property, in amenity value (use and enjoyment by occupant). Assume that from field inspection, your first step, you have determined that the subject vacant plot's highest and best use is residential because its neighbors are residential and the block and neighborhood is residential.

Your second step is then to check whether this projected highest and best use for residential improvement is permitted by zoning. Then, in the third step, go to the value plateau. Study the values in the neighborhood, the block, the house "next door." If these nearby lots are improved, study the improved values. Secure and validate and compare at least three recent sales of similar lots, similarly situated. Fourth step, come to your opinion of value and write your report.

HOW TO DO A COMMERCIAL LOT APPRAISAL

In our burgeoning suburban-exurban society which moves everywhere on its car wheels, one of your most important appraisal data sources for commercial appraisals is the office of the State Highway Superintendent, Auto Traffic Count Section.

States plan their road improvements and have received federal road grants based on the "ADTC," Average Daily Traffic Count which most highway departments take regularly at all important roads. These public records are available and invaluable to you when you appraise commercial lots.

Gas stations are not the only ones interested in the number of cars which pass in front of their doors. From fast food stores to now even funeral parlor drive-ins for visitations, the "ADTC" is critical to site feasibility and selection. In the final analysis, all other factors being acceptable for commercial improvements, the total number of passing car wheels with proper access make value in most commercial appraisals. Most commercial chains specify minimum "ADTC" count for their proposed site locations. You have to secure this information not only to satisfy clients with such specified requirements but also to compare your site to your comparable sites as one critically important value measure.

Obviously, zoning must permit the projected commercial use. Your appraisal should generally specify a purchase option subject to approval for the use contemplated and appraised. Your value will generally be based on recent sales of similar commercial lots for similar purposes in similar locations. I've bought, sold and appraised many gas station sites, for example, along Interstate Highway Interchanges. The selling prices were generally within 10 to 15% of each other, depending generally upon traffic count and proximity to the Interchange ramps. You can generally depend on the Market approach for your commercial lot appraisals.

In sum, step-by-step feasibility and valuation analysis on commercial lot appraisals is as follows:

● *First step,* get car count, curb cut laws, sign laws, zoning laws and determine whether and which permitted commercial usage is highest and best use.

● *Second step,* field inspect (walk) site and block, noting whether the size, shape and topography of the plot is conducive for commercial improvement and whether cut or fill is required.

● *Third step,* field check (drive) past the plot and in the vicinity, observing whether plot improvements (and signs) would have good visibility in both directions and whether cars are allowed to enter property from both sides of street.

● *Fourth step,* note all neighboring conducive and adverse usages in vicinity.

● *Fifth step,* secure comparable lot sales data and field inspect (using this checklist also) for comparison of each comparable used.

● *Sixth step,* write report (See Model Commercial Lot Appraisal in later section.)

HOW TO VALUE THE EFFECT OF TREES

In real estate appraising, trees enhance value as they stand, backdrop or screen the building, not for the intrinsic value of the wood in the trees.

A black walnut tree in Ohio sold recently for $30,000. Then its 57-foot long, 48-inch wide trunk was cut down and sawed into approximately 3 acres of veneer for fine furniture. Most black walnut trees run from $200 to $1,500 now, depending on height of trunk and diameter, if they can be sold before the tree rustler gets them. Trees are valuable intrinsically—walnut trees for veneer, timberland for newspapers and for our other needs. This is all value of course, but not for appraised residential value. For years, statisticians and textbook writers have attempted to measure and chart by diameters and heights and foot-dollars, so to speak, the effect trees have on residential value—a difficult task.

Your appraisal work is to make subjective opinions on value based on objective collection of data. To isolate the factor of trees and assign say $250 for the 60-foot high oak and $600 for the 20-foot high Japanese maple may be within the realm of arithmetic. What do you do when you appraise a lot on 1 acre with a stand of 85 average 60-foot high trees? Assign $38,000 to trees and $27,000 to building?

Stay away from tree arithmetic. Recognize that most buyers look for and believe that trees add value to residential properties. Note carefully whether the neighborhood features better homes on treed lots as they do in most such cases. Find your comparable sales from such locations if you are appraising such a property set amidst trees.

Appraisal reports which require Cost approaches as well as the primary Market approach should have some value ascribed to trees along with the amount stated for landscaping, but this again is subjectively fractioning your value. Look to the market mainly for similar comparables in timbered settings for your best opinions of value.

HOW TO MAKE LEASEHOLD LAND APPRAISALS

In the vast majority of your appraisal work, you will be dealing with land ownership fee simple where the owner holds the plot in fee simple use and exercises all rights not circumscribed or barred by zoning, covenants, restrictions, easement, or other limiting public or private control. In most of suburbia, building improvements on leasehold land are comparatively rare. In other countries, and particularly in our state of Hawaii, building improvements on leasehold land are the norm. If you work there, you will have more experience with this type of real estate interest.

However, you may get assigned occasionally to do an appraisal on leasehold land in certain areas and on certain types of properties. It is important to know that a 99-year lease spanning more than three generations is good enough for most banks to make mortgages on, the same as if fee simple were involved. You must read the lease carefully to make certain there is a 99-year lease or that there is at least 50 years left to run, with no right of reversion intervening during this period and with reasonable stated cost-of-living rent changes. Then this leasehold land can be considered as a marketable entity. Your Market approach utilizing fee simple comparables can be used to secure your best opinion of value for the whole improved property. The income approach, capitalizing the ground rent paid for the land lease, should be used to determine the value of the lessor's ground rent interest.

The step-by-step procedure is as follows: First estimate the value of the improved property as though it were owned in fee simple and unencumbered by a lease. The value of the leased fee is then determined and deducted from the estimated value of the unencumbered property. The resulting difference is accepted as the value of the leasehold (land), plus the improvements.

ILLUSTRATION: A one-family dwelling, located on 1 acre of leased land. Lease is 99 years, 60 years left on term, no reverter, renewable.

Estimated value of dwelling on 1 acre	$60,000
Less value of lessor's ground rent interest	3,000
Lessee's leasehold (land) interest, including building	57,000
Less depreciated building cost	40,000
Value of leasehold (land)	$17,000

A MODEL FEASIBILITY STUDY AND TRACT SUBDIVISION APPRAISAL REPORT

To conserve space but not usability as a handbook model, the following study-report has been condensed and exhibits referred to but not attached. Note especially environmental review data in the Land and Environmental Impact sections, the water and sewer comment in the Utilities section, zoning data in Local Authorities section and the ''Best Comparable'' selection in the Land Sales section. Also note the recommendations on option-purchase arrangements in the Feasibility section.

PROPOSED LAND SUBDIVISION

FEASIBILITY AND APPRAISAL REPORT

Appraiser *Ms. Anne Doe*   Date _____   Owner *Hope Realty, Inc.*
Subdivision *Not named yet*   Acres *197*
Location *Rt. 92 and My Ave., Suburbia*

This is a feasibility study and appraisal report on the above-identified proposed land tract subdivision.

The Land—There are 197 acres of undeveloped vacant land with 2,900 feet of frontage on Route 92, 1,500 feet of frontage on My Ave., with land not abutting public roads adjoining similar undeveloped land of others. The tract is located in the town of Suburbia, N.Y. pop. 10,000, 1,000 feet south of the incorporated Village of Suburbia, N.Y., approximately 50 miles northwest of N.Y.C. It is fully accessible from two road arterials, the numbered Route 92 and heavily trafficked My Ave. which runs between Suburbia and the Village of Arthur Falls 7 miles south. (See attached location map—Exhibit A.) There is an adverse view of a high tension 200 foot wide electric power easement with high towers bisecting the tract which would have to be considered in tract layout and in value of the subdivision lots. Heavy, fast traffic on both Rt. 92 and My Ave. will require subdivision layout which will minimize plot driveways entering directly onto these roads. The tract has approximately 15% wetlands according to field inspection, topographic maps and town zoning maps which show swampy flood plain. Careful site, layout, engineering, drainage and cut and fill studies will be critically necessary. (See attached geodetic topographic map—Exhibit B.) Gradient study also reveals approximately 5% terrain with grades exceeding 1 : 2. Terrain is well ground covered with good stands of trees on steep grades. There are no adverse smoke, fumes, landslide, subsidence, air traffic nor existing fill problems. The site is aesthetically pleasing with a majority of the acreage cleared former dairy farmland, a stream wending through the meadows and the timbered hills gracing the southern periphery of the tract.

The Community—Elementary and high school are within 2 miles. Local employment is basically low to moderate weekly wage warehouse, factory and service industry oriented within a 20-mile radius. Better paying salaries which could afford projected development are 40 to 50 miles to the south and east in New Jersey, Westchester and New York City. Interstate highway access to this site for commuting is excellent. Major shopping is 15 to 20 miles; local shopping is adequate and within 1½ miles. Local parks are limited. Tract layout should provide for parks and playgrounds. County parks are available within 15 miles. Closest hospital is 4 miles with excellent major highway access. Churches abound locally. The community has a master plan. There is no preliminary local approval on this tract and no record of a prior subdivision submission. (See attached Zoning Map, Exhibit C, with subject site sketched thereon.)

The Utilities—There is no public water nor public sewer in the town. Fire protection is volunteer. Electric and gas are in roads but only electric can be connected. Phone service is available. Garbage removal is by private carter. All streets around and to site are public and paved and maintained. The site is 1 mile from public transportation busses and 1½ miles to trains. Well diggers in area have records of nearby high yield wells averaging no more than 100 feet deep into sand and gravel aquifers. The stream which drains the site is mainly seasonal, drying to a trickle in the summer. It is highly doubtful whether State Health Dept. would approve this stream for discharge and dilution of effluent from a community sewer plant for the proposed subdivision. However, there is a village sewer plant with sewer main only 1,000 feet from subject site. Village officials stated they may sell sewer service to this subdivision on a connection charge contract basis. This would be critically important for site development and should be completely investigated and legally contracted for in advance of purchase and development.

Contact with Local Authorities—There is a combination Village and Town Engineer-building inspector, a Town Planning Board, a Zoning Board of Appeals and a Subdivision Ordinance as well as Zoning Ordinance and Master Plan. Town Boards meet on a regular and special basis. Zoning for this site shows R-15 (2.5 units per acre) residential one-family, 95%; R-.5 (1 unit per 2 acres) 5%. Clustering is permitted by special exception zoning procedures. This zoning is favorable since the tract lies at the edge of the existing developed village and conforms to current county and local planning which stresses building near existing built-up communities rather than spot rural tract development with community facilities and utilities. Future development in this area should follow this pattern and this site lies athwart this pattern.

Three Comparable Tracts—Town and Country Homes, an existing, recently built development on $15,000 (estimated) lots; Hill and Dale Estates with 125 plots half-built with some remaining lots (improved) for sale and sold for $19,000; Mountain Lake Estates with 200 lots on ½ acre $16,000 (estimated) lots; all developments cited are within 10 miles.

Environmental Impact Analysis—Aforementioned power line easements, wetlands and steep gradients can be coped with by cluster layout. Although water capability of subterranean aquifers in vicinity is reported good, a test well should be installed.

Demand for Housing This Area—Demand is good in moderate price range of $40,000 to $50,000 with basic demand from N.Y.C. commuters. An estimated typical lot price would be $16,000 for a typical lot of 15,000 sq.ft. Market demand is for single-family detached homes. Zoning permits clustering. This should be employed considering the comparatively large amount of low and hilly land and high cost of public road and utility improvements.

Development Cost Projection

```
Acreage  ..................................... 197 acres
Wetlands (15%)............................. 30 acres (no zoning credit)
Steep gradients (5%)........................ 10 acres (no zoning credit)
Utility easement ............................  7 acres (no zoning credit)
Net acreage for subdividing ................ 150 acres
R-15 Zoning (15,000 SF) 140 Acres × 2.0 Lots per acre = 280 lots
R-.5 Zoning (80,000 SF)  10 Acres × .4 Lots per acre =    4
                                        Total Lots 284
```

Raw Land Cost and Improvement Costs

Land.............197 Acres × $1,000 per acre $197;000
Est. Improvement Costs 284 lots @ $5,500.................... 156,000
      Total (say) $355,000
Value Projection.......284 lots @ $16,000.........................$454,000

LAND SALE COMPARABLES

Hennings to Jessup	Smith to Jones	Hoot to Hollar
Liber 1010/P. 140	Liber 1015/P.10	990/18
$140,000 Sales Price	$160,000 S.P.	$250,000
June 19___	Jan. 19___	Nov. 19___
Woolich, N.Y. Rt. 10	Exurbia, N.Y.	Exurbia
Sim. locat.	Sim. locat.	Inferior location
Sim. zoning	Sim. zoning	Inferior zoning
Sim. topo.	Better topo.	Sim. topo.
$1,000 per acre	$1,050 per acre	$850 per acre
140 acres	150 acres	300 acres
"Best Comparable"		

OPINION OF VALUE

Subject property adjusts at $1,000 per acre utilizing market approach to a total value of ONE HUNDRED NINETY SEVEN THOUSAND DOLLARS ($197,000)

FEASIBILITY

This site appears feasible for development of approximately 284 one-family homes on 15,000 sq. ft. lots, the highest and best use. Option-purchase arrangements should be made subject to engineering analysis, test well, contract sewerage and preliminary local subdivision approval.

_____   _____
   Dated   Ms. Anne Doe

A MODEL COMMERCIAL LOT APPRAISAL FOR A SUBURBAN "FAST FOOD" CHAIN STORE

The same site selection criteria which governed the tens of thousands of gasoline service stations which were installed during the sixties along the U.S. Interstate Highway system interchanges as well as on other major routes now govern "fast food" site selection.

Although the major oil companies have mainly stopped service stations location expansion, with some companies even contracting and closing down station outlets, "fast food" sites are still being found and improved in suburban and urban locations. As with service stations, fast food sites must be appraised based on market comparable sales of other fast food locations. Again, apples must be compared to apples. This particular use demands top locations in most cases, since such sites may be much higher valued than adjoining sites without the same requirements listed below.

Visibility, high traffic count, large sign permission, good access, adequate frontage, permissive zoning, adequate level space for building and parking improvements and a minimum local population in the vicinity are still key criteria. The following is an abbreviated appraisal of a commercial lot proposed for purchase and improvement with a chain-type fast food store, again mentioning but not including exhibits to save handbook space.

MODEL COMMERCIAL LOT APPRAISAL

Purpose of Appraisal—This appraisal is for the purpose of arriving at an opinion of the Fair Market Value of the subject property for sale on the open market under conditions prevailing Sep. 1, 19_____ and is based on a physical inspection of the parcel, analysis of the sale of comparable properties and consideration of all value factors.

Location—300 feet n/o easterly ramp Rt. 84, s/s Rt. 15, Mattrix, N.Y.

Size—200′ × 200′ square, level to road (See att. sketch, Exhibit B.)

Vicinity—Mattrix, N.Y. is a small incorporated city of 27,000 which has historically, geographically and topographically been located in the mountain pass of a 1,500 foot mountain chain, originally a railroad city because of its location and now being opened for development by Interstate Highway 84. (See Location Map Exhibit A.)

Legal—Tax Map City of Mattrix, Section 102, Bl.1 Lot 10. No survey.

Fair Market Value Definition—That which a ready, willing and able and knowledgeable buyer would pay an equally qualified seller in an arm's length transaction, neither acting under duress.

Environs and Economic Milieu—The property is readily accessible to major highways as well as city streets because of its prime location as the first plot permitted a building permit by Interstate Highway 300-foot rule from ramp. The city of Mattrix is an old railroad town with a depressed economic base 80 miles from N. Y. C. The site is located in the heart of a fairly new commercial highway strip at the edge of the city which is supplanting the city commercial district. This parcel is zoned commercial for its full width and depth permitting the proposed fast food restaurant use, and the site has prime ramp location. (See valuation discussion.)

Highest and Best Use—Based on location, topography, zoning, this parcel's highest and best use is for highway commercial.

Easements and Encumbrances—None known

Traffic Count—ADTC—25,000 cars per N.Y. State Highway Dept.

Assessment—$40,000

Method of Appraisal—Market Data Approach

Interest Appraised—Fee Simple

VALUATION—Sales throughout the area of similar plots with similar zoning and similar locations for similar improvement with fast food restaurants, have been reviewed and analyzed. Comparables have been adjusted for location, topography, road frontage, traffic count and market area. No time adjustments needed.

HILL to DOE	KAHN to ROE	RAM to SYM
Liber 2,000 P.102	1,800/10	1,500/15
$120,000 Selling Price	$105,000	$150,000
November, 19____	July, 19__	Jan. 19____
Rt. 84 and Rt. 100	Rt. 84 and Rt. 7	Rt. 84 and Rt. 15
Woolrich, Pa.	Hilldale, N.Y.	Mattrix, N. Y.
210′ × 170′	175′ × 250′	250′ × 200′
Burger King	Burger King	MacDonalds
Needed 2 feet fill	Needed 4-foot cut	North ramp same interchg.
Sim. locat. and count	Sim. locat. and count	Better traffic count
Adjusts $130,000	Inferior visibility	*Best comparable*
	Adjusts $125,000	Adjusts $135,000

OPINION OF VALUE—Considering all factors, particularly location, utility, "Best Comparable," road frontage, topography and size, a land value of ONE HUNDRED THIRTY FIVE THOUSAND DOLLARS IS ASCRIBED ($135,000) to the subject commercial lot.

Samuel T. Barash
Appraiser

Dated _____

Chapter 6

Techniques and procedures
for appraising
new construction

In this chapter I'll show you how to appraise new construction from plans and specifications.

After completion, of course, new construction can be appraised the same way you appraise existing construction. However, this chapter deals specifically with appraising *proposed* construction, using the tools of the builder, his plans and specifications. It is important that you know these proposed construction appraisal techniques so that you can also appraise for banks, government agencies and other clients who want to know what a property will be worth *before* it is built.

Skyrocketing land, construction and land improvement costs have effectively limited the market for new one-family homes to only one out of four families. The "average" new home is selling for over $55,000. Yet these same national surveys indicate that the "American Dream" still remains the new one-family home surrounded by its own lawns. Since proposed construction requires the same appraisal techniques for commercial-industrial properties as for residential, we have selected the basic one-family detached house for appraisal demonstration as still a representative sample.

You will be shown here actual building specification sheets as well as building sketches and you'll be given information on how to prepare your appraisal report from these building data. You will also find an important section in this chapter on how to estimate percentage of competition for staged construction mortgage payouts by your bank clients. Design standards for safe, sanitary, structurally rigid, functional and habitable new buildings are also stressed. Finally, there is a Model New Building Appraisal Report for you to follow and use in detail.

HOW TO REVIEW BUILDING SPECIFICATIONS

Building specifications, whether on standard government forms or on architectural narrative specification sheets, are an important adjunct to the building plans. The builder needs both to build the structure. You need both to appraise the proposed improved property on a proposed basis. Plans show graphically what the building will look like and the specifications spell out the proposed materials in detail. Plans and ''specs'' are an organic building whole and are always reviewed together.

An excellent specifications form for demonstration is the following VA-FHA Form, ''Description of Materials,'' which I have completed for sample purposes on a typical development type Bi-level dwelling. (See Figure 6.1.) This ''spec'' will be used throughout this chapter for review and model appraisal purposes in conjunction with the later plan sketches.

HOW TO REVIEW AND MEASURE
BUILDING PLANS FOR APPRAISAL DATA

When appraising existing buildings, you analyze and physically examine the community, the neighborhood, the block, the lot, as well as the interior and exterior of the structure. On proposed construction, you use the same appraisal process and techniques, except that you secure your quantity and quality data on the improvements from the two dimensional plans and specs instead of from the completed building. You benefit from ''internal'' information shown on these drawings and material forms rather than just being able to view the completed, covered three-dimensional product. However, as with building workmanship, the quality of your appraisal will depend on the quality and completeness of the plans and specifications you are given to review.

The following floor and plot plans demonstrate in sketch form the prior specifications and show an average 1,600 square foot Bi-level dwelling. In an actual proposed construction appraisal, you should have before you a package of architectural drawings including plan views, elevations and mechanical layouts, preferably ¼ inch = 1 foot-0 inches scale; minimum $1/_{16}$-inch scale. There should also be kitchen cabinet details, cross-sections and critical construction details in ⅜-inch scale as well as a fully dimensioned plot plan with all proposed grade elevations in $1/_{16}$-inch scale. If the building is being built to custom rather than for "speculative" sale, you also should be given the contract for review.

On existing construction, you tape and examine the structure to determine its size, amenities and the quality of its functional habitability. On proposed construction your tool is a 12-inch architectural ruler scale laid on plan and specs. However, the appraisal process remains the same. Examine all the documents carefully for safe, sanitary, structural, functional and habitable design and materials. You're in at the beginning, so to speak, on this type of appraisal. It's a good time to do an appraisal, a good time to measure the proposed worth and a good time to alert your client to noted deficiencies.

HOW TO DO A PROPOSED NEW BUILDING APPRAISAL REPORT

You have received plans and specifications from your client along with your appraisal assignment. When you inspect the neighborhood and building site, be certain to note whether the building is under construction and make photographs of such construction for your appraisal report.

Review the drawings and specs for completeness. Whatever the builder needs to build the structure with, you need to analyze and appraise properly. You can't see the quality of the kitchen without details and specs. You won't know if the property will be comfortable and efficient in heating cost if insulation specifications and location are not complete and detailed. You have to have it on paper in adequate detail to be able to value the proposed building properly for your client.

Analyze the drawings and specifications for safety, sanitation, function and habitability. Visualize these two-dimensional drawings transformed by sticks and mortar into a building on a site which has appearance, amenities, location, view and compatibility in its location.

Use your 12-inch scale to measure the building for your appraisal report. Measure the exterior foundation walls, add all bays and cantilevers. Measure the additional finished livable area in the lower level. Review all dimensions carefully. Are the closets deep enough? Do you see privacy for bedroom and bath access? Is the layout functional? Are the foundation and framing components sized for the spans? Are building spaces livable? Is fenestration adequate? Is building sited properly for drainage on the plot plan? Are there proper existing off-site and proposed on-site improvements? Don't be quick to depreciate the proposed construction as an "over-improvement" for the block and neighborhood. Such "over-improvement" has been the history of most construction in this country as available building lots have diminished and construction costs have soared.

Note this and all other data and measurements. Secure your comparables

FHA Form 2005
VA Form 26-1852

Form Approved
OMB No. 63–RO055

DESCRIPTION OF MATERIALS

No. _____

U.S. DEPARTMENT OF HOUSING AND URBAN DEVELOPMENT
FEDERAL HOUSING ADMINISTRATION

For accurate register of carbon copies, form
may be separated along above fold. Staple
completed sheets together in original order.

(To be inserted by FHA or VA)

☒ Proposed Construction

☐ Under Construction

Property address _____ 1 WEST STREET _____ City SUBURBIA _____ State U.S.A.

Mortgagor or Sponsor _____ EIGHTH FEDERAL S&L _____ 101 WEST ST. SUBURBIA
(Name)   (Address)

Contractor or Builder _____ BUILD-RITE INC. _____ SUBURBIA
(Name)   (Address)

INSTRUCTIONS

1. For additional information on how this form is to be submitted, number of copies, etc., see the instructions applicable to the FHA Application for Mortgage Insurance or VA Request for Determination of Reasonable Value, as the case may be.

2. Describe all materials and equipment to be used, whether or not shown on the drawings, by marking an X in each appropriate check-box and entering the information called for in each space. If space is inadequate, enter "See misc.", and describe under item 27 or on an attached sheet. THE USE OF PAINT CONTAINING MORE THAN FIVE-TENTHS OF ONE PERCENT LEAD BY WEIGHT IS PROHIBITED.

3. Work not specifically described or shown will not be considered

unless required, then the minimum acceptable will be assumed. Work exceeding minimum requirements cannot be considered unless specifically described.

4. Include no alternates, "or equal" phrases, or contradictory items. (Consideration of a request for acceptance of substitute materials or equipment is not thereby precluded.)

5. Include signatures required at the end of this form.

6. The construction shall be completed in compliance with the related drawings and specifications, as amended during processing. The specifications include this Description of Materials and applicable Minimum Property Standards.

1. EXCAVATION:

Bearing soil, type _____ SANDY LOAM

2. FOUNDATIONS:

Footings: concrete mix _____ 1-2-4 _____ ; strength psi 3000 # _____ Reinforcing _____

Foundation wall: material _____ CB 8" & 12" _____ Reinforcing _____ "DUROWALL"

Interior foundation wall: material _____ LALLY 4"-STEEL _____ Party foundation wall _____

Columns: material and sizes _____ LALLY 4"-STEEL _____ Piers: material and reinforcing _____

Girders: material and sizes _____ Sills: material _____

Basement entrance areaway _____ Window areaways _____

Waterproofing _____ CEMENT PARGE & ASPHALT _____ Footing drains PERFORATED ORANGEBURG

Termite protection _____

Basementless space: ground cover _____ ; insulation _____ ; foundation vents _____

Special foundations _____

Additional information: BOTTOM OF FOOTINGS MIN 3'-0" BELOW GRADE FOR ATTACHED GARAGE

Figure 6.1

FHA-VA DESCRIPTION OF MATERIALS, COMPLETED FORM

3. CHIMNEYS:

Material BLOCKS AND BRICK   Prefabricated (make and size) _____

Flue lining: material T.C.   Heater flue size _____ Fireplace flue size 8" x 8"

Vents (material and size): gas or oil heater _____ ; water heater _____

Additional information: _____

4. FIREPLACES:

Type: ☐ solid fuel; ☐ gas-burning; ☐ circulator (make and size) _____ ; Ash dump and clean-out _____

Fireplace: facing _____ ; lining _____ ; hearth _____ ; mantel _____

Additional information: _____

5. EXTERIOR WALLS:

Wood frame: wood grade, and species D.F./HEM/ CONSTR.   ☐ Corner bracing. Building paper or felt PAPER

Sheathing 3/8" PLY ; thickness 3/8" ; width 4x6 ; ☐ solid; ☐ spaced _____" o. c.; ☐ diagonal;

Siding ALUM ; grade INSULATED ; type _____ ; size 8" ; exposure _____" ; fastening ALUM NAIL

Shingles _____ ; grade _____ ; type _____ ; size _____ ; exposure _____" ; fastening _____

Stucco _____ ; thickness _____ "; Lath _____ ; weight _____ lb.

Masonry veneer _____   Sills _____   Lintels _____   Base flashing _____

Masonry: ☐ solid ☐ faced ☐ stuccoed; total wall thickness _____ "; facing thickness _____ "; facing material _____

Backup material _____ ; thickness _____ "; bonding _____

Door sills ALUM   Window sills _____   Lintels _____   Base flashing _____

Interior surface: dampproofing, _____ coats of _____ ; furring _____

Additional information: _____

Exterior painting: material PARAGON EXT. LATEX TRIM   ; number of coats 2

Gable wall construction: ☒ same as main walls; ☐ other construction _____

6. FLOOR FRAMING:

Joists: wood, grade, and species FIR HEM/CONST.; other _____ ; bridging METAL ; anchors _____

Concrete slab: ☒ basement floor; ☐ first floor; ☒ ground supported; ☐ self-supporting; mix 1:2:4 ; thickness 4 ";

reinforcing _____ ; insulation _____ ; membrane _____

Fill under slab: material RUN OF BANK ; thickness 8 ". Additional information: 4 MIL POLYETHELENE

7. SUBFLOORING: (Describe underflooring for special floors under item 21.)

Material: grade and species ½-D PLYSCORE

Laid: ☐ first floor; ☐ second floor; ☒ attic CATWALK sq. ft.; ☐ diagonal; ☐ right angles. Additional information:

LAID RIGHT ANGLES TO FLOOR JOISTS   ; size ½" ; type 4x8'

8. FINISH FLOORING: (Wood only.)   Describe other finish flooring under item 21.)

LOCATION	ROOMS	GRADE	SPECIES	THICKNESS	WIDTH	BLDG. PAPER	FINISH
First floor	L.R. HALL	#1	OAK	25/32	2¼"	15# FELT	POLYURETHANE
Second floor							
Attic floor	_____ sq. ft.						
Additional information:							

9. PARTITION FRAMING:

Studs: wood, grade, and species _EUR. HEM/CONSTR_ size and spacing _2 X 4 16" O.C._ Other ___
Additional information: ___

10. CEILING FRAMING:

Joists: wood, grade, and species _2 X 6_ Other ___ Bridging _2 X 4_
Additional information: ___

11. ROOF FRAMING:

Rafters: wood, grade, and species _2 X 8_ Roof trusses (see detail): grade and species ___
Additional information: ___

12. ROOFING:

Sheathing: wood, grade, and species _1/2" CD PLYSCORE Y.P._ ; ☒ solid; ☐ spaced ___ " o.c.
Roofing _ASPH. SHNGLES_; grade _240#_ ; size _3½ x 12_; type _SELF - SEALING_
Underlay _FELT_ ; weight or thickness _15 #_; size ___ ; fastening _GALV_
Built-up roofing ___ ; number of plies ___ ; surfacing material ___
Flashing: material _ALUM_ ; gage or weight ___ ; ☐ gravel stops; ☐ snow guards
Additional information: ___

13. GUTTERS AND DOWNSPOUTS:

Gutters: material _ALUM_ ; gage or weight _.027_ ; size _5"_ ; shape _OGEE_
Downspouts: material _ALUM_ ; gage or weight _.027_ ; size _2 X 3_ ; shape _BOX_ ; number _5_
Downspouts connected to: ☐ Storm sewer; ☐ sanitary sewer; ☐ dry-well. ☒ Splash blocks: material and size _10" x 36"_
Additional information: ___

14. LATH AND PLASTER:

Lath ☐ walls, ☐ ceilings: material ___ ; weight or thickness ___ Plaster: coats ___ ; finish ___
Dry-wall ☒ walls, ☒ ceilings: material _GYPSUM_ ; thickness _1/2_ ; finish _SMOOTH_
Joint treatment _TAPE + SPACKLE - 3 COATS_

15. DECORATING: *(Paint, wallpaper, etc.)*

Rooms	Wall Finish Material and Application	Ceiling Finish Material and Application
Kitchen	LATEX PAINT	GLOSS PAINT
Bath	CERAMIC TILE AND PAINT	GLOSS PAINT
Other	LATEX PAINT	SAND FINISH

Additional information: ___

16. INTERIOR DOORS AND TRIM:

Doors: type _FLUSH_ ; material _LUAN_ ; thickness _1 3/8"_
Door trim: type _CLAMSHELL_ ; material _W.P._ Base: type _CLAMSHELL_ ; material _W.P._ ; size _½ x ½"_
Finish: doors _STAIN + VARNISH_ ; trim _PAINT_
Other trim *(item, type and location)* ___
Additional information: ___

Figure 6.1 (Cont'd.)

94

17. WINDOWS:

Windows: type CASEMENT ; make CARADCO ; material W.P. ; sash thickness 1 3/4"

Glass: grade INSULATED ; □ sash weights; □ balances, type ; head flashing ALUM

Trim: type CLAMSHELL; material W.P. Paint LATEX ; number coats 2

Weatherstripping: type LEAF + TUBULAR ; material VINYL ; Storm sash, number

Screens: ☒ full; □ half; type ; number 13 ; screen cloth material FIBERGLASS

Basement windows: type HOPPER ; material ALUM ; screens, number ; Storm sash, number

Special windows

Additional information:

18. ENTRANCES AND EXTERIOR DETAIL:

Main entrance door: material PINE ; width 3' ; thickness 1 3/4" Frame: material PINE ; thickness 1 1/4"

Other entrance doors: material PINE ; width 2'-8"; thickness 1 3/4" Frame: material PINE ; thickness 1 1/4"

Head flashing ALUM Weatherstripping: type INTERLOCK ; saddles ALUM

Screen doors: thickness ; number ; screen cloth material ; Storm doors: thickness ; number

Combination storm and screen doors: thickness ; number ; screen cloth material

Shutters: □ hinged; □ fixed. Railings Attic louvers

Exterior millwork: grade and species SOFFITS, FASCIAS, Paint ALUM. ; number coats

Additional information:

19. CABINETS AND INTERIOR DETAIL:

Kitchen cabinets, wall units: material BIRCH, W.P. FIR PLYWOOD ; lineal feet of shelves 17' ; shelf width 11"

Base units: material SAME ; counter top PLASTIC LAMINATE ; edging SAME

Back and end splash PLASTIC LAMINATE Finish of cabinets STAIN + VARNISH ; number coats

Medicine cabinets: make CHEMCRAFT MODEL 1409 ; model

Other cabinets and built-in furniture BATH VANITY 40"

Additional information:

20. STAIRS:

STAIR	TREADS		RISERS		STRINGS		HANDRAIL		BALUSTERS	
	Material	Thickness	Material	Thickness	Material	Size	Material	Size	Material	Size
Basement	FIR	2"	FIR	2" x 12" TREADS	FIR	2x10	PINE	2x3		
Main										
Attic										

Disappearing: make and model number

Additional information:

Figure 6.1 (Cont'd.)

95

21. SPECIAL FLOORS AND WAINSCOT:

	Location	Material, Color, Border, Sizes, Gage, Etc.	Threshold Material	Wall Base Material	Underfloor Material
Floors	Kitchen	ASB. VINYL TILES - ARMSTRONG or EQUAL		WOOD	5/8" PLY
	Bath				

	Location	Material, Color, Border, Cap. Sizes, Gage, Etc.	Height	Height Over Tub	Height in Showers (From Floor)
Wainscot	Bath	MARLITE	48"	TO CLG	

Bathroom accessories: ☒ Recessed; material CERAMIC ; number 2 ; ☒ Attached; material CERAMIC ; number 3
Additional information:

22. PLUMBING:

Fixture	Number	Location	Make	Mfr's Fixture Identification No.	Size	Color
Sink	1	KIT	ELJER	EMORY	33 x 21	
Lavatory	1	BATH	ELJER	PRISCILLA	20 x 18	
Water closet	1	BATH	ELJER	HYGIENE	18"	
Bathtub	1	BATH	HAMLIN	K1306 A		
Shower over tub △		BATH				
Stall shower △						
Laundry trays						

△ ☒ Curtain rod   △ ☐ Door   △ ☐ Shower pan: material
Water supply: ☒ public; ☐ community system; ☐ individual (private) system. ★
Sewage disposal: ☒ public; ☐ community system; ☐ individual (private) system. ★
★ Show and describe individual system in complete detail in separate drawings and specifications according to requirements.
House drain (inside): ☐ cast iron; ☐ tile; ☒ other COPPER   House sewer (outside): ☒ cast iron; ☐ tile; ☐ other
Water piping: ☐ galvanized steel; ☒ copper tubing; ☐ other _____   Sill cocks, number 2
Domestic water heater: type INTEGRAL ; make and model _____ ; heating capacity
_____ gph. 100° rise. Storage tank: material _____ ; capacity _____ gallons.
Gas service: ☐ utility company; ☐ liq. pet. gas; ☐ other _____   Gas piping: ☐ cooking; ☐ house heating.
Footing drains connected to: ☐ storm sewer; ☐ sanitary sewer; ☐ dry well. Sump pump; make and model LAWN SPLASH BLOCK
_____ ; capacity _____ ; discharges into _____

Figure 6.1 (Cont'd.)

96

23. HEATING:

☒ Hot water. ☐ Steam. ☐ Vapor. ☒ One-pipe system. ☐ Two-pipe system.
☐ Radiators. ☐ Convectors. ☒ Baseboard radiation. Make and model _BURNHAM HEAT TRIM MODEL "R"_
Radiant panel: ☐ floor; ☐ wall; ☐ ceiling. Panel coil: material _____
☐ Circulator. ☐ Return pump. Make and model _____; capacity _____ gpm.
Boiler: make and model _BURNHAM Model RM 111H_ Output _106500_ Btuh.; net rating _96000_ Btuh.
Additional information: _WITH COMPLETE CONTROLS_

Warm air: ☐ Gravity. ☐ Forced. Type of system _____
Duct material: supply _____; return _____ Insulation _____, thickness _____
Furnace: make and model _____ Input _____ Btuh.; output _____ Btuh.
Additional information: _____

☐ Space heater; ☐ floor furnace; ☐ wall heater. Input _____ Btuh.; output _____ Btuh.; number units _____
Make, model _____
Controls: make and types _____
Additional information: _____

Fuel: ☐ Coal; ☐ oil; ☒ gas; ☐ liq. pet. gas; ☐ electric; ☐ other _____; storage capacity _275 GAL_
Additional information: _____
Firing equipment furnished separately: ☐ Gas burner, conversion type. ☐ Stoker: hopper feed ☐; bin feed ☐
Oil burner: ☐ pressure atomizing; ☐ vaporizing _____
Make and model _____ Control _____
Additional information: _____

Electric heating system: type _____ Input _____ volts; output _____ Btuh.
Additional information: _____
Ventilating equipment: attic fan, make and model _FAN 4400 LITE COMBO SWANSON MODEL 9100-36_; capacity _____ cfm.
kitchen exhaust fan. make and model _BATH FAN LITE COMBO SWANSON MODEL 411_
Other heating, ventilating, or cooling equipment _____

24. ELECTRIC WIRING:

Service: ☒ overhead; ☐ underground. Panel: ☐ fuse box; ☒ circuit-breaker; make _BRYANT_ AMP's _100_ No. circuits _4_
Wiring: ☐ conduit; ☐ armored cable; ☒ nonmetallic cable; ☐ knob and tube; ☐ other _____
Special outlets: ☐ range; ☐ water heater; ☐ other _____
☒ Doorbell. ☐ Chimes. Push-button locations _FRON DOORS_ Additional information: _____

25. LIGHTING FIXTURES:

Total number of fixtures _19_ Total allowance for fixtures, typical installation, $ _175⁰⁰_
Nontypical installation _____
Additional information: _____

DESCRIPTION OF MATERIALS

Figure 6.1 (Cont'd.)

97

26. INSULATION:

LOCATION	THICKNESS	MATERIAL, TYPE, AND METHOD OF INSTALLATION	VAPOR BARRIER
Roof			
Ceiling	6"	FIBREGLAS BLANKET STAPLED TO CEILING JOIST	INTEGRAL
Wall	3½"	EXTERIOR WALL STUDS + GARAGE COMMON WALL	FACING WARM SIDE
Floor			

HARDWARE: (make, material, and finish.) KWIKSET + STANLEY, BRASS FINISH

SPECIAL EQUIPMENT: (State material or make, model and quantity. Include only equipment and appliances which are acceptable by local law, custom and applicable FHA standards. Do not include items which, by established custom, are supplied by occupant and removed when he vacates premises or chattles prohibited by law from becoming realty.)

2 GAS + SMOKE ALARMS- PERFECT LINE SIA-SAF MODEL GSD-100

27. MISCELLANEOUS: (Describe any main dwelling materials, equipment, or construction items not shown elsewhere; or use to provide additional information where the space provided was inadequate. Always reference by item number to correspond to numbering used on this form.)

PORCHES:
FRONT + REAR ENTRANCE PLATFORMS ON 8" C.B. CHEEK WALL FOUNDATION

Figure 6.1 (Cont'd.)

98

TERRACES:

GARAGES:

ATTACHED - SPECS + CONSTRUCTION SIM. TO DWELLING

DOUBLE DRYWALL 1/2" STAGGERED JOINTS ON COMMON WALL

WALKS AND DRIVEWAYS:

Driveway: width _10'_ ; base material _SHALE_ ; thickness _4"_ ; surfacing material _ASPH Conc._ ; thickness _2"_

Front walk: width _3_ ; material _P.C._ ; thickness _4_ ". Service walk: width _3'_ ; material _P.C._ ; thickness _4"_

Steps: material _____ ; treads _____ "; risers _____ ". Check walls

OTHER ONSITE IMPROVEMENTS:

(*Specify all exterior onsite improvements not described elsewhere, including items such as unusual grading, drainage structures, retaining walls, fence, railings, and accessory structures.*)

BACKFILL AND FINISH GRADE TO PROVIDE POSITIVE RUNOFF FROM BLDG + LOT

LANDSCAPING, PLANTING, AND FINISH GRADING:

Topsoil _4"_ thick: ☒ front yard; ☒ side yards; ☐ rear yard to _15'_ feet behind main building.

Lawns (*seeded, sodded, or sprigged*): ☒ front yard ☒ side yards; ☒ rear yard

Planting: ☒ as specified and shown on drawings; ☒ as follows:

_1_ Shade trees, deciduous, _2_ " caliper.   _____ Evergreen trees. _____ ' to _____ ', B & B.

_____ Low flowering trees, deciduous, _____ ' to _____ '.   _6_ Evergreen shrubs. _____ ' to _____ ', B & B.

_____ High-growing shrubs, deciduous, _____ ' to _____ '.   _____ Vines, 2-year

_____ Medium-growing shrubs, deciduous, _____ ' to _____ '.

_____ Low-growing shrubs, deciduous, _____ ' to _____ '.

IDENTIFICATION.—This exhibit shall be identified by the signature of the builder, or sponsor, and/or the proposed mortgagor if the latter is known at the time of application.

Date _____   Signature _John Smith_

Signature _for Build-Rite, Inc._

FHA Form 2005
VA Form 26-1852

Figure 6.1 (Cont'd.)

from similar recently built and sold dwellings in similar locations. Analyze this proposed dwelling on a cost approach basis also, utilizing square foot, locally adjusted costs to arrive at an upper cost limit of value. However, the Market approach remains your primary approach to value, even on new construction, and should be stressed in your report. In your written report, refer to the plans and specifications (Figures 6.2 and 6.3) which you should also initial. (See also the design checklist and the model new building appraisal report in later sections.)

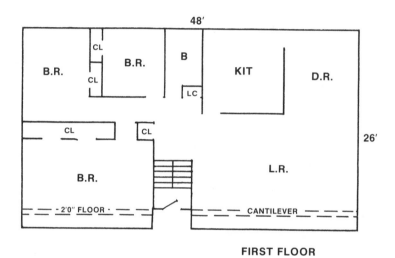

FIRST FLOOR

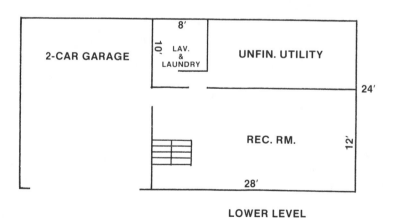

LOWER LEVEL

Figure 6.2

PLAN SKETCHES OF A 26′ × 48′ BI-LEVEL HOUSE

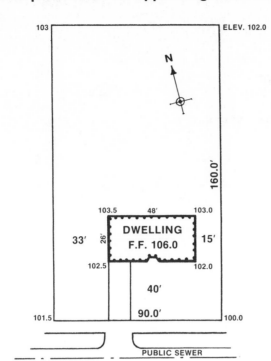

PLOT PLAN

Figure 6.3

PLOT PLAN WITH GRADE ELEVATIONS

HOW TO ESTIMATE PERCENTAGE OF COMPLETION
FOR STAGED CONSTRUCTION MORTGAGE PAYOUTS

The lender will often assign you to inspect the proposed construction which you appraised. You must then not only inspect during construction but you will also have to certify to the lender the percentage of completion for his staged mortgage payouts. The lender will generally specify inspection stages approximating the following:

FIRST STAGE—Foundation complete, not backfilled.

SECOND STAGE—Building erected, enclosed, mechanical roughing installed. No drywall.

THIRD STAGE—(Optional)—Insulation installed.

FINAL—Building and all on-site and off-site improvements completed.

The following cost breakdown of dwelling components is by approximate percentage cost and should help you certify completion percentages:

COMPONENT	% COST
Excavation and Foundation	10
Rough Carpentry and Lumber	11
Windows, Doors	2
Finish Carpentry and Lumber	9
Plumbing and Heating	11
Water and Sewer Connections	3
Roofing, Gutters and Leaders	3
Insulation, Weatherstrip	2
Drywall	13
Rough and Finish Hardware	1
Electric	4
Tile	3
Floors	3
Kitchen Cabinets, Vanity, Composition Floors	3
Clean-Up, Finish Grading	1
Walks, Landscaping, Drive, Parking	3
Plans, Specs, Survey, Permits	2
Job Overhead and General Overhead	16
TOTAL	100%

A CHECKLIST OF CHARACTERISTICS OF ACCEPTABLE DESIGN REQUIREMENTS FOR SAFE, SANITARY, FUNCTIONAL, HABITABLE NEW BUILDINGS

SITE DESIGN

— Land use harmonious
— Building placement satisfactory
— Noise control adequate
— Open space acceptable
— Traffic not adverse
— Site harmonious to surroundings
— Appropriate intensity of development
— Safe, convenient street, parking, walk access
— Utilities underground
— Access for all firefighting and other services
— Grading acceptable for access
— Lawns (4 inches topsoil)

BUILDING DESIGN

— Furnishability of living room, dining room, bedroom and other habitable areas
— Functional kitchens, no traffic through work triangle
— Functional baths, laundry
— Minimum clearances for equipment, dryer vent to outside
— Doors and openings, deadbolt locks for entrance doors
— Light and ventilation adequate
— Noise avoided or controlled
— Smoke detectors located properly

___ Drainage acceptable for erosion
control
___ Flood—lowest floor level above
recorded flood level
___ Planting meets local soil,
climate, orientation
___ Groundcover to prevent erosion
___ Decay protection, all wood
above ground or treated
___ Site details—fences, walls per
local custom
___ Common facilities—PUDs,
Associations, amenities

___ Materials acceptable
___ Safety glass in showers, sliding
doors
___ Lead-free paint specified
___ Safe, structurally rigid design
___ Soil investigation needed?
___ Seismic construction necessary?
___ Insulation meets R factors
___ Flashing adequate
___ Kitchen cabinets—functional
plan and manufacturer
labelled
___ Safety controls specified on
mechanical equipment
___ Sewage disposal sanitary
___ Marketability—design popular
in area

A MODEL NEW BUILDING APPRAISAL REPORT
(Attachments Omitted)

APPRAISER—Axel Swenson DATE—   *OWNER—John*
Smith PROPERTY—Proposed 1-Family Dwelling LOCATION—2 West
St., Suburbia LEGAL DESC.—Tax Map Sect. 108 Bł. 2 Lot 4
COUNTY—Kings County STATUS OF PROPERTY—Proposed Construc-
tion APPRAISED—Fee Simple

NEIGHBORHOOD—Major structures are typically frame, 1 to 20 years
old, 90% built-up, fair to good condition, owner occupied, residentially
zoned, shopping, schools and transportation accessible and adequate, a
stable middle class neighborhood in Suburbia, a mainly residential village
of 15,000, 40 miles northeast of New York City.

BLOCK—90' × 160', 14,400 sq.ft., interior lot, grades rear to front
mainly, all drainage positive, cleared, fully improved with existing paved
asphaltic concrete street, sidewalks, curbs, public sewer, public water,
underground electric, gas (not connectible), part of seven similar vacant
plots being improved for sale speculatively by John Smith, Builder, with
two lots already completed and occupied.

PROPOSED BUILDING DESCRIPTION—Plans and specifications pro-
pose a detached 26' × 48' dwelling, detached, aluminum siding, frame,
one-story Bi-level design, typical development type, with partially finished
lower level, two-car built-in garage, seven rooms, 1½ baths, three bedrooms, living room, dining room, kitchen, recreation room, unfinished
basement, oil hot water heat, asphalt roof shingles, concrete block foundations, oak floors, drywall interior, ceramic tile bath finish, aluminum gut-

ters and leaders, plans show a functional layout with adequate room sizes for furnishability, access and circulation, ample closets, kitchen design good for adequate storage, work surfaces adjacent to range, sink and refrigerator, no passageway through kitchen "work triangle," materials, design and layout are commensurate with type and price of proposed structure and meet current popular market demand, future economic life 50 years.

PHOTOGRAPHS—Attached plot and street photographs

QUALIFICATIONS—Attached appraiser's Qualification Sheet

VALUATION

Market Analysis Approach

Comparables	Sq.Ft.	Type	Rms	B.R.	B.	Const.	Gar.	Age Cond.	Price	Date
Subject	1,600	Bi-lev.	7	3	1½	Fr.	2 car	Prop.	—	—
1) 8 West St., Suburbia	1,600	Bi-lev.	6	3	1½	Fr.	2 car	NewG	$46,000	3/___
2) 4 West St., Suburbia	1,600	Bi-lev.	7	3	1½	Fr.	2 car	NewG	$48,000	3/___
3) 49 Seneca Ave., Suburbia	1,800	Ranch	7	3	2½	Fr.	2 car	1G	$52,000	12/___
4) 9 Old St., Suburbia	1,500	Bi-lev.	6	3	1½	Fr.	1 car	1G	$45,000	10/___

Comment

1) Same block, same bldg plan and spec, unfin. Rec. Rm. area, 80′ × 150′, 4% inferior
2) Adjacent, same bldg plan and spec, 90′ × 150′, "best comparable," equal
3) Similar location, larger dwelling, sim. imp., 100′ × 150′, 10% superior
4) Similar location, sl. smaller dwelling, less amenities, 80′ × 160′, 6% inferior

Cost Approach

First Floor 26′ × 48′ + *Lower Level* 10′ × 28′ + 8′ × 10′ = 1,600 SF × $22 = ...$33,600

Built-in garage (480 SF)—	700
Drive and walks—	300
Landscaping—	300

New (No Depreciation) Proposed Improvement Costs $34,900
Land Value (90′ × 160′)—   13,500

    Indicated Value by Cost Approach $48,400

VALUATION SUMMARY AND CONDITIONS—I certify that I have inspected the subject plot and its environs and examined and initialed the attached plans and specifications for the proposed building (plans and specs prepared by _____, dated _____). My valuation, which is based on these plans and specifications for the proposed improvements, is *FORTY-EIGHT THOUSAND DOLLARS ($48,000)*, founded on the Market Data and Analysis Approach, as of _____ , and is further conditioned on acceptable completion of the improvements in accordance with the aforementioned plans and specifications.

_____
    Date

APPRAISER
14 Main St., Suburbia

Chapter 7

How to appraise
the suburban one-family
dwelling

The one-family dwelling on its own lawn remains the "American Dream" house despite counteracting land and construction cost inflation. The single-family home still leads the suburban sales market and is probably your most important appraisal subject.

Changing population and life-style patterns which are causing purchase and occupancy of one-family homes by "extended families" and by affluent single persons, are also discussed in this chapter. Because of this changing occupancy and demand, local communities have reacted wtih zoning and planning controls. All these developments affect value.

You will also find here specific information on how to appraise the typical suburban "Ranch" one-story, the "Cape-Cod" 1½-story, the "Colonial" two-story, the "Bi-level" or "High-ranch," the "Split-level" and the "Townhouse." Finally, step-by-step instructions on an appraisal format, models of a "High-Ranch" Appraisal Report, a "Townhouse" Appraisal Report and a "Ranch" House Appraisal Report for a corporate transfer, are set down in this chapter for your use.

THE PREFERENCE FOR THE ONE-FAMILY DETACHED HOUSE

Whether existing or new, the majority of prospective house buyers prefer single-family, detached, one-story design. Countering this preference are some economic and population facts which may force changes in the future in this preference. Only one out of four buyers, for example, can afford the "average" $55,000 home, according to recent surveys. Such inflationary pressures will probably eventually affect the future size and design of homes. Questions like, "Does every child need his own bedroom?" and, "Does every person need his own bathroom?" may have to be answered negatively. Standards will probably go lower. Greater emphasis in the future will probably be on more prudent, rational use of residential space. More clustering, more townhouses, garden apartments, even some high-rises in the suburbs will be the answers.

However, you appraise in today's market. Today's, not tomorrow's buyer makes the market which you study for your appraisal report. He wants the one-family detached house on its own lawn. Also, the vast majority of the existing housing stock produced in the suburbs since WWII consists of one-family detached homes of typical development design. In all likelihood, you will be appraising this "American Dream" detached house in the suburbs for a long time.

HOW TO EVALUATE THE TREND TO "EXTENDED FAMILY" OCCUPANCY

Bureau of Census reports in the late seventies confirmed that basic changes have taken place in marriage and family living in the United States. The number of unmarried persons living with someone of the opposite sex doubled. The number of adults who had never married, ages 25 to 29, increased from 19% to 25%. These statistics confirmed what had been noted in the real estate field. The family unit so typical of suburban life for so long, is not now always the buyer and occupant. There is now common-law partner home ownership occupancy by man and woman. Many divorced and never married single persons also purchase one-family homes now. There is also "extended family" occupancy by married children as well as surviving grandparents in the same dwelling with the original household unit couple. This doubling-up has been made increasingly necessary for the many millions who can no longer afford to buy their own homes. A growing number of communities have legislated against this "multiple-family" occupancy of one-family homes. The market for houses with more bedrooms to meet this "extended-family" occupancy is growing. There is also a contrasting trend involving purchase of smaller one-family homes by affluent single persons. Husband and wife households accounted for less than 30% of the increase in household formations in the early seventies, reversing the previous decade of figures. These dramatic changes have resulted in a trend to buy smaller houses by men and women, divorced and single, suddenly or always living alone.

Many of these "singles," including women in our liberated age, are affluent. They are counted among the one in four who can afford the average $55,000 home. Yet, for function, convenience and life style, these affluent singles do not want larger homes with many bedrooms. They buy smaller homes, fee simple or condominiums. They also buy and rehabilitate "brownstone" attached homes in many city areas (covered in a later chapter). This need for smaller, denser housing with more amenities is also being countered by growing community no-and-slow growth and up-zoning controls.

Daily appraisal work requires constant analysis of these dynamic market and land use changes. Values are made by supply and demand. Census projections on our family formation statistics are no longer adequate to review for one-family homes demand. The statistics on single men and women coming of age, 25 to 35, must now be specifically analyzed in your area. These "singles" (as well as multiple-generation) double-ups have become an important factor in one-family appraising. As examples, when you appraise a proposed residential subdivision, you have to now research and report on this changed demand for one-family homes in your area from these "extended families." When you appraise for your seller-client so he can set a selling price on his one-family house with six bedrooms, you may not have to depreciate its value because it is a "white elephant" with little market appeal. Your area may now have a broadened "extended family" market demand with no zoning restrictions barring such occupancy.

HOW TO EVALUATE THE IMPACT OF "NO-GROWTH" ZONING PRACTICES

Local homeowners vote for no-growth and up-zoning because they fear a decline in property values and neighborhood amenities. They do not accept the changed smaller, denser, shelter needs of the young, the old, the childless, the "extended family" occupancy of larger homes because of economic necessity. Clustering has found some acceptance, especially when it's called "average density" like in the Ramapo, New York control regulations. However, Planned Unit Developments which usually involve a mix of housing including garden apartments, sometimes even high-rises, have not usually been accepted locally. Townhouses seem to be more palatable. However, the attached townhouse on a small plot is not always acceptable to the buyer who migrates from the crowded city looking for homes on their own suburban lawns. Quadruplex townhouses which are four townhouses designed to look like one large single-family house, sometimes find local acceptance.

More than a million more Americans have moved to rural areas since 1970 than those who moved from rural to city areas. This has, in turn, led to rebellion among the established residents of these rural regions against the demands of these migrants for better schools, roads and other social services.

The up-zoning and no-and-slow growth laws that have already resulted, directly affect the availability and value of existing housing stock as well as future development. For example, if my town legislates through zoning against new lower cost homes by requiring minimum 1,500-square foot, one-family houses, existing smaller homes become more valuable. If your town requires minimum 3-acre plots for one-family building permits, then existing homes on 15,000-square feet lots increase in value. If many towns now limit residential development to a maximum number of houses per year, then values of developable land plummet. Again, value is made by supply and demand. When these no-and-slow growth trends occur in your area and restrict supply, the values you consider and report on in your daily work are seriously affected.

HOW TO APPRAISE THE "RANCH" ONE-STORY HOUSE, THE "COLONIAL" TWO-STORY DWELLING, THE "BI-LEVEL" OR "HIGH-RANCH," THE "MULTI-LEVEL" OR "SPLIT-LEVEL" AND THE "TOWNHOUSE"

These various forms of the development type, one-family dwelling are the primary manifestations and most visible residential product of our suburban culture. They contrast with the denser multi-family low and high-rise types of shelter in our cities. They are the main focus of your appraisal work in suburban America.

These dwelling types have evolved during these several decades of suburb-building. They met popular demand rather than architectural fancies. The "Cape Cod," was ideally suited for post-WWII people buying a low cost finished one-story house with an unfinished half-story attic they could complete later. The "Colonial" with its traditional appearance, ample bedroom sizes and comparatively lower two-floor cost found many buyers. The "Bi-Level" is ideally suited for staying above high ground water tables and for delivering most livable square feet at lowest cost. The "Split Level" arose originally on sloping terrain but has since been built everywhere, even on level land. The "townhouse" is generally associated with open space and amenities in the suburbs. The "Ranch" is still the most expensive to build or buy and yet still the most popular. Photographs of development type, suburban, one-family homes follow:

Figure 7.1

"RANCH"
One-Story

Figure 7.2

"CAPE COD"
1½-Story

Figure 7.3

"COLONIAL"
Two-Story

Figure 7.4

"HIGH-RANCH" OR
"BI-LEVEL"

Figure 7.5

"SPLIT-LEVEL"

Figure 7.6

**"ROW" OR
"TOWNHOUSE"**

Since no one-family home properties are ever exactly alike, each appraisal report is never exactly like any other. Each report must be tailored individually for each dwelling. Yet a common appraisal thread of good practice runs through all good reports. Certain specific explanations, descriptions and statements should be included in each report. To help you make good, complete appraisal reports, step-by-step procedures on appraisal techniques follow, as well as a suggested appraisal report topical format.

Appraisal techniques on one-family homes involve an orderly step-by-step procedure:

First step, inspect the community, the neighborhood, the block, the plot. Measure the building exterior, examine the interior and exterior of the structure(s) and take photographs of front, rear and street scene.

Second step, collect data on the community, the area, economic conditions, community services, schools, taxes, assessment and zoning information, including all permitted usages for your determination as to highest and best use.

Third step, prepare the written report either on the client's appraisal form or on your own narrative appraisal format together with any necessary attachments such as plot plan, location map, building sketch and your appraisal qualifications sheet.

The following topic-by-topic format can be used for one-family home appraisal reports. It contains all elements generally required including the classical three-part approach to value.

ONE-FAMILY APPRAISAL REPORT FORMAT

IDENTIFICATION AND DESCRIPTION

Owner of Record—Property address, legal description, (section, block and lot and/or copy of deed description).

Neighborhood—Data on community, area, economics, community facilities, schools, immediate block and environs.

Site—Plot size, appearance, shape, corner or interior, gradients, road, utility improvements, views.

Assessment and Taxes—Including any special assessments.

Zoning—List all permitted and special exception uses, minimum plot sizes, note whether subject plot is conforming or non-conforming.

Highest and Best Use—If the existing residential use is highest and best use, state "present use."

Purpose of Appraisal—In most cases, for current market value.

Appraised—Fee simple or leasehold, condominium, cooperative or fee simple with homeowners association.

Contingent and Limiting Conditions—Subject to completion per plans if proposed construction, survey, termite inspection or any other noted condition in existing construction.

Future Economic Life—In most cases, 40 to 50 years minimum. If your client's forms do not call for this prophecy, it is well to omit it. See also Chapter 8 on Redlining and Urban Disinvestment.

Improvements—Dwelling and any attached or detached accessory structures on plot fully described for age, specifications, quality and condition.

VALUATION

Market Analysis of Recent Sales—The Market Data approach explained and a minimum of three recent sales of similar properties compared to subject. "Best Comparable" chosen and explained. Total value derived from Market approach stated.

Cost Approach—Multiply total habitable square feet by locally adjusted cost handbook factor. Exterior improvements like landscaping, walks, drives, garages added. Physical depreciation taken for age, wear and tear. Functional depreciation taken for items like poor layout, old kitchen, old bath and for the cost to modernize such items. Economic depreciation for adverse influences outside the property taken such as for heavy, fast traffic, industrial odors. Total depreciation is then deducted and land value added to secure total market value from this Cost approach. For example:

1,500 SF × $25	$37,500
Phys. Deprec. (age, wear and tear), Less	$3,000
Funct. Deprec. (semi-mod. kitchen), Less	1,000
Economic Deprec. (none), Less	0
Depreciated Improvements............................	33,500
Landscap'g (drive, walks, garage), Add	2,000
Land Value, Add	13,000
Total Market from Cost Approach	$48,500*

*(The theory of substitution states approximately that one should not buy when one could build cheaper. By this theory, then, the total value derived from the Cost approach would become the upper limit or final opinion of value, if the $48,500 is lower than the value derived from Market Data approach.)

Income Approach—Gross rent multiplier is theoretically taken from what similar houses would rent for if there is no rental market on one-family houses in the area; i.e., $400 monthly rental × 120 (gross rent multiplier) = $48,000 market value from income approach.

Opinion of Value—Set forth opinion of value as of specific date. State how value was derived, if from market analysis of comparable properties, if Cost approach was used or if Income approach was pertinent. In practically all cases, value is derived from Market Data approach.

Signature and Date.

Exhibits—Various, including location map, plot and floor sketches, tables, graphs, photographs, appraiser's statement of no present nor contemplated interest in the property, appraiser's qualifications sheet.

Other—A transmittal letter on appraiser's stationery forwarding the full report and including a summary digest of conclusions and opinion of value is helpful to client on extensive reports. An index sheet for lengthy reports is also often useful.

Stress the Market Data approach in your valuation investigation and discussion and opinion of value. Compare similar properties, similarly situated for location, size, amenities layouts, terms and conditions of sale. Try to avoid time adjustments. Find your "Best Comparable." (See Chapter 1.) Do not average or bracket.

WHEN AND HOW TO USE THE GROSS RENT MULTIPLIER

If there is not enough of a sales market in your area but there is an active rental market in homes with some sales, you can use the Gross Rent Multiplier Income approach, as your approach to value. For this approach, you collect data on the sales of houses which had been rented. Divide the sales prices by the monthly rental for a minimum of three rental comparables and apply the derived factor to the subject rental property. Thus:

	Sale		*Monthly Rental*		*Factor*
22 Low Street	$40,000	÷	$350	=	114
10 High St.	38,000	÷	325	=	117
5 Middle St.	42,000	÷	375	=	120

Assume that 5 Middle St. is the most similar and the gross rent multiplier chosen is 120. Then if your subject dwelling is renting for $350 per month and you consider it a fair rent, $350 × $120 gives a value of $40,000 for the property you are appraising.

However, there are very few such suburban areas where you can use this Gross Rent Multiplier approach. The Market Data approach is the correct approach for the vast majority of residential appraisals on one-family properties.

Similarly, the Cost approach is sometimes useful in new construction appraisals of one-family homes, but for most appraisals, use it only as secondary, upper limit control if your client's form or assignment instructions require it. (See prior Appraisal Report Form section for an explanation of such Cost approach upper limit use).

In general, use all approaches and their correlation for those assignments where they are needed, but depend on the Market Data approach as your primary or single approach to value on practically all dwelling appraisals.

A MODEL HIGH-RANCH APPRAISAL REPORT

To illustrate one-family home appraisals, there are three model appraisal reports in this important one-family suburban home chapter. This first model report on a High-Ranch which follows has been completed on a FNMA form so that you can have before you this type of traditional model to help you on similar assignments for clients who specify such a report.

A MODEL TOWNHOUSE APPRAISAL REPORT

You may receive appraisal assignments requiring a valuation "Letter of Opinion" without full narrative or form data. The requestor in such assignments is interested in your opinion of value based on your experience in real estate matters and value in the specific area. He apparently is also interested in paying a lower appraisal fee. Appraisers do issue such letters under such circumstances. However, it is an area fraught with uncertainty and problems for you and the client if good appraisal practice is not followed. You have to do the same field investigation, data collection, inspection and appraisal as if you were doing a full narrative or form report. The very same data you would secure for a full report must be kept available in your files. Your fee can only be adjusted for the amount of time you save in preparing a letter instead of a full report. The importance of a Letter of Opinion cannot be minimized. Once signed, you are as responsible for its statements as if it were a fully billed, complete report. The full file of data may someday have to be brought to court to back up your letter. The following model appraisal Letter of Opinion reports on a typical development type townhouse:

LETTER OF OPINION

Robert Mink, Esq.   September 1, 19___
Box 290, Suburbia, N.Y.   Re: 1-Fam. Dwg Appraisal

Dear Mr. Mink,

In compliance with your request, I have inspected the subject improved lot at 22 Mill Rd; Suburbia, N.Y. owned by your client, Ms Penny Welch. I have taken into account the entire value spectrum including architectural, amenity, site and location factors. Based on this complete review, which included a study of sales in the area utilizing the Comparable Market approach with all data placed and available in my files, description, analysis and opinion of fair market value is as follows. (Fair market value for this purpose is the highest price a property will bring in an open market after a reasonable sales period with a knowledgeable buyer and seller under no duress.)

Improved Residential Plot—20′ × 100′, town of Suburbia, pop. 10,000, _____ County, Maine, 20 miles from _____ , Tax Map Section 229, Bl. 4, Lot 5 in a 125-unit townhouse development, interior plot, level, well-drained, on fully improved paved street with curb, sidewalk, drainage, public sewer, public water, electricity, gas, good landscaping, assessment $34,000, taxes $1,250, location convenient to schools, transportation and community services, improved with a 12-year-old, brick and block masonry, two-story townhouse, 1-family, fully attached, seven rooms, three bedrooms, 1½ cer. tile baths, L.R., D.R., functional kit., fam. rm., full basement, drywall, flat built-up roofing, one-car built-in gar., covered conc. rear patio, gas H/W heat, central A/C, fair condition, vacant, interior needs cleaning, wet basement needs positive exterior grading away from foundation. Mill Rd has moderately fast traffic. Bldg has 1,560-sq.ft. livable area. Highest and best use is residential 1-family (present use), appraised in fee simple.

My opinion of value as of _____ is Forty Two Thousand Dollars ($42,000). I certify that I have no present or contemplated interest in this property which might affect my making this fair appraisal.

Sincerely,

JOHN DOE

APPRAISER, 2 Vue St., Suburbia

Date—September 1, 19_____

BUILDING SKETCH

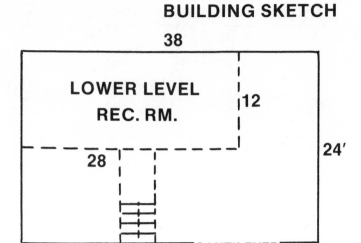

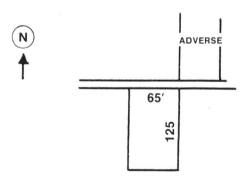

Lot Location Sketch including
the location of any adverse influences

Figure 7.7

BUILDING SKETCH AND FNMA APPRAISAL REPORT

RESIDENTIAL APPRAISAL REPORT

Borrower/Client		Census Tract	Map Reference	File No.

To be completed by Lender

Property Address 22 NEVERSINK PLACE

City SUBURBIA   County ORANGE   State N.Y.   Zip Code 10950

Legal Description BLOCK 2, LOT 10, SUBDIVISION OF MELLON FIELD OR ANGE COUNTY, N.Y.

Sale Price $ _____ Date of Sale _____ Property Rights Appraised ☒ Fee ☐ Leasehold ☐ DeMinimis PUD(FNMA only ☐ Condo ☐ PUD)

Actual Real Estate Taxes $1050 (yr) Loan charges to be paid by seller $ _____ Other sales concessions _____

Lender _____ Lender's Address _____

Occupant MILLICENT DAVIS   Appraiser JOHN DOE   Instructions to Appraiser CALL 914 783 4200 FOR APPT.

NEIGHBORHOOD

Location	☐ Urban ☒ Suburban ☐ Rural		Employment Stability	Good Avg. Fair Poor ☒ ☐ ☐ ☐
Built Up	☒ Over 75% ☐ 25% to 75% ☐ Under 25%		Convenience to Employment	☐ ☒ ☐ ☐
Growth Rate ☐ Fully Dev.	☐ Rapid ☐ Steady ☒ Slow		Convenience to Shopping	☐ ☒ ☐ ☐
Property Values	☐ Increasing ☒ Stable ☐ Declining		Convenience to Schools	☐ ☒ ☐ ☐
Demand/Supply	☐ Shortage ☒ In Balance ☐ Over Supply		Quality of Schools	☐ ☒ ☐ ☐
Marketing Time	☐ Under 3 Mos. ☒ 4–6 Mos. ☐ Over 6 Mos.		Recreational Facilities	☐ ☒ ☐ ☐
Present Land Use 100 % 1 Family ___% 2–4 Family ___% Apts. ___% Condo ___% Commercial			Adequacy of Utilities	☐ ☒ ☐ ☐
___% Industrial ___% Vacant			Property Compatibility	☒ ☐ ☐ ☐
Change in Present Land Use ☒ Not Likely ☐ Likely (*) ☐ Taking Place (*)			Protection from Detrimental Conditions	☐ ☒ ☐ ☐
(*) From _____ To _____			Police and Fire Protection	☐ ☒ ☐ ☐
Predominant Occupancy ☒ Owner ☐ Tenant ___% Vacant			General Appearance of Properties	☐ ☐ ☒ ☐
Single Family Price Range $ 35,000 to $ 45000 Predominant Value $ 40000			Appeal to Market	☐ ☐ ☒ ☐
Single Family Age 18 yrs to 22 yrs Predominant Age 20 yrs				

Note: FHLMC/FNMA do not consider the racial composition of the neighborhood to be a relevant factor and it must not be considered in the appraisal.

Comments (including those factors adversely affecting marketability) MOST PROPERTIES IN NEIGHBORITOD ARE SIMILAR, BUILT IN A DEVELOPMENT ABOUT 20 YRS AGO

SITE

Dimensions 65' X 125' = 8125 Sq. Ft. or Acres   ☐ Corner Lot

Zoning classification R-80   1-FAMILY RESID.   Present improvements ☒ do ☐ do not conform to zoning regulations

Highest and best use: ☒ Present use ☐ Other (Describe) _____

	Public	Other (specify)	OFF SITE IMPROVEMENTS		Topo	GENTLY ROLLING
Elec.	☒		Street Access: ☒ Public ☐ Private		Size	65 X 125
Gas	☒		Surface ASPH. CONCRETE		Shape	REGULAR RECTANGULAR
Water	☒		Maintenance: ☒ Public ☐ Private		View	POOR
San.Sewer	☒		☒ Storm Sewer ☐ Curb/Gutter		Drainage	POSITIVE
			☐ Sidewalk ☒ Street Lights			
☒ Underground Elect. & Tel.						

Is the property located in a HUD identified Flood Hazard Area? ☒ No ☐ Yes

Comments (favorable or unfavorable including any apparent adverse easements, encroachments or other adverse conditions) CONFORMING WELL DRAINED LOT ADVERSELY AFFECTED BY (TENANTED) POORLY MAINTAINED RESIDENCE ACROSS THE STREET (19 NEVERSINK PL) WHICH NEEDS PAINTING, DEBRIS + JUNK CARS IN YARD

IMPROVEMENTS

☒ Existing (approx. yr. blt.) 19 5 7	No. Units 1	No. Stories 1
☐ Proposed ☐ Under Construction		

Type (det, duplex, semi/det, etc.): DET
Design (rambler, split level, etc.): 1½-RANCH
Exterior Walls: ASB. SHINGLES

Roof Material: ASPH SHINGLES
Gutters & Downspouts: GALV ☐ None
Insulation: ☒ Ceiling ☐ None ☐ Roof ☒ Walls ☐ Floor

Window (Type): WD D.H.
☒ Storm Sash ☒ Screens ☒ Combination

Foundation Walls: CONCRETE BLOCK
☐ Crawl Space ☐ Slab on Grade
Comments: WELL MAINTAINED CONDITION

BSMT
96 % Basement ☒ Outside Entrance ☒ Concrete Floor
☐ Floor Drain ☒ Sump Pump 40 % Finished
Evidence of: ☐ Dampness ☐ Termites ☐ Settlement

Finished Ceiling: DRYWALL
Finished Walls: DRYWALL
Finished Floor: VINYL ASB. TILE

ROOM LIST

Room List	Foyer	Living	Dining	Kitchen	Den	Family Rm.	Rec. Rm.	Bedrooms	No. Baths	Laundry	Other
Basement									½		
1st Level	ı	ı	ı	ı				3	1		
2nd Level											

Total 6 Rooms 3 Bedrooms 1 Baths in finished area above grade.

INTERIOR FINISH & EQUIPMENT

Kitchen Equipment: ☒ Refrigerator ☒ Range/Oven ☐ Disposal ☐ Dishwasher ☐ Fan/Hood ☐ Compactor ☒ Washer ☒ Dryer ☐ None
HEAT: Type H/W Fuel GAS Cond. GOOD
AIR COND. ☒ Central ☒ Other 1 WINDOW ☒ Adequate ☐ Inadequate

Floors	☒ Hardwood	☐ Carpet Over	
Walls	☒ Drywall	☐ Plaster	
Trim/Finish	☒ Good	☐ Average ☐ Fair ☐ Poor	
Bath Floor	☒ Ceramic		
Bath Wainscot	☐ Ceramic ☒ MARLITE		

Special Features (including fireplaces):

ATTIC: ☐ Yes ☒ No ☐ Stairway ☐ Drop-stair ☐ Scuttle ☐ Floored ☐ Heated
Finished (Describe)
CAR STORAGE: ☐ Garage ☐ Built-in ☐ Attached ☐ Detached ☐ Car Port
No. Cars 0 ☐ Adequate ☒ Inadequate Condition
PORCHES, PATIOS, POOL, FENCES, etc. (describe)

PROPERTY RATING

	Good	Avg.	Fair	Poor
Quality of Construction (Materials & Finish)	☐	☒	☐	☐
Condition of Improvements	☐	☒	☐	☐
Rooms size and layout	☐	☒	☐	☐
Closets and Storage	☐	☐	☒	☐
Plumbing—adequacy and condition	☐	☒	☐	☐
Electrical—adequacy and condition	☐	☒	☐	☐
Kitchen Cabinets—adequacy and condition	☐	☒	☐	☐
Compatibility to Neighborhood	☐	☒	☐	☐
Overall Livability	☐	☒	☐	☐
Appeal and Marketability	☐	☒	☐	☐

Effective Age 20 Yrs. Est. Remaining Economic Life 40 Yrs.

COMMENTS (including functional or physical inadequacies, repairs needed, modernization, etc.)
NO GARAGE IN AREA WHERE GARAGES ARE STANDARD

ATTACH DESCRIPTIVE PHOTOGRAPHS OF SUBJECT PROPERTY AND STREET SCENE

Figure 7.7 (Cont'd)

121

VALUATION SECTION

Purpose of Appraisal is to estimate Market Value as defined in Certification & Statement of Limiting Conditions (FHLMC Form 439/FNMA Form 1004B). If submitted for FNMA, the appraiser must attach (1) sketch or map showing location of subject, street names, distance from nearest intersection, and any detrimental conditions and (2) exterior building sketch of improvements showing dimensions.

COST APPROACH

Measurements				No. Stories	Sq. Ft.
24'	x	38'	x	1	= 912
2'	x	21'	x CANTILEVER		= 42
	x		x		=
12'	x	28'	x F.N. BASEMENT	= 336 (BELOW GRADE)	
	x		x		=
	x		x		=

Total Gross Living Area (List in Market Data Analysis below) 954

Comment on functional and economic obsolescence: No GARAGE
IN AREA WHERE GARAGES ARE STANDARD

ADVERSE VIEW OF RUNDOWN PROPERTY.

ESTIMATED REPRODUCTION COST — NEW — OF IMPROVEMENTS:

Dwelling 954 Sq. Ft. @ $ 27 = $ 24900
Sq. Ft. @ $ =
Extras F.N. BASEMENT 336 S.F. @ 15.00 = 5000
CHAIN LINK FENCE = 400
Porches, Patios, etc. =
Garage/Car Port Sq. Ft. @ $ =
Site Improvements (driveway, landscaping, etc.) = 500
Total Estimated Cost New = $ 30800

Less	Physical	Functional	Economic
Depreciation $ 3000 $			$1000	= $ (4000)

Depreciated value of improvements = $ 26800
ESTIMATED LAND VALUE
(If leasehold, show only leasehold value) = $ 11500

INDICATED VALUE BY COST APPROACH = $ 38300

The undersigned has recited three recent sales of properties most similar and proximate to subject and has considered these in the market analysis. The description includes a dollar adjustment, reflecting market reaction to those items of significant variation between the subject and comparable properties. If a significant item in the comparable property is superior to, or more favorable than, the subject property, a minus (-) adjustment is made, thus reducing the indicated value of subject; if a significant item in the comparable is inferior to, or less favorable than, the subject property, a plus (+) adjustment is made, thus increasing the indicated value of the subject.

ITEM	Subject Property	COMPARABLE NO. 1		COMPARABLE NO. 2		COMPARABLE NO. 3	
Address	22 Neversink Rd	4 LINDEN DR SUBURBIA		21 BERRY LN SUBURBIA		7 GARDNER ST. SUBURBIA	
Proximity to Subj.		SIM DEVEL 1/2 MI. SO.		SIM DEVEL 1/2 MI. SO.		ADJACENT - CORNER	
Sales Price	$		$ 40500		$ 42000		$ 38000
Price/Living area	$	$ 44 ☑		$ 47 ☑		$ 39 ☑
Data Source		BUYER		BUYER		BROKER	
		DESCRIPTION	+(-)$ Adjustment	DESCRIPTION	+(-)$ Adjustment	DESCRIPTION	+(-)$ Adjustment
Date of Sale and Time Adjustment		7/1/77		8/1/77		8/10/77	
Location	FAIR	GOOD	-1000	FAIR		FAIR	
Site/View	FAIR	FAIR		GOOD		GOOD	-1000
Design and Appeal	FAIR	FAIR		FAIR		FAIR	
Quality of Const.	AV	AV.		AV		AV	
Age	20	18		22		20	
Condition	GOOD	GOOD		GOOD		FAIR	+1000
Living Area Room Count and Total	Total 7 B-rms 3 Baths 1½	Total 7 B-rms 3 Baths 1½		Total 7 B-rms 3 Baths 1½		Total 7 B-rms 3 Baths 1½	
Gross Living Area	954 Sq.Ft.	920 Sq.Ft.		900 Sq.Ft. +1000		980 Sq.Ft. +1000

122

MARKET DATA ANALYSIS

Basement & Bsmt. Finished Rooms	1+1 RANCH BASEMENT 334 S.F.	1+1 RANCH BSMT 306 SF	1+1 RANCH BSMT 290 SF	1+1 RANCH BSMT 340 SF
Functional Utility	FAIR	FAIR	FAIR	FAIR
Air Conditioning	1 (WINDOW) NONE	3 (WINDOW) -500	CENTRAL A/C -1000	1 (WINDOW) NONE
Garage/Car Port		1 (BUILT IN) -500	2 B.I. -1000	
Porches, Patio, Pools, etc.			GOOD LANDSCAPING -500	
Other (e.g. fireplaces, kitchen equip, heating, remodeling)		FIREPLACE -1000		
Sales or Financing Concessions				
Net Adj. (Total)		☐ Plus: ☒ Minus $ 3000	☐ Plus: ☒ Minus $ 4000	☐ Plus: ☐ Minus $ 0
Indicated Value of Subject		$ 37500	$ 38000	$ 38000
Comments on Market Data	Comp. #3 "BEST COMPARABLE, SIZE, LOCATION, AMENITIES			

☐ INDICATED VALUE BY MARKET DATA APPROACH .... $ 38000
☒ INDICATED VALUE BY INCOME APPROACH (If applicable) Economic Market Rent $ 325 /Mo. x Gross Rent Multiplier 120 = $ 39000

This appraisal is made ☒ "as is" ☐ subject to the repairs, alterations, or conditions listed below ☐ completion per plans and specifications.

Comments and Conditions of Appraisal: COST APPROACH IS UPPER LIMIT - INCOME APPROACH NOT PERTINENT BECAUSE OF SCARCITY OF HOUSE RENTALS - MARKET APPROACH IS BEST APPROACH BASED ON ADEQUATE SALES ACTIVITY IN AREA - COMPARABLE No. 3

Final Reconciliation: IS "BEST COMPARABLE"

This appraisal is based upon the above requirements, the certification, contingent and limiting conditions, and Market Value definition that are stated in
☐ FHLMC Form 439 /FNMA Form 1004B filed with client 8/15 19___ ☐ attached.

If submitted for FNMA, the report has been prepared in compliance with FNMA form instructions.

I ESTIMATE THE MARKET VALUE, AS DEFINED, OF SUBJECT PROPERTY AS OF 9/1 19 to be $ 38000

Appraiser(s) John Doe _____ Review Appraiser (If applicable) ☒ Did ☐ Did Not Physically Inspect Property

REVERSE

Figure 7.7 (Cont'd)

123

A MODEL APPRAISAL REPORT ON A
RANCH HOUSE FOR A CORPORATE TRANSFER

Americans are mobile, particularly corporation executives. These employees serve their corporations in many locations as they climb their career ladders. To minimize family relocation problems and foster good employee morale, many large corporations hire corporate transfer firms which specialize in such relocation. Some corporations still handle the transfers with their own real estate departments. Generally, two independent local fee appraisals for fair market value are secured, averaged if close or a third appraisal added if too divergent. Then an offer to purchase the dwelling is made to the employee-owner being relocated. He is generally given 45 to 90 days to try to sell it on the open market while the offer stands. If the offer is accepted, the transfer firm or corporate employer pays the owner his equity plus certain other costs, takes title and re-sells the property later. Criteria for continued use of the specific independent local fee appraiser are response time (usually seven days), appraised values compared to eventual selling prices, professionalism (conduct with occupant, ethics), detail and appearance of reports and fair realistic fees. Corporate transfer firms have diversified appraisal forms. Some have even abandoned form appraisals. However, practically all stress the market approach and require abundance of local, general and market sales data and sales exposure time projections in addition to opinions of value. The following narrative appraisal report embodies data usually needed on such appraisal reports, stresses the Market approach and gives detailed sales projections:

MODEL "RANCH HOUSE" CORPORATE
TRANSFER APPRAISAL

Owner-Transferee-Joseph Ames, Property Address—2 Corner Dr., Legal Desc.-Bl. 1, Lot 2, Acres Subdiv., Orange County, N.Y.

NEIGHBORHOOD—This improved plot is located in a good residential neighborhood of similar $45,000 to $55,000 one-family, 10- to 15-year-old homes on pleasant, rolling, typically 100' × 150' plots, neighborhood built up 100%, no vacancy, improving trend, accessible to good shopping, schools, transportation with estimated $21,000 average income and good pride of ownership evident throughout the area.

SITE—Lot size is 110 ' × 140', well-drained, level to rolling, located on a public paved street with curbs, sidewalk, street lights, public water, public sewer, gas, zoning one-family residential, 220-amp. service, good views of nearby lake, appraised fee simple, highest and best use—residential (present use).

IMPROVEMENTS—A one-story "ranch house," built 1969, six rooms, three bedrooms, two baths, floor area—1,400 sq. ft., entry-6' × 10', L.R.-14' × 20', D.R.-11' × 13', Kit.-13' × 15', B.R.-13' × 14', 12' × 12', 11' × 12', asph. sh. roof, frame wood siding, drywall interior, full basement, wood floor joists, gas hot water heat, central air cond., mas. firepl., wd. ample kit. cab., elec. Hot Point o/r, fan/hood, oak and carpet floors, cer. tile bath, asph dr.-standard construction quality, functional floor plan, ample closet space, panelled d.r., two-car attached frame garage added 1973, building and landscaping in good condition, house needs no apparent reconditioning for resale, no personal property included in appraisal.

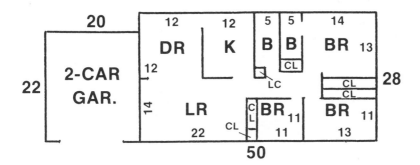

MARKETABILITY—Property is readily marketable within a three-month reasonable period at the established market value. It suffers from no economic nor functional depreciation. The market for such a dwelling in this area is good.

CERTIFICATION—I certify that I have personally inspected the exterior and interior of the foregoing described property and that I have no present nor contemplated interest in the property. In my opinion the market value as of September 1, 1977 is Forty Nine Thousand Dollars ($49,000) including Fourteen Thousand Dollars ($14,000) allocated to land value.

Dated: Harold Smith
                                                   Appraiser
                                                   4 Main St.
                                                   Suburbia

MARKET ANALYSIS

	Subject Property	Comparable #1 Desc.	ADJ.	Comparable #2 Desc.	ADJ.	Comparable #3 Desc.	ADJ.	Comparable #4 Desc.	ADJ.	Comparable #5 Desc.	ADJ.
ADDRESS	2 Corner Dr	22 Wells St.		6 Round Dr		3 Corner Dr.		19 Mack St.			
PROXIMITY TO SUBJECT	Suburbia	Suburbia		Suburbia		Suburbia		Suburbia			
DESCRIPTION OF IMPROVEMENTS	Desc.	SUBURBIA SIM. DEVEL.		SUBURBIA NEARBY BLOCK		SUBURBIA SAME BLOCK		SAME DEVEL. AROUND CORNER			
Rms.	6	8		7		6		6			
Bdrms.	3	4		4		3		3			
Bths.	2	2½	-600	2½		2		2			
Other Rms.		REC RM -1000 DEN -500		FAM. RM.							
LOCATION											
HOUSE SIZE	1400 S.F.	1650	-3500	1650	2500	1480	-1000	1400			
YEAR BUILT	1969	1969	+500	1969		1900	+500	1969			
CONDITION	Good	FAIR	+1500	Good		Good		Good			
QUAL. CONST.	Good	Good		Good		Good		Good			
LOT SIZE	110 x 140	75x120	+1500	100x150		100x160	-500	100x150			
FINANCING	CONV.	CONV.		CASH		FHA	-500	CONV.			
UTILITY	GOOD	GOOD		GOOD		GOOD		GOOD			
DESC. & ADJ.	2 CAR ATT.	2 CAR ATT.		2 CAR ATT		1 CAR ATT	+500	NO GAR	+1000		
FOR CHG MKT SINCE LAST SALE	STABLE	STABLE		STABLE		STABLE		STABLE			
SALES DATA	Last $46000 Current $52000	Date June Price $51000		Date Price $53000		Date July Price $49000		Date Aug. Price $48000		Date Price	
TERMS OF LAST SALE		CONV		CASH		FHA		CONV			
TOTAL ADJUSTMENT	+$	-$	-2000	-$	-4500	-$	-500	+$	+1000	+$	
INDICATED VALUE OF SUBJECT		$49000		$48500		$48500		$49000			

HOMES LISTED FOR SALE IN NEIGHBORHOOD IN COMPETITION WITH SUBJECT PROPERTY. Give brief description = list price — comparison to subject.

Figure 7.8

NARRATIVE APPRAISAL OF MODEL "RANCH HOUSE"

Chapter 8

Techniques and procedures for appraising urban one- to four-family homes

The chapter deals with appraisal techniques for urban residential properties. It reviews the economic and housing decline of many center areas of our cities during the past three decades and discerns the rise of many of these inner-city areas beginning in the sixties, emphasizing the effect these trends have on value.

One- to four-family existing urban homes constitute a major share of the national wealth of our country. "Redlining" or "urban disinvestment," with its impact upon the sale, occupancy and value of this vast national resource is described here.

You will find information on how to recognize the key signs which point to opportunities for real estate investors, rehabilitation builders and lenders in "turn-around" sections of our cities. There is a special section on how to appraise the popular "Brownstone" and similar masonry one- to four-family house found in so many of our older cities. Finally, there is a Model Rowhouse Appraisal Report.

KEY FACTORS IN THE DECLINE OF OUR CITIES

Since the early forties, many factors combined to cause rapid decline in our cities and erosion of our urban housing stock and values. The millions who moved out of the cities along the newly built highways were able to use cheap gas to go to work. Federal housing policies stressed new small home construction in the suburbs and largely unworkable urban renewal demolition and high-rise construction in the cities. These policies contributed greatly to the decline. The blacks who came to the cities from the rural south found that they could not find financing in their "redlined" areas which "blockbusters" helped to turn black. Aging industrial plants in many cities emptied. The cities in the Northeast and Midwest found their economic lifeblood draining to the "Sunbelt." For many years federal subsidies, defense plants and bases went South and Far West rather than to the older Northeast and Midwest cities.

All these factors depressed heavily many of our urban homes and values. Population movement became intense spurred by high family formation and a big "baby boom" in the decade after WWII. Big city neighborhoods deteriorated while suburbs grew rapidly. Even into the mid-seventies, census bureau figures reported that Northeast and Midwest cities continued to lose more people than they gained. However, there were some indications that population trends were stabilizing.

THE RETURN TO URBAN AREAS

The children of the white middle class which left the cities for the suburbs a generation ago appear to be returning to the inner cities now. A counter-cyclic complex of factors is causing this return to the cities as so many factors caused dispersal years ago. This reversal in the disintegration of our big city neighborhoods began as a grass roots movement in the mid-sixties, led by "urban pioneers." These pioneers were mainly young, affluent people seeking the diversity of urban life but also included "empty-nester" older people, ethnics and blacks. The skyrocketing cost of new suburban housing made rehabilitation of urban existing cheaper structures attractive. Concern for historic neighborhoods and structures mounted. Highway building programs slowed. Cost of commuting from suburbs soared. Urban renewal bulldozing halted and federal programs changed emphasis to housing rehabilitation and community re-development. Agencies like Housing and Urban Development (HUD) began to re-examine their programs and practices. These prior programs and sometimes corrupt practices had helped to destroy so many city neighborhoods by improper underwriting, foreclosure and property management policies.

Early portents of this revival occurred in places like Brooklyn Heights, Brooklyn, New York City, where as early as the late fifties, deterioration in this historic district slowed. Rooming houses were converted to resident ownership. Rehabilitation blossomed everywhere. By the seventies, prices ranged from $150,000 to $200,000 for houses which had traded slowly in 1960 for 10% of these figures.

This trend has appeared everywhere. Revitalization has been noted in New York City, Pittsburgh, Savannah, Ann Arbor, Cincinnati, Philadelphia, Boston, Seattle, Utica, Dallas, Chicago, Atlanta, Hartford, St. Louis, Washington, D.C., San Francisco and in many other cities.

These signs of change can be read easily by those of us who appraise successfully in our rapidly changing urban America. Account for these population pressures, changing legislation and economic pressures fairly and objectively in your appraisal reports and values. Appraisal techniques of the past which have contributed to ''redlining'' and ''disinvestment'' in city neighborhoods are relics of the past. They can no longer be used to appraise properly for a generation which appears to be coming back to the cities. The methodology of 30 years ago just doesn't work today. These modern, practical urban appraisal methods are detailed in later sections.

HOW TO EVALUATE "REDLINING"
AND "URBAN DISINVESTMENT"

Redlining, it is alleged, is a pattern of discrimination in which banks refuse to grant mortgage loans, regardless of applicants' creditworthiness, in specified areas because of alleged deteriorating conditions. Originally, it is said, lenders outlined these areas with a red line on city maps.

Banks generally base their underwriting analysis of loan applications on appraisers who can condemn a whole neighborhood by projecting ''economic decline'' and by estimating a short ''remaining economic life.'' Appraisal bank underwriting and even federal appraisal and underwriting FHA standards evolved in the thirties. ''Redlining'' may not only be blamed on racial attitudes, illegal now, but also on something of a state of mind which sees anything old as bad. Old neighborhoods and old properties were written off as bad in our appraisal reporting. Experienced appraisers taught apprentice appraisers that properties have almost a biological life cycle or ''remaining economic life.'' Those houses and neighborhoods which were old, even if sturdy, were depreciated and usually found no mortgages. With no mortgages available, values went down. Lenders' underwriting policies therefore became self-fulfilling prophecies. Appraisers who act as unqualified sociologists when they forecast ''economic life'' of neighborhoods also contribute greatly to these self-fulfilling prophecies.

But, the counter-trend of population movement, back to the cities, is clear. The trend of legislation is also clear. The Civil Rights Act of 1968, the Fair Housing Act of 1968, the Mortgage Disclosure Act of 1975, the Equal

Opportunity Act of 1975 all portend and implement this urban reversal. America has about an 80 million inventory of existing housing, our greatest national wealth. Much of this existing stock is in the cities. As in Europe, rehabilitation rather than demolition and new construction are beginning to revitalize our cities.

"Racial redlining" means that the "adverse feature" which a lender perceives as creating the "underwriting risk" or security risk," is the racial or ethnic composition of the residents of that area. A refusal to lend or the imposition of less favorable loan terms or conditions on account of racial make-up of a community is "racial redlining" and is illegal. It is barred by federal civil rights laws. In Laufman v Oakley Building and Loan Association, 408 F. Supp. 409 (S.D. Ohio 1976), the court said:

> ". . . imposition of barriers to occupancy in the form of higher mortgage-interest rates or refusal to make loans in connection with housing in changing neighborhoods works to discourage families, white and black, which could afford to purchase homes in such neighborhoods. The practical effect is to discourage whites . . . from moving into vacancies in "changing" neighborhoods, thereby inducing "white flight" . . .

"Redlining" is, of course, synonymous with that more dignified sounding term, "Urban Disinvestment." By any name, lack of institutional financing has directly contributed to the decay of our cities.

Remember, you are liable for your attitudes and appraisal reports. In the mid-seventies the Department of Justice filed lawsuits not only against several lenders associations but also against two of the five national appraisal organizations. The suits alleged that the organization required their appraiser members to practice appraisal according to "overtly racially discriminatory standards."

The American Society of Appraisers, a multi-discipline appraisal organization, led by its able Executive Vice President, Dexter D. MacBride, FASA, FSVA, former Chief Right-of-Way Agent, California Division of Highways, is trying to meet this serious challenge to appraisers and appraisal standards even though the ASA is not one of those under suit. This is a challenge to all appraisers since virtually all home loan appraisals made by the nation's institutional lenders are made by professional appraisers.

The ASA program:

1. All ASA organization documents, by-laws and rules were reviewed to assure fair, equal practices within the society.

2. A minority participation policy (within the society) was enunciated.

3. An "Equal Opportunity in Appraising" Committee was established and an Equal Opportunity Resolution was adopted.

4. Various society "Valutapes" on "Redlining and Appraisers" and on "Minority Opportunities" were incorporated into the ASA educational audio-library of Valutapes.

In addition to the above "in-house" action program, the ASA noted that appraisal (real estate) education has been characterized by "trade" teaching. Experienced appraisers taught young appraisers. There were no undergraduate or graduate university degree programs available anywhere in the United States. The ASA concluded that an accredited undergraduate and graduate program was needed, and together with Hofstra University on Long Island, New York began such a program in 1976. The later chapter on appraisal education details additional colleges and universities which are beginning degree programs in valuation science.

It appears inevitable that adequate financing will again become available in "redlined" city areas as these reversing population pressures, implementing legislation and income pressures increase. You have to be objective in attitudes, reports and values to avoid liability for improper or illegal reporting. An independent modern appraiser is truly independent and free of the appraisal myths of yesteryear. Redlining government lawsuits may affect superficial aspects but only good will of professionals can properly reflect and value changing suburban-urban real estate trends and values.

HOW TO KEEP UP WITH COUNTERVAILING TRENDS IN THE CITIES

There are other important reasons and key indicators for this countervailing return trend to sections of our cities. About 10 years ago, the "preservation" movement in America was recognized in law by the National Historic Preservation Act of 1966. Although seemingly innocuous, it set up a legislative vehicle for registering national and local historic landmark buildings and "districts" or neighborhoods. Landmark preservation commissions came into being mainly in urban areas.

There are key indicators here also. Is the home on a registered landmark site? Is it in a national or city historic register? Is there a Landmarks Preservation Commission in the area? Has the Secretary of the U.S. Department of Interior listed the district or neighborhood on his historic register?

The Tax Act of 1976 gave impetus to this National Historic Preservation Act of 1966. Opportunities for real estate investors, rehabilitation builders, lenders and home buyers multiplied. This will be detailed in the next section.

Also, keep up with trends in these constantly changing urban areas. One good way is by reviewing regular census reports on population. Changing patterns of life and life style are taking place in the United States and have important impact on appraisal work. Between 1970 and 1976, census reports show that the proportion of population aged 25 to 29 who never married increased substantially. The divorce rate more than doubled between 1963 and 1975. There are now three divorces for every five marriages. These important socio-economic indicators are additional signposts on this countervailing return road for many from the family-oriented suburbs to the cities. The high cost of homes in the suburbs versus the much lower cost in many sections of the city are not sufficient reasons. This modern American way of life for many apparently makes for less bedroom demand, less school demand and an increasing desire for city culture and amenities. This must all be considered when you estimate demand for urban one- to four-family homes.

HOW TO RECOGNIZE AND EVALUATE OPPORTUNITIES FOR REAL ESTATE INVESTORS, REHABILITATION BUILDERS AND LENDERS IN "TURN-AROUND" SECTIONS

You appraise for lenders, investors, builders, buyers and owners. In "turn-around" sections of the cities, where countervailing rehabilitation and preservation forces may be working amidst and against a backdrop of deteriorating conditions, your appraisal reports must meet the especially critical needs of your client.

As always, you should know your area indicators on a section-by-section, block-by-block basis. Is there a Neighborhood Revival or Preservation Committee? Are historic districts or properties involved? Are there committee publications which detail community efforts to keep people in neighborhoods as well as bring new people in? Are there presale building inspection programs in the city? These inspection programs were started in big cities like Detroit and Minneapolis and spread to many smaller cities in reaction to federal programs of the past which involved many foreclosures and led to much abandonment and decay. The Detroit inspection, for example, costs $92, covers basic livability, safety, heating, plumbing and electric systems and has brought long-term benefits. Are there recently rehabilitated buildings on the block? What is the trend of sales of building shells, of existing unrestored buildings, of rehabilitated buildings? Active, down, stable, up or runaway up, as in many popular city neighborhoods now?

The Tax Reform Act of 1976 gave impetus to the historic preservation of buildings and neighborhoods and is helping to combat the former practice of bulldoze and build rather than preserve. The act permits accelerated five-year depreciation for improvements on income producing certified historic structures. It also refuses write-off of demolition and construction costs on historic sites. In only one borough of New York City, the Brooklyn Landmark Commission identified 29 possible Landmark Districts with 89,000 housing units as potentially eligible. Also, if historic property is contributed for public use, tax deductions can be taken.

This appears to represent one of the greatest opportunities for low cost rehabilitation in cities today. Many Brownstone buildings have already been rehabilitated with a modern two-level duplex for the owner and smaller rental income producing apartments on the upper levels. Supportive to residential neighborhoods are viable commercial complexes. Restaurants, for example, are excellent adaptive uses for historic structures and service reviving residential areas. There are complexes like the Long Wharf project in Boston containing commercial, restaurants, appartments and offices. The Trolley Square in Salt Lake City is another excellent example of modern adaptation of historic structures to serve modern urban needs.

Rehabilitation of existing buildings in our cities is the apparent wave of the future. In Baltimore, a unit can be rehabilitated for one-third the cost of new construction. Federal programs now stress rehabilitation and community redevelopment. There is even a 3%, 20-year federal renovation loan program. The Bank of America in San Francisco set up a subsidiary to buy and renovate 30 houses and is expanding this program into other California cities. The Philadelphia National Bank invested $1 million in 95% and 100% loans in inner city Philadelphia areas in the mid-seventies and had only one delinquency in mortgage payments (because of a marriage break-up.)

There is a growing market, particularly among young people, ages 25 to 35. Chart this trend for your appraisal reporting, wherever it occurs, on a section-by-section and block-by-block basis. Revitalization of neighborhoods feeds upon prior rehabilitation. The word spreads among these young people as to the ''in'' neighborhoods, the ''good buys.'' Consider this in your valuation. It is a social and housing phenomenon which cannot be dismissed as transient. Your client needs full data to make his decisions in the light of these emerging opportunities.

HOW TO APPRAISE THE ONE- TO FOUR-FAMILY "BROWNSTONE"

From a trickle in 1968 to a strong flow by the late seventies, the ''movement back'' to the cities has resulted in rising values of city townhouses. Many such townhouses in New York City boroughs, for example, are called ''Brownstones'' because of the color of their stone facades. They are similar to row houses in Baltimore, Washington, Boston and even to attached frame houses in these and many other cities. (See Figures 8.1 and 8.2.)

Figure 8.1

THREE-STORY "BROWNSTONE" ROW HOUSE

Figure 8.2

TWO-STORY "BROWNSTONE" ROW HOUSE

Some are historic, most were built around the turn of the century. Generally there are fireplaces, hall pier mirrors, sliding doors, built-in China closets, wood wainscot, parquet floors, stained woodwork and sometimes even pull-chain, overhead type toilet tanks which work better than modern attached toilet tank-bowls. The buildings have mass, are suited for today's high energy costs and are generally of sturdy, superior construction.

Many of the New York City "Brownstones" have stoops, a Dutch architectural touch. The stoops lead to the parlor floor, are good for neighbors to sit on and socialize. Small boys also find stoops good for stoop ball.

How to appraise honestly, fairly and professionally in dynamic city neighborhoods where you note abandoned buildings, buildings being rehabilitated and new growth amidst decay? Some areas are easy. They've turned the corner. Of the 40-plus "Brownstone" areas in New York City and nearby New Jersey, for instance, about a dozen areas have become so popular that it's hard to find a building to rehabilitate and renovated homes sell for up to $200,000. Hoboken, New Jersey, for example, with its 45,000 residents, was formerly the drab and depressing environment where Marlon Brando did the movie "On the Waterfront." It had almost 2,500 housing units redone from 1972 to 1977 with many newcomers but with its ethnic heritage mainly remaining.

However, the inner city district areas, which are still in the throes of this change are the appraisal challenge.

There are various modern appraisal techniques you can use. The California Savings and Loan Regulations Commission has issued appraisal standards which seem very pertinent to this challenge:

(1) Select comparable sales from your market data which will avoid subjective time and location adjustments.

(2) Emphasize Market Data approach in one- to four-family home appraisals.

(3) Document thoroughly when you must take neighborhood adjustments.

(4) Use enough comparables. Normally three are enough but more should be used if neighborhood or time adjustments are necessary.

(5) The proposed sales price, if a buyer is involved, is one indication of market value.

(6) The Cost approach must be de-emphasized on one- to four-family urban appraisals.

(7) Adverse influences must be specific. Do not generalize. If you report a poorly maintained or abandoned house nearby, don't say "area," give the address and its proximity. Abandoned houses on the same

block would cause "economic depreciation" but evidence of re-habilitated houses or houses being rehabilitated in the immediate vicinity can counteract this depreciation.

(8) If your client's forms require an "economic life" statement, be specific in your best judgment, to the immediate block, not to the whole district or community.

(9) In the California regulations, in Detroit and Philadelphia, a number of lenders judge mortgage applications on the specific residential block involved and on the applicant's credit status rather than on the condition of the area where the property is situated. You can also use a guideline sketch similar to the following California Commission's sketch, Figure 8.3, to determine the proximity of localized adverse value affect. Note that the principal focus is given to conditions on those blocks and sides of blocks that are likely to most directly impact on the appraised property.

■ - PROPERTY BEING APPRAISED
— — — DOTTED LINES REPRESENT THOSE SIDES OF BLOCKS
WHICH MOST DIRECTLY IMPACT ON THE SECURITY PROPERTY

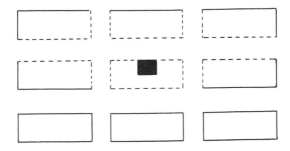

Figure 8.3

PROXIMITY SKETCH OF LOCALIZED VALUE EFFECT

A MODEL ROWHOUSE APPRAISAL REPORT

The following Model Appraisal Report has been prepared on the most recent edition of the FNMA 1004, Residential Appraisal Report. (See Figure 8.7 on pages 141-144.) This is considered particularly appropriate because the Form stresses under the Neighborhood section that "FHLMC/FNMA do not consider the racial composition of the neighborhood to be a relevant factor and

Figure 8.4

BROWNSTONE FRONT

Figure 8.5

BROWNSTONE REAR

it must not be considered in the appraisal.'' Also, FNMA has recognized urban revitalizing neighborhoods with positive actions. For instance, it committed to buy up to 800 home mortgages in St. Louis to stimulate bankers there to also recognize what is happening and originate home loans. To conserve space, attachments required by the Form such as location sketches have been omitted. Front, rear and street scene photographs, however, are attached. (See Figures 8.4, 8.5 and 8.6.) A location sketch similar to Figure 8.3 should also be included as well as a fully dimensioned building exterior sketch as shown in Chapter 7. For demonstration purposes and because the form requires its completion, the Cost approach box on the second page of the form has been completed. However, your market value should be derived from the Market Data approach.

Figure 8.6

STREET SCENE

RESIDENTIAL APPRAISAL REPORT

To be completed by Lender

Borrower/Client	File No.
Property Address: 14 HIGH ST. (CARROLL GARDENS)	
City: BROOKLYN County: KINGS State: NY Zip Code: 00000	Census Tract Map Reference
Legal Description	
Sale Price $ Date of Sale Property Rights Appraised [X] Fee [ ] Leasehold [ ] DeMinimis PUD(FNMA only) [ ] Condo [ ] PUD)	
Actual Real Estate Taxes $ 950 (yr) Loan charges to be paid by seller $ Other sales concessions	
Lender Lender's Address	
Occupant: THOMAS SMITH Appraiser: JOHN DOE Instructions to Appraiser: CALL OWNER FOR APPT 212-000-0000	

NEIGHBORHOOD

Location	[X] Urban	[ ] Suburban	[ ] Rural	
Built Up	[X] Over 75%	[ ] 25% to 75%	[ ] Under 25%	
Growth Rate [X] Fully Dev.	[ ] Rapid	[ ] Steady	[ ] Slow	
Property Values	[X] Increasing	[ ] Stable	[ ] Declining	
Demand/Supply	[X] Shortage	[ ] In Balance	[ ] Over Supply	
Marketing Time	[X] Under 3 Mos.	[ ] 4–6 Mos.	[ ] Over 6 Mos.	

Present Land Use 40% 1 Family 50% 2–4 Family ___% Apts. ___% Condo 2% Commercial ___% Industrial 8% Vacant ___%

Change in Present Land Use [X] Not Likely [ ] Likely (*) [ ] Taking Place (*)

(*) From ___ To ___

Predominant Occupancy [X] Owner [ ] Tenant 0% Vacant

Single Family Price Range $ 45000 to $ 75000 Predominant Value $ 60000

Single Family Age 75 yrs to 100 yrs Predominant Age 80 yrs

	Good	Avg.	Fair	Poor
Employment Stability	[X]			
Convenience to Employment	[X]			
Convenience to Shopping	[X]			
Convenience to Schools	[X]			
Quality of Schools		[X]		
Recreational Facilities	[X]			
Adequacy of Utilities	[X]			
Property Compatibility	[X]			
Protection from Detrimental Conditions	[X]			
Police and Fire Protection		[X]		
General Appearance of Properties	[X]			
Appeal to Market	[X]			

Note: FHLMC/FNMA do not consider the racial composition of the neighborhood to be a relevant factor and it must not be considered in the appraisal.

Comments (including those factors adversely affecting marketability) A VERY GOOD HISTORIC RESIDENTIAL DISTRICT OF MAINLY "BROWNSTONE" STYLES IN GOOD CONDITION WITH STRONG MARKET DEMAND GOWANUS CANAL, EASTERN BORDER OF DISTRICT WITH STRONG INDUSTRIAL ODORS, IS FAR ENOUGH AWAY TO HAVE NO ADVERSE AFFECT.

SITE

Dimensions 18' × 100' = 1800 Sq. Ft. or Acres [ ] Corner Lot

Zoning classification RES. Present improvements [X] do [ ] do not conform to zoning regulations

Highest and best use: [X] Present use [ ] Other (Describe)

	Public	Other (Describe)	OFF SITE IMPROVEMENTS		Topo	LEVEL
Elec.	[X]		Street Access: [X] Public [ ] Private		Size	18'×100'
Gas	[X]		Surface ASPH. CONCRETE		Shape	REGULAR
Water	[X]		Maintenance: [ ] Public [ ] Private		View	
San.Sewer	[X]		[X] Storm Sewer [X] Curb/Gutter		Drainage	POSITIVE
	[X] Underground Elect. & Tel.		[X] Sidewalk [X] Street Lights		Is the property located in a HUD identified Flood Hazard Area? [X] No [ ] Yes	

[ ] Other (specify)

Comments (favorable or unfavorable including any apparent adverse easements, encroachments or other adverse conditions) NARROW, TREE LINED, QUIET STREET ENHANCES RESIDENTIAL LIVING

Figure 8.7

FNMA APPRAISAL REPORT

IMPROVEMENTS

[X] Existing (approx. yr. blt.) 1902	No. Units 1
[ ] Proposed	No. Stories 2
[ ] Under Construction	Type (det, duplex, semi./det., etc.): ATT.

Design (rambler, split level, etc.): (BROWNSTONE) ROW D/H
Exterior Walls: BRICK AND STONE

Roof Material: BLT-UP
Gutters & Downspouts: COPPER

Window (Type): [ ] None [ ] Storm Sash [ ] Screens [X] Combination
Insulation: [X] Ceiling [ ] Roof [ ] Floor [ ] Walls [ ] None

Foundation Walls: BRICK
[X] 100% Basement [X] Outside Entrance
[ ] Crawl Space   Concrete Floor
[ ] Slab on Grade Evidence of: [ ] Dampness [ ] Termites [ ] Settlement
Floor Drain [X]   Sump Pump [ ]   70% Finished
Finished Ceiling: PLASTER
Finished Walls: PLASTER
Finished Floor: PINE ON SLEEPERS

Comments: EXCELLENT CONDITION

ROOM LIST

Room List	Foyer	Living	Dining	Kitchen	Den	Family Rm.	Rec. Rm.	Bedrooms	No. Baths	Laundry	Other
Basement									1/2	1	
1st Level	1	1	1	1	1		1		1/2		
2nd Level								3	1		

Total 7 Rooms   3 Bedrooms   1½ Baths in finished area above grade.

INTERIOR FINISH & EQUIPMENT

Kitchen Equipment: [ ] Refrigerator [X] Range/Oven [ ] Disposal [ ] Dishwasher [ ] Fan/Hood [ ] Compactor [ ] Washer [ ] Dryer

HEAT: Type Hot water   Fuel GAS   Cond. GOOD
AIR COND: [ ] Central [ ] Other [ ] Adequate [ ] Inadequate

Floors: [X] Hardwood [ ] Carpet Over			
Walls: [ ] Drywall [X] Plaster			
Trim/Finish: [X] Good [ ] Average [ ] Fair [ ] Poor			
Bath Floor: [X] Ceramic			
Bath Wainscot: [X] Ceramic			
Condition: [ ] Good [ ] Fair [ ] Poor			

Special Features (including fireplaces): MARBEL MANTEL TALL WINDOWS, ELEGANT MOLDINGS

ATTIC: [ ] Yes [X] No [ ] Stairway [ ] Drop-stair [ ] Scuttle
Finished (Describe): [ ] Floored [ ] Heated
CAR STORAGE: [ ] Garage [ ] Built-in [ ] Attached [ ] Detached [ ] Car Port
No. Cars ___ [ ] Adequate [ ] Inadequate   Condition ___

PORCHES, PATIOS, POOL, FENCES, etc. (describe):

PROPERTY RATING

	Good	Avg.	Fair	Poor
Quality of Construction (Materials & Finish)	X			
Condition of Improvements	X			
Rooms size and layout	X			
Closets and Storage	X			
Plumbing—adequacy and condition	X			
Electrical—adequacy and condition	X			
Kitchen Cabinets—adequacy and condition	X			
Compatibility to Neighborhood	X			
Overall Livability	X			
Appeal and Marketability	X			

Effective Age 20 Yrs.   Est. Remaining Economic Life 60 Yrs.

COMMENTS (including functional or physical inadequacies, repairs needed, modernization, etc.): STREET PARKING PERMITTED AND AVAILABLE

ATTACH DESCRIPTIVE PHOTOGRAPHS OF SUBJECT PROPERTY AND STREET SCENE

Figure 8.7 (Cont'd.)

VALUATION SECTION

COST APPROACH

Purpose of Appraisal is to estimate Market Value as defined in Certification & Statement of Limiting Conditions (FHLMC Form 439/FNMA Form 1004B). If submitted for FNMA, the appraiser must attach (1) sketch or map showing location of subject, street names, distance from nearest intersection, and any detrimental conditions and (2) exterior building sketch of improvements showing dimensions.

Measurements

18'	x	44'	x	2 No. Stories	= 1584 Sq. Ft.
18'	x	44'	x	1 (BASEMENT)	= 792
	x		x		=
	x		x		=
	x		x		=

ESTIMATED REPRODUCTION COST — NEW — OF IMPROVEMENTS:

Dwelling 1584 Sq. Ft. @ $ 30 = $ 47500

Extras FINISHED BAS'M'T = 5000

STOOP, W.I. FENCE = 2000

Porches, Patios, etc. ___

Garage/Car Port ___ Sq. Ft. @ $ ___

Site Improvements (driveway, landscaping, etc.) = 500

Total Estimated Cost New . . . . $ 55000

Less Depreciation $ 5000 | Physical | Functional | Economic

Less Depreciation $ 5000 . . . . $ (5000)

Depreciated value of improvements . . . . $ 50000

ESTIMATED LAND VALUE = $ 20000
(If leasehold, show only leasehold value)

INDICATED VALUE BY COST APPROACH . . $ 70000

Total Gross Living Area (List in Market Data Analysis below) 1584

Comment on functional and economic obsolescence: NO FUNCTIONAL NOR ECON. OBSOLESCENCE

The undersigned has recited three recent sales of properties most similar and proximate to subject and has considered these in the market analysis. The description includes a dollar adjustment, reflecting market reaction to those items of significant variation between the subject and comparable properties. If a significant item in the comparable property is superior to, or more favorable than, the subject property, a minus (-) adjustment is made, thus reducing the indicated value of subject; if a significant item in the comparable is inferior to, or less favorable than, the subject property, a plus (+) adjustment is made, thus increasing the indicated value of the subject.

ITEM	Subject Property	COMPARABLE NO. 1		COMPARABLE NO. 2		COMPARABLE NO. 3	
Address	14 HIGH ST.	22 HIGH ST.		10 CARROLL ST.		16 LOW ST.	
		DESCRIPTION	+(-)$ Adjustment	DESCRIPTION	+(-)$ Adjustment	DESCRIPTION	+(-)$ Adjustment
Proximity to Subj.		SAME BLOCK		3 BLOCKS NORTH		2 BLOCKS SOUTH	
Sales Price	$	$ 75000		$ 70000		$ 59000	
Price/Living area	$	$ 44 ☑		$ 44 ☑		$ 42 ☑	
Data Source		BUYER		DEED		BROKER	
Date of Sale and Time Adjustment		JAN '77		DEC 76		JUNE 77	+5000
Location		GOOD		GOOD		AVER	+5000
Site/View		AVER.		AVER		AVER	
Design and Appeal		GOOD		GOOD		GOOD	
Quality of Const.		GOOD		GOOD		GOOD	
Age		20 (EFF.)		20 (EFF.)		30 (EFF.)	+3000
Condition							
Living Area Room Count and Total	Total 7	B-rms 3	Baths 1½	Total 7 B-rms 3 Baths 1½		Total 6 B-rms 3 Baths 1	
	Total 8 B-rms 3 Baths 1½			Total 7 B-rms 3 Baths 1½			
Gross Living Area	1584 Sq.Ft.	1700 Sq.Ft.	-5000 ☑	1584 Sq.Ft.		1400 Sq.Ft.	+2000

Figure 8.7 (Cont'd.)

143

Basement & Bsmt. Finished Rooms			
Functional Utility			
Air Conditioning			
Garage/Car Port			
Porches, Patio, Pools, etc.			
Other (e.g. fireplaces, kitchen equip, heating, remodeling)	2 GOOD	2 GOOD	2 GOOD
Sales or Financing Concessions			
Net Adj. (Total)	☐ Plus; ☒ Minus $ 5000	☐ Plus; ☐ Minus $ 7000	☐ Plus; ☐ Minus $
Indicated Value of Subject	$ 70000	$ 70000	$ 69000

Comments on Market Data COMP. #2 (SAME SIZE RENOVATED DWELLING) IS BEST COMPARABLE

INDICATED VALUE BY MARKET DATA APPROACH .... $ 70000

INDICATED VALUE BY INCOME APPROACH (If applicable) Economic Market Rent $ _____ /Mo. x Gross Rent Multiplier _____ = $

This appraisal is made ☐ "as is" ☐ subject to the repairs, alterations, or conditions listed below ☐ completion per plans and specifications.

Comments and Conditions of Appraisal: _____

Final Reconciliation: MARKET APPROACH BEST APPROACH IN THIS POPULAR "BROWNSDALE" NEIGHBORHOOD WITH A STRONG MARKET DEMAND.

This appraisal is based upon the above requirements, the certification, contingent and limiting conditions, and Market Value definition that are stated in
☐ FHLMC Form 439 / FNMA Form 1004B filed with client JAN 1 ___ 19 __ ☐ attached.

If submitted for FNMA, the report has been prepared in compliance with FNMA form instructions.

I ESTIMATE THE MARKET VALUE, AS DEFINED, OF SUBJECT PROPERTY AS OF JULY 1 19 __ to be $ 70000

Appraiser(s) John Doe _____ Review Appraiser (If applicable) ☐ Did ☒ Did Not Physically Inspect Property

REVERSE

Figure 8.7 (Cont'd.)

144

Chapter 9

How to appraise apartments

This chapter is concerned with the appraisal of apartments. The impact of modern life styles and changing population patterns on apartment demand and appraising is evaluated here. The dynamic nature of our housing industry and economy, which constantly affects over- and under-supply of apartments on a regional basis, is also detailed. You'll find specific guidance on how to appraise those peculiarly American concepts of ''singles'' and ''senior citizen'' apartment complexes which evolved to supply these changing life styles and population patterns. A Model Apartment House Appraisal Report and a Model Senior Citizen Complex Appraisal Report are also illustrated here.

WHY APARTMENT VALUES WILL INCREASE

In terms of definitions, a garden apartment house is generally distinguished from multi-family high-rise apartment buildings by height, usually two- or three-story, and by low land density. There are also rent classifications: high rent, moderate rent and low rent apartment complexes. Apartments are further identified as rental, cooperative, condominium, subsidized and public housing. We will be concerned here mainly with suburban, rental garden apartment houses.

A complicated variety of socio-economic factors operate in the housing field to affect apartment supply and demand.

You do practical feasibility analyses when you evaluate these trends and their impact on apartment demand and values. These analyses are implied in your research or explicit in your appraisal reports. This feasibility approach is basic throughout this handbook, but it is particularly important in this apartment chapter. Apartment houses are generally bought for a profitable return on investment, unlike one- to four-family homes purchased for "amenity value." In new construction, feasibility analysis is generally what determines whether the project should be built. In existing apartment houses, feasibility analysis leads to determination of value and the projected present value of expected future returns.

Whenever you study the feasibility and value of an apartment house or complex, you are analyzing the market area, the neighborhood, the site, the location in terms of transportation, schools, shopping, churches, community facilities, noise, smoke, odors, existing or proposed improvements, their appeal to the market and the efficiency of the proposed plans or existing management. You also study population demographics and life styles in the nation, in the region and in your area for clues to current demand, continuing demand, values and future projections.

Sources for this information include:

- census reports,
- planning departments,
- county clerk offices,
- property transfer records,
- building inspector records,
- tax assessor records,
- libraries,
- chamber of commerce reports,
- utility company statistics,
- lawyers,
- real estate brokers and
- numerous national trade association publications.

Census reports, for example, show that by the mid-seventies, the median age of Americans was rising rapidly and the fertility rate dropped. The percentage of people over 65 was rising and the death rate declined. By the year 2030, census reports project that one out of six will be over 65, compared to one in 10 today. Most demographers believe this progressive "graying of America" will continue because of improved health care, effective contraception, liberalized abortion, easing of divorce laws, postponement of marriage and the changing role of women.

Countervailing this trend to an older society are the millions of "baby boom" children born from 1947 to 1961 who are moving through adulthood in the seventies and eighties.

Besides changing population patterns, there are also changing life styles. More "singles," those who marry later or not at all, those millions more who divorce and do not remarry, all contribute to our declining birth rate. Recent census statistics showed 2.8 million men and 4.4 million women divorced and not remarried.

There are always counter-trends. Many of these "singles," particularly the affluent ones, appear to have a desire to buy and live in one-family homes. However, the basic thrust of modern American demographics, life style and economics appears to be toward smaller shelter units and toward apartment living.

Regional pockets of over-built apartments and slowly reducing vacancy rates still spot our nation because of multi-family over-building in the late sixties and because of recession-inflation, high construction cost and high financing cost in the late seventies. However, the long-range trend appears to be for increasing overall apartment demand and values.

HOW TO RECOGNIZE AND EVALUATE REGIONAL CHANGES IN APARTMENT SUPPLY

These same dynamic population patterns have brought simultaneous housing boom and bust patterns to different regions of our nation in this last quarter of the twentieth century. So many young people in Southern California have made it a housing beehive of escalating values. This has not occurred just in California. Throughout the "Sunbelt," except for Florida and Georgia, population growth and jobs have combined with available financing to spur building of new shelter units and to accelerate resales of one-family units at a constantly inflating rate. Apartments in these areas have felt this surge too.

The older Northeast and Midwest cities and suburbs suffered decline. As industries moved from these older areas seeking modern plants, lower labor costs, lower energy costs and taxes, job seekers followed, leaving much of the inner cities to the poor while real estate values dropped in the suburbs.

Obsolete industrial areas in aging cities and their suburbs were not the only regional problem. In our free economy, the housing industry responds and often over-responds to supply housing demands whenever financing is available. It is the one industry composed of hundreds of thousands of developer-builder businessmen. Particularly with apartments because of their multi-unit nature, construction needs long lead time from planning to approvals to construction to rentals. All during various "easy money" financing years in the sixties and early seventies, millions of FHA and conventionally financed apartments were built . . . and over-built. When demand fell off because of recession and tight money, builders were caught, half built out and with untenanted complexes. Easy financing offered mainly through Real Estate Investment Trusts (REITS) spurred much of this over-building.

Most of these REITS of the sixties and early seventies were subsidiaries of institutional lenders. Once burned, these lenders were loath to venture into regions where apartments were still overhung, like in Florida and many parts of the Northeast.

Another brake on apartments was the inflation-escalated high cost of construction and high mortgage interest rates, making rents uneconomical. Many builders were forced to compete—particularly in the Northeast—for limited, government-subsidized, Section 8, multi-unit building funds backed by federal rent subsidies. Other builders found they could deliver apartments at lower rents acceptable to the market, particularly in older sections of cities and suburbs, often on historic buildings. They did this by rehabilitating existing housing, using conventional and private financing. Favorable tax write-off also has encouraged such rehabilitation and conversion to multi-family units.

Study and be alert to these changes and portents of changes in the money market, in the economy, in construction costs in the nation and in your area. Study census reports on a national, regional and local basis for population patterns and mobility. Housing turnover is generally associated with apartments. Many people used to opt for one-family home purchase when their rentals (they felt) got too high with no equity value resulting. With the high prices of one-family houses drawing an ever shrinking percentage of the market, this traditional reason for turnover in apartments may be affected. For whatever reasons, excessive turnover leading to inefficient and costly operation is the bane of apartment ownership. National apartment rental vacancies were down in the late seventies to 5% from 8% in the sixties. Know the vacancy rates in your own area and chart these changes. These are all key indicators for apartment appraising.

HOW TO APPRAISE "SINGLES" APARTMENT COMPLEXES

"Singles" apartment complexes began in the sixties to meet what some called the hedonistic life style of young people in those rebellious years. As with many innovations in housing, the concept began in California, then spread to other areas of the country in the early seventies. This type of housing no longer caters to and is advertised for singles only but has since broadened to a wider market.

These building improvements feature comparatively small but efficient apartments with one-bedroom and efficiency units predominating. For the affluent, there is usually the "studio" apartment. In "singles" parlance, this generally means a balcony studio-bedroom over the cathedral living room in addition to the basic one bedroom. Landscaping in these complexes is extensive. Amenities are emphasized including tennis courts, pools, Jacuzzis and recreational buildings. Usually, there are also scheduled "mixing" athletic-social affairs supervised and encouraged by paid directors.

As the rebellious sixties faded into the more mature seventies, these singles complexes built for the young changed into expanded "singles." Married couples, many older divorced people, retired people, even people with children, found these complexes with their many amenities appealing. Also, today's changed life styles with many people sharing life and shelter together without marriage appears to have broadened the market for this type of comparatively expensive apartment. Besides, two can live cheaper than one in these apartments which are expensive because of their many amenities. Turnover has always been high in these complexes and this expanded market appears to be a stabilizing force.

Although it is an exotic apartment variant, the singles complex is appraised using the same research approach, feasibility analysis tools and valuation techniques employed in any other multi-family appraisal.

The purpose of your feasibility study of a single apartment complex is always to determine the feasibility of building and renting a proposed project or, using the same premise, to determine the value of an existing project. Questions which are always posed for your appraisal answers include:

- What type of apartment mix is renting or would rent?
- Size of units?
- Proper, economic, competitive rent ranges?
- Amenities?
- Is there a projected continuing rental market?
- Projected near and future demand?
- Is location convenient for transportation, recreation, shopping, employment and community facilities?
- Competition in area?
- Does market study project future viability?
- Good design is not in the eye of the beholder. It is demanded by the apartment renter. Good storage design, including ample pantry, coat and kitchen closets, is a must. Landscaping, outdoor amenities, professional, efficient apartment management is necessary to compete successfully in most areas.

DETERMINING EXPECTED FUTURE YIELDS

Valuation techniques generally involve estimating the present value of the expected future yields. The objective is to determine a price at which the "singles" complex, proposed or existing, would be a good investment opportunity for a prudent investor. Many lenders and government agencies still require the outmoded three-approach valuation system of cost, market and income. For these clients, the classic "tripod" system must still be used. However, since apartment houses are built or bought for investment purposes, even these lenders and agencies, and certainly most of your buyers and builder clients, will be mainly interested in the results of your Income approach to value. On new construction, the Cost approach will have relevance. The Market approach would normally be best if there are enough sales of multi-unit properties in your area but it is often not possible to secure confirmed data on sales prices, terms and conditions for each comparable on these types of properties.

The Income approach depends upon your experience and good judgment. Critical to this approach is your capitalization rate which is generally determined by using one of the following three market-oriented techniques:

"Cap" Rate Method 1—Analyze *sales and income* data of recently sold similar properties, their selling prices and net income. Then divide selling price into net income to derive capitalization rate. Thus:

Net Income	÷	Selling Price	=	Capitalization Rate
($55,500)	÷	($540,000)	=	(10.3%)

"Cap" Rate Method 2—Usually, it is not possible to secure good enough market sales and income data needed for Method 1. One alternative then is to employ a *Built-Up* capitalization rate using accepted non-risk or safe rates applicable to government bonds, say. To such a safe rate, percentages are added for the management, non-liquidity and risk involved in investing and operating an apartment building rather than clipping safe bond coupon investment returns. Thus:

Government bond current rate 7%
Management rate 2%
Risk 1%
(Total) Capitalization rate 10%

"Cap" Rate Method 3—Similarly, a *Band of Investment* technique can be used to build up a capitalization rate by estimating the difference in risk involved in the various ownership and mortgage interests in the property. This technique is a composite of mortgage yield and equity yield, based on local market study, adjusted for the property's depreciation and including a "recapture" percentage representing capital return upon sale. For example, an owner has 40% equity investment in a property which is

burdened with a 60% first mortgage @ 9% interest. (Estimated that this equity would earn 8% if otherwise invested.) Thus:

Owner's equity (40% × 8%)	=	3.2%
First mortgage (60% × 9%)	=	5.4%
"Recapture" (50-year econ. life)	=	2.0%
(Total) Capitalization rate	=	10.6%

An equally critical element of this Investment Analysis Income approach is your informed analysis of the projected or existing operating statement and your determination from the statement of the gross rent roll and expenses, as to what the fair net income really is. These expenses include vacancy percentage, repairs, insurance taxes, management, labor, fuel, supplies, utilities, miscellaneous and reserve for replacement.

Although there are other income sub-approaches such as Land Residual and Property Residual techniques, the Building Residual technique is normally used to appraise apartment buildings. This technique involves capitalizing the building's derived net income and then adding land value secured from a study of local comparable land sales.

You proceed from feasibility to analysis to compilation of all project data to valuation analysis of operating statement to net profit before taxes, factored by the capitalization. This is the appraisal path you take to arrive at your final value, in dollars, for the subject singles apartment complex.

HOW TO APPRAISE "SENIOR CITIZEN" APARTMENT COMPLEXES

Like "singles" complexes, "senior citizen" complexes have evolved to meet demographic changes in our aging population. Prior sections of this chapter reviewed these dynamic population patterns involving so many changes in age groups, attitudes, location and desires of many millions of people. Shelter, a basic human need, has changed to meet these changing demographics.

What is the senior citizen complex? It can be the plush, high-walled, security-conscious, comparatively expensive, leisure-oriented, adult home-apartment communities mushrooming up in Southern California and in parts of Florida. It can also be the smaller, less expensive complexes of homes and apartments in other places like Lakewood, New Jersey or Springdale on the Hudson, New York. It apparently is destined to be everywhere in our nation in various forms. Some people like to retire to warmer climates in Florida and in the Sunbelt and in the Far West. Others like to stay within visiting distance of their children's families but want to live in separate adult communities with neighbors of like age groups and desires.

These complexes have to be specially designed for safety and convenience for the elderly. These special designs often include ramps, wider doors and hallways, generous bathroom areas with placement of fixtures at convenient elevations, adequate grab bars in tub and shower, wall switches and electric outlets mounted at minimum 18 inches and maximum 48 inches from floor. Room and apartment sizes generally are to smaller scale.

Location should be within a short walk of convenience shopping, near major shopping, adjacent to public transportation (or regular private in-house transportation to community facilities) and no more than a few minutes from a hospital.

Designed to appeal to a special if constantly growing market, "senior" complexes have suffered like all other apartment buildings from inflation, higher construction, financing and operating costs. The affluent elderly are a constantly growing minority. The poor elderly have had and appear to be having growing federal construction subsidy and rent supplement assistance. The middle class elderly retired have been finding it difficult to afford such shelter in the inflation ridden seventies. Federal programs encouraging rehabilitation of existing buildings by offering tax advantages are helping builders supply some of this growing market. However, builders and appraisers must be constantly aware of the difficulties and potential project failures inherent in this market.

As with any other type of apartment valuation, you also have to be ever alert to guard your client's interest by not only reporting your observations of the property fully but also by interpreting the data judiciously. For instance, an operating statement which shows comparatively low insurance cost, a physical inspection which shows poor upkeep, obviously causes a higher net income on the operating statement. If not alert, a higher economic appraisal results. It is not uncommon for a property to be milked, then sold.

Also, as with singles or any other apartment appraisal, "senior" complexes are built and bought not only for net return on investment but often also for the buyer's personal need for depreciation which he can use to offset income from other sources. For this income tax reason, there is a constant viable market in these types of properties. You have to be aware also of "leverage" situations where properties financed with large loan-to-value ratio mortgages may reduce income receipts because of higher mortgage principal and interest payments. However, this leverage situation may be exactly what the buyer is looking for, in terms of higher mortgage tax write-off on the interest payments.

Also, as with other types of apartment complexes, appraisal is normally based on good feasibility analysis, intensive informed study of the operation and, in most cases, on the Income approach. However, if confirmed adequate comparable sales are available for a Market approach to value, comparison items should include: location, type of construction, date of sale, terms and price, zoning, age, condition, quality, design, appearance, amenities, unit of comparison (either by dwelling unit, by room or per square foot of building area).

A MODEL APARTMENT HOUSE APPRAISAL REPORT

The following is an appraisal of a garden apartment house in a small city of 25,000 in the outer rim suburbs of a major Northeast city. Various portions of the report have been condensed and all appendices have been omitted including detailed rent roll, rent roll of comparables, comparable land sales chart, location map, detailed operating expense statement, key map, photographs, statement of contingent conditions, appraiser's qualifications sheet and transmittal letter.

OUTLINE AND PURPOSE OF APPRAISAL—The purpose of this appraisal is to determine current fair market value.

DATA ON CITY AND NEIGHBORHOOD—The city is Anytown, USA, population 25,000 about 50 miles northwest of Northeast City, population 3 million. Historically an agricultural seat and railroad junction, Anytown's economy became depressed during the past two decades as farmers moved from this area. The economy has been improving, mainly because the community college has had a major construction and student expansion. Although there are commuters from Northeast City who purchase homes in this area, practically all apartment tenants work or are students in this city of Anytown or in neighboring towns. Two major arterials, State Route 29 and Interstate Route 94 intersect here. Many manufacturing and warehouse plants are located along these major highways. Employment is stable in the area and is primarily "blue collar" factory and service with some higher demand from faculty at the college. One regional shopping area and six strip commercial centers service the city on its outskirts. There is a downtown business district which suffers from lack of ample modern parking facilities. The neighborhood is mainly one- to four-family homes with three other garden type apartment buildings located nearby. There is only one ten-story high-rise apartment building in the city. Because of high construction and financing costs, there are no apartments being built in the city and none before the planning boards for final approval. Consequently, there are practically no vacancies in the existing garden apartment buildings including the subject building being appraised. Prospects for continued rentals are good.

THE LAND—64,000 sq. ft. with 200 feet of frontage on High Street and 320 feet frontage on Low Street, corner plot. Grades, typical of this hilly area, roll up from the roads to the rear and sidelines. Land is terraced with adequate level areas for outdoor circulation and recreation. There is mature ground cover to control erosion on the slopes. There are adequate shade trees, lawn areas and asphaltic concrete paved parking areas for 90 cars.

UTILITIES—Electricity, gas, public water and sewer.

LEGAL—Tax Map, Anytown, Section 55, Block 55, Lot 26; Liber 1438, pages 363-367, Anytown City Clerk Deeds office.

COMMUNITY FACILITIES—Maximum six blocks from shopping, parks, schools and the college.

ZONING—M-R (Multiple-Residential)—permits maximum of 20 dwelling units per 20,000 sq.ft. with a maximum of 25% two-bedroom units. Present improvements conform.

APPRAISED—Fee simple.

HIGHEST AND BEST USE—Multiple-residential—present use.

ASSESSMENT AND TAXES—Anytown, Assessment $600,000 including $140,000 ascribed to land. Taxes—$21,000.

IMPROVEMENTS—The land is improved with a two-story frame, brick veneer, garden type apartment building, 20,700 sq.ft. per floor, total 41,400 sq.ft., 20 years, full basement, poured concrete foundations, $4/_{12}$ pitch composition shingle roof, aluminum double hung windows, masonry chimney, gas warm air heat, aluminum gutters and leaders, drywall interior walls, carpet on plywood floors, 59 apartments, 200 rooms, 82 bedrooms, 59 baths, copper plumbing, ample electric for all electric kitchens including range, refrigerator, dishwasher and garbage disposal. There is a laundry room and storage closet area for each apartment in basement. Improvements are in good, well-maintained condition.

VALUATION

Land Value—$192,000 @ $3 per sq.ft. from a comparable study of four similar sales detailed in appended Land Comparable Sales Analysis Chart.

Cost and Market Approaches. Cost approach is not pertinent because of age of improvements; Market approach is not feasible because of no recent sale of improved similar properties.

Income Approach

Fair stabilized rent roll for the subject property, in my opinion, is as follows (Based on analysis of appended comparable rentals chart.):

12—Efficiency units @ $215	$2,580
35—one-bedroom units @ 330	8,400
12—two-bedroom units @ 330	3,960
Monthly total	$14,940
say	$15,000

The actual rent roll, including 15 one-year leases being converted to month-to-month rentals as the leases expire, amounts to $15,200 monthly.

Total Estimated Gross Rental Yearly $180,000

Capitalization—(Using Income approach, Straight Line Depreciation, Building Residual technique and Band of Investment method to build up capitalization rate.):

First mortgage—75% @ 8.5%	=	6.4
Equity—25% @ 10.5%	=	2.6
Total	=	9.0
Remaining economic life—40 yrs.		
Recapture of capitalization rate	=	2.5
Total capitalization rate	=	11.5

Gross Annual Income $180,000

Vacancy (projected 2.5%) (actual 1%) ....__4,500__

Projected gross 175,500

Expenses

Taxes	$21,000
Fuel (oil)	12,000
Electric	2,000
Water	1,500
Insurance	5,500
Superintendent, mainten. supplies	12,000
Management	3,000
Reserve for replacement (10%)	5,500
Total	$ 62,500
Net income from land and buildings	113,000
Less interest imputed to land	
($192,000 × 9%)	17,300
Balance interest imputed to improvements	95,700
Capitalized ($95,700 divided by 11.5)	832,000
Add land	192,000
Total	1,024,000

Market Value from Income Approach $1,024,000

A MODEL SENIOR CITIZEN APARTMENT COMPLEX
APPRAISAL REPORT

The following is an appraisal of a *proposed* 320-unit senior citizen garden apartment type complex on 40 acres in a small town 30 miles south of a Northeast city of 2 million. Various portions have been condensed and all appendices have been omitted such as detailed rent roll, rent roll of comparables, comparable land sales chart, location map, topographic map, key map, county data book statistics, photographs, statement of contingent conditions, appraiser's qualifications sheet and transmittal letter. A major section of this report deals with feasibility since this is a proposed project.

OUTLINE AND PURPOSE OF APPRAISAL—The purpose of this appraisal report is to determine the feasibility of building and the value, when built, of this proposed senior citizen apartment complex.

DATA ON TOWN AND NEIGHBORHOOD—The town is Manytown, 30 miles north of Midwest City. The town has a population of 15,000, in a county of 210,000. It is mainly a bedroom area for its county environs and for commuters from Midwest City. The economy stabilized in the early seventies after a period of intense growth in the sixties spurred by commuter migration from Midwest City. This commuter rush has slowed considerably. There is an unincorporated town government, a 250-bed hospital, recently modernized, a still vital downtown business area and two modern shopping centers. There are several large military schools in the vicinity. Interstate Route 80 is nearby for arterial transportation. There are adequate, well-maintained, generally two-lane, roads throughout the township. There is public transportation to Midwest City by bus. The neighborhood is mainly scattered residential with strip commercial improvements on State Route 30 which runs past the proposed project. Because of high construction costs, high financing costs and reduced demand there is limited building now. This building is confined to one-family homes with no apartments being built nor planned for the immediate future. In the sixties, thousands of apartments were built in this area but the dearth of building since 1974 has reduced the vacancy rate to 4% currently. There are three apartment projects with 200 units within 2 miles which have average rentals of $225 and are designed and advertised for adult tenancy.

THE LAND—40.5 acres of wooded hillside which falls through three fairly level terraces to an escarpment along adjoining Rushing Creek. Views are pleasant. Access to the site is by three 50-foot wide, 200-foot long strips to three paved town roads which feed onto State Road 30, an arterial road. The acreage is abutted by the rear yards of 124 one-family homes on the west and north, by undeveloped similar land on the south and by Rushing Creek on the east. Testhole data reveals good bearing soils, no rock, some boulders which would not interfere with development.

UTILITIES—Electricity, gas, public water and sewers.

LEGAL—Tax Map, Manytown, Section 2, Block 14, Lot 3; Liber 1321, page 202, your County Clerk Deed office.

COMMUNITY FACILITIES—No convenient shopping within walking distance. Major shopping centers and downtown business district within 2½ miles, hospital 2 miles.

ZONING—R-3, Residential one-family—permits Senior Citizen housing as special exception use, 20 units per acre.

APPRAISED—Fee simple.

HIGHEST AND BEST USE—Residential, one-family.

ASSESSMENT AND TAXES—Vacant land, assessed at $40,000. Taxes $4,600 including $3,000 for public utilities special assessment funding.

PROPOSED IMPROVEMENTS—Preliminary plan by John Smith, P.E., proposes 20 garden apartment buildings, two-story frame, wood siding, 16 apartment units each building, 10,000 sq.ft. in each building, for moderate income by design and layout, slab construction, p.c. foundation walls, $4/12$ pitch comp. shingle roof, alum. d.h. windows, alum. gutters and leaders, drywall interior walls, carpet on plywood floors, copper plumbing, all electric kitchen including range and refrigerator. There are 320 proposed apartments. The typical apartment (280) is one bedroom, living room, kitchenette, bath. There are also 20 efficiency apartments and 20 two-bedroom apartments. One of the buildings, centrally located on the plot plan, has a full basement which opens to grade and is proposed for recreation hall use and for several small convenience shops. Roads shown on plan are proposed as private, cul-de-sac type layout with a loop perimeter collector road. Streets and parking are to be paved and drained to the adjoining creek. There is parking proposed for 400 cars.

VALUATION—Cost approach has been used since proposed improvements are involved. Market approach used for land valuation. Income approach not pertinent. Costs are from a national cost handbook, adjusted for local cost variations.

20 Bldgs @ 10,000 sq.ft. (incl. all equip.) × $28.50..........	$5,700,000
Grading, roads, drainage, utilities	400,000
Landscaping, walks, parking.....................................	75,000
Total Improvements	6,175,000
Land Value @ $1,100 per dwg unit	350,000
Total (say)...	$6,500,000

FEASIBILITY ANALYSIS—This study is to determine whether the proposed 320-unit senior citizen complex is feasible to build and rent. The land appears conducive to improvement from topography, testhole data and utilities availability. The question is whether 320 units would find moderate income rentals at current construction and financing costs. County planning survey statistics (see Appendix) indicate that there is a need in the county for 500 "senior" units annually during the next ten years, at low to moderate rent levels. Considering the comparatively large geographical area of the county compared to its population, the survey also indicates that this subject eastern area could absorb 75 units per year during this period. Directly across the river (but 30 miles away by bridge) is a 300-unit adult complex which has drawn about 25% of its residents as retirees from Midwest City. Approximately 100 units per year could be rented if otherwise feasible. The location of the property is acceptable for this type of improvement. The design and layout of the buildings appear commensurate with low to moderate income rentals. Special senior citizen features are included. The land is presently held by the developers of the proposed project under option @ $1,100 per unit, which appears to be justified as current market value based on study of comparable land sales in the county. However, a very serious bar to current senior citizen development at this site is current construction costs and the financing expense to fund these costs at current rates and then translating into feasible rent scales for this market.

Assuming a three-year buildout @ approximately 100 units per year and further assuming additional 15% cost increases over this three-year period, the total project cost can be estimated at $7.5 million. The complex is proposed for moderate income senior citizen rentals. In no way with conventional permanent financing at approximate 12% constant principal and interest payments can this high cost of construction be funded by moderate average rentals of approximately $250. For example, constant principal and interest payments of 12% for 90% permanent first and second mortgage financing would amount to more than $800,000 annually without even ascribing cost of equity capital. Compare this to the projected maximum of $960,000 gross annual receipts @ $250 average monthly rental. A full Income approach study is neither indicated nor pertinent within these obvious gross income-expense parameters.

CONCLUSIONS AND RECOMMENDATIONS

1. There is a moderate rental market which would absorb the proposed senior citizen rental complex in about three years.

2. The proposed "mix" of efficiency, one-bedroom and two-bedroom units is proper for the local and larger senior citizen market.

3. The maximum projected average rental is $250.

4. Projected construction cost, building and land improvements and raw land cost would be, at current level, $6.5 million. On a three-year build-out projection, approximately $7.5 million. This value is based on Cost approach.

5. This project is not feasible for development at "market rate" with either conventional or FHA-insured permanent financing because of the aforementioned construction costs and projected rental market.

6. The project should be considered only if the project developers can receive designation as sponsors of senior citizen housing under federal subsidized "Section 8" low-rent housing legislation together with low-rent supplements for tenants.

_____   _____
         Date   Signature

Chapter 10

Techniques and procedures for appraising commercial properties

This chapter explains commercial property appraising in terms of step-by-step procedures. It details the techniques which are used to appraise commercial properties, particularly in suburban areas.

Since accumulation of valid data is the first critically important step in any assignment, this chapter begins with directions on where to get such source data for commercial appraisals. The overriding importance to commercial property values of our suburban way of life is stressed here. The direct relationship good car access, car count and parking have on commercial values is also highlighted. I have also stressed the effect dynamic population movement and increased leisure time has had on recreational commercial values. Finally, this chapter details the Income approach as the specific technique for most suburban commercial appraisals.

WHERE TO SECURE SOURCE DATA FOR COMMERCIAL APPRAISALS

Every appraisal assignment, like every property, is unique. To solve each such singular appraisal problem and deliver clear, informative, factually correct appraisal reports, you proceed systematically to "touch every base." The first most important base in appraisal problem solving is systematic data accumulation. This is particularly important on commercial appraisals, where the economics of the times, the region, the locale are fundamental to successful operation, return on investment and, therefore, values.

There are many sources which you can systematically contact for data accumulation in a step-by-step procedure. These sources generally fall into the following broad groupings:

Step 1—U.S. Government—The census is the main source for statistics on commercial activity as well as population demographics. The Department of Commerce publications on business information and economic trends can be secured from the Superintendent of Documents. The Small Business Administration has much information on specific businesses. The U.S. Army Corps. of Engineers, Outdoor Recreation Department can be written to for data on recreation areas. Institutions like the Smithsonian Institute and the National Technical Information Center in Washington will do computer searches on specific topics. There are generally little or no fees for federal agencies; nominal fees for institutions.

Step 2—States—Various states have differing agency titles like Department of Economic Development or Department of Business Research. By whatever name, you can secure from your State Agency background data, maps and other data which would be invaluable to your appraisal report. State Departments of Labor give wage rates, employment statistics and labor trends. State Industrial Commissions and State Planning Departments are also excellent sources.

Step 3—Trade Associations—There are appraisal libraries at the American Institute of Real Estate Appraisers, the Society of Real Estate Appraisers and the American Society of Appraisers. The NARB in Chicago has a very extensive real estate library. There are also often trade association offices and publications covering many industries.

Step 4—County and Municipal Offices—These offices have available studies such as economics, population, land use, recreation, zoning, highway community facilities. Assessors' offices give assessment tax and equalization (true value to assessment) rates. Comparable market data sales can often also be secured from assessors. Engineer or building inspector offices, town clerks, zoning boards can give trends, maps and other important local data.

Step 5—Field Sources—Utility companies, banks, chambers of commerce have departments which maintain important data and publications on business trends. Real estate brokers, other appraisers, local newspapers, local libraries, competing businessmen in the industry being studied are other important sources for data accumulation on commercial appraisals.

HOW TO EVALUATE THE IMPACT ON COMMERCIAL VALUES
OF OUR SUBURBAN WAY OF LIFE

It is now house to car-to school-to car-to shopping center-to car-to work in suburban industrial office "parks" in most of suburban America. This life style has developed since WWII. It has not only affected the location and nature of our shelter types, but it has also affected the way we build, locate and value the commercial properties which service this way of life.

The automobile is the people mover in our suburban culture. The drive-in movie, fast food store, bank, photo shop are but a few examples of commercial enterprises which have proliferated in the modern suburb to accommodate this nation on wheels. The old "mom and pop," rural small motel for travelers has just about been made extinct by the 100-unit-plus modern motel, located near where the traffic flows off our Federal Interstate Highways onto other major arterials. The suburban shopping center needs three to four times the square foot area for parking that it has in its building for selling. Even resort areas with ski-slopes, marinas or other outdoor recreational commercial complexes which cater to "terminal" rather than "transient" overnight patrons are successful if modern road patterns can quickly and efficiently bring them their patrons. Modern America is car-oriented. The business which caters properly to this man-auto relationship is generally the successful business. The city and small town walk-in customer has become the suburban driver-shopper. Therefore, the first field step in appraising a commercial property in the suburbs is to analyze the location in relation to its car access, count and parking, as detailed in the following section.

HOW TO MEASURE GOOD CAR ACCESS, PARKING AND
TRAFFIC COUNT

Your source for accurate *car count* in front of or near the suburban commercial property being appraised is the State Highway Superintendent or State Public Works or Roads Department, Auto Traffic Count Section. Verification procedure should be systematic because current valid car count flow data is vital to value. The following field research steps should be taken:

Step 1—Contact the appropriate Auto Traffic Count Section. Their data is normally maintained in official auto traffic count ledger books, with car count locations by road name, number of cars, intersections and the dates counts are taken. The count is for average daily traffic.

Step 2—Assume there is an 18,000 average daily traffic count at the intersection of First Street and Route 34, Suburbia, New York. Relate this ADTC count of 18,000 cars to the property being appraised, located on First Street 450 feet south of the intersection of Route 34 and First Street.

Step 3—If car counts have not been taken, or not taken recently on First Street or Route 34, the proportionate amount of traffic on First Street may have to be approximated by counting cars on First Street. Most often though, in populous, busy areas where road building and maintenance operations depend on current adequate car count data, there will be available count data on either First Street or Route 34, adequate enough to proportion the 18,000 intersection ADTC.

Step 4—The next step is to relate this data to the site. For example, is a motel being appraised which gets its business mainly from overnight guests? Do most of the 18,000 cars whiz by in the middle of the day or does a good proportion pass in late afternoon and evening? Travelers don't check into motels early in the day (except in resort areas). If the state road agency does not have hourly car counts available, then you may have to go out again, click-counter in hand, to approximate the peak traffic flow.

Car access to the property is equally important to suburban commercial success and value.

- Is there adequate sight distance for slowing down and turning into the property?
- Does a curve, overgrown trees on another's property or difference in road elevation obscure the property sign until it is too late to brake safely?
- Are there acceleration and deceleration lanes or shoulders?
- Does the road in front of the property have a middle island which cannot be crossed?
- Does traffic on the opposite side therefore have to go half a mile or more before it can U-turn?
- Drive past the property on both sides of the street, noting carefully all these sight distance, turn and deceleration criteria.

While all these factors are critically important for your appraisal report and valuation, parking is of paramount importance in our car-oriented economy. Professional office building tenants require 4 square feet of parking for every square foot of floor space they rent. The neighborhood food center specifies maximum 4% parking gradients so that shopping carts left by shoppers don't roll into other cars and off the lot. The shopping mall "anchor" store won't sign up until it is assured of a 1 to 3.5 parking ratio. These are but a few examples of how important parking is to commerce in the suburbs. Review all parking plans on proposed construction appraisals carefully for adequate parking criteria. Tape measure parking facilities on existing commercial appraisals if original plans are not available to you.

HOW TO EVALUATE THE IMPACT OF DEMOGRAPHICS ON RECREATIONAL COMMERCIAL VALUES

The WWII baby boom generation which reached 30 in the seventies is bulging demographic population curves and affecting recreational life styles and commercial values. Recent surveys indicate $75 billion a year is spent in the U.S. on various recreational and leisure pursuits. U.S. government figures on spending report sports equipment, boats, etc. at a startling $9.4 billion. Americans are seeking more physically active recreation, like bicycling, tennis and jogging.

This trend is increasing not only in the West where climate encourages outdoor leisure pursuits but also in such sections as Washington, D.C. to Boston and the Pittsburgh to Chicago regions. There is increasing explosive demand for recreational sites and activities, many times water-oriented, within three to four hours from these megalopolises.

Increased leisure, population mobility, age demographics and income have made recreation the fastest growing and one of the largest American industries. Commercial properties such as ski-slopes, tennis centers and marinas are not the only manifestations of this trend. For example, ski-wear type clothes have become popular not just on the ski slopes. Ski-wear shops have proliferated to serve this trend.

The section in Chapter 11 which shows how to appraise specific recreational commercial properties must be related to the population demographics outlined here. However, probably more than in most other major industries, appraising commercial recreational properties means dealing with "trendy," sometimes even faddish, businesses. These recreation and leisure trends take people out of movie houses and onto tennis courts, away from bowling alleys and onto ski slopes, out of skating rinks and into racket clubs. Constant analysis is needed to keep abreast of these trends.

HOW TO USE THE INCOME APPROACH ON COMMERCIAL PROPERTY APPRAISALS

As in residential appraising, some clients, like the General Services Administration, still require, even for commercial appraisals, three approaches to value; namely, the Cost-Less-Depreciation, Income and Comparative or Market approaches. It is therefore important to know and use the three approaches for these clients. A current SBA Reviewers Appraisal Analysis form used by SBA staff appraisers to review narrative appraisal rights follows (this form illustrates this "tripod" approach described in previous chapters):

REVIEWER'S APPRAISAL ANALYSIS	PURPOSE OF APPRAISAL
(For use by Staff Appraiser in Reviewing Appraisal Reports)	☐ IN-LEASE ☐ ACQUISITION ☐ TRANSFER ☐ OUT-LEASE ☐ DISPOSAL

APPRAISER	FEE $	TYPE OF PROPERTY

CONTRACT NO.	CONTRACT DATE	TIME ALLOWED	NAME AND ADDRESS OF PROPERTY

EFFECTIVE DATE OF REPORT	DATE REVIEWED

REVIEWER	APPRAISED VALUE $	CASE NO.

INSTRUCTIONS

Items 1 through 45 are provided as an aid in answering Major Questions in Part VII.
Explain all negative answers on reverse (Part VIII). Comment fully on inadequacies and recommendations.
E - Excellent - Meets or exceeds specifications.
A - Adequate   - Meets minimum needs. Clarification may be desirable.
I - Inadequate - Does not meet needs. Revision or clarification necessary.

	ITEM	E	A	I		ITEM	E	A	I
I. FORM AND PRESENTATION	1. CONFORMANCE TO GSA SPECIFICATIONS (*As to format, inclusion and sequence of all significant items*)				**III. ANALYSIS AND TECHNIQUE (Con.)**	**E. MARKET APPROACH**			
	2. AREA, CITY, NEIGHBORHOOD DATA					30. LIST OF SALES AND OFFERINGS			
	3. LEGAL DESCRIPTION INCLUDED? ☐ YES ☐ NO					31. SAME LIST ADJUSTED TO CURRENT MARKET			
	4. PROPERTY DESCRIPTION, CONDITION, AND ADAPT-ABLE USE					32. SPECIAL CONDITIONS TO EACH SALE			
	5. INSURANCE AND TAX LOAD: PLANS, PHOTOS AND MAPS					33. RELATION OF SALE OR OFFERING TO SUBJECT PROPERTY - SIMILARITIES AND DIFFERENCES WEIGHTED			
	6. CERTIFICATION - STANDARD CLAUSES, SIGNATURE AND DATE					34. VALUE INDICATED AND JUSTIFICATION			
II. DELINE-ATION OF ASSIGN.	7. PURPOSE, INCLUDING DEFINITION OF VALUE				**IV. MACHINERY AND EQUIPMENT**	35. DESCRIPTION AND CONDITION			
	8. HIGHEST AND BEST USE - FOR LAND - FOR TOTAL PROPERTY					36. ANALYSIS OF UTILITY			
						37. VALUE FOR IN-PLACE USE (*If applicable*)			
	9. STATEMENT OF LIMITING CONDITIONS					38. VALUE FOR OFF-SITE USE " "			
III. ANALYSIS AND TECHNIQUE	**A. LAND VALUE BY COMPARISON**					39. FAIR RENTAL ESTIMATE " "			
	10. ADEQUATE LISTINGS				**V. FAIR RENTAL**	40. LOGICAL RELATIONSHIP TO COMPARABLES			
	11. DATE AND CONDITIONS OF EACH SALE					41. BASED ON INTEREST PLUS CAPITAL RECAPTURE (*If applicable*)			
	12. SAME LIST ADJUSTED TO CURRENT MARKET					42. DOES ESTIMATE REFLECT CONTEMPLATED LEASE PROVISIONS? ☐ YES ☐ NO			
	13. SIMILARITIES AND DIFFERENCES WITH SUBJECT PROPERTY				**VI. CORRE-LATION AND VALUE**	43. CORRELATION OF ESTIMATES			
	14. LOGICAL CONCLUSION					44. THE APPROACH THAT IS CONTROLLING: _____			
	15. MAP SHOWING COMPARABLES					45. VALUE CONCLUSION			
	B. LAND RESIDUAL TECHNIQUE (*If used*)							YES	NO
	16. LOGICAL CONCLUSION					46. IS THE APPRAISAL PROBLEM CLEARLY STATED?			
	C. COST APPROACH					47. IS THE PROPERTY ACCURATELY DELINEATED AND DESCRIBED?			
	17. COST ESTIMATES				**VII. OVERALL EFFECTIVENESS**	48. IS THE BEST AND MOST PROFITABLE USE OF THE PROPERTY STATED, AND USED FOR BASIS OF VALUE?			
	18. DEPRECIATION - PHYSICAL					49. IS SUPPORTING DATA ACCURATE?			
	19. DEPRECIATION - FUNCTIONAL					50. IS CONCLUSION LOGICALLY RELATED TO SUPPORT-ING DATA?			
	20. DEPRECIATION - ECONOMIC					51. ARE ALL ESSENTIAL ITEMS INCLUDED?			
	21. LAND VALUE ADDED? ☐ YES ☐ NO					**IS THE REPORT RECOMMENDED:**			
	22. SUMMATION VALUE					52. AS A BASIS FOR CONTEMPLATED ACTION?			
	D. INCOME APPROACH					53. WITHOUT FURTHER CLARIFICATION?			
	23. GROSS ANNUAL RENT BY COMPARISON					54. FOR FEE PAYMENT?			
	24. VACANCY AND CREDIT LOSS					**AS EVIDENCED BY THIS REPORT:**			
	25. EXPENSE AND FIXED CHARGES INCLUDING RESERVES FOR REPLACEMENT					55. DOES THE APPRAISER'S PANEL RATING SEEM APPROPRIATE?			
	26. NET ANNUAL INCOME FROM RENT					56. WOULD YOU RECOMMEND THIS APPRAISER FOR OTHER SIMILAR ASSIGNMENTS?			
	27. METHOD OF CAPITALIZATION								
	28. CAPITALIZATION RATE - JUSTIFIED								
	29. VALUE								

GENERAL SERVICES ADMINISTRATION

GSA   1305

Figure 10.1

GSA APPRAISAL ANALYSIS FORM

The Comparative or Market Data approach is always the best approach to value commercial vacant sites and determine land values on improved commercial properties. If enough similarly situated and zoned recent land sales, adequate for comparative adjustment analysis, cannot be found, then residual land valuation techniques must be employed. (This will be fully described and illustrated in Chapter 11.) The Market approach is occasionally used on improved special commercial properties, such as gasoline service stations, where location and land value are paramount and improvements are fairly standard.

The Cost approach, of course, is used to secure replacement value for insurance purposes on commercial appraisals. Yet, even on comparatively new commercial buildings where actual cost can be determined without much subjective depreciation "guess-timating," the Cost approach is usually not pertinent. A commercial building's value is based on the rents or returns on investment it generates, not on what it cost to build.

In sum, it is important to mainly rely on the Income approach for accurate value conclusions on most improved commercial property appraisals. This Income approach is therefore stressed in this section and in the companion Chapter 11 which demonstrates specific commercial property appraisals.

The *Income approach* is an appraisal technique which uses the expected net income flowing from a property to determine how much investment is needed to produce this net income. This capital amount of investment is then certified as the present value of the property since investors normally purchase commercial properties for a return on their investment. The following procedure is done systematically to ensure correct application of this Income approach:

Step 1—*Net Income* anticipated from the commercial property being appraised is secured by first estimating gross income. It is important that a vacancy percentage (usually up to 10%) be deducted and that the total gross rents be checked in the market by comparison with similar properties similarly situated. From this total estimated gross rent (less vacancy allowance), operating expenses are then deducted. These generally include insurance, taxes, maintenance, fuel, utilities and reserve for replacement and management. The remaining income is the net income, before depreciation, flowing from the building and land. Accurate determination requires systematic data collection and good judgment.

Step 2—*Rate of Capitalization* is then determined. (See also Chapter 9 for explanation and examples of capitalization rates.) The best way is to analyze market data of recent similar properties sold, their selling prices and net income of the properties sold. Thus,

Net Income divided by Selling Price equals Capitalization Rate.

If a capitalization rate cannot be secured by this market data method because of inadequate sales and income data, there are alternatives. Since investment return is involved, a rate can be built up by taking a non-risk rate like government bonds and adding percentages for management, non-liquidity and risk. Thus, if 6% is a current bond rate, then 1% each for management, non-liquidity and risk would give a total 9% capitalization rate.

Similarly, a *Band of Investment* technique can be used to build up a capitalization rate by estimating the difference in risk to the various interests in the property. Thus, if there is a 60% First Mortgage @ 8% and a 40% Owners Equity estimated @ 9% then 60% @ 8% + 40% @ 9% plus a recapture rate of 2½% on a 40-year economic life would give a 4.8% + 3.6% + 2.5% = 10.9% Capitalization Rate.

Step 3—*Land Value* is then secured by analyzing recent similar land sales and using the *Building Residual technique* to determine the value of the building. This is done by multiplying the land value (found by Market approach) by a percentage of interest needed to service such land investment or value. The resulting amount of income imputable to land is then deducted from the net income of the property and the remainder is then processed to determine the building value. If land value cannot be found in the market because of inadequate sales data, then *Land Residual* technique can be utilized. In this technique, building and operating costs are estimated, net income from the building is determined, and this income is deducted from the total income produced by land and building. The resulting income imputable to land is then capitalized to find the land value. (There is also a *Property Residual* technique which is used when the known factors are net income, the useful economic life of the building, the capitalization rate and the land value. This technique is used to determine the total improved property value. Land value secured from the Market approach is always best, however. These various Residual techniques should only be used as a last resort in the absence of sales.)

Step 4—*Economic Life* remaining in the building is then estimated. The capitalization rate previously secured is applied for the period of the remaining economic life to find the value of the building.

Examples—The type of property and the type of rental generally determine the method of capitalization used. If there is a long-term, high-quality lease involved, say a 20-year lease with a triple A tenant, then annuity compound interest tables can be used. (A Selected Compound Interest table follows.) More often on smaller suburban commercial properties, rentals are on a short-term basis. Straight line depreciation and capitalization methods are used.

SELECTED COMPOUND INTEREST TABLE

Present Value of $1

(Invested at end of each year)

Years	6%	7%	8%	10%	12%
1	0.943	0.935	0.926	0.909	0.893
5	4.212	4.100	3.993	3.791	3.605
10	7.360	7.024	6.710	6.145	5.650
20	11.469	10.594	9.818	8.514	7.469
30	13.764	12.409	11.258	9.427	8.055
40	15.046	13.332	11.925	9.779	8.244
50	15.761	13.801	12.233	9.915	8.305

Example 1—(Using Compound Interest Annuity table for a property with triple A tenant, long lease)

Annual net income ....$ 50,000

Interest (8%) imputed to Land Value ($100,000)................. 8,000

Annual net income imputed to building ....$ 42,000

(Remaining economic life 30 years, interest rate 8%. Then from Compound Interest Annuity table, present value of $1 invested each year @ 8%, 30 years is $11.258)

Building value $42,000 × $11.258 ....$473,000

Add land value.. 100,000

TOTAL $573,000

Example 2—(Using straight line depreciation and Band of Investment Capitalization Rate for a property with short-term rents)

Annual net income ....$ 77,000

Less interest imputed to land ($100,000 × 8%) 8,000

Balance imputed to building ....$ 69,000

(Capitalization rate from Band of Investment technqiue, First Mortgage—60% @ 8.5% = 5.1%; Equity 40% = 3.6%; plus 40-year economic life = 2.5% = Total Capitalization Rate of 11.2%)

Building Value $74,000 ÷ 12% $616,000

Add Land Value 77,000

TOTAL $693,000

Example 3—(Using Built-Up Capitalization Rate method derived from interest paid on high-grade secure investments like government bonds and adding percentages to cover management, liquidity and risk factors involved in real property investment.) (This method is for property with short-term rents.)

Annual Net Income...$100,000

Less interest imputed to land ($100,000 × 8%).................. 8,000

Balance to building...$ 92,000

(Capitalization built up from current interest on government bonds—6%; management—2%; liquidity—1%; risk—2%; Total—11% Capitalization)

Building value $92,000 ÷ 11% $836,300

Add land value... 100,000

TOTAL $936,300

The techniques, procedures and examples in this commercial appraisal chapter are demonstrated further in Chapter 11 which follows on how to appraise specific commercial properties.

Chapter 11

How to appraise
five common types
of commercial property

This chapter follows up the general techniques and procedures given in Chapter 10 for appraising commercial properties. In this companion chapter, details are given on how to appraise specific types of commercial properties. Typical small suburban neighborhood commercial shopping complexes, convenience stores and fast food outlets are covered. You will also find procedures here on how to do feasibility appraisals on professional buildings. The booming leisure-recreation industry, including tennis centers and ski slopes, is also covered here. There is a section on how to appraise nursing homes, one of the fastest growing health care businesses in "graying" America. Appraisal of the modern motel in suburbs is an important part of this chapter. For illustration, office and field use, there is also a complete Model Motel Appraisal Report including exhibits.

HOW TO APPRAISE THE NEIGHBORHOOD COMMERCIAL COMPLEX, THE "CONVENIENCE" STORE AND THE FAST FOOD OUTLET

The shopping center concept with its larger "anchor" store(s), its smaller "satellite" retail stores, its adequate parking for efficient shopping on a planned site is a modern suburban development. Strip commercial zoning has also caused much building of free-standing, mainly one-story retail stores along many arterial suburban roads. Other comparatively recent commercial developments spawned in the suburbs are the "convenience" store and the fast food outlet store. These "convenience" and fast food stores can be found in shopping centers or standing free on commercial road strips in practically every suburban community. We will not be concerned here with the large regional centers featuring several department stores and hundreds of satellites. We will be dealing mainly with the appraisal of neighborhood centers generally anchored on a 20,000 to 40,000 square foot food store with usually about the same amount of space for satellite retail stores.

The following steps are taken to appraise neighborhood shopping centers:

Step 1—The property is considered as an unsubdivided whole, not as separate buildings.

Step 2—The trading area of the center is investigated. Where do the shoppers come from? A shopping center serves and is dependent on its trading area. Research into the trading area must include—(a) population growth or decline, (b) transportation road network and any proposed changes, (c) employment, (d) competition. State Economic Commissions are good sources for obtaining figures on spendable income of households. A neighborhood center needs about 2,500 households to support its usual chain food mart, banks and about 20 smaller retail service stores. (Regional stores, for instance, are designed to service a minimum of 50,000 families.) It is important to know that generally weak economic areas affect regional centers more than neighborhood shopping centers which specialize in food and necessity shopping.

Step 3—Shopping centers, depending on size, have their own drawing power for motorist shoppers because of the concentration of numerous stores in one place. However, even here, car count, car access, site visibility and adequate parking are most important and should be carefully investigated (see Chapter 10), especially for these smaller neighborhood centers.

Step 4—The site, on existing or proposed centers, is then carefully field checked and analyzed in terms of location, zoning, utilities, topography, competition, taxes and highest and best use.

Step 5—The existing or proposed improvements are then analyzed. Modern construction specifications generally involve open span interiors with 30 to 60 feet between columns, well-lighted and air-conditioned, with resilient floors. Obsolescent features in older buildings would be close column spacing, immovable partitions, poor delivery access, inadequate parking area.

Step 6—The Market Data approach (except for land and for analysis of comparable rentals) is not applicable. The Income approach is used to determine shopping center value.

Step 7—From the gathered source data, a market survey report is then completed, including exhibits, statistics and data dealing with location, competition, car count, access parking, trading area, household spendable income trend forecasts and earnings expectancy.

Step 8—The valuation portion of the report is then completed. On neighborhood shopping centers, the Income approach is used to capitalize income into value. On existing neighborhood centers, particularly those with several years of experience with rentals, the Income approach is particularly pertinent. These actual rental amounts received, based on lease percentages of sales, provide a firm foundation for the appraisal process of capitalizing these verified or actual, rather than forecast, returns. Also, on these small neighborhood centers, land value can often be determined by market data analysis of land sales of similarly situated commercial sites. (On larger regional sites, where the Market approach can usually not locate good sales data, residual techniques, including the Cost approach to find and deduct building value are used to determine land value.) What is most important in this valuation procedure is the determination of the capitalization rate. The market study, the trend projections, the durability of the income flow are all basic criteria for judging whether, for example, a high 12% capitalization rate should be used or a low 9%. (See Model Shopping Center Appraisal Report in later section in this chapter.)

Other products of our modern way of life, the free-standing "convenience" and "fast food" stores are now everywhere in the suburbs. Fast food chains like MacDonalds and Burger King have expanded from their birthplace in the suburbs into storefront locations in the cities and even internationally. "Convenience" chain stores like the "7-11" (Southland Corporation) totalled 30,000 stores recently, grossing $7.5 billion annually. A "7-11" type store needs a busy street (corner preferred) with plenty of traffic (minimum 15,000 ADTC). Land costs are generally about $40,000 to $100,000. The 2,500-square foot building costs about $30 a square foot. These franchise stores have established sales and value patterns. However, this modern American drive-in life style of fast eating and convenience shopping is catered to not just by these chain giants. It is also serviced by smaller group and individual retail stores.

Commercial real estate in the suburbs is dynamic. For example, many neighborhood gas stations were made obsolete by the Federal Interstate System. Later, these sites, and many times the buildings on them, were converted to other uses. In most cases, because of good local neighborhood location, these gas stations (pumps removed or left in for self-service) became "convenience'' fast shop stores or fast food stores (see Figure 11.1). In three New York counties, for example, one enterprising dairy bought up about 50 old neighborhood gas stations, converted them into free-standing convenience stores and even sold gas (self-service) on some of the sites. Pizza parlors, chicken take-out stores, individual and small chain hamburger stores also took these sites and established others throughout our suburbs. The suburban way of life has transformed our nation's eating and shopping habits. The appraisal of a ''convenience'' store or fast food outlet in this dynamic industry is done using the following procedure:

Step 1—The location of the property in its economic environment must be carefully studied. Determining highest and best use carefully is particularly important in commercial store appraisals. First, the region is studied. Housing starts, building permits for commercial construction, population trends, industry and utilities are carefully analyzed.

Step 2—The immediate environs are then field inspected and data gathered and analyzed including transportation, car count, road network, trading area, spendable income, competing and other commercial usages in the vicinity.

Step 3—The property is analyzed including review of the deed description, land dimensions, easements, zoning, taxes, topography, utilities, soil conditions, building description, condition, maintenance and management.

Step 4—Comparable market data and photographs must be accumulated on recent sales and rentals of similar properties similarly situated.

Step 5—Valuation of the property is then accomplished, usually by using the Income approach to capitalize net income derived from rentals. In this method, the net income is secured by deducting from investigated effective gross rentals, operating expenses, taxes, insurance, reserve for replacement, maintenance, management. (If the income is net, these deductions are not taken). This net income is then capitalized by straight-line depreciation (estimated remaining economic life divided into 100) plus capitalization rate, built up from Band of Investment technique or from adjusted ''safe'' rate. (See Chapter 10.) If a long-term secure lease is involved, compound interest tables (like Inwood premise tables) can be used. In all cases, careful valuation analysis is done by Market approach to study sales, rental data, land values in many cases and to provide a firm foundation for the Income approach.

HOW TO DO FEASIBILITY-APPRAISAL REPORTS ON PROPOSED AND EXISTING PROFESSIONAL BUILDINGS

Doctors, attorneys, accountants and other professionals rarely practice nowadays from their own homes or in small individual office buildings. Not only in the suburbs but even in urban areas, designed and managed professional office buildings now cater to professionals.

Many of these are special-purpose professional buildings like medical arts buildings. In these buildings, doctors of various specialties each rent or buy about 1,200 square feet (and up) of office space. This particularly important new building also answers modern medicine's need for clustering doctors of varying specialties to give typical "one-stop" referral service to patients. On a financing as well as medical need basis, this type of medical professional building has proliferated because doctors are considered prime triple-tenants by lending institutions, for building construction and permanent loans. Also, growth of group medical practice fostered in such professional buildings has been steady. In 1946, there were 404 groups with 3,500 doctors. By the mid-seventies, there were 8,500 groups with 67,000 doctors. Many of these medical professional buildings are owned by some of the doctors who tenant them. Ownership on a partnership or condominium basis is important to them because depreciation for income tax purposes can amount to about $2 a square foot for doctors in the 50% tax bracket. This expanding type of professional building has also spun off various formats. Because hospitals get their business from referrals by doctors, hospitals often will lease land to a group of doctors for an office building for little or nothing. This will also save the physician time in commuting from his office to the hospital and will keep the hospital filled with referrals.

This new type of professional building, the medical office building, has emerged from the changing nature of health care. The medical arts building requires more plumbing, interior partitions, sophisticated heating/cooling, stain-proof carpets and is more expensive to build than the usual office building. It usually rents for about $2 more per square foot than other office space. Units are usually 1,200 to 2,000 square feet. Roof spans are normally trussed for clear span and maximum flexibility on partition placement and future alterations. Parking in suburban locations, particularly, must be ample, preferably a 1-to-4 ratio, building to parking. The buildings are generally pleasantly landscaped and require good road network and access into the site.

Feasibility studies of these proliferating medical arts office buildings as well as other types of small professional buildings are accomplished as follows:

Step 1—Research the market to identify prospective tenants for proposed sites. This should include study of tenant requirements as well as typical sizes of offices in demand.

Step 2—Research the market to identify population, economic trends, existing and proposed competition.

Step 3—Forecast rental period needed to absorb the square feet proposed.

Step 4—Study the proposed site in terms of its location, accessibility,

Figure 11.1

CONVENIENCE STORE CONVERTED FROM NEIGHBORHOOD
GAS STATION

Figure 11.2
PROFESSIONAL OFFICE BUILDING

physical aspects, dimensions, subsurface, zoning, utilities and other neighboring influences.

Step 5—Project construction costs, overhead and profit.

Step 6—Project cash flow.

Step 7—Project operating costs, depreciation and tax aspects.

Step 8—Review whether the proposed design is appropriate for prospective tenants including facilities to be improved by tenants as well as special amenities for special type office buildings.

Step 9—Valuation of the proposed smaller type office building is generally based on the Income approach, capitalizing projected rents verified by market study. On newly constructed office buildings, the Cost approach can be used to confirm value derived from Income approach. On such new construction, subjective depreciation amounts generally do not have to be estimated. On existing buildings the matured rent roll is analyzed, compared to and verified by market data and then capitalized, using the Income approach as the best road to value.

HOW TO APPRAISE A TENNIS CENTER AND A SKI SLOPE COMPLEX

The booming leisure-recreation industry is setting new records. Recent surveys counted 11 million skiers and 30 million tennis players. In this trendy, some say faddish, recreation business, the bowlers of yesteryear become the tennis players of today and the former hockey enthusiasts are now found on ski slopes.

What this has done to the ice hockey rink business, for example, is to depress usage and values. In addition, surveys show, construction cost inflation has pushed skating rink start-up costs to over $1 million while average grosses are only $150,000. This makes new construction unfeasible. The same general problems affect new construction of bowling alleys.

Even though these trends affect the type of activity currently popular, the overall leisure-recreation industry graph line appears to be constantly up. An affluent middle class and a generation of post-WWII babies bulging demographic charts with their outdoor, sports-oriented life style appears to assure continued overall growth to this industry. The appraiser's job is to keep constantly informed on these dynamic trends for his projections, his values and his clients.

The game of tennis, for instance, is still booming but the construction of new tennis centers is slowing down. Lenders are becoming concerned that the supply of courts is not only beginning to meet the demand but also that inflation again has pushed construction and utility costs up dramatically. Electric bills are very high for indoor tennis centers (with those high ceilings). They must be heated in winter and cooled in summer. The commercial tennis club's key to success is low construction costs and few amenities. Those clubs which offer good playing courts and not too many other frills like pools, Jacuzzis and other amenities are the successful ones now. A typical eight-court operation must have 70% court occupancy to break even. Energy costs are most important. "Prime time" average costs of $11 to $12 per hour and annual fees of members are being raised to meet these inflating costs.

These upper limit costs appear to have halted tennis expansion. Squash, platform tennis and racquet ball, with their smaller playing court needs and reduced costs (some with bubbles for year round use), appear to be taking up the "slack" and becoming popular. This "trendy" business continues to change. The manifestations of increased leisure time, income and mobility may alter in form. However, the solid base for recreational real estate, albeit its changing forms, remains. Discretionary income, or disposable income for other than necessities, has tripled during the sixties and seventies to make this recreation industry the fourth largest and fastest growing in our nation today.

A tennis center is appraised as follows:

Step 1—Whether proposed or existing, the region, its economy, its population, its growth trends, are first studied.

Step 2—Where are the tennis players? Where will they come from? How far will they travel? Is the proposed or existing location properly located for this projected or actual clientele. These are the main questions which must be answered by the appraisal tennis location analysis.

Step 3—What is the competition? In an all-year tennis climate, locate every public and commercial tennis court in a reasonable driving time distance, depending upon type of roads. In the Northeast and West, where winter shuts down outdoor play, where are the competing tennis buildings, tennis bubbles? Is the area tennis oriented? There may be 30 million tennis enthusiasts but this area may be high on racquet ball, or golf or strictly recreation water-oriented. Usually, competitive public and commercial tennis facilities and their occupancy percentages will generally answer this question.

Step 4—Study the proposed site then and determine whether a tennis center is its highest and best use based on the market study, its location, its transportation aspects, its access by auto, its parking, its zoning and neighboring usages.

Step 5—The property's physical aspects are then studied. Are its dimensions proper for the comparatively large building needed? Is there room for adequate parking and landscaping? Are there any easements which may affect function? Is the topography conducive or will grades cause excessively costly cut or fill? Are subsoil conditions conducive for bearing, maintenance of level playing surfaces and drainage? Are utilities, including water and sewer, adequate? If an existing building, is its structure and condition modern, functional and well-maintained? (Talk to the player-customers also.)

Step 6—Comparable market data is then accumulated on recent sales (if any) of land for tennis centers or of tennis centers as well as comparable data on court rental fees in competing centers.

Step 7—The property is then valued. Since there are investment commercial properties, it may be of interest to know that tennis playing surfaces cost from $8,000 to $20,000 per court depending upon the type of surface. The tennis building will cost $10 up per square foot, without equipment involved in amenities, like pools, lockers, gymnasiums. Interesting, but not pertinent to market value. Value of tennis centers is secured from the Income approach. Since this is a "trendy" business, subject to the vagaries of players, energy costs and inflation, the capitalization rates must, of necessity, be comparatively high. The buyer-builder investor expects a high return on his capital investment because of the nature of the business. Since there is usually no long-term secure lease, straight line depreciation plus a capitalization rate method of capitalization (see Chapter 10) can be used to capitalize the net income market value.

Ski slope complexes cater to a growing horde of skiers. Yet here too these recreation properties are subject to trends. The recent climate changes when there was comparatively little snow west of the Continental Divide gave the western ski slopes their worst season since the thirties. Yet, even then, almost $2½ billion was grossed, doubling records set seven years previously. Ski lift tickets went from $5 to $15 during the same period.

As with tennis centers, a ski area is a unique and special-purpose property. It has lifts, trails and supporting facilities and buildings, generally including food and beverage service, ski shops, equipment rental and ski schools.

Appraisal of a ski-slope complex includes the following (the non-skier appraiser may have to sub-contract field inspection to an expert):

Step 1—Physical Aspects—Analyze the ski terrain with its grades, trees, altitude, skiability and ability to maintain the area.

Step 2—Weather and Climate—Study the snow quality records, frequency, quality, dependability, air temperatures, winds, sunshine, length of season.

Step 3—The Dimensions of the Slope—Analyze the width, length and vertical elevation of trails for various levels of skiers.

Step 4—Layout—Study the capacity of the slope to maintain the demand flow and the layout and condition of the trails.

Step 5—Lifts—Analyze the type and condition of the ski lifts.

Step 6—Supporting Amenities—Analyze the type, nature and condition of building-food-beverage-services-shops-bar-ski school-parking.

Step 7—Skier Density—Is skier traffic flow proper? Generally 10 to 20 skiers per acre depending on the trails are acceptable to the market. Also, research indicates that more than 4,000 skiers at a ski slope cannot generally be handled. Much less makes the operation uneconomical. Another important usage criterion is the season length. Generally, 100 days of skiing is needed to make a slope profitable.

Step 8—The Market—Study the market in terms of the region forecast of potential skier-visits. Analyze the probable type of skier to determine whether the existing or proposed type and quality of facilities will meet the projected skier demand.

Step 9—Feasibility Checklist

- Labor availability and cost
- taxes
- environmental constraints
- land cost (many U.S. ski areas are land leased from U.S. government)
- access road
- construction and maintenance costs
- utility availability and cost
- ticket cost (will the type of population in the area pay the necessary going rate now?)
- insurance premium cost (recent court decisions have held ski slopes responsible for slope accidents with large awards resulting in much higher premiums)
- competition (including both existing and proposed or expanded ski areas).

Step 10—Valuation—Ski areas are speculative businesses. There aren't many sales of ski areas, so we cannot generally secure a capitalization rate by comparing sales prices to net income. The practical approach to ski slope appraising is to capitalize the net income using a Band of Investment technique. (See Chapter 10.) For all the reasons previously cited, we are dealing with non-secure, fluctuating, speculative cash flow. The rate of return investors would expect under such circumstances would probably be about 15%. Of course long-established ski areas with overall good management and record of profit returns would rate better than proposed or new complexes. Unless the land value is separately needed for tax purposes, valuation of the ski slope complex is done by dividing the net income by the capitalization rate to arrive at current market value. (See Chapter 10.)

HOW TO DO FEASIBILITY-APPRAISAL REPORTS ON NURSING HOMES

During the next half-century, the number of people over 65 will double to 52 million, to one out of every six people. In the mid-seventies, there were 1¼ million over 65 in nursing homes.

When an older person needs help with dressing, shopping, meal preparation, personal chores or medical attention and when these needs cannot be filled by family or community services, nursing home care is indicated. Some homes specialize in personal or custodial care and are known as "intermediate care" homes or residential homes. Others offer 24-hour nursing and are known as "skilled nursing facilities." There are private or proprietary homes operated for profit, and non-profit homes operated by charitable, religious, sometimes public bodies. We are concerned here with the appraisal of homes operated for profit.

The care of the aged is a big business in "graying" America. It is financed mainly by U.S. government Medicare and Medicaid payments. Care standards are mainly set by the federal government and administered by the states. Construction standards for new and altered homes are established by the U.S. Department of Housing and Urban Development.

The federal government sets their standards for services as well as safety and sanitation. Each state must follow these standards when it inspects homes that receive Medicare and Medicaid money. States follow their own standards in inspecting and licensing all other nursing homes. All states require and issue licenses. In general, these involve setting standards and controls on licensing, location, safety, fire safety, cleanliness and facilities.

In the mid-seventies, widespread nursing home financial and care abuses were found. These abuses were mainly eliminated through industry reforms, increased government surveillance, law enforcement and closing of many homes which were structurally deficient.

Research for feasibility appraisal reports on nursing homes should include the following checklist:

BASIC NURSING HOME REQUIREMENTS

1. State Licensed?

2. Home Administrator *Licensed?*

3. *Certified* for Government Programs?

4. *Special Services* Provided?

PHYSICAL CRITERIA

1. *Location* convenient? Near hospital? Accessible for doctors, employees, visitors?
2. *Safety*—Well-lighted? Non-slip floors? Handrails in halls? Grab bars in baths?
3. *Fire Safety*—Meets code (Life Safety Code of NFPA-No. 101—for new as well as altered buildings)? Minimum two exists each floor? 44-inch doors? 8-foot corridors? Proper ramps? Emergency lights at exits? Two-hour ratings for stairwells, interior walls, ceilings, floor finish? Fire, smoke detection and alarm and sprinkler systems? Automatic dampers in ducts? (Existing homes may receive certain variances if approved by local authorities.)
4. *Bedrooms*—Open onto hall? Window? Maximum four beds per room? Nurses call bell at each bed? Chairs, closet, dresser drawers for each patient?
5. *Cleanliness*—Kitchens sanitary as well as bedrooms, baths and other areas?
6. *Lobby, Activity Room, Special-Purpose Rooms*—Pleasant, large enough and functional?
7. *Hallways*—Handgrips on walls? Can wheel chairs pass?
8. *Dining Room*—Attractive, clean? Food tasteful and served well.
9. *Toilet Facilities*—Near bedrooms? Grab bars? Adapted for wheelchair use? Nurses bell call? Non-slip surfaces?
10. *Grounds*—Pleasant? Ramps?
11. *Services*—Physicians available in emergencies? Hospitalization available nearby? Nurses aides on duty in intermediate homes? Rehabilitation specialists available? Dietician?

Valuation of a nursing home is mainly done by using the Income approach as the best approach to value. However, nursing homes are a highly specialized business, expanding greatly to meet a growing demand. This specialized business is funded mainly by the U.S. government which has set not only care and construction standards but also valuation standards.

Information on construction standards is in FHA Booklet 4514.1. Reference 4450.1 is for cost estimation/cost data for nursing homes. Valuation procedures and requirements are in HUD Handbook 4600.1 which gives procedures for the Section 232 program for nursing homes and/or intermediate care facilities.

A nursing home must follow these governmental standards to receive funding. Its appraisal must also follow these government appraisal standards. These standards still require the three-approach, correlated, Cost-Market-Income approach and this is how you proceed:

Step 1—*Analyze Location*—The analysis of the site, existing or proposed, should include consideration of prominence. Is the site known, appealing to the public, yet not in a too busy or noisy locale? Are there available services, staff? Is it near a hospital? Is it well-located for access by doctors, visitors? Is it in a growth pattern? Is it isolated, on a secondary road network or in an undesirable commercial or industrial environment?

Step 2—*Analyze Zoning and Neighboring Usages*—Is site properly zoned? Any inharmonious neighbors or land zoned for airports, heavy industrial, commercial, noisy traffic, truck terminals, railroad sidings?

Step 3—*Analyze the Property*—Site level or gently sloping? Contours all right for function and efficient maintenance?

Step 4—*Analyze Personal Services*—Are barbers, beauticians nearby for ambulatory patients? Is there adequate on-site parking for doctors, staff and visitors?

Step 5—*Analyze Economic Considerations*—The extent, quality and expected duration of earning capacity of the nursing home is then analyzed. Is the home eligible to receive patients under federal, state and local requirements so that it can have as large a market as possible? (Public rates being paid as well as local health insurance program rates must be determined. By government-rate set regulations, in nursing homes operated for profit, there can also be a return or profit recognized which compensates the owner of the nursing home business for promotional effort in operation of the facility and for the business risk involved.)

Step 6—*Analyze the Proposed or Existing Improvements*—Use previously cited checklists to collect data for review, description and analysis of the improvements for the appraisal report.

Step 7—*Collect Sales Data*—Be most circumspect in analysis of sales of nursing homes. Many homes have been "sold" from one corporation to another "dummy" corporation or to a related individual to kite values and government payment rates. The State Department of Health is usually a prime source of sales data since it collects such data in its licensing work.

Step 8—*Analyze Cost*—Use Cost handbooks to secure costs for application of the Cost approach.

Step 9—*Estimate Income*—Gross income is predicated on number of beds available. The rates charged are on a daily, weekly or monthly basis and depend on the kind and quality of accommodations and services rendered. Occupancy for a typical home will be about 85% according to government figures. For purposes of income estimates, 93% is an absolute maximum, per HUD handbook.

Step 10—*Estimate Value*—The HUD agency divides income into two parts. Approximately 75 to 85% of the net income is capitalized for the realty and non-realty. The residual of 15% to 25% income is attributed to the proprietary earnings (profit for business operation and risk). This breakdown is checked by market data analysis of homes which are leased to operators. If the appraisal is being done on a fee basis for the HUD agency, this breakdown of the income must be done. Otherwise, the usual commercial appraisal process of capitalizing the net income is done and checked by market and sales approaches. In nursing home appraisals, market comparison items are location, quality of construction, accommodations, services offered and a per bed, per annum dollar adjustment. Replacement cost (less depreciation) is secured from cost handbooks. The Income Approach should be relied on for final value in the correlation of the appraisal approaches. Again, great care must be used in analysis of operating statements of nursing homes to make certain that valid data is capitalized.

HOW TO APPRAISE A MOTEL

There are various types of modern motels. Airport motels reflect increased air traffic. In the cities, one checks into large motor-hotels, mainly over 250 rooms. In resort areas, equally large motor hotels cater to leisure-time vacationers. In the suburbs and along major roadside locations, the typical 100-unit-plus, modern motel caters mainly to the businessman and family travelers. We will be working here with suburban roadside motels.

The Interstate System, which has laid a highway network across our land, has changed the motel industry. The average 30-unit "Mom and Pop" roadside motel has been by-passed and is becoming extinct. The Howard Johnson, the Holiday Inn, the Ramada Inn franchise type and company-owned motel as well as many independent, modern 100-unit motels have taken over at many of these highway interchange ramp locations. As with our whole economy, gasoline availability is the spectre for motels. However, with the energy-saving 55 mph speed limit, people drive shorter distances which is good for motel occupancy rates and business. Severe winters curtail business. Recent national all-year vacancy rates in suburban motels were 40%. "One-day" rentals and the very nature of the business demands that a large reserve of rooms be available for those periods when needed. For example, seasonal average national monthly occupancy ranges from over 80% to off-season lows of 47%. Occupancy trends are critical to the business and to values. Equally critical to value analysis is income breakdown. Recent data reports on income of typical suburban roadside motels showed a national average ratio to total sales of (rounded) 58% for room, 27% for food and 15% for bar sales. Rate per room is of course the prime contributor to gross income. Inflation and increasing demand have brought the rate up for such suburban-highway motels to a recent average daily cost of $22. Practically all modern chain or independent motels are tied into computers for efficient, convenient reservation systems.

Budget motels like Regal 6, Motel 6, Day Inns and other chains and independents evolved in the late sixties to counter these rising costs of lodging and supply a larger economy-minded market of travelers. These economy motels usually have similar modern room space and facilities, some even with pools. They generally offer no food, have no banquet halls, bars nor meeting rooms. They always locate near restaurants. Their rates are about 40% to 50% lower and reflect their lower construction and operating costs. Occupancy rates approximate 80%.

Architecturally, the typical suburban roadside motel has 100 units as a basic, efficient modern size. Each room unit is about 260 square feet. Furnishings are typically functional. Public areas, lobbies, meeting halls, banquet rooms, dining areas, pools, service areas generally add 200 square feet more per room (economy motels excepted, of course). Most suburban roadside motels are two-story construction. Necessarily of repetitive design because of function and cost, motel fronts are often heavily detailed with stone facades and other colorful designs for maximum advertising effect. Parking in these motels must be ample and convenient. The typical parking layout permits the guest to park in front of his motel room or very close to it. For guest rooms, employees, restaurant guests and trucks, the typical suburban roadside motel needs a minimum of two parking spaces per room. Conventional motel construction takes over a year; some chains, particularly budget motels, use precast modular construction.

Motels are a special-use type of commercial-residential business. People reside overnight. Yet, the vacancy rates are extremely high compared to other commercial-residential businesses like apartment houses. Analysis of this special nature is also basic to the appraisal of motels. In this competitive and speculative industry, whenever I have bought, sold or appraised modern motels, I have used the following nine-step field and office checklist and appraisal procedure:

Step 1—*Field Review Location*—For proposed feasibility review or for appraisal of existing motels, location is the most important consideration. Is there good visibility? Access from an Interstate highway or major arterial? Population back-up in vicinity of 40,000? Near a 300-bed hospital? Near a University with a student population of 10,000? Other backup locational influences?

Step 2—*Review Special Motel Considerations*—What is the traffic count? How does it flow? Peak hourly counts? Is location accessible from major highways without excessive interchange turns, detours or necessity of complicated directional signs? If an economy motel is involved, are there acceptable restaurant(s) nearby? Also, for budget motels, does the site have at least 150 feet of frontage (250 feet if an affiliated restaurant is involved), with no dimension less than 150 feet? For any modern motel, is it or will it be tied into a computer for efficient reservations? For other than some economy motels, can a liquor license transfer or issuance be guaranteed? Is existing management history all right? Do local police records show any pattern of morals raid-arrests? If an interchange site, how far to nearest exits which have motels?

Step 3—*Analyze Zoning and Other Controls*—How many units per acre permitted? (Budget motels require as many as 60 units per acre.) Minimum setback, yard, coverage, parking requirements? Do maximum sign size or sign height requirements restrict visibility? Is motel use by zoning right or by special exception? Is the existing motel non-conforming to present zoning ordinance? Would temporary closing for fire or other reason void the non-conforming usage? For proposed motels, do building regulations permit prefab construction? For existing motels, is there a record of unsatisfactory performance of private motel sewage and/or water systems in Health Department records? Any road changes contemplated?

Step 4—*Analyze the Site*—Topography grades acceptable? Dimensions alright? Is there enough frontage to face motel properly for maximum visibility and function? Enough depth for parking at rear guestrooms and for service facilities? Subsoil acceptable for bearing? No evidence of erosion on existing sites? Good all-year stream for dilution of effluent from private motel sewer system? If no public water, does well give good yield? Is the proposed or existing site the number one site at the interchange ramp or highway junction? (Best location makes for best value. Motels cluster near each other and near good traffic counts.) Any adverse neighbors? Smoke, odors, noise, undesirable views? Steep highway grade in front of motel with revving truck engines at night? Existing or proposed competition in vicinity?

Step 5—*Analyze the Building Improvements*—For proposed or existing motels, does the plan or building show safe, sanitary, durable, structurally acceptable construction? Exterior materials needing minimum maintenance? Interior surfaces and furniture capable of sustaining heavy wear and easy maintenance? Bath materials water-resistant? Design of halls, exits, stairs, windows per national and local fire safety standards? Space sizes of rooms, corridors, restaurants, public areas, pools meet accepted standards and competition? If a chain type motel is involved, are room design and layout similar to others? (Some people like to frequent same chain where they feel at home in similar style rooms everywhere.) Age of improvements? Condition? Does furniture need replacement? Is a new roof needed? Exterior or interior paint? Level of maintenance acceptable? Clean? Restaurant facilities ample for motel? Grounds, pool, in acceptable condition? Ample parking? Condition of paving? Adequate room for truck parking? Kennel for pets?

Step 6—*Analyze Income-Expenses*—This is a special-use business which is subject to many factors affecting successful operation and appraised value.

Occupancy rates in region, in area, in this motel? Is trend up or down? Percentage room-food-liquor ration in average line? Supplies, labor, management, advertising, insurance, utilities, taxes, maintenance expenses in average industry line? Is trend up or down? (Typical sources for this commercial comparison data are motel chains, associations, motel and hotel accountant specialists who publish data and federal and state agencies. However, the most important source is always field investigation through brokers, assessors, owners, attorneys regarding income-expense and sales data of similar motels in similar locations.)

Step 7—*Collect Market Data*—From these same sources, market sales data (and net profit data, if possible) should then be collected. Since many such motels are of highway interchange type or similar to many other affiliated or chain motels, adequate recent comparable sales data even in other states can usually be found. Motels are a business and the Income approach is usually the correct approach. However, in a good recent sales market, the appraiser can test properly operating statements, income forecasts, effective gross income and fair net income. If the market data is good enough, similar enough, recent enough and properly verified, the Market approach can then be used to find current value. Market comparison data criteria include room rentals, occupancy rates, location, size, age, condition, date of sale, type of construction, room sizes, financing, land area (room for expansion) and sale price per room.

Step 8—*Estimate the Value*—As previously stated, the Income approach of capitalizing the net income is usually the best approach for commercial motel appraisals. The Market approach is very important for checking and comparing income, expense and sales data, or the market data can be used to derive a gross multiplier for the Income approach. In this method, each comparable sale price is divided by each net income to secure a multiplier factor. After appraisal verification and analysis, a final factor is chosen from the comparable data and is used to multiply the net income of the subject motel (i.e., Comparable Sales Price $2,600,000 ÷ $350,000 Net Income equals 7.43 factor). In most cases, however, such complete market data is not obtainable or verifiable. Then, the "Band of Investment" technique (see Chapter 10) can be utilized to build up a capitalization rate since motels have a comparatively speculative nature. Unless separate land value is needed for tax purposes, value is derived from capitalizing total income without separately considering the land. The Cost approach is rarely used. Even on new construction, most lenders and appraisal clients want to know what the motel will return on investment and its resulting worth rather than what it had cost to build. For those clients who request the Cost approach also or the old three approaches to value, standard cost handbooks can be used. Also, an additional criterion for comparison is construction cost per room. In the late seventies, such average construction cost was $25,000 per room.

Step 9—*Write the Report*—Because of the voluminous nature of most motel appraisal reports, it is normally desirable to do complete reports. This includes a transmittal letter so that client can have a quick outline of the value found, "up front," without having to immediately read through the whole report. An Index of report sections is also helpful. The narrative description, the valuation section, the exhibits, the photographs, the maps, sketches, statistical charts, appraiser's qualifications and other addenda should be systematically presented and preferably bound in a folder for this type of report. (See Model Motel Appraisal Report which follows.)

A MODEL MOTEL APPRAISAL REPORT INCLUDING
TRANSMITTAL LETTER, INDEX AND EXHIBITS

The following is a complete format for a motel appraisal report. It contains cover sheet, letter, index sheet, condensed narrative sections and addended exhibits.

(COVER SHEET)

APPRAISAL OF
100-UNIT MOTEL
LOCATED OFF INTERSTATE ROUTE 84
ON _____ ROAD, _____, N.Y.
for
HIGHHILL MOTEL CORP., OWNER
by

SAMUEL T. BARASH
REAL ESTATE APPRAISER   DATED _____

INDEX

Page

APPENDIX

Samuel T. Barash

Residential	**REAL ESTATE APPRAISER**	**Estates**
Commercial	**R D 1 - P. O. Box 130**	**Condemnation**
Industrial	**Lakes Road - Monroe, N.Y. 10950**	**Assessment Appeals**
Testimony	**914-783-4240**	**V A Appraiser - Inspector**

Mr. _____, Pres.   Date

HighHill Motel Corp.

_____ Road

_____, N.Y., 10000

Dear Mr. _____,

     In compliance with your request for current market value of the motel building you own on leased land on _____ Rd., _____, N.Y., I have examined the interior and exterior of the building improvements and inspected the site.

     My review also included a study of the property environs and all factors affecting value. Market value is defined as the highest price a property will bring in the open market after reasonable sales exposure, presupposing a knowledgeable, able buyer and informed seller, neither under duress. I further certify that I have no future nor contemplated interest in this property.

In my opinion, the market value of the property, as of
_____, is ($2,255,000) TWO MILLION TWO
HUNDRED FIFTY-FIVE THOUSAND DOLLARS.

Sincerely,

Samuel T. Barash

DETAILED OUTLINE OF APPRAISAL—The purpose of this ap-
praisal is to estimate current market value of the 100-room motel located on
_____ Rd., _____, N.Y. as of _____.
The motel building improvements are sited on land leased for 99 years. For
appraisal purposes, this long-term lease is considered the same as if the
land were held in fee. Such long-term leases are customarily considered the
equivalent of fee simple ownership by lending institutions who regularly
make long-term mortgage loans on such properties. (There are permanent
mortgage loans on this property where the lessor has subordinated his fee to
a certain extent so that the lessee could receive these institutional loans.)
LOCATION, ENVIRONS AND ECONOMIC MILIEU—The subject
property is located on the north side of _____ Rd., 300 feet
e/o the easterly ramp of the Route 84 Interstate Highway Interchange,
_____, N.Y. This is a small city of 30,000, historically a
trading center for a large, mainly rural region because of the city's location
in a mountain pass with old roads, railroad and now the Interstate Highway
funneling through. The site is about 75 miles northwest of New York City.
The motel mainly services travelers on Route 84, which is the closest
northerly bypass around New York City connecting New England and the
Midwest. The motel is also readily accessible to local streets. It has prime
location because of the federal highway rule which prohibits states from
receiving federal highway funds if they permit driveway entry within 300
feet of Interstate ramps. This property is 300 feet distance from the ramp.
Since the highway opened, commercial development in this vicinity has
increased, supplanting the older shopping section in the city. In addition to
this motel built five years ago, there is also an adjoining 120,000 sq. ft.
shopping center on the north, anchored by a 60,000 sq. ft. discount store.
Additional strip commercial improvement further from the ramp has also
taken place recently. The economy of the region is static. This county also
suffers from the general economic ills of the Northeast. Industry in the area
is mainly warehouse, not labor intensive. Unemployment is above national
averages. Local labor for the motel is available at comparatively moderate
rates. This is a Holiday Inn modern motel, five years old. There are several

small, 20- to 40-unit, older, "Mom and Pop" type motels in the city but no other modern competitive motels served by modern computerized reservation systems. The nearest modern comparable amenity motel is 18 miles away where several modern motels with approximately 350 rooms are congregated. There are no new motels planned within a 25-mile radius.

THE LAND—5.2 acres of land on the north side of _____ Rd., 300 feet from the easterly Route 84 ramp. There is 575-foot road frontage and 490 feet depth, a regular plot. Topography is steep, contouring up from the road. There is a vista view of the mountains and the pass through which Route 84 runs. Visibility of the site from all directions is excellent. When the motel was built five years ago, an extensive cut-and-fill landmoving operation terraced this steep terrain so that a 550-foot long by 200-foot deep level "shelf" for building and parking improvements was created. Resulting slopes are plant and sod covered, stable with no visible erosion.

EASEMENTS AND ENCUMBRANCES—The motel is on land which is leased for 99 years, @ $10,000 per year for the first 20 years, then increases every three years using the U.S. (All States) Cost of Living Index, base year 1990. Lease is net, net.

TRAFFIC COUNT—24,000 Average Daily Traffic Count per N.Y. State Highway Department, as of _____.

ASSESSMENT—$1,700,000.

TAXES—$51,000.

UTILITIES—Electricity, private sewer system, individual well.

ZONING—CS (HIGHWAY COMMERCIAL)—Permits general highway commercial including retail, banks, service stations, motels, shopping centers. Subject conforms in usage to all requirements.

LEGAL—HighHill Motel Corp. is the lessee of land and motel owner-operator. CHOK Realty Corp. is land owner-lessor. Tax Map City of _____, N.Y. Section 56, Block 4, Lot 2; Deed Book 1306, Page 322.

BUILDING IMPROVEMENTS—This is a 100-unit, one- and two-story masonry motel. The one-story section is 80′ × 100′; the attached two-story guestrooms section is 60′ × 360′ for a total of 52,800 sq. ft. including basic guestroom size of 13′ × 27′ with tile bath, drywall, carpet, no basement, flat roof, typical Holiday Inn furnishings, conference meeting rooms, restaurant, bar, lobby, 20′ × 40′ outdoor pool, kennel. Rooms face front and rear off a center hall. There is paved parking, front and rear, for 175 cars. Condition of improvements very good, Circulation around building is good with maximum 4% gradients. Access driveway from the public road has a maximum 8% gradient. Drainage is positive to front paved swales which then run through ample size culverts to a heavy stream south of the property.

VALUATION

MARKET DATA—No recent sales of similar properties could be found. There has been a comparative dearth of motel construction in the Northeast and in this region during the past five years because of lack of financing and comparatively high construction costs. This has made existing motels more profitable and upped occupancy rates and revenues. Occupancy in this inn was 74% for the year (up 7% from previous year), for the region 69%, for this roadside type 70%, according to Holiday Inn figures. Average room rental for this motel was $21.58, up from $20.58 in previous year and above the national average of $20.97 for highway type motels.

INCOME APPROACH—The following gross actual income has been compared to local and regional room rates, food and beverage revenues and verified to be effective gross income for appraisal purposes.

Room Revenue $591,299	
Food Revenue 293,212	
Beverage Revenue 171,614	
Total ....(rounded)	$1,056,000

EXPENSES (rounded)

Supplies $510,000	
Management, labor 75,000	
Advertising 21,000	
Franchise fees 41,000	
Utilities 32,000	
Maintenance, repairs 32,000	
Taxes 51,000	
Land rent 10,000	
Insurance 9,000	
Total $781,000	

NET INCOME (Gross less expenses) $275,000

Capitalization Rate of 12.2% has been built up from analysis of the First Mortgage of 60% @ 8½% interest equals 5.1% owner's equity 40% @ 9½% equals 3.8%; 30-year life equals 3.3% depreciation (straight line) for a total capitalization rate of 12.2%. This compares well with data from national motel studies which show that modern motels sell for about 7 to 8½ times net earnings (these factors are the reciprocals of 14.3 to 11.8 percentage capitalization rates). Considering the age, location, condition, rising income trends of this motel, this capitalization rate of 12.2% appears justified also by market analysis. Thus:

$275,000 ÷ 12.2% (or multiplied by 8.2) = $2,255,000

In my opinion, therefore, value derived from the Income approach

for the subject property, checked by market data analysis, as of
_____, is ($2,255,000) TWO MILLION TWO HUNDRED
FIFTY-FIVE THOUSAND DOLLARS.

Dated   Samuel T. Barash

(A COPY OF THE RECORDED SHORT-FORM MOTEL LAND LEASE
IS APPENDED HERE, INCLUDING A METES AND BOUNDS LAND
DESCRIPTION.)

	Samuel T. Barash	
Residential	**REAL ESTATE APPRAISER**	Estates
Commercial	**R D 1 - P. O. Box 130**	Condemnation
Industrial	**Lakes Road - Monroe, N.Y. 10950**	Assessment Appeals
Testimony	**914-783-4240**	V A Appraiser - Inspector

QUALIFICATIONS

Samuel T. Barash holds a B.S.S. Degree from the College of the City of
New York with graduate work at New York University and Columbia
University in Real Estate and Allied Studies.

He has been in the real estate field since 1947, including 15 years as a
supervisory appraiser with the New York Regional Office of the Veterans
Administration, territory all of New York State except the Buffalo region,
and seven years as Chief Appraiser for the Newark, N. J. Loan Guaranty
Office of the Veterans Administration covering all of New Jersey.

In this capacity, he has appraised personally and supervised the appraisals
of over 300 fee and staff appraisers, averaging more than 12,000 appraisals
per year to values in excess of $250 million each year, including numerous
residential development tracts.

He has lectured on appraisal at colleges, government seminars and has
been qualified in many courts throughout the metropolitan area.

Mr. Barash is a licensed Real Estate Broker in Chester, N.Y., residing and
appraising in Orange County, N.Y. since 1959, with appraisal office on
Lakes Road, Walton Lake, Orange County, Town of Monroe, N. Y.
10950.

Figure 11.3
SUBURBAN ROADSIDE MOTEL

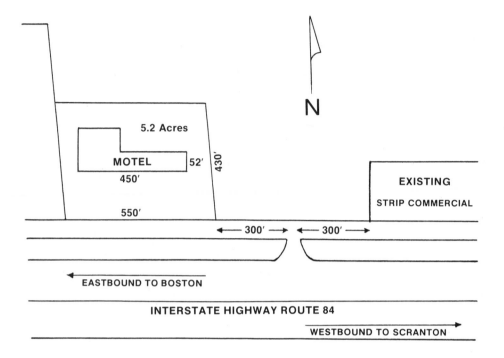

N

5.2 Acres

MOTEL 52'   430'

450'

550'

300'   300'

EXISTING

STRIP COMMERCIAL

EASTBOUND TO BOSTON

INTERSTATE HIGHWAY ROUTE 84

WESTBOUND TO SCRANTON

**LOCATION - DETAIL
SKETCH**

HIGHHILL MOTEL CORP.,   , N.Y.
(NOT TO SCALE)

Figure 11.4

MOTEL LOCATION SKETCH

Chapter 12

How to appraise
industrial properties

This chapter details the techniques of industrial property appraisals. It surveys how industrial development has been spread by suburbanization and the Interstate Highway System. Industrial plant location and labor supply criteria as well as sources for appraisal data accumulation are given here. The mounting impact of environmental controls on industrial location and function are also demonstrated. The historic local practice of zoning all low, wet wasteland for industrial use is shown to be obsolete now because of environmental flood controls. Northeast industrial obsolescence in contrast to "Sunbelt" growth is also evaluated here. There are sections on how to appraise specially designed industrial buildings, buildings with universal appeal and "mini-warehouses." A Model Industrial Warehouse Appraisal Report is also in this chapter.

HOW SUBURBANIZATION AND HIGHWAYS SPREAD INDUSTRIAL DEVELOPMENT

For a large majority of industries, a central location in an established industrial corridor is no longer required. The same forces which have spread suburban housing throughout our country since WWII have also affected industrial locations. Industry now often prefers suburban sites to keep up with demand from an expanding population and to follow its labor supply. The network of fine interstate highways has freed industry from dependence on railroads. Larger available suburban land parcels have made possible one-story industrial buildings with more efficient layout, production, storage, parking and receiving areas.

Accompanying this industrial suburbanization has been the trend of many manufacturers to lease rather than to own. This has given rise to "industrial parks" in the suburbs. A "park" contains a number of one-story buildings built on one large parcel, managed by one owner. These buildings are usually built on speculation, and designed for universal tenant appeal rather than for special industrial use. These "parks" fulfill another industrial need since they can control influences within their "parks" which inhibit or affect industrial usage. In this regard zoning regulations of municipalities are often different since many zoning codes permit higher uses (such as residential) in industrial areas. This usually leads to friction and sometimes affects continued operation of industrial usages. "Parks" generally appeal to relatively small companies.

These broad changes in the type and location of industrial buildings have also affected the appraisal process. Pre-WWII multi-story and specialized industrial buildings in dense urban locations were mainly appraised using the Income approach. Now the past several decades of Interstate highway building and accompanying suburbanization have created a large mass of free-standing, modern, one-story industrial buildings and industrial "parks." This industrial wealth of similar modern buildings being regularly rented and sold has made possible the use of the more objective Market approach to appraise many of these industrial properties.

This modern appraisal process for analyzing, reporting and estimating the value of most modern industrial buildings generally breaks down into the following broad steps. (Later sections of this chapter give specific examples.)

Step 1—Analyze the location—Is it well located? Ample labor supply? Good truck and rail transportation? Favorable tax structure? Acceptable environmental impact?

Step 2—Analyze the site—Room for expansion? Adequate parking? Acceptable gradients? Ample water, sewer and power?

Step 3—Analyze the existing or proposed building—Flexible layout? Adequate ceiling height? Adequate bay width between columns? Fireproof, sprinklered construction? Efficient processing, storage and office space? Condition and structural stability of building? Watertight integrity of roof, exterior and openings?

Step 4—Analyze the operation—Check tenancy and turnover records on existing properties; project fair rentals on proposed properties. Analyze expenses and income to derive net income.

Step 5—Estimate the value—Wherever sufficient recent sales of similar properties are available, use the Market approach, adjusting for differences.

(See later sections of this chapter for industrial property comparable rating charts.) Use the Income approach where there are inadequate sales of similar industrial properties, or for specialized, unique industrial buildings. In the Income approach, capitalize projected or adjusted actual net rents. The depreciated Cost approach can sometimes be used to help estimate the value of specialized industrial buildings which can be altered for another, more typical, marketable use. (See example in later chapter section.)

Step 6—Write the appraisal report—From accumulated field and market data, write the narrative and valuation report.

WHERE TO SECURE APPRAISAL DATA

Although our population is highly mobile and many people do move where growth and jobs are, most industries want to know they have an assured labor supply in a community before they locate there. This is the mission of State Industrial Development Agencies. They disseminate information on labor supply and other data to companies looking for sites in order to attract more industry to their states.

The first step in every appraisal assignment, whether on a proposed or existing industrial property, is to gather data. Such State Industrial Development Agencies are only one source of such data. Data sources for industrial property appraisals generally fall into the following broad groupings:

Group 1—U.S. Government—The census is most important for statistics on industrial activity and on population. The Superintendent of Documents, U.S. Government Printing Office, Washington, D.C., can be contacted for Department of Commerce and Small Business Administration publications on specific industries and economic trends.

Group 2—States—State Agencies for Economic Development, State Departments of Commerce, Departments of Labor and State Planning Commissions have important data on industries, wage rates, employment statistics and labor trends.

Group 3—Trade Associations—Many industries have association offices and publications.

Group 4—County and Municipal Offices—Economic, population, land use, zoning, highway, community facility studies, assessment equalization and tax rates. All these studies can usually be had for the asking in these local offices. Comparable market sales data on recent industrial sales can be located in county and local assessors' offices.

Group 5—Field sources—Information on industrial and business trends, lists of vacant industrial land and buildings can be secured from utility companies, banks and Chambers of Commerce. Real estate brokers, particularly those specializing in industrial properties, members of the Society of Industrial Brokers, are important sources for data accumulation on industrial property appraisals.

HOW ENVIRONMENTAL CONTROLS AFFECT INDUSTRIAL VALUE

The Federal Pollution Act of 1972 requires all industries to eventually use best available technology to control pollution of waterways. Fines can be up to $10,000 a day. Under the Act, industries must secure a pollution discharge permit from the state which administers the Act or from the Federal EPA if the state does not oversee the permit review. The Clean Air Act of 1970 controlled the emission of pollutants into our air.

The appraisal of an industrial property, proposed or existing, involves the estimation of the present value of future benefits involved in its ownership. If the function is jeopardized or curtailed by these mounting environment pollution concerns, then value is similarly affected.

Careful field analysis can expose such environmental risks affecting industrial development, function and value. The following environmental checklist is specifically designed for industrial pollutant discharges. You can use this checklist when you make your field inspection of the industrial property under appraisal and when you consult with local authorities. It will help you cover the environmental field data you need for narrative and valuation reports on industrial properties.

INDUSTRIAL POLLUTANT DISCHARGES CHECKLIST

	YES	NO
DISCHARGES INTO WATERWAYS		
Solid waste	_____	_____
Incinerator residue	_____	_____
Sewage	_____	_____
Garbage	_____	_____
Sewage sludge	_____	_____
Munitions	_____	_____
Chemical wastes	_____	_____
Biological materials	_____	_____
Radioactive materials	_____	_____
Heat	_____	_____
Wrecked equipment	_____	_____
Rock	_____	_____

Sand	———	———
Cellar dirt	———	———
Industrial waste	———	———

DISCHARGES INTO AIR

Sulphur oxides (combination of fossil fuels, oil and coal)	———	———
Particles	———	———
Hydrocarbons	———	———
Carbon monoxide	———	———
Photochemical oxidants (smog)	———	———
Nitrogen oxides	———	———

POLLUTION DISCHARGE PERMITS

State permit issued	———	———
Federal permit issued	———	———

APPRAISING INDUSTRIAL PROPERTY ON WETLANDS

The age-old practice of communities zoning all their low, wet "waste" land for industry, is now mainly obsolete because of environmental flood controls. Look at almost any local zoning map drawn before 1970 and you will find the high land marked for residences and the low land for industry. Many of these zoning ordinances also permit "higher" usages like residences in these low areas. Unfortunately, all of the suburban building since WWII has made many of these areas flood-prone. These level plains, covered with buildings and paving often become flooded from upstream runoff.

The National Flood Insurance program became law in the mid-seventies. It provides that no federal government loans may be made, guaranteed or insured when the property is located in an identified flood-prone area, unless the community has adopted effective land use controls and the property is covered by flood insurance. Most communities are participating in this national flood control program.

Many of these areas bar new construction in strips as much as one-quarter mile wide on each side of streams. Wetlands, fresh water tidal marshes and swamps will not be issued permits by the EPA or state agencies for filling, draining or building.

Much of the suburban wetland in America zoned for industry can no longer be developed.

This nationwide bar to wetland building improvements has become in-

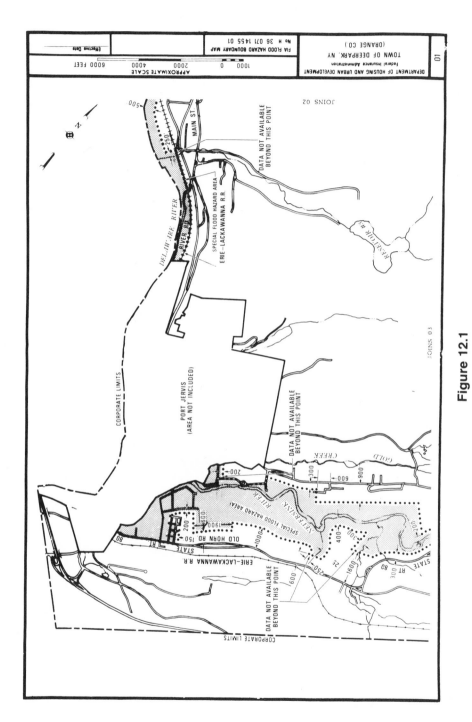

Figure 12.1

FLOOD HAZARD BOUNDARY MAP

200

These maps may not include all Special Flood Hazard Areas in the community. After a more detailed study, the Special Flood Hazard Areas shown on these maps may be modified, and other areas added.

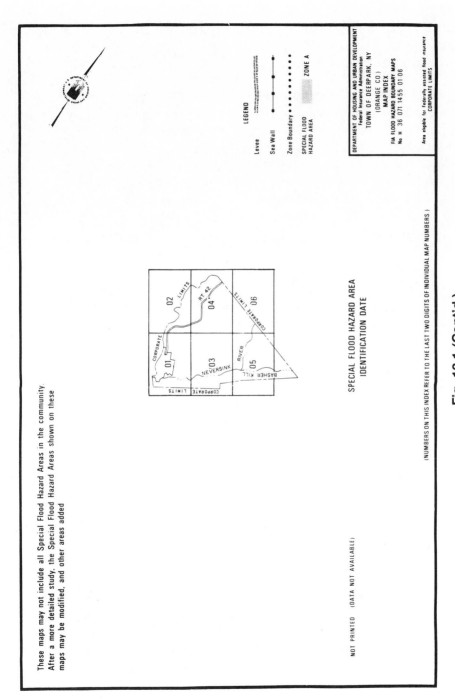

NOT PRINTED (DATA NOT AVAILABLE)

LEGEND

Levee ....

Sea Wall ●━━━●━━━●

Zone Boundary ●●●●●●●●●●●

SPECIAL FLOOD
HAZARD AREA   ZONE A

DEPARTMENT OF HOUSING AND URBAN DEVELOPMENT
Federal Insurance Administration
TOWN OF DEERPARK, NY
(ORANGE CO)
MAP INDEX
FIA FLOOD HAZARD BOUNDARY MAPS
No H 36 071 1455 0106

Areas eligible for federally assisted flood insurance
CORPORATE LIMITS

SPECIAL FLOOD HAZARD AREA
IDENTIFICATION DATE

(NUMBERS ON THIS INDEX REFER TO THE LAST TWO DIGITS OF INDIVIDUAL MAP NUMBERS)

Fig. 12.1 (Cont'd.)

creasingly effective and is especially affecting industrial development and appraisals. The following is a flood hazard appraisal procedure. (See also "Environmental Restrictions Checklist," Chapter 5.)

Step 1—Check whether in flood hazard area—When you appraise property or existing industrial property, your feasibility or appraisal investigation first determines whether the site is in an identified flood hazard area. The local Town Engineer or Building Inspector has flood maps which you can review. The Housing and Urban Development Agency, Federal Insurance Administration, Washington, D.C. can also be contacted for area flood maps for your own files. (A sample Town of Deer Park flood hazard map is on page 201.)

Step 2—Determine whether flood insurance applies—If the industrial building is in an identified flood hazard area, ascertain whether the property is covered by flood insurance.

Step 3—Verify community land use controls—Contact local authorities to make certain that land use controls on wetlands have been adopted into law. Otherwise, the subject property will be ineligible for government loans or conventional loans guaranteed or insured by the government. This inability to readily secure financing materially affects marketability and value of the property under appraisal.

NORTHEAST INDUSTRIAL OBSOLESCENCE VERSUS SUNBELT GROWTH

In the last two decades, the number of manufacturing establishments rose in the South and Southwest and declined materially in the Northeast and Midwest. These older Northern and Western sections suffer from very high energy costs, obsolete urban transportation systems and obsolete urban industrial plants. Although many Canadian and other foreign companies have replaced many of the companies which have departed from these northern areas, the overall loss of industrial facilities and jobs to the "Sunbelt" has been heavy.

In industrial appraising especially, you estimate value for a specific industrial property against this broad regional backdrop of economic pressures. For any individual appraisal to have current value meaning, a larger study must first be made in the light of these continuing dynamic demographic and economic trends. When appraising industrial properties, the following important preliminary questions must first be answered before the quality and condition of the property can be evaluated.

1. *Growth or decline area?* Is the property in a growing or declining location? What are the economic trends in the region?

2. *Tax structure?* Are the local and state taxes heavy? Do tax assessment policies favor industrial or residential properties? What is local kilowatt cost for electricity for industrial use? Is it competitive with other regions?

3. *Transportation?* Railroad available? Rail costs? Location and condition on road network?

4. *Competitive businesses?* Have they been moving into the area or away to greener economic pastures? Are there many vacant industrial plants in the area? Are there countervailing trends, such as foreign industries coming into a declining Northeast area?

5. *Population trends?* Are the young people, the labor force, moving in or away? What are the demographic trends?

HOW TO APPRAISE SPECIALLY DESIGNED INDUSTRIAL BUILDINGS

Except for industrial "parks," most industrial buildings are generally created to meet a specific functional need of an industrial user. This contrasts with commercial buildings which are mainly built to secure rental return on investment or residences which are generally erected to return capital profit on investment by the builder. Resale of industrial buildings after original user abandonment, usually involves modification of the building for the new user. Generally the sales price must be depreciated to reflect the cost of such changed use.

Here is a specific example of how sales prices (and/or appraisals) are depreciated to reflect the cost of such changed industrial usage. Assume a 20-year-old, 30,000 square foot, one-story masonry building in a good suburban location, near road and rail networks, originally designed and previously used for manufacturing. This industrial building was built with ample fenestration, including exterior wall and skylight windows to provide good natural light for manufacturing processes. The original user has relocated to a "Sunbelt" location. Manufacturing is no longer an economically viable, typical use in the subject area. However, because of strategic location near excellent Interstate highways and railroads, warehousing has become a prime user of industrial space in this area and is the highest and best industrial use of the subject property.

From recent comparable sales data of warehouse type properties in the vicinity, the subject building should sell for $480,000, or $16 a square foot, including land, if it were designed for materials storage and handling. To convert it to a building secure and functional for warehousing would involve closing off the windows and skylights, adding two loading docks with doors and upgrading the office space at an estimated cost of $75,000.

Thus:

$480,000.....Value from Market data, if converted for warehouse use ($16 per sq.ft.).

−75,000.....Less cost of closing fenestration, adding loading docks with doors and upgrading office space.

$405,000.....Depreciated current value of property in as-is condition ($13.50 per sq.ft.).

Industrial appraising is more complicated than commercial and residential appraising because of this special nature of many industrial buildings. High turnover rate of industrial tenants due to hard economic times, or by tenants' attraction to another region (Northeast vs. Sunbelt) leaves many specially designed industrial buildings vacant for long periods of time.

A modern plant was built near the author's town in the early seventies to manufacture prefabricated housing. It was over 60,000 square feet, masonry, one-story construction (small balcony office space), with very high, 28-foot ceilings to handle very heavy duty traveling cranes. When the housing boom collapsed in this Northeast region, the manufacturer-owner was foreclosed by his lender for mortgage non-payment. The building has remained vacant, used for only a short while thereafter as a weekend flea market. Because of its unusual special industrial design in a non-market area and because it is not economically feasible to adapt it for other uses, property value has been affected seriously. This comparatively modern building cost over $1 million to build. Its present value would be far less.

The best approach for industrial property appraising is the Market approach. Yet specially designed buildings are often too dissimilar because of their special function and design for effective comparison with sales of similar buildings similarly situated. Often, the Income approach must therefore be utilized as the next best method. Such special purpose buildings deserve high capitalization rates and downward stabilization of current income on existing occupied properties or lowered projected income on proposed properties to reflect such limited marketability.

The following is an appraisal marketability analysis procedure for industrial properties:

Step 1—Analyze location—Is property remote from highway and rail transportation? Is there an ample local labor supply within convenient commuting distance? Is it in a crowded area where materials receiving and shipping will be delayed and costly?

Step 2—Analyze parking—Is there adequate employee parking for the designed or contemplated highest and best industrial use?

Step 3—Review loading facilities—Can materials move in, through and out of the building efficiently? Is there a flexible layout? Adequate space between column bays?

Step 4—Check ceiling height—Are ceilings too high or too low for projected typical users?

Step 5—Check environmental impact—Any air or water pollutants? All permits in hand? (See prior pollutants discharge checklist in this chapter.)

Step 6—Analyze design—Is building specially designed for a unique use? Does it vary in major specifications from typical industrial space?

Step 7—Check if fireproof—Sprinklers installed? Water supply adequate for fire safety?

Step 8—Analyze utilities and facilities—Are lighting and power service adequate for projected industrial uses. Are office space and sanitary facilities adequate?

Step 9—Do construction review—Check condition of roof, flashings, exterior paint, structural stability and watertight integrity of walls and roof.

Step 10—Analyze adaptability—Is building on its plot and location reasonably adaptable to other than designed use? What is highest and best use?

HOW TO APPRAISE INDUSTRIAL BUILDINGS WITH UNIVERSAL APPEAL

In contrast to specially designed industrial buildings, those properties with universal tenant appeal generally are adaptable to other than original use. These modern universal appeal buildings can be found in both suburban free-standing and industrial "park" locations. The characteristics which give them better marketability and values are the following:

1. Flexibility in layout.
2. Adequate electric service (440 V).
3. One-story, fireproof, sprinklered buildings.
4. Efficient receiving, loading, processing, storage and shipping.
5. Commensurate office space.
6. Adequate parking.
7. Adequate room for expansion.

Such buildings can be readily compared to similar properties. The Market approach is therefore the best approach wherever there is adequate sales activity. It is important to secure recent comparables, if possible, to avoid having to adjust subjectively for time of sale. Individual criteria are rated as inferior, equal or superior. Sales prices are usually adjusted in total (including land) using gross square feet of these industrial buildings as units of comparison. (See Model Appraisal Report, Comparable Criteria Rating Chart in the last section of this Chapter as an example of such rating and total square adjustment.) For this Market approach on industrial appraisals, you can usually use the following adjustment criteria to compare the subject property to the other similar properties which have sold recently:

1. Location—Describe and compare.
2. Time—Choose recent sales.
3. Land value—Describe and compare.
4. Parking—Describe and compare.
5. Layout—Describe and compare.
6. Ceiling height—Describe and compare.
7. Light—Describe and compare.
8. Column spacing—Describe and compare.
9. Loading facilities—Describe and compare.
10. Age of improvements—Describe and compare.
11. Room for expansion—Describe and compare.
12. Office facilities—Describe and compare.
13. Railroad availability—Describe and compare.
14. Trucking facilities—Describe and compare.
15. Utilities—Describe and compare.
16. Quality and condition—Describe and compare.
17. Rentals—Describe and compare.
18. Zoning—Describe and compare.
19. Price per square foot—Include land.

HOW TO APPRAISE "MINI-WAREHOUSES"

The "mini-warehouse" is an important new industrial warehouse concept, evolved in the South in the early seventies. This new type of industrial building has spread to most other areas. It is basically a one-story building of built-in-place masonry or prefabricated steel construction (see Figure 12.2) divided into cubicles ranging from about 25 to 600 square feet each.

The site is usually fenced and protected by watchmen. In most installations, renters can have access from 6:00 a.m. to midnight; some are open 24

Figure 12.2
"MINI-WAREHOUSE"

hours. Buildings contain up to 700 units, are fireproof, site lighted at night, open seven days a week. They are normally located in areas which have dense suburban apartment developments. Many of the tenants are apartment dwellers who need additional storage space or mobile homeowners, or contractors who may need storage area for their materials, or merchants with excess inventory.

The buildings normally are not heated, some are not lighted in their interior, with rental unit sizes usually ranging from $5' \times 5'$ to double $10' \times 30'$. Each unit has its own $3'$ door or garage type door, equipped for locking. Monthly rates from $10 to $80 a month. Turnover and vacancy rates are comparatively high because of the nature of the tenancy but there is an average gross rental of $4 per square foot annually.

Appraisal of a proposed or existing mini-warehouse involves the following:

Step 1—Analyze the locale—Is there a 40,000 population within a 10-minute drive? Are there numerous apartment projects in the vicinity? Are there shopping centers in the vicinity with numerous small satellite stores set on slabs, no cellar, limited storage?

Step 2—Analyze the site—If existing, is it fenced? Building fireproof? Site lighted for security? Paved circulation about buildings? Drainage positive off site? No ponding water after rains? Watchmen and management controls?

Step 3—Inspect the improvements—Condition of building, of roof, of exterior, of doors, of interior partitions should be field reviewed. If prefab steel, are there any unrepaired damaged panels? If masonry, any structural cracking, water entry?

Step 4—Analyze the operation—Check tenancy records, turnover rate. Is vacancy rate higher than 15%? Is there a 24-hour access? Is it needed? Analyze the expenses and income.

Step 5—Estimate the value—On existing properties, use the Income approach to capitalize verified net income derived from rentals. Net income is secured by deducting operating expenses, taxes, insurance, reserve for replacement, maintenance and management expenses from investigated effective gross rentals. This net income is then capitalized by using straight line depreciation plus a capitalization rate built up from Band of Investment technique or from adjusted "safe" rate (see Chapter 10). Since light construction and high turnover in rentals is involved in mini-warehouses, comparatively fast depreciation (ranging down to 20 years) and high capitalization rates (ranging up to 16%) are usually appropriate.

A MODEL INDUSTRIAL WAREHOUSE APPRAISAL REPORT

The following is a narrative appraisal of a medium-size, free-standing modern masonry industrial warehouse building in a small town of 15,000 in the outer rim suburbs of a major Northeast city. Various portions have been condensed and all appendixes omitted, including location map, key map, photographs, statement of contingent conditions, appraiser's qualification sheet and transmittal letter.

OUTLINE AND PURPOSE OF APPRAISAL—The purpose of this appraisal is to determine current fair market value.

DATA ON CITY AND NEIGHBORHOOD—The town is Yourtown, USA, population 15,000, about 50 miles northwest of Northeast City, population 8 million. Historically a railroad junction, this town's economy dwindled as railroad influence waned. When Route 18 was improved as a limited access highway about 10 years ago, new industries, mainly of warehouse nature began to locate near highway interchanges as truck shipping supplanted the railroads. Employment is mainly factory and material handling in the area. The town's "bedroom areas" are also inhabited by a substantial proportion of higher paid commuters who work in Northeast City. There is one modern strip shopping center in the town as well as a small, old commercial district. Labor supply is ample in the area. There are many similar one-story industrial free-standing buildings and one industrial park in the town, with the majority of the industrial space similar and comparable to the subject warehouse in design and usage. The balance is manufacturing. About 20 miles west and 20 miles north there are two small cities in this county which have a number of large, old, multi-story, mill-type industrial buildings with considerable square feet, vacant over one year. There are no vacant industrial buildings in the town. Rentals of similar warehouse space average $2.75 per square foot. Prospects for continued full industrial occupancy appear good for the comparatively modern industrial space in this area. There are no additional buildings in construction or planning at this time with costs for similar construction risen to $19 per square foot.

THE LAND—Three acres with 300-foot frontage on Meadow Road. Grade is level. Building is positively drained with minimum gradient to side and rear swales which run off to a stream at rear. There is asphaltic paved parking for 30 cars. There is ample room for expansion.

UTILITIES—Electricity, individual septic system, public water.

LEGAL—Tax map, Yourtown, Section 10, Block 20, Lots 4 and 5, Liber 1240 pages 10-11, County Clerk's office.

COMMUNITY FACILITIES—Incorporated town, public water, no sewers, volunteer fire.

ZONING—I-(1)—Light industrial—permits by right, veterinarian, business school, non-nuisance industry, office building, utility, research building, warehouse. Special exception use, motel, restaurant, gravel extraction, one-family dwelling. Present warehouse use is fully conforming.

APPRAISED—Fee simple.

HIGHEST AND BEST USE—Warehouse industrial, present use.

ASSESSMENT AND TAXES—Yourtown assessment $250,000 including $35,000 ascribed to land. Taxes $7,800.

IMPROVEMENTS—The land is improved with a five-year-old, one-story masonry block, brick and aluminum panel front facade in industrial warehouse building, poured concrete reinforced foundation on spread footings, 22-foot high structure, 900 square feet finished office space, loading dock, two overhead doors, sprinklers, 400-amp. service, suspended heaters, 40 feet between columns, good layout for warehouse operations, fenced parking area, building 100 × 200, 20,000 sq. ft.

VALUATION—Market data comparison has been used as the best approach to value because there have been adequate recent sales of similar modern industrial buildings similarly located. The building is owned and used by its owner, a beer distributor. No rentals are involved. Neither the Income nor Cost approaches are considered pertinent. A Comparative Analysis Rating Chart follows:

COMPARABLE CRITERIA	Sale #1	Sale #2
Address	22 Low St. Yourtown	14 High St. Yourtown
Proximity to subject	1 mile	1000 feet
Location	Inferior	Equal
Zoning	Equal	Equal
Age	Older	Newer
Land size	1 acre	Equal
Parking	Equal	Equal
Quality and condition	Equal	Equal
Room for expansion	Limited	Equal
Utilities	Public sewer, water	Public sewer, water
Column spacing	Inferior	Equal
Shopping, receiving	No rail, equal truck	Rail, equal truck
Ceiling height	16 feet	20 feet
Rentals	Owner occupied	Owner occupied
Office facilities	Equal	Equal
Date of sale	6 months	9 months
Time adjustment	None (recent)	None (recent)
Sale recorded	County clk. Lib 15/24	1494/10-12
Principals	Roe Co. to Joe Co.	Hill Co. to Dale Co.
Price per square foot (including land)	$19	$21

This abbreviated comparative analysis of Sales #1 and #2 (three comparables should normally be used) yields the following value conclusions. Sale #1 is better than subject in some ways such as public sewers but has inferior location, no room for expansion and an inferior layout with narrower column bays. Sale #2 is equal in practically all aspects to subject except for smaller size of property, public sewers and is newer. The indicated value appears to be $21 per sq. ft. for the 20,000-sq. ft. subject building including land, considering Sale #2 an adjusted equal comparable and the "best comparable."

CERTIFICATION—I certify that I have personally inspected the exterior and interior of the described property and that I have no present nor contemplated interest in the property. In my opinion, the market value, including land, of the subject property, as of _____, is *Four Hundred Twenty Thousand Dollars ($420,000).*

Dated _____   John Smith

                                  Appraiser _____

Chapter 13

Techniques and procedures for appraising mobile home parks and mobile homes

Mobile homes and mobile home parks are appraised in this chapter. The age patterns of our people, thier modern life style and particularly the economics of housing today are shown here as the basis for mobile home popularity. Federal government financing loan guarantees and national mobile home construction standards are also stressed here because of their increasing impact on this growing section of the housing market. There is an important section on how to make a feasibility study for a proposed Mobile Home Park. Checklists for inspection of mobile homes are also furnished. There are step-by-step procedures on how to appraise proposed and existing mobile home parks, vacant lots for mobile home placement, mobile homes on rental lots and mobile homes on lots owned in fee simple. This chapter concludes with a Model Mobile Home Park Appraisal Report as well as a Model Mobile Home Appraisal Report.

FACTORS AFFECTING GROWTH OF MOBILE HOMES

A Mobile Home is a transportable structure, exceeding 8 feet wide by 32 feet long. Most modern mobiles are 12 feet and 14 feet wide by up to 70 feet in

213

length. An Expandable Mobile Home is a mobile home which has one or more room sections which telescope out to expand the home after delivery to the site.

Yet the term "mobile" is a misnomer. Many think of them as recreational or travel trailers. Actually, most mobile homes are permanent homes which rarely leave their sites once placed.

The statistics are impressive. By the mid-seventies, 8 million Americans were living in 4.5 million mobile homes. The industry has been subject to the same recession-boom economic forces as conventionally built housing. Yet the mobile homes industry has managed to deliver, in most recent years, from 30% to 50% of the single housing units built in the U.S. As many as 600,000 mobile units a year have been manufactured and sold.

The millions of post-WWII babies are contributing strongly to this surge. In the mid-seventies, the under-30 age group represented more than 42% of all mobile homeowners. The mobile home is furnished—instant housing. It appears to satisfy the modern life styles and housing needs of millions of suburbanites. Probably most important, it appeals to those millions who want single housing. They cannot afford the average $55,000 conventionally built home but can afford the average $14,000 mobile home. Mobile homes account for over 75% of all homes sold under $30,000. The average cost of a conventional house appears to be rising twice as fast as the average income of families who do not own one. So the demand for mobile homes will no doubt continue and increase.

THE EFFECT OF U.S. GOVERNMENT GUARANTEES OF MOBILE HOME FINANCING

By the early seventies, the Federal Government began to recognize the impact of mobile homes on the housing market. The VA, the FHA, the Farmers Home Loan Agency began to encourage, under various laws, less costly financing with loan guaranty and other programs. Federal national standards on construction of mobile homes and parks are supplementing manufacturer association standards. The H.U.D. agency brought thousands of mobile homes to house whole communities stricken by national disasters. Enabling legislation under various programs authorized the purchase of mobile homes with loan terms up to 15 years. The Truth in Lending Act helped to inhibit excessively high financing charges for mobile homes.

These are major examples of the effect of government entry. However, by the very fact of its entry, the government has recognized the growing importance of this mobile home sector. Once considered housing "jungles," many trailer parks lined the highways of this country. Now, young married, retirees, middle and lower middle income people are primary buyers, rather than poor transients. Zoning and neighbors continue to mainly oppose expansion of modern residential mobile home parks, particularly in the populous Northeast. However, this appears to be changing. When the government entered this field, so did many more institutional lenders. Planners, courts and legislators are starting to equate the newer mobile homes built under uniform industry and government standards with conventionally built housing.

Traditionally, lenders limited financing terms on mobile homes to about 10 years. Higher interest rates of about 12% on mobile homes always compared unfavorably to typical 20- to 30-year, 8½% to 9½% mortgages on conventional housing. So even though mobile homes cost less, monthly payments are comparatively high. However, with liberal government mortgages like FHA 15-year terms and general lender awareness of better quality of modern mobile homes and parks, financing appears to be easing. Also, since smaller down payments are required on mobile homes, purchase becomes even more feasible for most buyers.

HOW TO MAKE A FEASIBILITY STUDY FOR A PROPOSED MOBILE HOME PARK

Newer mobile home parks are changing the former image of trailer park "jungles" and helping to overcome local resistance. There are travel trailer parks. There are retirement parks with up to 2,500 spaces and extensive recreational facilities. There are government subsidized rental parks where H.U.D. subsidizes rentals of low income tenants. There are mobile home subdivisions where lots are sold. And there are regular rental parks.

We will be concerned here with the regular rental parks with about 300 spaces. This type of park has paved streets, sidewalks, curbs, lights, recreational facilities, public and/or community water and sewer plants. Typical spaces are 50′ × 100′. There are concrete pads, concrete patios and concrete sidewalks on the mobile home spaces. There are usually no more than six to eight spaces per acre.

Mobile homes appear to be answering the market demand for under $30,000 single unit housing. However, problems have accompanied this growth. Like apartment dwellers, tenants in mobile home parks in many areas have few legal rights. They may be faced with large rent increases without warning. Complaints regarding parks and mobile homes in general include grievances, site problems, park rules, high financing charges, high fire fatality rates, high wind damage and inadequate warranties. Investors have also lost tenants and their parks because of such complaints, overall poor location and poor management. Abusive and rip-off practices are being regulated in certain areas. New York has its Property Law 233, a Bill of Rights for tenants and other states are beginning to follow this lead. In some parts of the U.S., particularly in the South and West, there may be too many parks in one area. For all of the above reasons, feasibility analyses and feasibility sections of appraisal reports are critically important.

The following step-by-step feasibility appraisal guideline procedure and feasibility checklist are set up for field inspection data collection of tracts proposed for mobile home rental parks. These aids should help you supplement the market analysis and income/expenses projections for your narrative feasibility and valuation reports. (See also model Mobile Home Park Appraisal Report in the later section of this chapter.) In all cases, clients should be advised to buy tracts only on an option basis subject to receiving zoning variance or other full municipal and other authority approvals for the mobile home park.

GUIDELINE PROCEDURES FOR FEASIBILITY/APPRAISALS
ON
PROPOSED MOBILE HOME RENTAL PARKS

Step 1—Check zoning—If a zoning violation is involved, the proposed park is not feasible. If there is no zoning or if variances can be secured, it is feasible if otherwise well-located and marketable.

Step 2—Check location—A proposed park should be free from and not substantially contribute to adverse scenic or environmental conditions and be conducive for residential purposes to meet Federal guidelines and renters' desires. Convenient to schools, shopping, transportation, arterial roads, community facilities? Affected by unacceptable physical hazards such as subsidence, floods, noxious gases, traffic hazards or danger from fire or explosion? (See later field checklist.)

Step 3—Investigate public water/sewer—Individual water and sewer systems are not appropriate for proposed parks, especially if there are competing parks in areas which do have public utilities.

Step 4—Review proposed layout and site—A proposed park should provide good community service and maintenance with the development well laid out with an attractive appearance. Plans should include all weather roads, positively drained. There must be on-site parking for each pad permitted, or convenient street parking on wide enough streets. Electricity, laundry facilities, on site or nearby, and mail service must be available. Are proposed pad sizes adequate for mobile home placement? Are topography, subsoil conditions, soil bearing and site drainage conducive to development? Are neighboring usages existing or zoned for residential? Are there adverse commercial or industrial neighbors? Any deed restrictions and covenants which affect mobile home placement?

Step 5—Study values—Secure, validate and compare a minimum of three recent sales of similar tracts similarly located, purchased for or zoned for mobile home improvement.

Step 6—Write feasibility/appraisal report—Analyze collected data, come to opinion of value, write your report, using Market approach technique.

The following Feasibility Checklist supplements the preceding step-by-step procedure and should help you collect field data for a mobile home park feasibility/appraisal report:

FEASIBILITY STUDY FOR A MOBILE HOME PARK
A FIELD CHECKLIST

PARK _____ACRES _____ DATE _____
LOCATION _____OWNER _____

The Community	Miles	Utilities and Misc.	Yes No
1. Schools		16. Public water, sewer	
2. Jobs		17. Well yields ample	
3. Local shopping		18. Soil percolates	
4. Major shopping		19. Fire protection	
5. Parks		20. Street lighting	
6. Churches		21. Garbage removal	
7. Hospitals		22. Police protection	
8. Nearest mobile park		23. Paved street to site	
		24. Public transportation	
The Land	**Yes No**	25. Growth area	
9. Accessible		26. Zoned for mobiles	
10. Adverse views		27. Max. 6 per acre	
11. Adverse traffic		28. Bldg req'ts feasible	
12. Smoke or fumes		29. Envirm'tl feasible	
13. Flooding			
14. Acceptable soil			
15. Acceptable topo			

List 3 comparable parks and rentals for each:
1. _____ $ _____
2. _____ $ _____
3. _____ $ _____
Demand for mobile home spaces in area _____
_____
Typical space size in area _____
Typical space rental in area _____
Remarks (key to above numbers) _____
_____
_____
_____

WHAT TO LOOK FOR IN CHARACTERISTICS OF SAFE, SANITARY, FUNCTIONAL, HABITABLE MOBILE HOMES

Most mobile homes built today are 12 feet and 14 feet wide by up to 70 feet long, include a living room, a kitchen with range and refrigerator, a dining area, one or two bathrooms, built-in cabinets and closets, free-standing furniture, drapes, carpets, floor covering, heating, water heater and optional extras like fireplaces, bay windows, special trim, wood shingles. Tie-downs to avoid wind damage and skirts around the base of the homes are required in most areas.

As the housing environment in mobile home parks has improved, so have mobile homes. (An excellent source for data on construction standards is the Mobile Homes Manufacturers Association, Dept. B, Box 201, 14650 Lee Road, Chantilly, Va.) A shield is affixed near the front door of mobile homes which meet ANSI A 119.3, a construction standards booklet for "Installation of Mobile Homes Including Mobile Home Park Requirements," sponsored by manufacturer associations and by the National Fire Protection Association. These standards are required now by almost all states. Because of these and federal uniform safety standards, and because of location in modern parks, modern mobile homes today do not appear to suffer from rapid depreciation as they did in prior years. Also, the 12-foot and 14-foot wide mobiles have, with their better spaces and design, made obsolescent the former 8-foot and 10-foot wide models.

The following Inspection Checklist for mobile homes and parks is for field use and for data collection for the appraisal report:

MOBILE HOME AND PARK INSPECTION CHECKLIST

MOBILE HOME NAME _____ MODEL # ____ SERIAL # ____
LOCATION _____ OWNER _____
PARK _____ LOCATION _____

CONSTRUCTION—MOBILE HOMES

1. FRAME—Sight along center beam for straightness, deflection
2. SIDING—Check that screws are non-ferrous or protected
3. STRUCTURAL—Check required map certificate that home built for winds, snow load this area

PARKS

1. Meets zoning requirements __
2. Paved streets _____
3. Curbs, sidewalks _____
4. Public or locally approved sewer and water _____
5. Off-street parking or wide enough streets to park _____
6. Adequate electric, underground

_____

4. ANCHORS—Ties required most areas
5. STUDS—usually 2 × 3 with siderail, sometimes 2 × 4
6. FLOOR—Good quality homes bolt floor to steel frame
7. ROOFS—Usually 30 ga. steel, one piece
8. WINDOW, DOORS—Min. 10% floor area for vent and fire exit safety—2 exit doors remote from each other
9. WATER HEATER—Closed off from living quarters
10. CONDITION—Siding, windows, floor, appliances, furniture, smoke detector
11. REPAIRS—Make up list
12. CERTIFICATES—Compliance shield near front door—Map certificate

7. Residential area _____
8. No hazards to occupants ____
9. Community facilities nearby
10. Adequate size space (min. 50′ × 100′) _____
11. Acceptable landscaping _____
12. Garbage removal _____
13. Commensurate recreational facilities _____
14. Skirts required _____
15. Condition of facilities _____
16. Views _____
17. Overall appearance _____
18. Entry fees _____
19. Good park regulations _____
20. Leases available_____
21. Local recorded violations ____
22. Rent schedule_____
23. Set-up fees _____
24. Room for expansion _____

HOW TO APPRAISE A BUILDING LOT FOR MOBILE HOME PLACEMENT

Procedures for appraising a building lot for mobile home placement include the following steps:

Step 1—Check location—Convenient to schools, shopping, community facilities, transportation? Affected by adverse influences such as noise, odors, unsightly views, heavy, fast traffic?

Step 2—Inspect lot—Size adequate for mobile placement, topography, paved road to site, subsoil conditions, soil bearing, positive drainage, ground cover, public utilities or satisfactory well yields and soil percolation for private utilities?

Step 3—Check amenities—Trees, views, neighboring usages, recreational facilities?

Step 4—Investigate controls—Zoning permits mobile homes? Variance possible? Assessment? Taxes? Do deed restrictions and covenants affect mobile home placement?

Step 5—Study values—Study improved lot values in neighborhood, block and adjacent properties. Secure, validate and compare a minimum of three recent sales of similar lots similarly situated.

Step 6—Write appraisal report—Come to your opinion of value and write your report, using Market approach technique.

HOW TO APPRAISE A MOBILE HOME ON A LOT OWNED IN FEE SIMPLE AND ON A RENTED LOT

Government appraisal forms require the retail book value from recognized books which give current market value of new and used mobile homes, be inserted on their appraisal forms. As with the fading Three-approach technique to value on conventional homes, you have to know how to use these market books and complete these government forms as required. The following publications can be used to complete this Cost approach required on ·government forms:

Mobile Home Blue Book
    Judy-Berner Publishing Company
    10060 W. Roosevelt Road
    Westchester, Illinois 60153

Unicomp Directory of Used Mobile Homes
    United Compilation, Inc.
    P.O. Box 237
    Libertyville, Illinois 60048

National Automobile Dealers Association Mobile Home Appraisal Guide
    National Mobile Home Appraisal System
    P.O. Box 1407
    Covina, California 91722

Marshall & Swift Residential Cost Handbook
    Marshall & Swift Publication Company
    1617 Beverly Boulevard
    Los Angeles, California 90026

Boeckh Building Valuation Manual
    Boeckh Publications
    American Appraisal Associations, Inc.
    525 East Michigan Street
    P.O. Box 664
    Milwaukee, Wisconsin 53201

However, you should rely primarily on the Market approach for your opinion of value by securing and analyzing at least three actual recent sales of similar mobile homes in the vicinity.

Appraisal techniques for mobile homes on lots owned in fee simple, involve the following step-by-step procedures:

Step 1—Inspection—Community, the neighborhood, the block, the plot (using checklist for vacant lot, previous section). Measure the mobile home exterior, examine the interior and exterior of the mobile home (use construction checklist in prior section) and take photographs of front, rear and street scene.

Step 2—Collect data—On the community, the area, economic conditions, community services, schools, taxes, assessment and zoning information, including whether mobile homes are permitted by right or by exception, whether a mobile home as it exists on plot is a conforming or non-conforming usage.

Step 3—Prepare written report—Either on the client's appraisal form or on your own narrative appraisal format, using Market approach. Attach plot plan or sketch, location map, building sketch and your appraisal qualification sheet. Contingent conditions to include a clause making value subject to approval or continued local permit for mobile home usage.

Appraisal techniques for mobile homes on rented lots in a mobile home park involve the following procedures:

Step 1—Inspect the park—Use Mobile Home Park Inspection Checklist in previous section.

Step 2—Measurement—Tape the mobile home exterior, examine the interior and exterior of the mobile home. Take photographs.

Step 3—Prepare written report—Same as fee simple lot procedure above but omit land value. Add attachments. Advise client that value is contingent upon there being no transfer nor ''commission'' fees payable to park owner upon sale of mobile home.

A MODEL MOBILE HOME PARK APPRAISAL REPORT

The following is a Mobile Home Appraisal Report with a condensed narrative and omitting cover sheet, letter, index sheet and addended exhibits, such as comparable rentals rating chart, location detail sketch, appraiser qualifications and photographs. Investors buy or build mobile home parks for return on their capital investment. The Income approach is therefore used to derive opinion of value on mobile home parks. If there are enough sales of parks available, market analysis can be used to check value. Cost approach is not pertinent. Valuation by Income approach has been based on total income flow from land and improvements. If land value is separately needed, say for an assessment appeal, it can be derived by using residual techniques (see Chapter 10).

DETAILED OUTLINE OF APPRAISAL—The purpose of this appraisal is to estimate current market value of the 300-space mobile home park on the southwest corner of _____ Rd and _____ Rd, _____, N.Y. as of _____.

LOCATION, NEIGHBORHOOD AND COMMUNITY INFLUENCES—The subject property is located on the S/W/C of _____ Rd and _____ Rd about 600 feet east of the easterly ramp of Route _____ Interchange in the town of _____, N.Y. This town is about 55 miles northwest of Northeast City. Within the last 15 years, this town mushroomed from a quiet agricultural area of less than 3,000 to its current population of 14,000, many of whom commute to work in and near Northeast City. In the past four years, growth has slowed because of the general Northeast economic recession. The site is readily accessible to the major State Route _____ by ramp nearby and to local streets. There is a city of 25,000 with schools, churches, shopping about 3 miles away. There is a small local shopping area in front of the park on the same road. Other neighboring usages include residences, mobile homes on privately owned individual lots, several seasonal bungalow colonies and two working dairy farms. There are no adverse neighborhood usages affecting the subject with noise, smoke, odors or incompatible views. Because many of the neighboring towns zone out or restrict mobile homes severely, this subject mobile home park has no nearby park competition. The nearest comparable parks are about 15 miles away. there are no new parks planned within a 20-mile radius. There is a strong demand for mobile home spaces which can be expected to continue.

THE LAND—There are 46 acres of land with 150 feet of road frontage on _____ Rd and 500 feet of frontage on _____. Grades are level at front, roll down gently to a stream which drains the parcel, then rise up to a wooded area at rear. There are pleasant views of farmland and hills to the west. Visibility of park's signs is excellent from the arterial as well as from the local streets. Land is well drained by the stream, with no improvements on low portions. Steeper slopes are plant and sod covered with no visible erosion.

UTILITIES—Public water, public sewer, electricity.

TRAFFIC COUNT—30,000 ADTC on arterial road _____, as of _____, 5,000 ADTC on access road to property.

EASEMENTS AND ENCUMBRANCES—None known.

ASSESSMENT—$1,900,000, with $1,200,000 allotted to land and $900,000 to administration building and mobile homes.

TAXES—$67,000.

ZONING—RA (Residential) and C (Commercial). RA zoning (about 85% of site) permits one-family residential and up to eight mobile home units per acre in a mobile home park by special exception. Commercial (15%) permits a variety of highway commercial uses including retail, gas stations, banks. The existing mobile home park conforms.

LEGAL—WALLKILL MOBILE HOME PARK, INC. is the owner. Town Map Section 122, Block 2, Lot 1, Deed Book 1101, page 100.

HIGHEST AND BEST USE—Mobile home park, present use.

IMPROVEMENTS—A one-story, five-year-old, masonry building, 40′ × 60′, serves as utility, office and recreation building. Interior has asphalt tile floor, drywall, four lavatories, lounge area, vending machine room, laundry room and a large open recreation room. Building is in good condition.

There are 300 mobile home sites, with each space a minimum 50′ × 100′. Each site has a 180 square foot concrete patio and a 3-foot concrete sidewalk to street. The streets are 30 feet wide with a 3-foot concrete sidewalk, concrete curbs, storm sewers and are paved with asphalt paving. Each site has underground utility connections. The stream which drains the site is part of site's "open recreational space" and has paved walks, benches, ponds, a softball baseball field and is an attractive amenity. Park management requires one type of aluminum skirting on each mobile home. Spaces are clean, well-tended, with tow hitches under trailers or masked with plantings. Condition of this five-year-old park is good, with streets in good condition, garbage collection areas clean and open areas well-maintained. There are only seven vacant spaces but these have already been rented and are awaiting setup of mobile homes.

VALUATION—Market data—No recent sales of similar properties found. Rents for similar mobile spaces in the country range from $90 to $120. Average recent cost of building a mobile home park has increased because of scarcity of allowable sites, building restrictions and inflation to about $5,000 per space plus raw land cost. The Cost approach, however, has not been used because it is not pertinent. The Income approach has been utilized to determine value.

INCOME APPROACH—The following fair gross rent has been obtained from contacting all similar parks in the area. Their rentals have been adjusted for features of the subject. Vacancy rate is a low 5% because of strong demand and few available spaces in area.

Gross annual rental income (300 × $110/mo.) $396,000
Other income (laundry, vending, setups)............. 16,900
    Gross Income (rounded) $413,000
EXPENSES (rounded)
       Vacancy ....$ 21,000
       Management and labor.............. 24,000

Utility charges		31,000
Cleaning and supplies		3,000
Grounds maintenance		2,000
Repairs and maintenance		6,000
Taxes		67,000
Advertising		4,000
Reserves for replacement		11,000
Insurance		8,000
	Total	$177,000

Net Income (gross less expense)......................$236,000

A capitalization rate of 14% has been built up using Band of Investment technique. First Mortgage of 65% @ 10% interest equals 6.5%; owner's equity 35% @ 10% equals 3.5%; 25-year life equals 4% depreciation (straight line) for a total capitalization rate of 14.0%.

Thus $236,000 \div 14\% = \$1,686,000$.

In my opinion, therefore, value for the subject property derived by the Income approach based on market data analysis of comparable rent schedules as of _____ is ($1,686,000) ONE MILLION SIX HUNDRED EIGHTY SIX THOUSAND DOLLARS.

Date _____ John Appraiser _____

A MODEL MOBILE HOME APPRAISAL REPORT

The following Mobile Home Appraisal Report is an actual report which was completed as a VA assignment. All identifying information has been deleted and the second page of the report which contains contingent certification, date and signature, is omitted. Note that blue book retail book value is requested on the form (item 5G) but that the reasonable value is estimated (item 15) from the Market approach:

Form Approved
OMB No. 76–S74005

VETERANS ADMINISTRATION
MOBILE HOME APPRAISAL REPORT

1. NAME AND ADDRESS OF PERSON OR FIRM MAKING REQUEST	2. LOAN NUMBER
Michael A.	LHM

3. LOCATION OF MOBILE HOME	4. IF PRESENTLY FINANCED WITH VA LOAN, SHOW LOAN NUMBER AND LOCATION OF LOAN FILE
Sunset Knolls Mobile Home Park Town of	None

5A. YEAR	5B. MANUFACTURER (Include make)	5C. MODEL NUMBER	5D. SERIAL NUMBER	5E. LENGTH	5G. RETAIL BOOK VALUE
197_	_____Homes, Inc.			70	not found
				5F. WIDTH 12	5H. NAME OF BOOK Blue Book

6. CONDITION OF UNIT AND COST OF REPAIRS

DESCRIPTION	CONDITION	COST OF REPAIRS	DESCRIPTION	CONDITION	COST OF REPAIRS	DESCRIPTION	CONDITION	COST OF REPAIRS
TIRES	Good	None	REFRIGERATOR	Good	None	DOORS	Good	None
HITCH	"	"	STOVE	"	"	PAINT	"	"
OUTSIDE PANELING	Fair	"	KITCHEN SINK	"	"	SUBFLOOR	"	"
WINDOWS	Good	"	CABINETS	"	"	GARBAGE DISPOSAL	None	"
ROOF	"	"	HOTWATER HEATER	"	"	DRYER	None	"
FLOOR	"	"	FURNACE	"	"	DISHWASHER	None	"
WALLS AND CEILING	"	"	BATHROOM	"	"	AUTOMATIC WASHER	Good	"
COUCH AND CHAIRS	"	"	BATHROOM FIXTURES	"	"	AIR CONDITIONER	None	"
DRAPES	"	"	CARPETING	"	"	EVAPORATIVE COOLER	None	"
DINETTE SET	"	"	BEDS	"	"	GARBAGE COMPACTOR	None	"

7. ADDITIONAL EQUIPMENT (Condition and description of any repairs and repair cost.) (If additional space necessary, use Item 18, "Remarks".)

All furnishings including B/W Zenith 19" TV, oil tank, stereo, kitchen equipment including toaster, silverware and additional sets of curtains bedding and sheets are included.

Condition is almost new with some very minor handling dents in outside panelling.

(ATTACH PHOTOGRAPHS HERE— 2 VIEWS)

8. TOTAL COST OF REPAIRS	9. MEETS MPR'S	10. THIS MOBILE HOME HAS:
$ None	[X] YES [ ] NO	[X] EMERGENCY EGRESS FROM SLEEPING ROOMS [X] TWO EXIT DOORS REMOTE FROM EACH OTHER [X] SMOKE DETECTION DEVICE

11. MOBILE HOME WAS MANUFACTURED FOR USE IN THIS GEOGRAPHIC AREA	12. OCCUPANCY DATA
[ ] YES [ ] NO [X] UNABLE TO ASCERTAIN (If "NO", indicate area)	2 B.R., Den, K., L.R. Bth

13. COMPARABLE SALES (List three)

LOCATION OF UNIT	DATE OF SALE	NEW	USED	YR., MAKE AND MODEL	PRICE	SIZE	CONDT.	EQUIP.	TERMS	IND. VALUE OF SUBJ.
Sunset Knolls Mobile Home Pk	8/20/-		X	197- Double wide Dunhill	$ 8700	24 x 56	Good	None	Conv	$ 8750
" " "	8/11/-		X	197- Sunrise	$ 6000	12 x 65	G	None	Conv	$ 8750
" " "	7/17-	X		197- Olympian	$ 10600	14 x 65	G	None	C	$ 8750

14. I ESTIMATE "REASONABLE VALUE" (Do Not complete for liquidation appraisal, complete Items 16 and 17)	15. ESTIMATED REASONABLE VALUE
[X] "AS IS" [ ] "AS REPAIRED"	$ 8750

VA FORM **26-8712**

540684

Figure 13.1

MODEL MOBILE HOME APPRAISAL REPORT FORM

Chapter 14

Techniques and procedures for appraising condominiums, cooperatives and planned unit developments

This chapter deals with appraising condominiums, cooperatives and planned unit developments (PUD's). It sketches the 2,500 years of history which led up to the appearance of condominiums on the U.S. housing scene. The "condo's" increasing share of the housing market today is evaluated. There is a detailed, step-by-step appraisal checklist on horizontal, low-rise and high-rise condominiums as well as techniques for reviewing master deeds. There is also an item-by-item comparison section covering condominiums, cooperatives, planned unit developments and cluster developments. For specific how-to-do-it appraisal purposes, there is a Model Condominium Appraisal Report of a horizontal condominium unit and an excellent Department of Housing and Urban Development Glossary of condominium special words.

HOW CONDOMINIUMS CAME TO THE U.S. HOUSING SCENE

Condominiums are everywhere in the U.S. now. They came here via Babylon, where a second floor apartment deed was first recorded in 434 B.C.

The Roman Senate, over 2,000 years ago, enacted a law permitting Romans to own individual units in multi-unit buildings. Puerto Rico in 1951 passed the first U.S. condominium law. The U.S. Housing Act of 1961, Section 234, extended government mortgage insurance to condominiums.

All of the states now have their own differing condominium laws. A recently nationally recommended model Uniform Condominium Law will probably be enacted soon by most states. This should simplify condominium processing and appraising in this fast-spreading ancient legal development solution of our modern problem of land scarcity.

THE "CONDO" MARKET TODAY

To appraise a condominium today and in the future, you have to first appreciate its pluses, minuses and trends. Condominium is a Latin word meaning joint ownership or control. When applied to housing, it means individual ownership with unrestricted right to disposal of one's unit in a multi-unit project. The land and all other parts of the project are held in common with owners of the other units. The unit owner can take income tax deductions for taxes and mortgage interest the same as in conventional housing because his unit can be individually mortgaged. Other advantages in successful projects include less expensive carrying costs and maintenance costs. Disadvantages include high legal costs for structuring the condominium documents, inexperienced, under-financed developers and often too much, too expensive common recreational facilities constructed for too few actual sales.

Yet, despite this comparatively complicated legal structure and some history of unsuccessful projects, the long-term condominium trend is definitely up. By the late seventies, 5% of all single-family units in the U.S. were being sold as condominiums. This percentage appears bound to increase as land continues to become scarcer and more expensive in urban-suburban areas. Housing forecasters predict that 50% of the U.S. population will live in some form of condominium housing by the year 2,000.

Condominiums are an increasingly popular method of satisfying the universal desire for home ownership. It is also providing a sophisticated means of using scarce land and air space in metropolitan areas to extend home ownership to many who could not otherwise afford it.

HOW TO REVIEW MASTER DEEDS AND APPRAISE
LOW-RISE, HIGH-RISE AND HORIZONTAL CONDOMINIUMS

When you appraise condominiums, you can be involved in a marvelous variety of construction. The "condo" is only a form of ownership. It can be in a high-rise building (over six stories), a low-rise, an attached townhouse, or even a detached single unit building. The condominium owner pays taxes and in return gets tax deductions. He also contributes to upkeep of common areas, hallways, grounds, streets and to amenities like pools, tennis courts, etc. Condo residential projects may consist of high-rises, groups of low-rises, groups of attached or detached single units (''horizontal'') or in combination. Condos can also be office buildings, medical buildings, industrial buildings, shopping centers standing alone or in combination with housing projects. Condos can be newly structured or can be conversions of existing buildings, like conversions of rental apartment buildings to luxury condominiums. High-rise and low-rise condos have other individual ownerships above and/or below individual units while horizontal units like condo townhouses do not. In all types of condominiums, the land below the structure is owned in common by all owners as one part of the common elements.

The basic difference which distinguishes condominiums from fee simple ownership is the deed. A conventional property deed on an improved property owned in fee simple describes the plot in two dimensions, length and width, all around its boundaries and includes all improvements within these described boundaries. A condominium Master Deed also describes the land in two dimensions, but then goes on to describe the building(s) and others on the land in three dimensions including depth/height. This ''air space'' or volume type of deed description can best be visualized by considering, say, a two-bedroom living unit in a low-rise six-story condominium. This unit's deed description would start at one corner of the entry foyer floor, describe the distances and directions around the floor of the entire living unit (beneath the paint film and floor finish), come back to the same entry foyer corner, then go *up* that corner to the ceiling, go all around the ceilings back to the same beginning point to encompass and describe the legal ownership of that two-bedroom condominium unit. The owner of the unit would get only a short deed, identifying his unit by a designated number and referring to the Master Deed which is recorded and filed legally with local authorities. The Master Deed also describes the common elements which all unit owners share in ownership and in maintenance charges, including streets, utilities, recreational amenities, parking, lights, grounds, building structure (outside of each unit's paint films and floor finishes, generally) and building foundations, basements and roofs.

FEASIBILITY-APPRAISAL CHECKLIST

A feasibility and/or appraisal checklist for a new or existing condominium should generally include the following step-by-step procedures:

*Step 1—Inspect Site and Location—*Inspect and review for location, access to transportation and arterial road facilities, market characteristics, construction, site coverage, light, air and view. Is the plan functional in terms of access by car and by walks to project units and common elements including recreational facilities? On existing properties, check for owner-tenant ratio (i.e., tenant occupancy versus owner occupancy). A high tenant occupancy usually means a poor sales market.

Step 2—Analyze Master Deed and By-Laws—On existing project, review the Declaration in the Master Deed and By-Laws, on new proposed projects review the Prospectus for number of units and project information on rights, conditions and limitations. The review should include the following:

(a) Is there adequate safeguard against developer having "locked" the condominium into long-term agreements or self-serving covenants?

(b) Does the language prevent unnecessary control by developer over an extended period of time by the legal language or by developer retaining ownership of 51% or more of units?

(c) Does the language preempt powers of the unit owner's Board of Directors and delegate these powers to professional management companies without possibility of change by the majority of owners?

(d) Is there unrestricted resale right by unit owners or is there a "right of first refusal" given to the Association? Are any restrictions against leasing of units limited to periods of less than six months?

(e) Are by-laws, use restrictions and rules of conduct not dictatorial and on the same basis for all unit owners? Do by-laws contain the right for owners to petition for changes in the government of the condominium?

Step 3—Inspect and Analyze Competitive Projects—Complete a market analysis, including inspection and review of competitive projects. This analysis should include community and local data on schools, utilities, services, transportation, roads, jobs, shopping, parks and churches. Competitive projects are reviewed for housing demand, sales activity and price ranges. This special review on competitive condominium projects should also include comparison data on location, type and quality of construction and of common elements including amenity facilities.

Step 4—Analyze the Project on a Staged Basis—Determine whether the subject condominium building is part of a phased project and if so, note the stage. Review carefully the ratio of units built, sold and occupied compared to the common elements provided and built for such stage. For example, in an existing condo, are the amenities, such as tennis courts, in or promised?

Step 5—Check Whether Ownership Interests Are Fair—Check the Master

Deed or Prospectus for the percentage of ownership interest schedule. These schedules typically calculate the unit owner's interest in common elements based on the value of his unit or on the square foot area of his unit compared to the total net salable area of all units. Thus, if all units are similar, then one unit would have a fair $1/100$ ownership interest in a 100-unit project. Or if there are various types of units, then one unit's value of square feet can be measured against total project value of square feet to derive equitable ownership interests.

Step 6—Check Whether Parking Is Adequate—Is there adequate owner plus guest parking? Is parking convenient?

Step 7—Check if Commercial or Other Interests—Check if commercial or industrial condominium unit ownership interests are also involved and if they are harmonious with the residential interests.

Step 8—Analyze Budget—Analyze budget including adequacy of reserves for maintenance and replacement of common elements. On existing condominiums, your inspection of the grounds, roads, public halls, recreational amenities, building exteriors and other common elements should indicate whether the budget is adequately funding maintenance and replacement. On both proposed and existing projects, your market analysis of comparable projects and their budget assessments, should also confirm whether there is adequate operating budget and reserves in the project under appraisal.

Step 9—Analyze Monthly Assessment—Analyze monthly assessments. On proposed projects, has the assessment charge, as usual, been under-estimated? On existing projects, is the assessment adequate to cover maintenance and reserves?

Step 10—Inspect for Any Required Repairs—Inspect for and list any repairs needed in condominium common elements of project and/or in the individual unit being appraised.

Step 11—Review Organizational Documents—On existing projects, review recent meeting minutes of Council of Co-Owners, the current financial statement and the condominium budget. If monthly assessment and reserve is too low compared to current prevailing market conditions, estimate a "fair" monthly condominium assessment.

Step 12—Write the Condominium Narrative Summary—Summarize data collection from Steps 1 through 11.

Step 13—Complete the Appraisal Report—The Market approach to value should be used for all residential condominium projects. If your report is being done for VA or FHA, their instructions require that Cost and Income approaches to value shall also be used for horizontal condominum resale units. As with other types of residential ownership appraisals, however, the Market approach even on these government forms should be the main approach to value. Your appraisal report on an existing condominium unit should be based mainly upon comparable sales of other units within the same building or project, provided they are resales by individuals rather than the builder-developer. Comparable sales from other projects should be carefully analyzed, if used. As always, comparables should be recent, arms-length, have comparable rights and responsibilities and comparable location, square footage and exposure in the structure or project along with other appropriate elements. (See model condominium narrative summary, photographs and appraisal report in final section of this chapter.)

HOW TO DISTINGUISH CONDOMINIUMS FROM COOPERATIVES, PUDS FROM CLUSTER DEVELOPMENTS

Your day-to-day appraising will be increasingly concerned with condominiums as this form of ownership takes its increasing share from conventional fee simple ownership of real estate. There is also the cooperative form of housing ownership. Cooperatives have some similarity to condominiums but they must be clearly distinguished for purposes of type of ownership and appraisal. Also important for proper appraisal is a clear understanding of the modern planning concepts of planned unit development (PUD) and cluster development.

The cooperative means cooperative or joint operation of a housing development by those who live in it. In a cooperative, the cooperative corporation owns all the property including the individual units. A member of a cooperative does not directly own his dwelling unit. He owns a membership stock certificate in the cooperative corporation. This certificate also entitles him to exclusively occupy his individual unit and to help operate the cooperative corporation as a Board member or voter. The corporation not only holds title to the whole property but it also pays the mortgage payments, taxes and other obligations to finance and operate the development. Each member pays his proportionate share of the annual budget. Each member is entitled to his proportionate share of the real estate taxes and mortgage interest paid by the corporation for his personal income tax statement. If a member wants to leave the cooperative, he sells his membership certificate (not his unit) in accordance with value and rules set forth in the cooperative corporation By-Laws.

The fundamental difference between a cooperative and a condominium is that a cooperative corporation owns everything and a condominium association owns nothing. A condominium owner owns his individual estate (or unit) and an individual interest in the common estate (or common elements). An owner of an individual condo unit pays his own mortgage and taxes as well as his monthly assessment for common element costs. The condo owner can sell or lease his unit directly, sometimes having to give first refusal to purchase for a limited time to the Condominium Council representing the other owners.

A planned unit development (PUD) differs from a Condominium and cooperative in that PUD homeowners own the land on which their dwelling is situated and belong to a Homeowner Association which holds the common lands and other recreational facilities of their PUD project. This is in contrast to condos where the unit owner holds title to the air space of his units plus an undivided interest in the land under his unit as well as in the other common lands and improvements in the project. PUDs allow mixtures of all types of zoning so that different varieties of housing can be combined with commercial, office buildings, shopping and even industrial buildings. Whole new neighborhoods have been created by the use of PUDs. In their largest forms, PUDs become new towns.

A cluster Development is another modern concept which evolved to cope with vanishing open space and urban sprawl. Most zoning codes today include clustering which generally means putting the same number of housing units permitted by the zoning on smaller lots. This results in surplus land which can be left as open space or improved with recreational facilities. To planners, clustering generally means attached units. To communities not yet ready for attached units, clustering means detached houses on smaller lots. In all cases, a cluster development means cost savings for the developer, for the buyers and for later public maintenance since streets and utilities are shortened. These comparatively modern, sophisticated concepts, whether singly or in combination, as in PUDs, are making dramatic changes in the real estate market and creating new interesting appraisal assignments. An appraisal checklist for an existing PUD unit, for example, should include the following special steps:

Step 1—Review recorded covenants, conditions and restrictions to be certain that there is mandatory homeowners association membership with a required periodic assessment to support the common areas owned by the Homeowners Association. Such common areas usually include one or more of the following: swimming pools, tennis courts, bridal path, bike trails, community building, ball diamonds, private street, green-belt areas and other possible common areas.

Step 2—Review articles of incorporation of the PUD Home Association, as in Step 1.

Step 3—Review Association By-Laws, as in Step 1.

Step 4—Review the deed which conveys common lands to the Association.

Step 5—Review the recorded map.

Step 6—Inspect the common area to determine that all common improvements are finished.

Step 7—Determine that common areas and amenities to be owned by homeowners association are free and clear of liens, or if in an existing PUD, that such clear conveyance has been made.

Step 8—Review assessment for adequacy of funding maintenance and replacement of common areas and amenities.

MODEL CONDO NARRATIVE SUMMARY AND APPRAISAL REPORT

The following is a model narrative summary and VA report form of an actual recently completed condominium appraisal report. Identifying data has been omitted. On the completed VA form, note particularly condominium data in Item 13 on easements, Item 15 on condominium certification, Item 17H on reserves and Item 21 on square foot rate, which includes proportionate share of common element replacement costs:

CONDOMINIUM APPRAISAL
NARRATIVE SUMMARY REPORT

_____ Drive, Spring Valley, N.Y.
Unit No. _____ of The
_____ Condominium Group 1

V.A. No. _____

The project is located in the Village of Spring Valley, N.Y. in the county of Rockland at the intersection of _____ Blvd. and _____ Turnpike. Rockland County is 33 miles north of N.Y.C. along the Hudson River with a population of approximately 235,000. Spring Valley is a comparatively densely developed portion of the county with regional shopping 3 miles from the project and local shopping within ¼ mile. Schools, libraries, parks, hospitals and all community facilities are convenient within 4 miles. Village of Spring Valley police and volunteer fire protection cover this area. There is bus commuter service to N.Y.C. and major arterial N.Y.S. Thruway access is 2 miles from the project.

Twenty-eight buildings and 206 horizontal, two-story (and basement) condominium "townhouse" units are shown on the attached plot plan by _____, with 186 units, one- and two-bedroom types, built and occupied. Occupancy percentage is 85%. This Group 1 comprises 14.7 acres with land gently rolling and improved with private roads, curbs, sidewalks, landscaping, street lights, Spring Valley sewer and water. There is a recreation area with pool, tennis courts, paddle ball, handball, basketball, clubhouse, with title remaining in developer but available to unit owners for $100 yearly fee. This recreational area will also serve the rest of the 44 acres and approximately 1,000 total units (including the 206 in Group 1) if and when constructed. The recreational facilities appear adequate.

Parking for 331 cars; a 1½ + to 1 ratio appears adequate considering that parking is also permitted on _____Drive, a public road which splits the project. Assessment fee is $54 per month and covers water charges, road and snow maintenance, landscaping maintenance, garbage removal, exterior building maintenance. Although the project appears to be in a well-maintained condition since its inception five years ago, analysis of its operating budget shows no provision for reserve. A "fair" market condominium assessment fee should be $70 instead of its current $54 per month. Two similar condo projects in Rockland County are _____ in Suffern with a $75 monthly charge and _____ in New City with a $65 charge for similar common elements. The subject project appears to be efficiently managed with grass cut, streets clean and building exteriors being painted on a regular schedule.

Light, air, views are good, with the rolling terrain and some existing tree stands adding amenities. The project layout is good for circulation, traffic collection and has convenient parking. Percentages of interest in common elements are based on square feet of units and appear fair.

Real estate market in Rockland County has been slow during the past two years. However, in this $38,000 to $48,000 price range and particularly in this development during the past six months, there has been increased activity with good demand for two-bedroom units.

The rights, conditions and limitations of the Master Deed and By-Laws of the condominium have been reviewed for effect upon Reasonable Value and have been considered in the Estimated Reasonable Value on the following Form 26-1803, V.A. Appraisal Report.

_____   _____
        Dated   Samuel T. Barash
                                              Appraiser

VETERANS ADMINISTRATION
RESIDENTIAL APPRAISAL REPORT

CASE NUMBER: 0000000

1. MAJOR STRUCTURES	A. TYPICAL COND.	B. BUILT-UP	C. AGE TYPE BLDG.	D. OWN OCCUP.	E. VACANCY	F. ZONING	G. LAND USE CHGS.	2. PROP-ERTY IS	3. BLDG. WARRANTY IN FORCE?
NEIGHBORHOOD	GOOD	30 %	1 TO 10	80 %	0 %	MULTIPLE RESID.	STABLE	☒ OCCU-PIED □ VACANT	□ YES ☒ NO □ UNKNOWN
BLOCK	GOOD	100 %	5	95 %	0 %	11	STABLE		

4. STATUS OF PROPERTY
☒ A. PROPOSED □ B. PREVIOUSLY OCCUPIED □ C. EXISTING, NOT PREVIOUSLY OCCUPIED □ D. ALTERATIONS, IMPROVEMTS. OR REPAIRS

5. CONSTRUCTION COMPLETED BEFORE DATE HEREOF
□ A. WITHIN 12 CALENDAR MOS. ☒ B. MORE THAN 12 CALENDAR MOS.

□ E. REFINANCING - VETERAN AP-PLICANT OWNS AND OCCUPIES RESIDENCE AS HOME

6. NAME AND ADDRESS OF FIRM OR PERSON MAKING REQUEST (Complete mailing address. Include ZIP Code)
MORTGAGE CORP.
___ ST.
___, N.Y.

7. PROPERTY ADDRESS (Include ZIP Code)
___ DRIVE
SPRING VALLEY, N.Y.
(UNIT NO. ___, HEIGHTS CONDO)

8. TYPE OF PROPERTY
☒ HOME □ MOBILE HOME LOT

9. MANDATORY HOME ASSOCIA-TION MEMBER-SHIP?
☒ YES □ NO

10A. NO. BLDGS. 1
10B. NO. LIVING UNITS 1

11. LOT DIMENSIONS

12. DESCRIPTION				SPLIT LEVEL	7	NO. ROOMS	I	DINING ROOM		CAR GARAGE		GAS		CEN. AIR COND.
DETACHED	☒	WOOD SIDING	CINDER BLOCK	% BASEMENT	100	BEDROOMS	2	KITCHEN	I	CAR CARPORT		UNDERGRD. WIRE		TYPE HEAT. & FUEL
SEMI-DET.		WOOD SHINGLE	STONE	SLAB		BATHS	1	FAMILY RM.	I	WATER (Public)	☒	SEWER (Public)	☒	GWA
ROW		ALUM. SIDING	BRICK & BLOCK	CRAWL SPACE		1/2 BATHS	2	RECREATION UTILITY RM.	I	WATER (Comm.)		SEWER (Comm.)		ROOFING DESCRIP.
CONDOMINIUM	☒	ASB. SHINGLE	STUCCO	YRS. EST. AGE	5	LIVING RM.	I	FIREPLACE		WATER (Ind.)		SEPTIC TANK		A/S
		BRICK VENEER	STORIES	2										

13. LEGAL DESCRIPTION
UNIT ___ OF HEIGHTS CONDOMINIUM

14. TITLE LIMITATIONS, INCLUDING EASEMENTS, RESTRIC-TIONS, ENCROACHMENTS, HOMEOWNERS ASSOCIATION AND SPECIAL ASSESSMENTS, ETC.
DEEDED EASEMENTS TO USE IN COMMON WITH ALL OTHER UNIT OWNERS - TO USE ALL UTILITIES - TO CONTINUE ALL NECESSARY ENCROACHMENT OF HIS UNIT ON ANY OTHER - EASEMENTS BY BOARD OF MANAGERS FOR MAINTENANCE PURPOSES

15. OFFSITE IMPROVEMENTS
A. STREET SURFACE: BT
B. STREET ACCESS □ PRIV. ☒ PUB. CONDOMINIUM
C. STREET MAINT. □ PRIV. ☒ PUB. CONDOMINIUM

D. ADD'L. IMPROVEMENTS
☒ STORM SEWER
☒ SIDEWALK
☒ CURB/GUTTER

16. REPAIRS NECESSARY TO MAKE PROPERTY CONFORM TO APPLIC. MPR'S $

17. REMARKS (Complete A through F. Use supplemental sheet or reverse, if necessary.)

A. DETRIMENTAL INFLUENCES: NONE INCLUDING AIRPORTS

B. REAL ESTATE MARKET IN COMMUNITY: ACTIVE RECENTLY THIS PRICE RANGE

C. HIGHEST AND BEST USE: RESIDENCE PRESENT USE

D. FEDERAL FLOOD HAZARD MAP ISSUED? ☒ YES □ NO (If "Yes," complete item 17E)
E. PROP. IN SPECIAL FLOOD HAZARD AREA? □ YES ☒ NO

F. EXPLAIN DEPRECIATION: PHYSICAL-AGE, NORMAL WEAR & TEAR (NOMINAL-5 YRS OLD)

I HEREBY CERTIFY THAT THE INFORMATION CONTAINED IN THE PLANS, SPEC AND CONDOMINIUM ORGANIZATIONAL DOCU-MENTS HAS BEEN REVIEWED AND ALL CONDOMINIUM ELEMENTS HAVE BEEN REVIEWED TO ARRIVE AT THE ESTIMATE OF REASONABLE VALUE IN THIS APPRAISAL REPORT.

TOTAL ESTIMATED COST OF REPAIRS $ 0

18. MARKET DATA

ITEM	SUBJECT PROPERTY	COMPARABLE NO. 1		COMPARABLE NO. 2		COMPARABLE NO. 3	
ADDRESS		UNIT ___, ___ DRIVE		UNIT ___, ___ DRIVE		UNIT ___, ___ PLACE	
SALE PRICE		$ 37,000		$ 45,000		$ 46,000	
TYPE OF FINANCING		CONVENTIONAL		CONV.		CONV.	
		DESCRIPTION	ADJ.	DESCRIPTION	ADJ.	DESCRIPTION	ADJ.
DATE OF SALE		9/1/—	$	7/15/—	$	9/1/—	$
					$ -1,000		$ -1,000

236

VA FORM 26-1803

VA CONDOMINIUM UNIT APPRAISAL REPORT FORM

Figure 14.1

LOCATION				
SITE IMPROVEMENT	Good	Good	Good	Good - Adjacent Block
AGE/CONDITION	5 Good	5 Good	5 Good	5 Fair -3000
GARAGE/CARPORT	None	None	None	None
CONSTRUCTION	Frame	FR	FR	FR
PORCHES, POOL, ETC.	Condo Amenities	Same	Same	Same
	Semi-Att Open Porch	Row	Sem Att Open Porch	Sem Att Open Porch

Model B-S / Model B-S / Model B4 / Model D-S

ROOM COUNT/SIZE:

ROOMS	BDRMS	BATH	S.F. AREA	ROOMS	BDRMS	BATH	S.F. AREA	ROOMS	BDRMS	BATH	S.F. AREA	ROOMS	BDRMS	BATH	S.F. AREA
7	2	2	1244	6	1	1½	1100	7	2	2	1244	7	2	2	1244

NET ADJUSTMENT (Show (+) or (−) adjustment): +3000 / +1000 +6500 / +2500 +3000 / −1000 / −3000

INDICATED VALUE OF SUBJECT PROPERTY: $43000 / $43500 / $44000 / $43000

19. PROPERTY SHOWS EVIDENCE OF (Check)
☐ TERMITE ☐ DRY ROT ☐ DAMP-NESS ☐ SETTLE-MENT

20. ESTATE (Check)
☒ A. FEE SIMPLE ☐ B. LEASE-HOLD ☒ NO EVIDENCE

21. REMAINING ECONOMIC LIFE (Years) MAIN 40 OTHER

23. DATA

DESCRIPTION	CONDITION
ROOF	A/S	G
FOUND.	P.C.	G
BSMT.	Full	G
FLOORS	H/W	G
INT. WALLS	Drywalls	G
BATH FINISH	Ceramic	G
GUTTERS	Alum	G

24. EQUIP.

DESCRIPTION	DEPR. VALUE
Hotpoint Refrig-Syns	$100
" Washer	75
" D/w	100
" Dryer	75
Caloric Range 5 Yrs	75
TOTAL	$425

25. OTHER IMPROVEMENTS

DESCRIPTION	DEPR. VALUE
Finished Bsmt Rec Rm	$1500
Storms/Screens (Alum)	200
✱ Item 22 Rate Per Ft	
Includes Percentage Share of Cost of Common Elements	
TOTAL	$1700

22. COST APPROACH

MAIN 1244	CU.	SQ. OTHER
RATE PER FT.	$ ✱ 34	
REPLMT. COST	$42300	
PHYSICAL DEP.	$1200	
FUNCTIONAL	$	
ECONOMIC	$	
TOTAL DEP.	$1200	
DEPR. COST	$41100	
TOTAL DEPR. COST OF IMPR.	$41100	
OTHER IMPR. AND EQUIP.	$2125	
LAND VALUE (Condo)	$ −	
TOTAL DEPR. COST OF PROP.	$43200	

26. ANNUAL TAXES
GENERAL $1472 SPECIAL $ OTHER $

27. DOES PROPERTY CONFORM TO APPLICABLE MINIMUM PROPERTY REQUIREMENTS? ☒ YES ☐ NO (If "No" explain on reverse)

28. ESTIMATE FAIR MONTHLY RENT TIMES RENT MULTIPLIER (If applicable) Not Applicable × $ = $

29. RECONCILIATION

A. MARKET APPROACH	B. COST APPROACH	C. INCOME APPROACH (If applicable)
$43000	$43200	$ N. A.

30. I ESTIMATE "REASONABLE VALUE" ☒ "AS IS" ☐ "AS REPAIRED" ☐ "AS COMPLETED" $

31. ESTIMATED REASONABLE VALUE $43000

32. SIGNATURE OF APPRAISER Samuel T. Beach

33. DATE SIGNED

NOTE: No determination of reasonable value may be made unless a completed appraisal report is received (38 U.S.C. 1810). I HEREBY CERTIFY that (a) I have carefully viewed the property described in this report, INSIDE AND OUTSIDE, so far as it has been completed; that (b) it is the same property that is identified by description in my appraisal assignment; that (c) I HAVE NOT RECEIVED, HAVE NO AGREEMENT TO RECEIVE, NOR WILL I ACCEPT FROM ANY PARTY ANY GRATUITY ANY GRATUITY OR EMOLUMENT OTHER THAN MY APPRAISAL FEE FOR MAKING THIS APPRAISAL; that (d) I have no interest, present or prospective, in the applicant, seller, property, or mortgage; that (e) in arriving at the estimated reasonable value I have not been influenced in any manner whatsoever by the race, color, religion, national origin, or sex of any person residing in the property or in the neighborhood wherein it is located. I understand that violation of this certification can result in removal from the fee appraiser's roster.

VA FILE COPY 5

Figure 14.2

PHOTO OF CONDOMINIUM UNIT

Figure 14.3
PHOTO OF CONDOMINIUM AMENITIES

CONDOMINIUM GLOSSARY

The following HUD glossary (HUD-365-H(4) of special words is specific to condominiums and should help you appraise in this rapidly growing real estate field.

Figure 14.4

GLOSSARY OF CONDOMINIUM SPECIAL WORDS

ABSTRACT—A summary of the history of the legal title to a piece of property.

AMORTIZATION—Provision for gradually paying off the principal amount of a loan, such as a mortgage loan, at the time of each payment of interest. For example, as each payment toward principal is made, the mortgage amount is reduced or amortized by that amount.

APPRAISAL—An evaluation of the property to determine its value. An appraisal is concerned chiefly with market value—what the unit would sell for in the market place.

ASSESSMENT (Operating)—Proportionate share of the budgeted annual cost to maintain physically the common areas and elements of a condominium and to maintain sufficient reserves to assure financial stability. The annual assessment is reduced to monthly charges payable to the Association of owners.

ASSESSMENT (Special)—An assessment for some special purpose or because of inadequate budgeting of operating expenses.

CAVEAT—A warning or notice to take heed such as a clause in a document which is meant to be a warning.

CERTIFICATE OF TITLE—Like a car title, this is the paper that signifies ownership of a unit. It usually contains a legal description of the unit and its relationship to the condominium.

CLOSING COSTS—Cost in addition to the price of a unit and its undivided interest in the common estate including mortgage service charge, title search, insurance and transfer of ownership charges paid each time the unit is resold or refinanced.

CLOSING DAY—The date on which the title for property passes from the seller to the buyer and/or the date on which the borrower signs the mortgage.

COMMON AREA OR COMMON ESTATE—Generally, this encompasses all of a condominium which is not specifically delineated and described as dwelling or commercial units.

COMMON OR UNDIVIDED INTEREST—Joint ownership with other fee owners of all land and areas within the structures that are not described as individually owned units. The interest is defined by a percentage of a total area but not actually divided into individual parts.

CONDOMINIUM ASSOCIATION, ASSOCIATION OF OWNERS, CONDOMINIUM ASSOCIATION BOARD OF DIRECTORS, OR COUNCIL OF CO-OWNERS—The governing body of a condominium, elected by and from among the owners upon conveyance of titles to the individual owners by the Grantor. Its authority to operate comes from the Declaration. It must operate within the framework of the Bylaws.

CONDOMINIUM REGIME—The mode of self-rule established when condominium documents are recorded. The term also refers to all the documents necessary to legally constitute a condominium and to permit it to operate as such.

CONVEY—To transfer title from one person to another.

COVENANT—A promise usually in the form of a recorded agreement when used as a part of the language of real estate.

COOPERATIVE HOUSING—A housing corporation or a group of dwellings owned by residents and operated for the benefit of resident members of the corporation by their elected Board of Directors. The resident occupies but does not own his unit. Rather, he owns a share of stock or membership certificate in the total enterprise.

DECLARATION—A document which contains conditions, covenants and restrictions governing the sale, ownership, use and disposition of a property within the framework of applicable State condominium laws.

DEED—A document used to transfer a fee simple interest in the unit together with an undivided interest in the common estate in the case of condominium title transfers.

DELINEATE—To describe the physical boundaries of a dwelling unit in a condominium.

DEPRECIATION—A decline in the value of a dwelling unit as the result of wear and tear, adverse changes in the neighborhood and its patterns, or for any other reason.

EASEMENT RIGHTS—A right of way granted to a person or company authorizing access to or over the owner's land. Water, sewer and electric companies often have easement rights across private property.

EASEMENT—A right or privilege a person or group of people may have in property owned by one or more other persons.

ENCUMBRANCE—A claim or lien attached to real property, such as a mortgage or unsatisfied debt incurred with respect to the property.

EQUITY—Increase in value of ownership interest in the unit as the owner reduces his debt by paying off his mortgage, and from market value appreciation.

ERNEST MONEY OR SUBSCRIPTION MONEY—The deposit money given to the seller by the potential buyer to show that he is serious about buying the dwelling. If the deal goes through, the earnest money is applied against the downpayment. If the deal does not go through, through no fault of the seller, it may be forfeited.

ESCROW FUNDS—Subscription or downpayments required to be held unused, until the condominium regime is recorded on the property and titles are conveyed to each buyer. Escrows are usually used in each resale situation. The deed is held in escrow until all conditions of the sale (including any prepayments) have been met. Other escrow accounts are used to accumulate monthly tax and insurance payments until the taxes and insurance are actually due.

GRANTOR—The owner of the property which is being subdivided into a multiple number of individual unit estates under a condominium regime.

LATENT DEFECT BOND—One type is an assurance required by HUD-FHA that defects due to faulty materials and workmanship, which are found within a year of the date of completion, will be corrected.

LEASEHOLD INTEREST—The right to use a property under certain conditions which does not carry with it the rights of ownership.

LIABILITY AND HAZARD INSURANCE—Insurance to protect against negligent actions of the Association of owners and damages caused to property by fire, windstorm and other common hazards.

LIEN—A claim recorded against a property as security for payment of a just debt.

MORTGAGE COMMITMENT—The written notice from the bank or other lender saying that it will advance the mortgage funds in a specified amount to enable one to buy the unit.

MORTGAGE DISCOUNT "POINTS"—Discounts (points) are a one-time charge assessed by a lending institution to increase the yield from the mortgage loan to a competitive position with the yield from other types of investments.

MORTGAGE INSURANCE PREMIUM—The payment made by a borrower to the lender for transmittal to HUD-FHA to help defray the cost of the FHA mortgage insurance program and provide a reserve fund to protect lenders against loss in insured mortgage transactions. In the case of an FHA insured mortgage this represents an annual rate of one-half of one percent paid by the mortgagor on a monthly basis to FHA. Non-government mortgage insurance companies have a similar premium.

MORTGAGE LOAN (INDIVIDUAL UNITS)—The amount loaned by the lender (mortgagee) to the individual owner (mortgagor) necessary to purchase the unit.

MORTGAGE LOAN (PROJECT)—Provides money to the builder/developer to acquire the land and construct the condominium. This loan should be paid off in full by the cash and individual mortgage loans that come into existence when all sales have been consummated. At such time the condominium individual units must be free and clear of all liens and all individual unit mortgages must be first mortgages assumed by owners of the units.

MORTGAGE LOAN (HUD-FHA INSURED)—The lender is insured by HUD-FHA against default by the mortgagor to induce the lender to lend a larger sum to the purchaser. The loan limits are established by HUD-FHA.

MORTGAGOR—The homeowner who applies for, receives and is obligated to repay a mortgage loan on a property he has purchased.

MORTGAGEE—The bank or lender who loans the money to the mortgagor.

PLAT AND PLANS—Drawings used by surveyors and architects to show the exact location of utilities, streets, buildings and units within the buildings, in relation to the boundary lines of the total property. They may also show units, common areas and restricted areas.

PREPAID EXPENSES—The initial deposit at time of closing, for taxes and the subsequent monthly deposits made to the lender for that purpose. Hazard insurance is not a mortgage payment under the individual unit mortgage.

REPAIR AND MAINTENANCE—The costs incurred in replacing damaged items or maintaining housing systems to prevent damage. In a condominium the owner is responsible for repairing and maintaining the dwelling unit and the condominium Association is responsible for repairing and maintaining the common areas. The owner only pays his proportionate share of the cost to the Association.

RESERVE FUNDS (REPLACEMENT)—Funds which are set aside in escrow from monthly payments to replace common elements, such as roofs, at some future date.

RESERVE FUNDS (GENERAL OPERATING)—Funds which are accumulated on a monthly basis to provide a cushion of capital to be used when and if a contingency arises.

STATUTE—A law passed by a legislative body and set forth in a formal document, for example the Horizontal Property Act of Puerto Rico.

TAXES—Local real estate assessments which are levied on the individual units and not on the condominium Association.

TITLE—The evidence of a person's legal right to possession of property, normally in the form of a deed.

TITLE COMPANY—A company that specializes in insuring title to property.

TITLE INSURANCE—Special insurance which usually protects lenders against loss of their interest in property due to unforeseen occurrences that might be traced to legal flaws in previous ownerships. An owner can protect his interest by purchasing separate coverage. A mortgagee's policy, as distinguished from an owner's policy, usually protects only the lender in an amount equal to the outstanding balance of the mortgage loan.

TITLE SEARCH OR EXAMINATION—A check of the title records, generally at the local courthouse, to make sure you are buying the dwelling from the legal owner and that there are no liens, overdue special assessments, other claims, outstanding restrictive covenants or other defects in title filed in the record.

UNDIVIDED INTEREST—In condominium law, the joint ownership of common areas in which the individual percentages are known but are not applied to separate the areas physically. This situation is similar to the joint ownership of an automobile or home by husband and wife.

UNIT VALUE RATIO—A percentage developed by dividing the appraised value of a unit by the total value of all units. The percentage attaches to the dwelling unit and determines the percentage of value of the common estate attached to that unit, the percentage of votes the owner of the unit has in the government of the common estate, and the percentage of operating costs of the common area the respective unit owner must bear.

Chapter 15

How to make real property assessment appraisals and assessment appeals

This chapter examines the real property tax system, analyzing all its archaic ways and the differing assessment methods used by our local taxing authorities. The tax system's ever-increasing affect on our shelter cost and economy is also detailed. I also describe here how assessments and tax bills are determined and how property is appraised for assessment purposes.

Because of the nature of the system and the many taxing jurisdictions with different assessment laws, procedures and assessors, many properties are assessed unfairly, not equally and too high.

Keeping in mind the rebellious attitude of many property taxpayers, there are also several important sections on how the aggrieved property owner or his appraiser makes and files an assessment appeal, how he checks for correctness of assessor's public record property cards, how formal assessment appeals are filed and how grievance hearings and assessment court suits are handled. A sample Assessment Record Card is exhibited together with a Model Review of Assessor's Records as well as a Model Appraisal Report for Market Value filed to appeal a too high assessment.

HOW THE REAL PROPERTY TAX SYSTEM WORKS

In the 4th Century, B.C., Athens levied taxes on land, houses and slaves. Colonial America taxed real and personal property. Most property taxes are now on real estate rather than on personalty.

The property tax is critical to local school and governmental finances. Theoretically, the property tax is not only necessary to pay for community services but equitable in that it taxes those whose wealth in property makes demand for such services.

However, as set up, staffed and administered, the property tax system is often inequitable. Tax districts, city, county, school district, sewer, water, etc., number in the tens of thousands in this country and rarely assess similarly when properties in neighboring districts are compared. A third of our states require that properties be assessed at 100% of market value, yet practically all of these many thousands of taxing districts assess at fractions of full market value ranging generally from ½% to less than 50%, usually because of poor administration, poor current market data, poor politics and untrained, often over-burdened personnel. Not only do inequities abound between districts but often even between classes of properties in the same district. Commercial-industrial properties are often under-assessed deliberately in one community compared to residential properties and vice-versa in another community, depending on many factors. Desire for certain types of "ratables" and sometimes pure politics—the desire to get re-elected—are many times more influential than market value and equity. There are taxpayer furors now over tax "exemptions" given to religious and educational properties. Agricultural and forest land, special reduced assessment districts, further reduce total ratables in many localities.

As inflation has increased real estate values drastically, so have assessments and resultant taxes soared to a point where taxpayers are rebelling and limiting their taxes and services as in California's "Proposition 13." In 28 states, "circuit-breaker" or "homestead" legislation has had to be enacted to provide relief to homeowners through a system of tax credits and rebates when property tax payments exceed a certain percentage of family income.

To work within the archaic assessment taxing system, you must understand its basically simple theory. Real property, usually on a certain day each year, is legally and tentatively assessed along with all other property in the district, then placed on a legal assessment "roll" by the legally appointed or elected assessor, ordinarily at some fraction of current market value. From this roll, taxes are collected by dividing the total dollar amount the district needs to spend by the total dollar amount of the assessment roll. The resulting "tax rate" is then used to multiply each property assessment for total taxes to be collected.

WHAT THE ASSESSOR DOES

The assessment process in this country, once mainly political and still always responsible to the electorate, is becoming more professionalized and in many localities computerized. The elected or appointed assessor, who still has full unsupervised authority to set assessments in most localities, generally receives information and copies of deeds on all sales in his district. He maintains and updates public record files on each property based usually on a percentage of current market value. He delivers his assessment roll for publication by the legal date in his locality each year and is responsible for at least the initial receipt and processing of all appeals on his assessment.

Court decisions in California, New Jersey and New York have struck down lower court rulings that permitted assessors to assess at a percentage of market value and to utilize construction costs rather than market value. In California and New Jersey, courts have also held that state systems of financing schools with property taxes which give better localities better schools are illegal under their state constitutions. These decisions are already affecting assessment procedures and school financing in these states and in other areas also. However, tax assessment is still mainly a "Balkanized" field and complete detailed knowledge of local practice is the key for successful tax appeals.

HOW ASSESSORS ASSESS PROPERTIES

Most assessors, once elected or appointed in most states, get very little guidance from their state capitols. This makes for a rather high degree of individuality in assessment practices and assessments and for a low degree of uniformity and comparability. This is apparent even in two such populous states as New Jersey and New York. New Jersey has a Real Property Appraisal Manual which is based mainly on charts of square foot costs requiring regular updating. New York issued a Manual in 1957 but has not kept it current. In 1970, New York began to compile a new Assessors Handbook which has still not been completed. Most other states have similar legal requirements for assessors but very little guidance to ensure uniformity. Most states use equalization techniques to level out inequities between localities. These equalization ratios are derived by statistically comparing selling prices of properties (or current appraisals if there are no sales) with assessed values of these sold properties. The resultant ratio is then applied by locality as an adjustment factor.

The assessor works mainly alone in this difficult field, beset by irate taxpayer-voters, and must constantly attempt to keep his many properties current for each annual tax roll. He suffers many times from inaccuracies in prior public record descriptions of property improvements and is generally unable legally to enter premises to verify inaccuracies or later improvements. He can, like appraisers, "count" tax stamps on recorded deeds to secure selling prices but he, like appraisers, must verify each sale for it to have value meaning. Many times, with his mass of data and deadlines, this is not possible.

Assessment revaluations throughout a district are done by the assessor, or more usually, ordered from private appraisal companies. This is often necessary because of aforementioned court decisions requiring 100% market valuation. Sometimes re-evaluation is done because politically it is not usually wise to raise tax rates and excite inevitable voter reaction.

HOW TO APPRAISE MARKET VALUE FOR ASSESSMENT PURPOSES

The aggrieved property owner or his appraiser must start first by checking the public records in the assessor's office. Later sections in this chapter will give step-by-step procedures for this review. Here however, we assume that the aggrieved property owner is not satisfied with written and verbal assessment explanations and hires you to give him a report on the value of his property for assessment appeal purposes.

Simply, you generally use the Market Data approach for this type of assessment appeal appraisal to arrive at your opinion of current market value. Fortunately, the chaotic "Balkanized" nature of assessment procedures with assessors setting fractions of market value generally on properties is not your problem. If it is residential or vacant land, get your comparable sales, your "best comparable" if possible, and give your best opinion of value. If it's industrial or commercial and you don't have a good sales market of similar comparables, arrive at your best opinion of value through the income approach. But unless you're working with, say, a newly built property, don't use the cost approach as your primary path to value simply because the assessor did.

HOW TO MAKE AND FILE AN ASSESSMENT APPRAISAL

When the property owner hires you to appraise his property for assessment appeal purposes, your techniques for securing current market value do not differ materially from nonassessment appraisals, but the environment you will appraise in differs markedly. First step, go to the assessor's office and ask to see the assessment record on your property. It is a public record and open to you. Second step, check the card thoroughly for errors in description. Third step, since the assessment value is usually based on the Cost approach, check all computations for correct arithmetic. Fourth step, review the public record cards for as many similar properties as you can identify to see if you can determine assessment inequities as they apply to your property. Perhaps such a review and its results will convince the assessor to adjust your assessment without proceeding to more formal written appraisals and appeals.

If the appraisal must be filed with an appeal, determine the proper appeal agency (states differ), get the right grievance date and secure all data on the method of filing the formal appeal.

HOW TO CHECK FOR CORRECTNESS OF ASSESSOR'S PUBLIC RECORDS

The model appraisal review of a sample Michigan Assessment card in a later section of this chapter is really an example of what is usually the first step in the assessment appeal process. Assessor's records, the record card, any related assessment information on the property being appealed as well as any assessor's data on other properties in the district are open to public review. If incorrect data is found on the assessor's record card (and I have found new perfect assessment cards), take the matter up with the assessor. At this stage, you are dealing with public facts on record, not opinions. If there are errors of fact, the assessor has the authority to correct these errors and change values at this preliminary stage of the assessment appeal process, when he later prepares his tax roll.

The next review step involves checking the local tax rate. This rate of assessment is important and refers to the percentage of the full market value of the subject property at which it is assessed. In order to determine the rate of assessment, divide the market value of the property into the assessed value. If the resultant rate is, say, 50% and is more than the average rate of assessment for other similar properties or for the district, there is a complaint of inequity. Securing lists of properties which have sold and comparing them to their assessed values, can be time-consuming but may be worthwhile. In New York, court decisions permit use of the state equalization rate in assessment suits. Reviewing the assessments of similar unsold properties can be a good method to determine inequity, if not value.

HOW TO FILE FORMAL ASSESSMENT APPEALS

Most localities in most states have complaint forms for aggrieved property owner taxpayers. Some states are more cooperative than others. Oregon is very informative; it even puts appeal instructions on a cartoon form, perhaps to make the pill less bitter. In all states, generally, this form must be secured and completed properly and submitted on or before the deadline grievance date or dates, for it to affect the proposed assessment if relief is granted. The following

GENERAL INFORMATION AND FILING REQUIREMENTS
FOR COMPLAINTS ON REAL PROPERTY ASSESSMENTS

Who may complain? Any person aggrieved by an assessment (i.e. an owner, purchaser or tenant who is required to pay the taxes pursuant to a lease or written agreement) may file a complaint (a written statement under oath). He may complete the complaint himself, or his representative or attorney may complete it for him.

What assessment can be reviewed? The only assessment that can be reviewed is the assessment on the current assessment roll tentatively completed by the local assessor. The right to a review is based on a timely filing of a written verified complaint. A separate complaint must be filed for each separately assessed parcel.

When and where must complaint be filed? The complaint must be filed in the assessing unit in which the property is located (i.e. city, town or village) with the assessor on or before grievance day or with the board of review on grievance day. If property is located in a village, a complaint must be filed with the town assessor (or board of review) or the village assessor, or both, if the complainant wishes his complaint reviewed by both.

When is grievance day? In most towns, grievance day is the third Tuesday of June, except that in towns in the County of Erie, it is the first Tuesday of August; in towns in the County of Monroe, it is the second Tuesday of July; and in towns in the County of Suffolk, it is the third Tuesday of July. In Nassau County which has county assessment, grievance day for towns is the third Tuesday in May. In Tompkins County, which has county assessment, grievance day for towns is the third Tuesday in June. In cities, grievance day must be ascertained from specific charter provisions and the assessor's or the city clerk's office should be contacted. Most villages conduct grievance day on the third Tuesday of February but since there are some that do not, the village clerk should be consulted.

Grievance Day Procedure

1. Your verified statement, plus any supporting statements, records, and other relevant information may be used to support your complaint.

2. You may appear personally, with or without your attorney or other representative, to support the statements contained in the complaint and attachments.

3. You may have your attorney or other representative appear personally without you to support the complaint.

4. You may mail your complaint for review, but it must be received by the board of review no later than grievance day. Although mailing your complaint is the least desirable procedure, you should do so if you or your representative cannot appear personally. The failure to file your complaint on time closes off your right for court review.

5. The board may require you or your representative to appear personally, or to submit additional evidence. If you willfully refuse or neglect to do so, or to answer any material question put to you, you probably will be unable to obtain any reduction in assessment from the board of review.

6. Determinations of the board. The board may determine the final assessment to be the same as, or higher, or lower than the original assessment. However, the board cannot reduce your assessment to an amount lower than you claimed on your complaint. If you are not satisfied with the determination of the board of review, your next step is to seek a court review.

INSTRUCTIONS FOR COMPLETING THE COMPLAINT

Grounds for complaint. There is a presumption under the law that the assessment made by the assessor is correct. The burden of proof is with you, the complainant, to overcome this presumption. To obtain a correction of your assessment, you must show that the original assessment is erroneous by reason of inequality, erroneous by reason of overvaluation, or illegal. No other grounds can be allowed.

1. **Erroneous assessment** - by reason of inequality.

a. If you believe your property is assessed at a higher percentage of full value than the average of all other properties on the same assessment roll, you may claim an erroneous assessment by reason of inequality.

2. **Erroneous assessment** - by reason of overvaluation.

a. If you believe the assessed value of your property is greater than the market value of the property, you may claim an erroneous assessment by reason of overvaluation.

b. To establish the market value of your property, you should supply the kind of information set forth in 1 (c) above.

3. **Partial exemptions.** If your application for an exemption has been denied, you may claim an erroneous assessment by reason of inequality or overvaluation.

4. **Illegal assessment** - where the assessor has no authority to assess the property.

Figure 15.1

COMPLAINT FORM ON FILING REAL
PROPERTY ASSESSMENT APPEALS

For example, if you prove the market value of your property is $20,000, an assessment of $15,000 would show that it is assessed at 75 percent of market value. If you show that all other property on the average is assessed at 50% (i.e. by using the state equalization rate for the assessing unit), you can claim a reduction of your assessment to $10,000.

b. You must show the market value of your property in order to develop the percentage of market value represented by the assessment. Then you must show that this percentage is higher than the average percentage at which all other properties are assessed.

c. To establish the market value of your property, the following information would be useful:

1. Purchase price of the property, if recent.
2. Offering price of your property, if recently offered for sale.
3. Professional appraisal of your property.
4. Cost of construction if recently built.
5. Rental information, if property is rented.
6. Income and expense information, if property is commercial or industrial.
7. Purchase price of comparable property recently sold.

d. To establish the average percentage of full value at which property is assessed on the assessment roll, the following information would be useful:

1. The latest state equalization rate for your assessing unit (county, city, town or village). Equalization rate data is available for inspection at the offices of the State Board of Equalization and Assessment in Albany, or copies may be obtained for a small fee.
2. Market values and assessments on a sample of other properties on the roll.
3. Statements of the assessor or other local official.

a. Property totally exempt. Certain real property of certain organizations and agencies is totally exempt from real property taxation (for example, churches, colleges, etc.). If your claim is that the assessment is illegal because the property should be totally exempt, you should supply the board of review with information upon which they may make their judgments. (NOTE: If your claim relates to a **partial** exemption such as a veteran's or aged exemption, the assessment is not illegal, but erroneous denial of your application for exemption may constitute an erroneous assessment; see item 3 above).

b. Property outside the assessing unit. If your property is physically located totally outside the boundaries of the assessing unit, the assessment on this property is illegal. You must produce facts showing that no part of the property in question was physically located within the assessing unit on taxable status day.

c. Property cannot be identified from description. If you think your property cannot be located from the description on the assessment roll, your assessment may be illegal.

Amount of reduction on complaint is limited by amount claimed. The amount by which you believe your assessment should be reduced cannot later be changed after you enter this amount on the complaint and file it. For example, if you claim an erroneous assessment by reason of overvaluation and seek a reduction of $2,000, you cannot in any later action claim some larger amount than the $2,000 as the reduction sought.

Further, the board cannot grant a greater reduction than the amount you request, even if circumstances should show that a larger reduction is warranted.

Penalty for false statements: A person making false statements on a complaint is guilty of an offense punishable by law.

Figure 15.1 (Cont'd.)

New York State form EA 38-a (4-72)200000 "General Information and Filing Requirement for Complaints on Real Property Assessments" (Figure 15.1) is a typical appeal form with good explanations and instructions.

Property owners are not your only assessment appraisal clients. Communities who must defend taxpayer's assessment law suits in court also hire appraisers to complete written reports and testify in court.

HOW TO APPEAR AND TESTIFY AT GRIEVANCE HEARINGS IN ASSESSMENT COURT SUITS

Any person affected by an assessment—an owner, a purchaser, a tenant required to pay taxes pursuant to a lease, an attorney or representative appraiser—may appear before the Grievance Assessment Review Board.

Be well-prepared and ready to show the Board all the information you

Michigan Department of Treasury
L-4188

STATE TAX COMMISSION
RESIDENTIAL

Appraisal Record Card

COUNTY _____
Township _____
Village _____
City _____

DATE OF TRANSFER	GRANTEE'S NAME	ADDRESS	REVENUE STAMP	VERIFICATION SALE PR.	MAP NO.	BOOK NO.	PAGE NO.	PARCEL CODE NO.

Property Address _____ St. Ave.

Building or Alteration Permit   Date   Amount $

DESCRIPTION AND LAND SKETCH

Sec. _____ T. _____ R. _____

IMPROVEMENTS

LAND

Dirt — Level
Gravel — Rolling
Paved — Low
Curb — High
Sidewalk — Landscaped
Water — Swamp
Sewer
Electric
Gas

LAND VALUE PLUS IMPROVEMENTS COMPUTATION

LOT SIZE	DEPTH FACTOR	EQUIVALENT FRONTAGE	RATE	TRUE CASH VALUE
			$	$

LAND IMPROVEMENT   VALUE NEW   % COND.

Well
Septic System
Paved Drive
Fence
Landscaping

TOTAL LAND PLUS IMPROVEMENTS $
TOTAL BUILDINGS $
TOTAL TRUE CASH VALUE $

Person Interviewed _____
Examined by _____ Date _____

PROPERTY TYPE

Residential	Acreage
Resort	Platted
Suburban	Improved
	Vacant

YEAR	ASSESSED VALUATION	BOARD OF REVIEW	TAX COMMISSION
	$	$	$

Figure 15.2
MICHIGAN
ASSESSMENT RECORD CARD

PLAN

4. Interior

Type			
Single Family	Trim & Decoration:	Flab.	Ord.	Min.
	No. Inside Window Trim		
Frame	Size of Closets:		
Wood	Large	Ord.	Small
	Number of Closets:		
Year Built:	Many	Ord.	Few
	Drywall		
	Plaster		
Year Remod.	Paneled Wainscot		
	Hardware Qual.		

Number Rooms		5. & 6. Floor & Ceilings	
Basement		Foyer Fl.	
1st Floor		Kit Fl.	
2nd Floor		Other Fl.	
Baths		Coved Ceilings	
Total Bedrooms		
	Plaster	Drywall

Insulation		7, 8, 9. Foundation & Basement	
Ceiling		Crawl Space	s.f.
Entire		Slab House	s.f.
None		Basement	s.f.
	Height to Joists	ft.

1. Exterior		
Wood	Concrete Block	
Aluminum	Concrete Walls	
Brick	Asphalt Tile	s.f.
Block	Recreation Room	s.f.

10. Floor Support		
Joists	x	o.c.
Unsupported Length		ft.
Sill Plate:	Yes	No
Diag. Sub-Floor	x	
Ply. Sub-Floor	x	
Center Support		

2. Windows		
Many	Few	
Large	Small	
Wood Sash		
Metal Sash		
Double Hung		
Hor. Sliding		
Double Glass		
Storms & Scr.		

11. Heating & Air Conditioning

Gas - Forced Warm Air	
Oil - Forced Warm Air	
Gas	Oil	Coal
Wall Fur.	Floor Fur.	
Stove or Space Heat	
Steam Radiators	
Forced Warm Water	
AIR CONDITIONER	tons

3. Roof		12. Electric
Hip	Amps Service	
Gable	No. & Qual. Elec. Fixtures:	
Front Overhang	Ex.	Ord.	Min.
Other Overhang	No. Electric Outlets:	
Eavestrough	Many	Ord.	Few

Chimney Type		
Brick	Block	
Stone	Metal	
Asphalt Shingles		

13. Plumbing $

No. of Baths	
Cer. Tile Walls	
Cer. Tile Floor	
Plastic Tile Walls	
Extra Stool	
Extra Wash Bowl	
Water Heater:	Gals.	Gas	Elec.
	Well	Septic Tank

14. (see front of record card)

15. Built-In Items $

Open	Range
Disposal	
Hood & Fan	
Dishwasher	
Refrigerator	
Incinerator	
Water Softener	
Fireplace	
Vanities	
Cupboard Length	
Cupboard Quality	

16. Porches		
Wide	Deep	Type

17. Garage		
Year Built		
Attached		Separate
Cars		Condition
Wide		Deep
Walls		
Floor		
Doors		
Common Wall		
Other Walls		
Ceiling		

Priced by	
Date	
Checked By	
Date	

CLASS

Typical Classes of Other Houses in this Neighborhood

Neighborhood is ☐ Improving ☐ Stable ☐ Declining

Condition for Age

Effective Age

ITEM OR NO. STORIES	SQUARE FEET	UNIT COST	BASE VALUE	DEPR. & OBSOL. % GOOD	DEPR. VALUE
		$	$		$

Total Depr. Value $ _____

COST MOD. ____ x ____ E.C.F. ____ %

True Cash Value $ _____

Figure 15.2 (Cont'd.)

have. Bring not only your written appraisal report but also the results of your review of the assessor's public records, including, if possible, a sufficient list of similar properties which are assessed lower than subject. If there is inequitable assessment because the equalization rate has not been adhered to properly on the subject assessment, bring this data also.

If the appeal is rejected, the property owner must determine whether to go to court. This legal expense must be related to the amount which can be saved. Generally, only large land tracts, multiple dwellings or commercial-industrial property owners can afford this last-resort procedure. It is most important for the property owner or his representative to make certain that the suit is filed by the required legal filing date after rejection by the Grievance Assessment Review Board. This date varies widely because of the many counties and localities within the states.

You should also review Chapter 21 on how to testify in court as an expert witness if you are called either by the taxpayer or by the locality in an assessment court suit. Principals, procedures and your court demeanor are the same as in any other court testimony.

A MODEL APPRAISAL REVIEW OF A SAMPLE MICHIGAN RESIDENTIAL ASSESSMENT RECORD CARD

The following card (Figure 15.2) is used in Michigan and is a good example of assessor's public record cards on property.

If you have been hired by the taxpayer, review this important record carefully:

1. Does the card have land description which compares properly with the deed description?
2. Are the land computations correct?
3. Does the property actually have paved streets and sidewalks as shown?
4. Has the property declined from the "improving" neighborhood rating shown?
5. Are all depreciating on-site and off-site influences included and are calculations correct?
6. Are the building improvements described correctly?
7. Is building measured correctly?
8. Is square foot computation correct?
9. Age? Specifications? Grade and quality of improvements correct?

Review carefully. You may save your client time and money at this beginning point.

A MODEL APPRAISAL REPORT FOR MARKET VALUE

Recently I completed the following appraisal report which has had certain title, cover exhibits and other identifying data omitted and has been condensed. I later testified as an expert witness before the court-appointed Referee on the assessment suit. A substantial reduction in assessment and taxes resulted.

MODEL APPRAISAL REPORT

I am a real estate appraiser, residing at Lakes Road, Walton, N.Y. and I am fully acquainted with the subject land and its environs. My professional qualifications are detailed in the attached exhibit.

I have reviewed the survey of the lands of _____, Town of _____, done by _____, L.S. on Dec. 8, 19____. I have considered the later northeasterly assemblage of 8.745 acres on 9-20-____ as well as the sale-deletion of 6.2 northerly acres from the original tract, making a current total holding by _____ and h/w _____, of 84.26549 acres improved with a one-family old farmhouse in fair to poor condition and dilapidated barn and outbuilding. I have reviewed sales of properties similarly situated and have considered existing usages, topography, zoning, location, highest and best use and all factors affecting value. The land is being zoned to R-80 Residential (one-family—min. 80,000 sq. ft.) (Exhibit D Location Map).

The property has poor both-side access from a one-lane, poorly surfaced road, aptly named Hardscrabble Rd., located between _____ and _____. The topography is pocketed with approximately 30% low meadow subject to flooding and ponding, and the balance is steep slate outcrop according to personal inspection and according to the attached surveyor's report by _____ dated _____, Exhibit B, which I have also reviewed. The access, topographic and subsoil limitations completely bar the property's highest and best use development for residential purposes and severely limit its permitted zoned use for large-scale horse farm value. It has no value for dairy farming topographically, because of its marginal, non-productive soils, and within the current economic milieu. The land currently is being used to stable three riding horses by the owner; the old farmhouse is tenanted, in structurally poor condition. A valuation grid analysis, Exhibit C, details my investigation of comparable sales.

My opinion of value is SIXTY-SEVEN THOUSAND FIVE HUNDRED DOLLARS ($67,500), including $21,000 ascribed to the tenant house, $1,100 to the dilapidated barn with the land valued @ $550 per acre.

Date _____

Samuel T. Barash
Real Estate Appraiser

Chapter 16

How to do

condemnation appraisals

This chapter deals with condemnation appraisals of properties being acquired for public purposes. It covers the background, definitions and modern trends of such special condemnation concepts as "just compensation," "cost to cure," "fair market value," "before and after appraisals," "full and partial takings," "damages to remainder" and "highest and best use." Most federal agencies follow "Uniform Appraisal Standards for Federal Land Acquisitions." Step-by-step appraisal procedures and a copy of these guideline federal standards for written appraisal reports are therefore included in this chapter. There is an important section on how to appraise aerial, utility, scenic and other easement and leasehold interests which are taken for public use. Indian lawsuits are covered here as they relate to appraisals and land titles. A step-by-step appraisal procedure and a graphic illustration of riparian rights are also included. There is an important section on appraising properties affected by fast-spreading, controversial, ultra-high-voltage electric transmission lines. Finally, for a practical workaday guide in this very special appraisal field, there is a Modern Condemnation Report.

CONDEMNATION APPRAISAL BACKGROUND,
CONCEPTS AND TRENDS

In the 1600's, a Dutch jurist, Grotius, formulated the concept of "eminent domain." He declared that the property of subjects is under the eminent domain of the state. When the state acts to use such property for public use, it is bound to make good the private loss. Our Constitution's Fifth Amendment required that "just compensation" be given for private property taken for public use. Various condemnation concepts continued to develop in the 19th Century in reaction to ruthless right-of-way acquisition practices by railroads. By 1880, most states had passed laws defining that any special benefits caused by the proposed R.O.W.'s could not be offset for value purposes against the portion of property taken. The Heilbron case at the turn of the century, (Sacramento Southern Railroad Company v. Heilbron, 1906, 159 Cal. 408) on appeal, defined "just compensation." It declared, "The highest price estimated in terms of money which the land would bring if exposed for sale in the open market with reasonable time allowed in which to find a purchaser, buying with knowledge of all the uses and purposes to which it was adapted and for which it was capable."

Other basic acquisition concepts continued to evolve. "Before and after" acquisition appraisals, generally with two separate sets of comparables, became necessary because two separate appraisals had to be done on condemnation appraisals to be able to appraise the value of the portion of property being taken. The terms, "full and partial takings" were used to describe various types of condemnation acquisitions. Often a "partial" taking became a "full taking" even though not initially needed for the public improvement. "Remainder parcels" landlocked by partial takings were often subsequently purchased to avoid condemnation litigation on "severance damages" to remainder. The term "cost to cure" became the appraisal concept and tool used to estimate value when an existing structure or other improvement had to be modified by the taking agency or by owner because of a partial taking. The term "flowage" came into condemnation legal and appraisal use to cover acquisitions involving flooding of lands for dams and other water-related projects. Some states required "full compensation" in excess of "just compensation" by legislating that condemnors pay for all losses by owner. "Right-of-way" condemnations involving "changes in road grade," in most states permitted payment only to those owners who had some portion of their property actually taken.

"Highest and best use" became critically important in condemnation appraising of "partial takings," "flowage," "clearance" for urban renewal or on other types of acquired easements because the very fact of the taking often changed the highest and best use and value of what was left.

Public bodies and quasi-public agencies like utility companies supplanted railroads as main condemnors. Roads, including the Interstate Highways, clearance for renewal in the cities and high voltage lines for energy distribution overlaid our land mainly during the second half of this century. Proper appraisals became extremely important because these agencies which were doing the takings, generally used their R.O.W. appraisals to set maximum amounts for payment for property taken. Often, these agencies had policies of offering 25% or less of these maximum appraisal figures when they negotiated with property owners. Many times owners, particularly homeowners, took these lower offers because they were unable to afford the long delays and legal-appraisal costs which are not compensable. This special appraisal field of condemnation which has been so dependent on the courts for its background, concepts and definitions is still evolving, through law, a new and apparently more liberal approach in this latter quarter of the 20th Century. Public and quasi-public R.O.W. employees have historically pictured themselves often as adversary to the property owner in appraisal reviews and negotiation as well as in condemnation litigation. Laws in many states and in federal land acquisition appraisal practice are beginning to identify these public employees as representatives of the people, required to represent the public but also to represent the affected owner to see that he receives the highest price the property would command in the open market. This trend appears to be strengthening even unto a number of states now requiring compensation for business dislocation damages and good will, better notice to condemnees, small claims procedures adopted in smaller takings to avoid legal costs, homeowner relocation costs and sometimes even tenant relocation costs and damages.

The "corridor concept" of one R.O.W. corridor for multiple highway, utility and other public use is beginning to be utilized in overall public condemnation planning to avoid often conflicting and multiple community and private dislocation. Recent environmental protection legislation requires that the environmental effect of a public improvement be considered through impact studies covering radiation, air, water, solid waste, pesticides and noise pollution.

The market price revealed by appraisers' comparable studies reveals only the cost to the buyer. After years of extraordinary condemnation expansion, legislation appears to be recognizing that the cost to the public in many condemnations, may be far greater.

STEP-BY-STEP APPRAISAL PROCEDURES ON FEDERAL
LAND ACQUISITIONS

The booklet, "Uniform Appraisal Standards for Federal Land Acquisitions," was issued by the U.S. government in the mid-seventies and is used as an appraisal guideline by most federal agencies when they acquire property for U.S. purposes. These standards resulted from an interagency land acquisition conference whose purpose was to set standards of fairness and efficiency in condemnation which would be a model for state as well as federal practice. Many government agencies like the U.S. Army Engineers contract to hire independent appraisers. The following step-by-step appraisal procedure is a working outline for appraising in federal land acquisitions. It can also be used as a good general guide for local, non-federal condemnation appraisals when supplemented by contact with attorneys involved for advice on condemnation law in the subject state.

STEP 1—Confer with counsel—Whenever the property to be appraised may be involved in an eminent domain proceeding, you should confer with your client's lawyer for guidance on the laws affecting the valuation.

STEP 2—Review Federal Controls and Collect Data—

(2a) The criterion for just compensation is the fair market value of the property, generally as of the time of the taking. A specific dollar amount opinion, not an estimate range, is required. The Supreme Court has ruled that the "market price" which arises from the "haggling of the market is being sought," not any special values for sentimental, family or other special value associated with the property.

(2b) Highest and best use for the property should be considered, not remote or speculative uses. Normally, existing use in most appraisals represents the highest and best use because of existing economic pressures. However, supply and demand, competitive properties, use conformity, size of the land, existing or possible improvements, zoning, deed restrictions, vicinity trends must all be considered.

(2c) Prior sales of the same property, reasonably recent and not forced, are the best evidence ("best comparable") of market value.

(2d) All sales of the subject property in the last 10 years should be included.

(2e) The Comparable approach is the best approach to value. When there are adequate sales, there should be very little consideration of other approaches. Cost is recognized as the least reliable approach. The Income approach which can only be used on some investment type properties should not even be used then when there are reasonable sales of similar properties. In capitalizing income for value, only income which the property itself will produce is considered, not income from the business conducted on the property.

(2f) When comparing sales to subject property, the basic rating elements are time, motivation, location and similarity of highest and best use as well as physical and economic aspects. Market value at time of taking, not enhancement of value because of the taking, is the rule. However, federal law, unlike most states which have varying legislation on this question, requires that the amount of the benefit, if any, affecting the remainder parcel because of the public project, must be dedicated or "set off." This is set off not only against the "severance damage" on the remainder parcel but also against the entire award of just compensation. For example, there can be no federal award where a project has caused the remainder to become more valuable than the original parcel because of say, lake frontage, frontage on a better road, more convenient access or to become a prime commercial site. (Most states differ here in that these benefits can be offset against remainder damages, not against the taking parcel.)

(2g) Under federal law, unlike most states, compensation is paid for "takings" not "damages." Thus, the federal "severance damage" rule allows only such loss in value to the remaining land as may be due to the particular land taken. It does not include damages resulting from the use of adjoining land taken from other persons. For example, when an airfield is expanded and flights over a property are so low as to affect its enjoyment and diminish its value, the appraiser cannot use noise, vibration and lights affecting other properties not subject to the easement as justification to ascribe consequential damages to the subject property.

(2h) The "before-and-after method" is the preferred appraisal method of determining compensation in partial takings. First, estimate the market value of the entire unit, then subtract the market value of what remains. The difference is compensation, including both value of the land taken and any diminution of value in the remainder. "Severance damages" as such is not separately appraised nor awarded.

(2i) The "unit rule" is important in federal condemnation. First, this unit rule requires that property be valued initially as a whole rather than by its various lessor, lessee, etc. interests. Secondly, different elements of a tract of land are not to be separately valued and added together.

(2j) Offers to purchase a property made by the government during negotiation may not be used as appraisal documentation for later condemnation litigation.

(2k) Prices paid by condemnor for similar properties will not be accepted as appraisal comparables by most federal courts.

STEP 3—Secure and Review the Legal Description—It is most important that you obtain an accurate legal description of the property rights to be appraised and that these exact rights be appraised. This description should be verified in the field by personal inspection and by comparison with surveys, official local maps and with available recorded legal descriptions. Descriptions may not always contain reference to easements or other exceptions. You may have to get this information from interviews, inspection of the property, abstracts of title, insurance policies or other related documents.

STEP 4—Reviewing the zoning—Zoning is an important factor in evaluating property and zoning restrictions must be reviewed and recited in the appraisal report. For example, a more profitable (higher and better) use of the property than the use at the time of the taking can be considered if it is allowed by zoning.

STEP 5—Write the Report—Whether appraising for federal agencies or for condemnees, you should prepare the text of the appraisal report using the guidance contained in the following four-part appraisal report model taken from the booklet, "Uniform Appraisal Standards for Federal Land Acquisitions." As stated in prior sections, the Market approach is the best approach in federal condemnation appraisals. Many states give rights of "discovery" in condemnation cases which means that your appraisal reports will usually be secured in advance of trial by opponents and that your comparables, arithmetic and all other data will be fine-combed.

For this and all other reasons in condemnation appraising, you have to always be competent, unbiased and never an advocate. Your comparables cannot be chosen to make a higher or lower case. Try to please everyone, especially your client and you wind up later in condemnation court in adversary process, displeasing everyone including the judge and your client.

B–1. *Contents of appraisal report:* The text of the appraisal report shall be divided into four parts as outlined below:

Part I—Introduction

1. *TITLE PAGE*. This shall include *(a)* the name and street address of the property, *(b)* the name of the individual making the report, and *(c)* the effective date of the appraisal.

2. *TABLE OF CONTENTS*.

3. *LETTER OF TRANSMITTAL*.

4. *PHOTOGRAPHS*. Pictures shall show at least the front elevation of the major improvements, plus any unusual features. There should also be views of the abutting properties on either side and that property directly opposite. When a large number of buildings are involved, including duplicates, one picture may be used for each type. Views of the best comparables should be included whenever possible. Except for the overall view, photographs may be bound as pages facing the discussion or description which the photographs concern.[109] All graphic material shall include captions.

5. *STATEMENT OF LIMITING CONDITIONS AND ASSUMPTIONS*.

6. *REFERENCES*. If preferred, may be shown with applicable approach.

Part II—Factual Data

7. *PURPOSE OF THE APPRAISAL*. This shall include the reason for the appraisal, and a definition of all values required, and property rights appraised.

8. *LEGAL DESCRIPTION*. This description shall be so complete as to properly identify the property appraised. If lengthy, it should be referenced and included in Part IV. If furnished by the Government and would require lengthy reproduction, incorporate by reference only.

9. *AREA, CITY AND NEIGHBORHOOD DATA*. This data (mostly social and economic) should be kept to a minimum and should include only such information as directly affects the appraised property together with the appraiser's conclusions as to significant trends.

10. *PROPERTY DATA:*

a. Site. Describe the soil, topography, mineral deposits, easements, etc. A statement must be made concerning the existence or nonexistence of mineral deposits having a commercial value. In case of a partial taking, discuss access both before and after to remaining tract. Also discuss the detrimental and hazardous factors inherent in the location of the property.[110]

b. Improvements. This description may be by narrative or schedule form and shall include dimensions, cubic and/or square foot measurements, and where appropriate, a statement of the method of measurement used in determining rentable areas such as full floor, multitenancy, etc.

c. Equipment. This shall be described by narrative or schedule form and shall include all items of equipment, including a statement of the type and purpose of the equipment and its state of cannibalization. The current physical condition and relative use and obsolescence shall be stated for each item or group appraised, and, whenever applicable, the repair or replacement requirements to bring the property to usable condition.

Any related personalty or equipment, such as tenant trade fixtures, which are not attached or considered part of the realty, shall be separately inventoried. Where applicable, these detachable or individually owned items shall be separately valued.

d. History. State briefly the purpose for which the improvements were designed, dates of original construction and major renovation and/or additions; include, *for privately owned property*, a ten-year record as to each parcel, of all sales and, if possible, offers to buy or sell, and recent lease(s); if no sale in the past ten years, include a report of the last sale.

e. Assessed value and annual tax load. Include the current assessment and dollar amount of real estate taxes. If the property is not taxed, the appraiser shall estimate the assessment in case it is placed upon the tax roll, state the rate, and give the dollar amount of the tax estimate.

f. Zoning. Describe the zoning for subject and comparable properties (where Government owned, state what the zoning probably will be under private ownership), and if rezoning is imminent, discuss further under item 11.

Part III—Analyses and Conclusions

11. *ANALYSIS OF HIGHEST AND BEST USE*. The report shall state the highest and best use that can be made of the property (land and im-

provements and where applicable, machinery and equipment) for which there is a current market. The valuation shall be based on this use.

12. *LAND VALUE*. The appraiser's opinion of the value of the land shall be supported by confirmed sales of comparable, or nearly comparable lands having like optimum uses. Differences shall be weighed and explained to show how they indicate the value of the land being appraised.

13. *VALUE ESTIMATE BY COMPARATIVE (MARKET) APPROACH*. All comparable sales used shall be confirmed by the buyer, seller, broker, or other person having knowledge of the price, terms and conditions of sale. Each comparable shall be weighed and explained in relation to the subject property to indicate the reasoning behind the appraiser's final value estimate from this approach.

14. *VALUE ESTIMATE BY COST APPROACH, IF APPLICABLE*. This section shall be in the form of computative data, arranged in sequence, beginning with reproduction or replacement cost, and shall state the source (book and page if a national service) of all figures used. The dollar amounts of physical deterioration and functional and economic obsolescence, or the omission of same, shall be explained in narrative form. *This procedure may be omitted on improvements, both real and personal, for which only a salvage or scrap value is estimated.*

15. *VALUE ESTIMATE BY INCOME APPROACH, IF APPLICABLE*. This shall include adequate factual data to support each figure and factor used and shall be arranged in detailed form to show at least *(a)* estimated gross economic rent or income; *(b)* allowance for vacancy and credit losses; *(c)* an itemized estimate of total expenses including reserves for replacements.

Capitalization of net income shall be at the rate prevailing for this type of property and location. The capitalization technique, method and rate used shall be explained in narrative form supported by a statement of sources of rates and factors.

16. *INTERPRETATION AND CORRELATION OF ESTIMATES*. The appraiser shall interpret the foregoing estimates and shall state his reasons why one or more of the conclusions reached in items (13), (14), and (15) are indicative of the market value of the property.

17. *CERTIFICATION*. This shall include a statement that Contractor has no undisclosed interest in property, that he has personally inspected the premises, date and amount of value estimate, etc.

Part IV—Exhibits and Addenda

18. *LOCATION MAP*.[111] (Within the city or area.)

19. *COMPARATIVE MAP DATA*. Show geographic location of the appraised property and the comparative parcels analyzed.

20. *DETAIL OF THE COMPARATIVE DATA*.

21. *PLOT PLAN*.[111]

22. *FLOOR PLANS*.[111] (When needed to explain the value estimate.)

23. *OTHER PERTINENT EXHIBITS.*

24. *QUALIFICATIONS.* (Of all Appraisers and/or Technicians contributing to the report.)

[109]As noted, *supra* p. 11, all photographs should show the identification of the property, the date taken, and the name and address of the person taking the photograph.

[110]Detrimental and hazardous factors are present to some extent on practically all properties, with some areas and properties having much more serious factors of this nature than are normally found. Appraisers should determine the types of nuisances and detrimental factors present, such as odors, undesirable businesses, dumps, land fills, noxious weeds, etc. With respect to farm properties it is especially important that appraisers consider the area hazards such as noxious weeds, incidence of hail, floods and droughts, and annual variations in crop yields. Appraisers should list and describe all factors that may be undesirable and estimate the extent of their effect.

[111]All maps and plans may be bound as facing pages opposite the description, tabulation, or discussions they concern.

HOW TO APPRAISE EASEMENTS AND LEASEHOLD INTERESTS BEING CONDEMNED

All the rights (the bundle'') in property go to the owner except those belonging to the state (police, eminent domain, taxation and escheat), and also excepting those rights diminished by easements going to others. The appraisal of easement rights-of-way is specially concerned with the nature of the easements and the laws which are applicable to such condemnations. You are also specially concerned here with valuations involving only portions of the property, and problems involving severance and special benefits. Easements give the right to someone other than the owner to one or more of the ''bundle of rights'' owned by the owner in fee. There are many types of easements, scenic, subsurface, surface and above surface including pipeline, utility, road, slope, flowage, waterway, access, ''cube easement'' in subsurface subway condemnation, air rights, aviation, facade, temporary easements, etc. Ancient Indian treaties even affect the ''bundle,'' and in many states cloud legal title. For example, during the middle seventies, an Indian suit by the Penobscot and Passamaquoddy tribes based on a 200-year-old treaty, seriously affected appraisals and paralyzed most real estate sales on 12 million acres in Maine.

There are comparatively new types evolving such as development easements which bar development of farms and other open lands to control urban sprawl and retain farming and open space. There are aerial rights over highways for building residential and other structures (which sometimes become filled with carbon monoxide from the cars which flow underneath.)

Rights-of-way may be acquired in fee or by easement. If by easement, the owner of the fee continues to pay taxes. Easements are property rights. They may be permanent or temporary. They usually involve only a portion although they may apply to the entire property.

Appraisal of leasehold interests is dependent upon rules of law. In federal acquisitions, the value of a "leasehold is the present worth of the amount, if any, by which the current fair market rental (of the building improvements, say) exceeds the rent which the tenant is obliged to pay under the terms of his lease for the term taken by the government." Thus, the tenant has no compensable property right, unless the rent he has to pay is less than the fair market rent for that period his interest is taken from him. There are differing state laws on leasehold condemnation. Here also, you have to consult with your client's attorney for guidance on local law on leaseholds before you complete your data collection and write your appraisal report.

A step-by-step procedure for appraising easement and leasehold interests is as follows:

STEP 1—Determine Applicable Laws—Consult your client's attorney.

STEP 2—Determine the Nature of the Easement or Leasehold—From deed descriptions, insurance policies, title abstracts, recorded deeds, recorded maps, surveys, taking documents, leases, lease descriptions, personal site and improvements inspection, determine the exact location, geography, nature and conditions of the easement or leasehold under appraisal.

STEP 3—Complete the "Before" Appraisal—From your collected data, complete the "Before the Taking" appraisal portion of your report. This involves appraising the entire property based on highest and best use, relying on the Market approach mainly.

STEP 4—Complete the "After" Appraisal—Complete the "After the Taking" appraisal portion. This involves appraising what is left of the property after the taking, first ascertaining whether highest and best use has been changed by the taking. It preferably also involves a different set of comparables, if possible. This "before and after" is the best method and is the one given most credence by courts for award of compensation for the takings. When the "after" appraisal amount is subtracted from the "before" amount, it shows market value for the part taken. This method also shows best what the market says about value of damages or special benefits to the remainder. Other methods or appraisal approaches involve: (1) Valuing the part taken less any net severance damages to the remainder and, (2) valuing both taking and remainder parts by adding value increments. Both of these latter methods are not recommended in federal condemnations and have not been accepted in many state courts.

STEP 5—Write the Appraisal Report—Write your report on either your client's form or your own narrative form. However, regardless of what form you use, carefully triple-check all comparable data, all arithmetic and all sources. As in the prior section on federal condemnation, your report in most states is subject to legal "discovery." You can expect it to receive a thorough item-by-item adversary review before and during trial.

STEP 6—Prepare for trial—From the moment you accept the condemnation appraisal assignment, you should be preparing not only for the written appraisal report but also for trial. Whether later settled by negotiation or not, you should assume that you will be testifying as an expert witness. Again, in your report, during discovery hearings and in court, you have to be specially careful in your written material, your testimony—composed, unruffled under cross-examination and unbiased—expressing your expert opinions on value, never an advocate. (See Chapter 21, How to Testify in Court.)

HOW TO APPRAISE RIPARIAN RIGHTS

In federal condemnation, the Commerce Clause of the Constitution, or so-called "navigation servitude" governs. Under this clause, there are reserved to the Federal Government, very broad powers over navigable waters which appraisers must bear in mind when valuing riparian (under water) land. Navigable waters are the public property of the nation. Previously, land riparian to a navigable stream did not receive payment for the value of the land attributable to the flow of the stream when condemned by the U.S. This included not only port site value, power site value, riparian rights of access to the water but also other factors such as boating, fishing and hunting. However, federal legislation in the early seventies not completely tested in the courts, affected these prior principles of riparian law. The "Uniform Appraisal Standards" federal guidance booklet recommends that appraisal be made on two alternative bases: (1) on the basis of no value attributable to access to and riparian location on navigable waters and, (2) on the basis of value attributable to riparian access and location.

State laws vary. New Jersey law is a good example of riparian definition. "Riparian lands consist of lands flowed by tidewater and location below the natural mean highwater line along the shore or bank of the waterway. Title is in the State of New Jersey, which may lease or grant such lands to persons who apply and pay rent therefor. . . . If tide-flowed lands are illegally filled in so as to exclude the tidewater . . . the line is considered still located where it naturally existed before the illegal filling in. . . . Normally the owner of upland adjoining the waterway has . . . prior right to apply for a lease of grant. . . . The exterior waterward extent of granted or leased lands is established by two lines . . . the bulkhead line to which lands may be filled in and the pierhead line to which piers may be built but under which the tide must be permitted to flow . . .'' (See following Pierhead-Bulkhead Lines Illustration, Figure 16.1.)

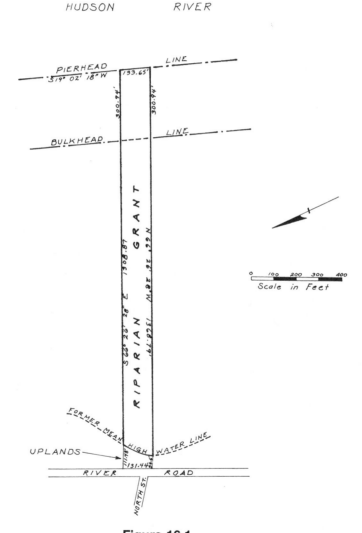

Figure 16.1

PIERHEAD/BULKHEAD MAP

Appraising properties affected by such riparian rights involves the following distinct steps:

STEP 1—Determine Whether Preemptive Rights Are Involved—Even though the owner of the adjoining uplands has not applied for nor received a grant nor lease for the riparian lands, his preemptive right to do so confers additional value to his property. Your comparables should reflect such riparian values.

STEP 2—Determine Whether a Grant or Lease Exists—If a grant or lease does exist, you appraise the value of the upland and the value of the riparian land under water to the pierhead line, whether a pier actually exists or not.

STEP 3—Determine Whether Land Is Filled or Bulkheaded—Appraise the value of the improved riparian land and the upland, including enhancement because of the improvement.

STEP 4—Determine Whether a Pier Exists—Depending on type and condition, appraise the property including the pier.

ULTRA-HIGH-VOLTAGE ELECTRIC TRANSMISSION LINES

There are new highways spreading across America, highways carrying energy, ultra-high-voltage lines. Electric utility companies, armed with the power of eminent domain are stringing these uninsulated wires which carry up to 765,000 volts on towers up to 175 feet high in rights-of-way 250 feet wide. These cross-country transmission lines began with 138,000-volt lines in 1916, then went to 230,000 volts on most of the 10,000 miles in use today. In the early fifties, the first 345,000-volt line was installed in Ohio; in the late sixties, the first 765,000-volt line. The economics are that a 350,000-volt line carries five times what a 138,000-volt line does and a 765,000-volt one 30 times more at a relatively small increase in installation cost.

These fast-proliferating lines have spread their rights-of-way across West Virginia, Virginia, Kentucky, Michigan, Indiana and New York. Farmers in Ohio and New York have faced these utility line bulldozers with pitchforks to stop these lines, but they continue to spread while law suits increase.

Appraisals of properties affected by these transmission lines are also faced with a whole new set of evolving value effects. Louise B. Young in her book *Power Over People*, reported as a scientist and property owner affected by an Ohio transmission line on the results of her investigation. Problems included shock to animals or people passing or working under the lines and noise up to 85 decibels in the vicinity. She also reported that Soviet research on electrical substation workers showed that people regularly exposed to the electrical fields of these installations, experienced deteriorating health, nervous disorders, cardiovascular changes and increased evidence of sexual impotence. Light bulbs hand-held under these lines light up. Electric utility power companies contend that if objects are grounded under the lines, steady state currents can't build up.

In general, appraisers cannot look to federal legislation or uniform standards to assist in valuation of effects. States vary. For example, in the late seventies, New York permitted construction to start on a line which will have 700 steel towers and 122 miles of ultra-high-voltage lines within a 250-foot R.O.W. No permit for energizing the line was given pending hearings on environmental effects of the line. The N.Y. Public Service Commission staff report later advised that "chronic exposure would probably cause biological effects on humans and animals." The report further recommended that the line being constructed in a condemned 250-foot R.O.W. have a 550-foot wide zone under the lines within which homeowners would be given option to sell or have their homes relocated.

This is a new, very important and rapidly expanding R.O.W. field. On an appraisal basis, you have to be alert to state law in your locality on these ultra-high transmission lines and be ready to measure the value effect on impacted properties still evolving from developing scientific investigation. Your main yardstick, as always, is the market. If sales of affected properties are influenced in terms of value and resistance by buyers, then these controversial lines and their impact can be measured properly. Look to the market always.

A MODEL CONDEMNATION REPORT

The following condemnation appraisal report has been condensed, omitting cover sheet, index, letter of transmittal, photographs, contingent and certification condition sheet, maps, qualification sheet and all identifying data:

PURPOSE OF APPRAISAL—This appraisal is made for the purpose of arriving at an opinion of the Fair Market Value of the subject property if offered for sale on the open market under conditions prevailing _____ and is based on a physical inspection of the parcels, analysis of sales of comparable properties and consideration of all factors which affect value including amenities, depreciating influences, zoning, utility, location, topography, present and potential uses.

LOCATION OF LAND—This is in the Town of _____ approximately 2½ miles west of Village of _____ at the intersection of _____ Turnpike, (County Rd. 1) and _____, in Southeastern Orange County, approximately 45 miles from New York City. See Location Map, attached.

DESCRIPTION OF THE PROPERTY BEFORE TAKING—Property involved is 127 acres of rolling, mainly cleared land approximately bisected by the _____, _____, the road proposed for realignment and widening by Orange County. The property also abuts a town highway, _____, on the east.

TOPOGRAPHY—The parcel has rolling, generally cleared, upland acres with a stream at the westerly end of the property. It is well drained.

ZONED—Town of _____ Zoning ordinance established RR zone which principally permits agriculture and cattle raising operations on minimum 20-acre lots and one- and two-family residences on 60,000 sq. ft. lots.

AREA AND NEIGHBORHOOD—The property is located at the edge of a rural hamlet called _____ which services its rural environs with country stores, post office, equipment store, etc. Within the past 10 years, residential development has accelerated as the New York Metropolis spilled residential commuter development into _____ Orange County. This area, however, because of its distance from the Route 17 arterial highway, has seen some speculative activity but very little building activity. With tight money, gasoline cost affecting commuters and economic recession, the future for large-scale residential development in this area is, in the appraiser's opinion, non-existent.

HIGHEST AND BEST USE—The property's highest and best use is for agricultural, animal raising, breeding or dairy operations. Although the unusually long road frontage on two roads and its location adjacent to the hamlet of _____ would facilitate potential for residential building, this is a very minor value affect because of location and economic factors discussed in the previous paragraph.

EASEMENTS AND ENCUMBRANCES—Drainage and access for maintenance easements at four locations as shown on Taking Map sheets 12 through 15, _____, Road No. 1, _____ (attached).

IMPROVEMENTS—There is a 100-year-old farmhouse, and two barns in fair condition. There is a small shed between the barns which has collapsed and has no value. There are one-story sheds attached to the rear of the large barn which are in poor condition and have no value. There are barbed wire and wood post farm fences.

METHOD OF APPRAISAL—In my opinion, the acquisition will have no effect on the value of the farmhouse because of its comparatively deep setback from the road widening. Therefore, the farmhouse was given a value which would be the same both before and after the acquisition. The two barns, however, which are in structurally fair to good condition (see photos attached), are structurally and functionally completely damaged by the road widening. The Market Data approach to value was the only appraisal method used to estimate value of land. Depreciated replacement method was used to estimate value of damaged barns and fences. The land was appraised as it existed just before the taking and again immediately after the taking. The difference in these values will be the total damages to the property resulting from the taking.

INTEREST APPRAISED—Fee Simple.

MARKET APPROACH TO LAND VALUE
BEFORE TAKING COMPARABLES

Seller-Buyer	Date	Location	Acres	Liber/Page Price	Analysis
Doe, et al to L&G Assoc.	—	—	83.87	1937/ 196 276,771	No buildings, better location— $3,350 per acre
Jones to Smith	—	—	42.73	1958/ 737 $110,000	No buildings, better location— $2,574 per acre
Masters to Do Company	—	—	65.83	1939/ 276 $115,494	No buildings, equal location-steeper topography with large % unusuable and—$1,754 per acre
Subject			127		Subject compares to above sales @ $2,000 per acre for land value.

BUILDINGS

FARMHOUSE 3,500 sq. ft. × $15 =	$52,500	
Less Depreciation (Physical)	24,000	(Wear and tear, age)
(Functional)	4,000	(Old facilities)
(Economic)	2,500	(Slow market)
Depreciated Cost—Farmhouse..........$22,000		

LARGE BARN
26.5 feet × 89 feet × 2-Story = 4,725 sq. ft. × $6 = $28,500

Less Depreciation	(Physical)	12,000 (W&T, age)
	(Functional)	0
	(Economic)	1,500 (Slow market)
Depreciated Cost—Large Barn $15,000		

```
SMALL BARN 2,070 sq. ft. × $7 =    $14,500
   Less Depreciation    (Physical)       5,500    (W&T, Age)
                        (Functional)         0
                        (Economic)       1,000    (Slow market)
   Depreciated Cost—Small Barn............$8,000
```

```
   TOTAL DEPRECIATED COST HOUSE
   AND 2 BARNS.................................... $45,000
       Farm Fencing 16,256 feet × .30 ...................4,800
       Land Value 127 Acres @ $2,000 ...............254,000
       BEFORE TAKING TOTAL VALUE............$304,000 (Rounded)
```

DESCRIPTION OF THE TAKING

As described in County Maps, attached, regarding Subject R.O.W. Parcels No. 34A and 34B, the taking basically involves fee simple acquisition by Orange County of 3.722 acres of land of the subject property for purposes of widening and realigning _____ Turnpike, _____ No. 1 which bisects this farm. Taking plans also show easement areas in four locations for drainage and access for maintenance purposes. The taking line runs through the front wall of the large barn and almost coincides with the front wall of the small barn requiring demolition and removal. The taking also causes need for replacement of 409 rods or 6,756 feet of farm fencing.

EFFECTS OF THE TAKING

The taking has measurably affected the buildings and improvements. Since the highest and best use of this parcel is for agricultural-animal husbandry usages, demolition of barns and farm fences caused by the taking, materially affect usage and value. Land is reduced by 3.722 acres and is so valued by the appraiser on an acreage basis.

VALUE AFTER THE TAKING

To estimate the value of the property after the taking I have used the same land sales as in the previous situation. Farmhouse, as previously stated, has no damages from taking. Farm fencing needs replacing. Both two-story barns are considered 100% damaged by taking, since to set-back the front walls and to re-orient entrances to side ramps would render their structure and function obsolete, non-functional and uneconomical. The barns are set 2 feet to 4 feet above road. Widening and regulation on 50% bank gradients would effectively bar access and usage. (See Taking Map attached.) Thus,

Farmhouse ....$ 22,000

Farm fence 16,256 feet − 6,756 feet * taken
= 9,500 feet × .30   2,850
*(6,756-feet fence needs 15 rolls and 450 posts
and labor = $2,027)

Large barn and small barn 100% damage**   0
**(depreciated cost of barns $23,000)

Land—123.27 acres (after taking) × $2,000 246,556

    Value of property after the taking $271,406

        Say $271,500

SUMMARY OF VALUES

Value before taking
  127 Acres and improvements $304,000
Value of the remainder as a result of
  the taking
  123.27 acres and improvements 271,500

    Total Damages* $ 32,500
    *Damages—
    3.722 acres Land @ $2,000 = $ 7,444
    Large barn......................... 15,000
    Small barn......................... 8,000
    6,756 feet fencing @ $.30 2,027
                           $32,471

  Say...$ 32,500

Chapter 17

Government housing programs: appraisal requirements and techniques

This chapter on government housing programs details government appraisal requirements and techniques. There is a section on how to keep up with these changing programs and appraisal standards. There is a companion section on how to use data from these many government sources to help you appraise. This chapter also shows how to appraise for and work with important government and government-supported housing agencies like FNMA, HUD-FHA and the VA. There is a Model VA Application and a completed Appraisal Report.

HOW TO KEEP UP WITH THE IMPACT OF CHANGING GOVERNMENT PROGRAMS

Federal government policies and agencies have a critical impact on the housing market. Our urban-suburban nation today, where we live and the kind of shelter we inhabit, was mainly mapped, designed and fostered by the FHA, the VA and other U.S. government housing agencies and policies. Although the FHA and VA are not as strong now, government housing and monetary policies have in recent years helped to make or break the housing industry. From the mid-thirties into the sixties, FHA-VA led the development of middle-class housing as suburban residential and other development "spread" from our cities. In recent years, agencies such as Housing and Urban Development (HUD) have been pumping money into housing for the elderly, rent supplements for the poor and other subsidized programs.

The government's influence on housing pervades our whole economy. Prior chapters are replete with illustrations of government effect on housing, appraisal techniques and requirements. Later sections of this chapter list the many federal sources for appraisal data collection. However, there are several general bases which need regular touching to keep up with these government programs and their affect on appraising. First, of course, is regular review of daily national newspapers, periodicals, business and housing publications. Second and specifically important to federal data collection, is subscription to the U.S. Superintendent of Documents, Washington, D.C. mailing list of government publications. Once you have written to the Superintendent for this list, he will send you regular mailings which list all recent publications by all U.S. agencies. You can then order those you need for nominal cost. This mailing list will help keep you alert to government data in housing and real estate and is an invaluable general appraisal tool.

HOW TO USE GOVERNMENT DATA IN YOUR APPRAISAL WORK

Systematic accumulation of data in the real estate marketplace and from other sources is the heart of the appraisal process. Each appraisal assignment is unique. First, the appraisal question is defined, then the data to answer the question is accumulated from local, state and/or federal sources. Finally, the appraisal report is written from this investigation and data collection process. The following is specific to Federal Government data resources. Agencies like the FHA, VA and FNMA have had major historical and current impact on housing. Their appraisal requirements and techniques are detailed below. However, there are many other agencies with missions other than housing, which are important sources for appraisal data collection. These agencies and their appraisal requirements are also in the following sources list for appraisal data collection. Many of these agencies, particularly the VA, also use independent fee appraisers to do some or most of their appraisals.

Department of Census—This is probably the single most important source for vital statistics and for various useful studies like those on household and family formation characteristics.

Housing and Urban Development (HUD)—This mammoth housing agency also incorporates the Federal Housing Administration (FHA). Basic national building codes like the FHA Minimum Property Standards for single and multiple dwellings are available here. Current topical publications like

Standards for Solar Heating have been issued recently. Numerous research and miscellaneous statistical housing publications are also available. Important data such as flood maps originate here.

Veterans Administration (VA)—The Loan Guaranty Division of the VA is probably the best-run, most scandal-free government housing agency. Since WWII, it has continued to guaranty the financing of new and used housing for veterans, featuring no down payment and no ceiling on mortgage loans. Since 1944, only a small percentage of properties VA has guaranteed have been foreclosed. This program has guaranteed about 10 million mortgages and there are still 25 million eligible veterans. The VA mainly uses FHA minimum property building standards but has its own appraisal procedures. It is involved in home loan guarantees, mobile home, direct loan, condominium loan and specially adapted paraplegic grant programs. Independent fee appraisers do these VA appraisals which are reviewed by VA staff appraisers.

Department of Commerce—This Department publishes a monthly review which summarizes economic trends. Their housing analysts also issue housing reports.

Department of Interior—This Department has basic charge of most of U.S.-owned land. It has a number of pertinent Bureaus and Services—The Bureau of Indian Affairs, Bureau of Land Management, Bureau of Reclamation, Fish and Wildlife Service and the National Park Service. For example, if information on geology or mining is needed for an appraisal assignment, the Department of Interior, with these many arms, is the source.

Environmental Protection Agency (EPA)—This newest of major agencies is a major source for data on pollution involving solid waste, air, water, pesticides, radiation and noise. Government or other development projects which could affect the environment all need approved impact statements prior to construction.

Federal National Mortgage Association (FNMA) ("FANNY MAY")— FNMA is the world's largest mortgage banker now and the nation's largest single supplier of funds for homes and apartments. It is a secondary lender, buying and selling mortgages, originated by lenders. This giant lender, chartered by Act of Congress, is now privately controlled although still federally supervised. FNMA handles its own individual loans. It also administratively processes project loans for the Government National Mortgage Association (GNMA—"Ginny May"). The "National Neighborhood Policy Act" of the late seventies focused national attention on the preservation of our greatest national wealth, our neighborhoods and homes. FNMA has been in the lending forefront in regard to speaking out against "redlining" (see Chapter 8). This giant lender, like the VA, has its own appraisal forms and appraisal guidelines. (See later section for sample appraisal forms.) It also uses independent fee appraisers.

Farmers Home Administration (FmHA) (Dept. of Agriculture)—The FmHA makes home and farm loans in rural areas and grants for rural community development. The FmHa is a very important financing influence in our exurban areas, particularly during tight money times and in those rural areas which have limited conventional lending. It is an important source for data on farm and home sales and for other rural statistical data.

The Internal Revenue Service (IRS)—The IRS requires appraisals in connection with certain estate and gift tax issues. Real estate appraisal techniques employed are the Market Data, Income and Replacement Cost approaches. It does not use a standardized appraisal form. IRS Publications 561 and 592 identify some of the valuation issues involved in tax laws, and assist individuals and appraisers in evaluating the fair market value of property donated. The format of appraisals submitted should include:

(a) Appraiser's qualifications

(b) Statement of value and how the value was obtained

(c) Description of the property

(d) Bases of appraisal, including any restrictions limiting use of the property

(e) Three-approach method

(f) Land and buildings valued separately

(g) Signature and date

Department of Army Engineer Corps—The Corps and other government agencies follow the basic guidelines in "Uniform Appraisal Standards for Federal Land Acquisition." (See Chapter 16 on condemnation.) This and other data are available from Directorate of Real Estate of the Corps which is regularly involved in major condemnations and construction projects affecting the economy and appraisal work in all regions.

General Services Administration (GSA)—The GSA acquires, manages, services and disposes of government real property. This government real estate unit obtains about 1,900 appraisals yearly from staff appraisers or by contract with independent appraisers. GSA Forms 1241D and 1241A on definition of appraisal terms and specifications for narrative appraisal reports follow at the end of this section. They illustrate the traditional three-approach method of value which most government appraisal agencies still require.

OTHER GOVERNMENT AGENCIES

Other agencies which have important real estate functions and are good federal data sources include the Department of Justice, the Federal Bureau of

Investigation, the Federal Aviation Agency, the Federal Home Loan Bank Board, the Forest Service of the Department of Agriculture, the Navy Department, the Small Business Administration, the Post Office and the Health, Education and Welfare Departments. The FAA, for example, is a prime source for data, maps and information when appraising in areas affected by airports. The SBA in its loans to businessmen and in its work during natural disasters, no longer has its own appraisal staff. As an additional example, the HEW, in its enforcement of the Rehabilitation Act of the early seventies, is a prime source for standards requiring that buildings serving the public be readily accessible to the handicapped.

HOW TO WORK WITH FNMA, HUD-FHA AND VA HOUSING AND APPRAISAL REQUIREMENTS

GSA Form 1241A (Figures 17.1 and 17.2) dates back to the mid-sixties even though it is for appraisal guidance now. FNMA Form 1004 (Figure 17.3) was revised by the Federal National Mortgage Association in the mid-seventies to streamline its appraisal reporting, to stress that racial composition is not a relevant appraisal factor and to emphasize the Market approach. These forms typify the slowly evolving changes taking place in government appraising, following what is happening in the private sector.

The single Market approach in residential appraisals and the one-approach method in all types of other appraisals, as promulgated by the American Society of Appraisers and practiced by many modern appraisers, is still not completely accepted by most government agencies. To quote Dexter D. MacBride, the brilliant Executive Vice-President of the ASA, "One of the problems of the FNMA form is its insistence upon questionable areas of documentation related to residential appraising. The Cost approach is vestigial in most instances. To be a relevant tool the form needs further improvement." However, it does appear that government appraising is slowly de-emphasizing the Cost approach. Yet, when you work with government requirements or appraise for a government agency, it is important that you still know and use this traditional three-approach system of correlating cost, income and market data to secure your opinion of value.

The FHA since 1934 led the development of middle class housing in America. It pioneered in subdivision planning and fostered suburban growth. Yet, later in the sixties and early seventies, under HUD, it helped destroy many inner areas of our cities. The "HUD-FHA" neighborhoods in Detroit and throughout the United States with their tens of thousands of demolished, boarded-up and abandoned homes is a legacy of these inept government policies and housing scandals. These scandals ruined many unethical, incompetent appraisers. Urban renewal, under HUD-FHA, was stopped in the early

GENERAL SERVICES ADMINISTRATION

DEFINITION OF TERMS
Contract For Appraisal Report

INSTRUCTIONS. Definitions applicable to this contract for appraisal report are checked below:

1. ☐   HIGHEST AND BEST USE. The most profitable likely use, within the realm of reasonable probability, to which real and related personal property can be put or adapted, and for which there is a current market.

2. ☐   FAIR MARKET VALUE (MARKET VALUE). The highest price estimated in terms of money which the property will bring if exposed for sale in the open market by a seller who is willing but not obligated to sell, allowing a reasonable time to find a buyer who is willing but not obligated to buy, both parties having full knowledge of all the uses to which it is adapted and for which it is capable of being used.

3. ☐   FAIR MARKET VALUE FOR LEASING PURPOSES (FMVLP). The definition is the same as 2, above. This heading is applicable only to In-Lease Appraisals used in connection with appraising a whole or part of a property, and is intended to limit the use of such reports to leasing purposes.

4. ☐   SPECIAL USE VALUE.

    a. The marketable measure of the value to a known user of a specialized type property to provide usefulness, service, or profitableness above the value of the property if vacant. (Examples: This value could apply to a lessee in possession; an adjacent property holder; or a public body.)

    b. The price which the Government would be justified in paying for a facility specially designed and constructed for its use, or for an existing facility on which alterations are made to meet special Government requirements. This definition also applies to property specially constructed or remodeled for lease to the Government.

5. ☐   SALVAGE VALUE. The price expectable for the whole improvement (for example, a building), or part of the whole improvement (for example, a plumbing fixture), for removal from the premises for use elsewhere.

6. ☐   SCRAP VALUE. The price expectable for a part of a property for sale and removal from the premises for the reclamation of the value of the basic material itself (for example, copper), and not for use as originally intended.

7. ☐   INSURABLE VALUE. The reproduction cost of insurable items (construction above ground) of all buildings and appurtenances, less accrued physical depreciation.

8. ☐   SEVERANCE DAMAGE. Loss in value to the remaining property as a result of the taking of a part of the whole property; the diminution of the market value of the remainder area as a result of the severance of the part taken.

9. ☐   JUST COMPENSATION. In condemnation, the dollar amount to which the owner is entitled for the taking of private property, as of the date of taking, to make him whole. Usually it is based on Fair Market Value plus additional awards for certain legally allowable types of damages. In partial takings it is generally measured by the difference between the Fair Market Value of the property as a whole, immediately before and unaffected by the taking, and the Fair Market Value of the remainder immediately after and as affected by the taking.

10. ☐   FAIR ANNUAL RENTAL. Annual monetary amount reasonably expectable for the right to the agreed use of real and related personal property as established by competition in the rental market. If market information is unavailable, it is that annual amount which will amortize the value of the remaining capital investment, plus a fair rate of interest return during the remaining useful life of the rented property.

    a. SERVICED. The same as defined above including all services as specified under the terms of the lease.

    b. UNSERVICED. The same as above exclusive of the cost of operating services such as heat, light, cleaning, etc.

GSA-WASH DC 69-222-4   **GSA** FORM **1241D**

Figure 17.1

GSA DEFINITION OF APPRAISAL CONTRACT TERMS

GENERAL SERVICES ADMINISTRATION

SECTION 3 - SPECIFICATIONS FOR THE GSA ANALYTICAL NARRATIVE APPRAISAL REPORT

GENERAL - In the preparation of this report, the Contractor shall follow current professional appraisal practices giving consideration to three approaches to value, namely, the Cost Less Depreciation, Income, and Comparative (or Market) approaches, unless otherwise specified in this contract. Should certain approaches or requirements covered in these specifications not be applicable to the assignment, the contractual obligation can be fulfilled by identifying that approach or requirement together with a brief explanation for its omission (i. e. an appraisal involving land valuation only). Of necessity, supplementary specifications will be furnished requiring additional data in the appraisal of highly specialized properties or under other unusual circumstances.

FORMAT - The report shall be bound, in book-fashion, in the left margin, in a durable cover with an identification of the property on the face thereof. The paper used shall be a good grade bond of size 8-1/2 by 11 inches. All pages shall be numbered consecutively, including all exhibits, and each important heading shall be shown in the Table of Contents. To provide uniformity for GSA files, the text shall be divided into four parts as outlined below.

PART I - INTRODUCTION

1. TITLE PAGE. This shall include (a) the name and street address of the property, (b) the name of the individual making the report, and (c) the effective date of the appraisal.

2. TABLE OF CONTENTS.

3. LETTER OF TRANSMITTAL.

4. PHOTOGRAPHS. Pictures shall show at least the front elevation of the major improvements, plus any unusual features. There should also be

views of the abutting properties on either side and that property directly opposite. When a large number of buildings are involved, including duplicates, one picture may be used for each type. Views of the best comparables should be included whenever possible. Except for the overall view, photographs may be bound as pages facing the discussion or description which the photographs concern. All graphic material shall include captions.

5. STATEMENT OF LIMITING CONDITIONS AND ASSUMPTIONS.

6. REFERENCES. If preferred, may be shown with applicable approach.

PART II - FACTUAL DATA

7. PURPOSE OF THE APPRAISAL. This shall include the reason for the appraisal, and a definition of all values required, and property rights appraised.

8. LEGAL DESCRIPTION. This description shall be so complete as to properly identify the property appraised. If lengthy, it should be referenced and included in Part IV. If furnished by GSA and would require lengthy reproduction, incorporate by reference only.

9. AREA, CITY AND NEIGHBORHOOD DATA. This data (mostly social and economic) should be kept to a minimum and should include only such information as directly affects the appraised property together with the appraiser's conclusions as to significant trends.

10. PROPERTY DATA -

   a. SITE - Describe the soil, topography, mineral deposits, easements, etc. A statement must be made concerning the existence or nonexistence of mineral deposits having a commercial value.

   b. IMPROVEMENTS - This description may be by narrative or schedule form and shall include dimensions, cubic and/or square foot measurements, and where appropriate, a statement of the method of measurement used in determining rentable areas such as full floor, multitenancy, etc.

   c. EQUIPMENT - This shall be described by narrative or schedule form and shall include all items of equipment, including a statement of the type and purpose of the equipment and its state of cannibalization. The current physical condition and relative use and obsolescence shall be

stated for each item or group appraised, and, whenever applicable, the repair or replacement requirements to bring the property to usable condition.

Any related personalty or equipment, such as tenant trade fixtures, which are not attached or considered part of the realty, shall be separately inventoried. Where applicable, these detachable or individually owned items shall be separately valued.

   d. HISTORY - State briefly the purpose for which the improvements were designed, dates of original construction and major renovation and/or additions; include, for privately owned property, a five-year record as to each parcel, of all sales and, if possible, offers to buy or sell, and recent lease(s); if no sale in the past five years, include a report of the last sale.

   e. ASSESSED VALUE AND ANNUAL TAX LOAD. Include the current assessment and dollar amount of real estate taxes. If the property is not taxed, the appraiser shall estimate the assessment in case it is placed upon the tax roll, state the rate, and give the dollar amount of the tax estimate.

   f. INSURANCE - Give the estimated rate per thousand and the annual cost of adequate insurance coverage (not necessarily present coverage).

   g. ZONING - Describe the zoning for subject and comparable properties (where Government owned, state what the zoning probably will be under private ownership), and if rezoning is imminent, discuss further under item 11.

PART III - ANALYSES AND CONCLUSIONS

11. ANALYSIS OF HIGHEST AND BEST USE. The report shall state the highest and best use that can be made of the property (land and improvements and where applicable, machinery and equipment) for which there is a current market. The valuation shall be based on this use and if made for disposal purposes, shall also include suggested method(s) of disposal.

12. LAND VALUE. The appraiser's opinion of the value of the land shall be supported by confirmed sales of comparable, or nearly comparable lands having like optimum uses. Differences shall be weighed and explained to show how they indicate the value of the land being appraised.

13. VALUE ESTIMATE BY COST APPROACH. This section shall be in the form of computative data, arranged in sequence, beginning with reproduction or replacement cost, and shall state the source (book and page if a national service) of all figures used. The dollar amounts of physical deterioration and functional and economic obsolescence, or the omission of same, shall be explained in narrative form. This procedure may be omitted on improvements, both real and personal, for which only a salvage or scrap value is estimated.

14. VALUE ESTIMATE BY INCOME APPROACH. This shall include adequate factual data to support each figure and factor used and shall be arranged in detailed form to show at least (a) estimated gross economic rent

or income; (b) allowance for vacancy and credit losses; (c) an itemized estimate of total expenses including reserves for replacements.

   Capitalization of net income shall be at the rate prevailing for this type of property and location. The capitalization technique, method and rate used shall be explained in narrative form supported by a statement of sources of rates and factors.

15. VALUE ESTIMATE BY COMPARATIVE (MARKET) APPROACH. All comparable sales used shall be confirmed by the buyer, seller, broker, or other person having knowledge of the price, terms and conditions of sale. Each comparable shall be weighed and explained in relation to the subject property to indicate the reasoning behind the appraiser's final value estimate from this approach.

16. INTERPRETATION AND CORRELATION OF ESTIMATES. The appraiser shall interpret the foregoing estimates and shall state his reasons why one or more of the conclusions reached in items (13), (14), and (15) are indicative of the market value of the property.

17. CERTIFICATION. This shall include statement that Contractor has no undisclosed interest in property, that he has personally inspected the premises, date and amount of value estimate, etc.

PART IV - EXHIBITS AND ADDENDA

18. LOCATION MAP*. (Within the city or area)

19. COMPARATIVE MAP DATA. (Show geographic location of the appraised property and the comparative parcels analyzed.)

20. DETAIL OF THE COMPARATIVE DATA.

21. PLOT PLAN*.

22. FLOOR PLANS*. (When needed to explain the value estimate)

23. OTHER PERTINENT EXHIBITS.

24. QUALIFICATIONS. (Of all Appraisers and/or Technicians contributing to the report.)

*All maps and plans may be bound as facing pages opposite the description, tabulation, or discussions they concern.

GSA ^{FORM} 1241A

GSA WASH DC 65- 129 43

Figure 17.2

GSA SPECIFICATION FOR NARRATIVE APPRAISAL REPORT

RESIDENTIAL APPRAISAL REPORT

File No. _____

To be completed by Lender

Borrower/Client		
Property Address		
City	County	State	Zip Code
Legal Description		Census Tract	Map Reference
Sale Price $	Date of Sale	Property Rights Appraised ☐ Fee ☐ Leasehold ☐ DeMinimis PUD ☐ (FNMA only ☐ Condo ☐ PUD)
Actual Real Estate Taxes $	(yr) Loan charges to be paid by seller $	Other sales concessions
Lender		Lender's Address
Occupant	Appraiser	Instructions to Appraiser

NEIGHBORHOOD

Location	☐ Urban	☐ Suburban	☐ Rural
Built Up	☐ Over 75%	☐ 25% to 75%	☐ Under 25%
Growth Rate ☐ Fully Dev.	☐ Rapid	☐ Steady	☐ Slow
Property Values	☐ Increasing	☐ Stable	☐ Declining
Demand/Supply	☐ Shortage	☐ In Balance	☐ Over Supply
Marketing Time	☐ Under 3 Mos.	☐ 4–6 Mos.	☐ Over 6 Mos.

Present Land Use ____% 1 Family ____% 2–4 Family ____% Apts. ____% Condo ____% Commercial
____% Industrial ____% Vacant ____%

Change in Present Land Use ☐ Not Likely ☐ Likely (*) ☐ Taking Place (*)
(*) From _____ To _____

Predominant Occupancy ☐ Owner ☐ Tenant ____% Vacant
Single Family Price Range $ ____ to $ ____ Predominant Value $ ____
Single Family Age ____ yrs to ____ yrs Predominant Age ____ yrs

	Good	Avg.	Fair	Poor
Employment Stability	☐	☐	☐	☐
Convenience to Employment	☐	☐	☐	☐
Convenience to Shopping	☐	☐	☐	☐
Convenience to Schools	☐	☐	☐	☐
Quality of Schools	☐	☐	☐	☐
Recreational Facilities	☐	☐	☐	☐
Adequacy of Utilities	☐	☐	☐	☐
Property Compatibility	☐	☐	☐	☐
Protection from Detrimental Conditions	☐	☐	☐	☐
Police and Fire Protection	☐	☐	☐	☐
General Appearance of Properties	☐	☐	☐	☐
Appeal to Market	☐	☐	☐	☐

Note: FHLMC/FNMA do not consider the racial composition of the neighborhood to be a relevant factor and it must not be considered in the appraisal.

Comments (including those factors adversely affecting marketability) _____

SITE

Dimensions _____ = _____ Sq. Ft. or Acres ☐ Corner Lot
Zoning classification _____ Present improvements ☐ do ☐ do not conform to zoning regulations
Highest and best use: ☐ Present use ☐ Other (Describe) _____

OFF SITE IMPROVEMENTS			
		Topo	
	Other (specify)	Size	
Street Access:	☐ Public ☐ Private	Shape	
Surface		View	
Maintenance:	☐ Public ☐ Private	Drainage	
☐ Storm Sewer	☐ Curb/Gutter		
☐ Sidewalk	☐ Street Lights		

Elec. ☐
Gas ☐
Water ☐
San. Sewer ☐
☐ Underground Elect. & Tel.

Is the property located in a HUD identified Flood Hazard Area? ☐ No ☐ Yes

Comments (favorable or unfavorable including any apparent adverse easements, encroachments or other adverse conditions) _____

IMPROVEMENTS

☐ Existing (approx. yr. blt.) 19____ ☐ Proposed ☐ Under Construction

No. Units ____ No. Stories ____

Type (det., duplex, semi/det., etc.) ____

Design (rambler, split level, etc.) ____

	Exterior Walls			Insulation	
				☐ None ☐ Floor	
				☐ Ceiling ☐ Roof ☐ Walls	

Roof Material ____

Gutters & Downspouts ☐ None

Window (Type): ☐ Storm Sash ☐ Screens ☐ Combination

Foundation Walls ____

BSMT. ☐ % Basement ☐ Outside Entrance ☐ Concrete Floor

☐ Crawl Space ☐ Slab on Grade

Evidence of: ☐ Dampness ☐ Termites ☐ Settlement

☐ Floor Drain ☐ Sump Pump ____ % Finished

☐ Finished Ceiling ☐ Finished Walls ☐ Finished Floor

Comments ____

ROOM LIST

Room List	Foyer	Living	Dining	Kitchen	Den	Family Rm.	Rec. Rm.	Bedrooms	No. Baths	Laundry	Other
Basement											
1st Level											
2nd Level											

Total ____ Rooms ____ Bedrooms ____ Baths in finished area above grade.

INTERIOR FINISH & EQUIPMENT

Kitchen Equipment: ☐ Refrigerator ☐ Range/Oven ☐ Disposal ☐ Dishwasher ☐ Fan/Hood ☐ Compactor ☐ Washer ☐ Dryer

HEAT: Type ____ Fuel ____ Cond. ____

AIR COND: ☐ Central ☐ Other ____ ☐ Adequate ☐ Inadequate

	Floors	Walls	Trim/Finish	Bath Floor	Bath Wainscot
	☐ Hardwood	☐ Drywall	☐ Good	☐ Ceramic	☐ Ceramic
	☐ Carpet Over	☐ Plaster	☐ Average	☐ Fair	☐ Poor

Special Features (including fireplaces): ____

ATTIC: ☐ Yes ☐ No ☐ Stairway ☐ Drop-stair ☐ Scuttle ☐ Floored ☐ Heated

Finished (Describe) ____

CAR STORAGE: ☐ Garage ☐ Built-in ☐ Attached ☐ Detached ☐ Car Port

No. Cars ____ ☐ Adequate ☐ Inadequate Condition ____

PROPERTY RATING

	Good	Avg.	Fair	Poor
Quality of Construction (Materials & Finish)	☐	☐	☐	☐
Condition of Improvements	☐	☐	☐	☐
Rooms size and layout	☐	☐	☐	☐
Closets and Storage	☐	☐	☐	☐
Plumbing—adequacy and condition	☐	☐	☐	☐
Electrical—adequacy and condition	☐	☐	☐	☐
Kitchen Cabinets—adequacy and condition	☐	☐	☐	☐
Compatibility to Neighborhood	☐	☐	☐	☐
Overall Livability	☐	☐	☐	☐
Appeal and Marketability	☐	☐	☐	☐

Effective Age ____ Yrs. Est. Remaining Economic Life ____ Yrs.

PORCHES, PATIOS, POOL, FENCES, etc. (describe) ____

COMMENTS (including functional or physical inadequacies, repairs needed, modernization, etc.) ____

ATTACH DESCRIPTIVE PHOTOGRAPHS OF SUBJECT PROPERTY AND STREET SCENE

FHLMC Form 70   FNMA Form 1004

Figure 17.3

SAMPLE FNMA APPRAISAL FORM

VALUATION SECTION

Purpose of Appraisal is to estimate Market Value as defined in Certification & Statement of Limiting Conditions (FHLMC Form 439/FNMA Form 1004B). If submitted for FNMA, the appraiser must attach (1) sketch or map showing location of subject, street names, distance from nearest intersection, and any detrimental conditions and (2) exterior building sketch of improvements showing dimensions.

COST APPROACH

Measurements	No. Stories	Sq. Ft.	ESTIMATED REPRODUCTION COST — NEW — OF IMPROVEMENTS:
x	x	=	Dwelling ___ Sq. Ft. @ $ ___ = $
x	x	=	___ Sq. Ft. @ $ ___ =
x	x	=	Extras ___ =
x	x	=	___ =
x	x	=	Porches, Patios, etc. ___ =
x	x	=	Garage/Car Port ___ Sq. Ft. @ $ ___ =

Total Gross Living Area (List in Market Data Analysis below)

Comment on functional and economic obsolescence:

Site Improvements (driveway, landscaping, etc.) = $ ___

Total Estimated Cost New = $ ___

Less — Physical | Functional | Economic
Depreciation $ ___ | $ ___ | $ ___ = $ ( )

Depreciated value of improvements . . . . . = $ ___

ESTIMATED LAND VALUE = $ ___
(If leasehold, show only leasehold value)

INDICATED VALUE BY COST APPROACH . . . . $ ___

The undersigned has recited three recent sales of properties most similar and proximate to subject and has considered these in the market analysis. The description includes a dollar adjustment, reflecting market reaction to those items of significant variation between the subject and comparable properties. If a significant item in the comparable property is superior to, or more favorable than, the subject property, a minus (-) adjustment is made, thus reducing the indicated value of subject; if a significant item in the comparable is inferior to, or less favorable than, the subject property, a plus (+) adjustment is made, thus increasing the indicated value of the subject.

ITEM	Subject Property	COMPARABLE NO. 1		COMPARABLE NO. 2		COMPARABLE NO. 3	
Address							
Proximity to Subj.							
Sales Price	$		$		$		$
Price/Living area	$		$		$		$
Data Source							
		DESCRIPTION	+(−)$ Adjustment	DESCRIPTION	+(−)$ Adjustment	DESCRIPTION	+(−)$ Adjustment
Date of Sale and Time Adjustment							
Location							
Site/View							
Design and Appeal							
Quality of Const.							
Age							
Condition							
Living Area Room Count and Total	Total	B-rms	Baths	Total	B-rms	Baths	Total	B-rms	Baths	Total	B-rms	Baths
Gross Living Area	Sq.Ft.		Sq.Ft.		Sq.Ft.		Sq.Ft.

284

MARKET DATA ANALYSIS

Basement & Bsmt. Finished Rooms

Functional Utility

Air Conditioning

Garage/Car Port

Porches, Patio, Pools, etc.

Other (e.g. fireplaces, kitchen equip., heating, remodeling)

Sales or Financing Concessions

Net Adj. (Total) ☐ Plus; ☐ Minus $ ____ ☐ Plus; ☐ Minus $ ____ ☐ Plus; ☐ Minus $ ____

Indicated Value of Subject $ ____ $ ____ $ ____

Comments on Market Data ____

INDICATED VALUE BY MARKET DATA APPROACH . . . . $ ____

INDICATED VALUE BY INCOME APPROACH (If applicable) Economic Market Rent $ ____ /Mo. x Gross Rent Multiplier ____ = $ ____

This appraisal is made ☐ "as is" ☐ subject to the repairs, alterations, or conditions listed below ☐ completion per plans and specifications.

Comments and Conditions of Appraisal: ____

Final Reconciliation: ____

This appraisal is based upon the above requirements, the certification, contingent and limiting conditions, and Market Value definition that are stated in

☐ FHLMC Form 439 (____)/FNMA Form 1004B filed with client ____ 19 ____ ☐ attached.

If submitted for FNMA, the report has been prepared in compliance with FNMA form instructions.

I ESTIMATE THE MARKET VALUE, AS DEFINED, OF SUBJECT PROPERTY AS OF ____ 19 ____ to be $ ____

Appraiser(s) ____ Review Appraiser (If applicable) ____ ☐ Did ☐ Did Not Physically Inspect Property

FHLMC Form 70   REVERSE   FNMA Form 1004

Figure 17.3 (Cont'd.)

seventies after leveling the hearts of many cities. Although the FHA is no longer a major force in housing, its Minimum Property Standards publications still are the one main national building and planning code today. HUD grants and rent supplements are now also helping to support such pioneering urban rebuilding efforts like the Urban Reinvestment Task Force run by the Federal Home Loan Bank. This Task Force has successfully spurred reinvestment and rebuilding in Philadelphia and in other areas.

The Veterans Housing Acts of the early seventies expanded eligibility of veterans and the activity of this important agency in housing. Mobile home loans and condominium loans were added to the VA home loan, direct loan and paraplegic grant programs. By the latter half of the seventies, the VA was guaranteeing over 300,000 loans per year totalling over 10 billion dollars. This scandal-free agency has developed its own appraisal procedures and forms even though it mainly uses FHA Minimum Property Standards for building and planning requirements.

The following four important elements are generally involved in government appraising and in working with government housing agencies:

ELEMENT 1—Timeliness—Above all, government appraisal reports must be timely. The best report loses its current value if it is not completed and returned within the required assignment period. Most housing agencies specify five days.

ELEMENT 2—Market Approach—Most housing agencies ask for the correlated three-approach method. Yet, most emphasize the Market approach in their guidance instructions and in their review of appraisal reports. (See Chapter 16 on Condemnation and government acquisition, for example.)

ELEMENT 3—Documentation—All appraisal reports for government agencies need specific documentation, particularly in the Market Data Analysis approach to value. For example, guidance instructions for completion of the FNMA appraisal report require similar sales comparables, each less than six months old, all in the same neighborhood with all data sources listed, like deed records, brokers, buyers, etc. If any of these specifications cannot be met, the appraiser has to attach an explanation as to the reasons for selecting comparables which do not meet these criteria.

ELEMENT 4—The Review Process—Practically all important government housing agencies have a review system of appraisal. Appraisal reports from outside independent appraisers are reviewed for accuracy, completeness and documentation. Reviewers are authorized to question appraisal reports and do field spot inspections of regular as well as questionable reports. It is important that the appraiser understand and be able to work with this review system and submit any additional documentation when requested. However, the independent appraiser has to always give his best independent opinion of value.

The reviewer's job is to ensure adherence to agency requirements, not to enforce uniformity of opinion.

A SAMPLE FNMA APPRAISAL FORM

The following FNMA Residential Appraisal Report Form 1004 has become most important in the housing industry because FNMA is involved in the financing of so many homes. This form is required for appraisals on all single-unit home mortgages offered by originating lenders to FNMA for purchase. It is prepared by an appraiser nominated by the lender-seller with the form typed or printed, dated and signed by the appraiser. Guidelines stress that appraisers cannot downgrade a neighborhood by marking it "declining" unless they report actual specific property sales which demonstrate this declining trend. All blanks have to be completed. An exterior sketch of the building, a location map showing location, and front, rear and street scene photographs of the property are required. Timeliness of the report date, comparables and opinion of value are stressed.

A MODEL VA APPLICATION AND APPRAISAL REPORT

Figures 17.4 and 17.5 are model completed VA application and appraisal report forms. These two forms, 26-1805, and 26-1803, are two parts of a VA ingeniously interleaved, nine-page, carbonized application/appraisal certificate "package." The data on the application lines up with and is transcribed into the appraisal and certificate forms when the application is filled in. The application should therefore be typed and carefully prepared to avoid impeding the processing. A copy of the executed or proposed contract, and plans and specifications on new or not previously occupied construction, should be attached. Four copies of the legal description should also be attached. The appraisal report can be typed or printed by pen. You complete the Appraisal Report 26-1803 in accordance with the following steps:

Step A—Verify Name of Municipality and County—The VA does its filing by county. Add the county to Item 7 if not already inserted.

Step B—Verify Lot Dimensions—Review the legal description or survey and correct lot dimensions in Item 11 when needed.

Step C—Check Legal Descriptions—In Item 13, if condominiums or P.U.D.'s are involved, return assignment to the VA if these special exhibits are not attached.

Step D—Review Survey and Legal Description for Restrictions—In Item 14, enter limitations or note "None Known."

Form Approved
OMB No. 76-R0231

VETERANS ADMINISTRATION

REQUEST FOR DETERMINATION OF REASONABLE VALUE (Real Estate)

CASE NUMBER

0000000

On receipt of "Certificate of Reasonable Value" or advice from the Veterans Administration that a "Certificate of Reasonable Value" will not be issued, we agree to forward to the appraiser the approved fee which we are holding for this purpose.

1. STATUS OF PROPERTY			2. CONSTRUCTION COMPLETED BEFORE DATE HEREOF	
☐ A. PROPOSED	☐ B. PREVIOUSLY OCCUPIED EXISTING, NOT	☒ C. PREVIOUSLY OCCUPIED	☐ D. ALTERATIONS, IMPROVEM'TS, OR REPAIRS	☐ E. REFINANCING-VETERAN APPLICANT OWNS AND OCCU-PIES RESIDENCE AS HOME	☐ A. WITHIN 12 CALENDAR MOS. ☒ B. MORE THAN 12 CALENDAR MOS

3. NAME AND ADDRESS OF FIRM OR PERSON MAKING REQUEST (Complete mailing address. Include ZIP Code.)

Ready Funding Corporation
000 Anywhere Drive
Alltown, U.S.A.

4. PROPERTY ADDRESS (Include ZIP Code)

0000 Sycamore Lane
Yourtown, Whiten County
U.S.A. 10000

5. TYPE OF PROPERTY	6. MANDATORY HOME ASSOCIATION MEMBERSHIP?	7A. NO. BLDGS.
☒ HOME		1
☐ MOBILE HOME LOT	☐ YES ☒ NO	7B. NO. LIVING UNITS 1
8. LOT DIMENSIONS	100' x 150'	

9. DESCRIPTION	WOOD SIDING	CINDER BLOCK	SPLIT LEVEL	NO. ROOMS	DINING ROOM	CAR GARAGE	GAS	CEN. AIR COND.
☒ DETACHED	WOOD SHINGLE	STONE	% BASEMENT 50	5	KITCHEN	CAR CARPORT	UNDERGRO.WRE	☒ TYPE HEAT. & FUEL g.h.w
SEMI-DET.	☒ ALUM. SIDING	BRICK & BLOCK	SLAB	BEDROOMS 3	FAMILY RM.	WATER (Public)	SEWER (Public)	
ROW	ASB. SHINGLE	STUCCO	CRAWL SPACE ☒	BATHS 1½	UTILITY RM.	WATER (Comm.)	SEWER (Comm.)	ROOFING DESCRIP. A/S
CONDOMINIUM	BRICK VENEER	STORIES 1	YRS. EST. AGE 15	LIVING RMS. 1	FIREPLACE 1	WATER (Ind.) ☒	SEPTIC TANK ☒	

10. LEGAL DESCRIPTION

Block 1, Lot 12 of Map of
Rolling Woods filed Whiten
County Clerk

11. TITLE LIMITATIONS, INCLUDING EASEMENTS, RESTRIC-TIONS, ENCROACHMENTS, HOMEOWNERS ASSOCIATION AND SPECIAL ASSESSMENTS, ETC.

R.O.W to Public Highway
Utility Easements
Lake Rights

12. OFFSITE IMPROVEMENTS			
A. STREET SURFACE: BT		D. ADD'L IMPROVEMENTS	
B. STREET ACCESS ☒ PRIV. ☐ PUB.		☐ STORM SEWER	☐ SIDEWALK
C. STREET MAINT. ☒ PRIV. ☐ PUB.		☐ CURB/GUTTER	

14. REMOVABLE EQUIPMENT INCLUDED IN PURCHASE PRICE OR COST			
☒ RANGE OR COUNTER TOP UNIT	☐ DISHWASHER	☐ REFRIGERATOR	
☐ AUTOMATIC WASHER	☐ DRYER	☐ WALL-TO-WALL CARPETING	
☒ OTHER(S) (Specify) Alum S/S			

13. VETERAN PURCHASER'S NAME AND ADDRESS (Complete mailing address. Include ZIP Code)

John Smith
10 Doe Drive
Yourtown, U.S.A. 10000

15A. OCCUPANT'S NAME	15B. TELEPHONE NO.	16A. BROKER'S NAME	16B. TELEPHONE NO.
Vacant	000-0000	Fairview Elm Realty	300-3000
17. DATE AND TIME AVAILABLE FOR INSPECTION	18. KEYS AT (Address)	19. NAME OF OWNER	
By appointment ☐ AM ☐ PM	Broker	Henry Hill	

Figure 17.4

A MODEL VA APPLICATION FORM
FOR REQUESTING APPRAISALS

VA FILE COPY 1

20. COMPLIANCE INSPECTIONS WILL BE OR WERE MADE BY

☐ FHA ☐ VA ☒ NONE MADE

21. NUMBER OF MASTER CERTIFICATE OF REASONABLE VALUE (If any)

22. PROPOSED SALES CONTRACT ATTACHED
☐ YES ☒ NO

23. CONTRACT NO. PREVIOUSLY APPROVED BY VA THAT WILL BE USED

24A. NAME AND ADDRESS OF BUILDER (Include ZIP Code)

24B. TELEPHONE NO.

25A. NAME AND ADDRESS OF WARRANTOR (Include ZIP Code)

25B. TELEPHONE NO.

26. PLANS (Check one)
☐ FIRST SUBMISSION ☐ REPEAT CASE (If repeat case, complete Item 27)

27. PLANS PREVIOUSLY PROCESSED UNDER VA CASE NO.

28. ANNUAL REAL EST. TAXES (If exist. construction)
$ 1400

29. COMMENTS ON SPECIAL ASSESSMENTS AND/OR HOMEOWNER ASSOCIATION CHARGES

None known

30. SHOW BELOW: Shape, location, distance from nearest intersection, and street names. Mark N at north point.

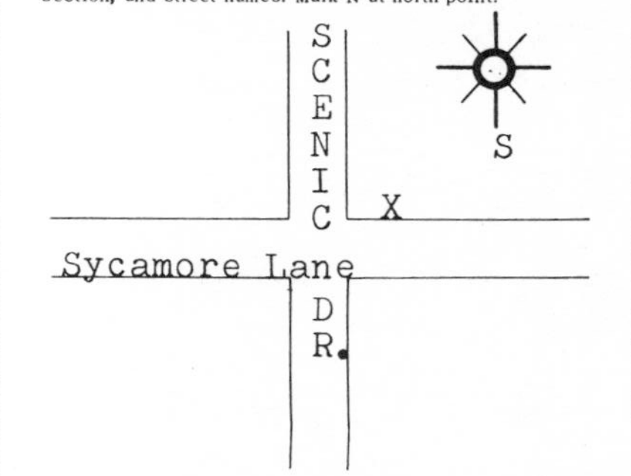

N
S   C   E   N   I   C
X
Sycamore Lane
D
R.

EQUAL OPPORTUNITY IN HOUSING - NOTICE

Federal laws and regulations prohibit discrimination because of race, color, religion, national origin, or sex in the sale or rental or financing of residential property. Numerous state statutes and local ordinances also prohibit such discrimination.

Non-compliance with applicable antidiscrimination laws and regulations in respect to any property included in this request shall be a proper basis for refusal by the VA to do business with the violator and for refusal to appraise properties with which the violator is identified. Denial of participation in any program administered by the Federal Housing Administration because of such violation shall constitute basis for similar action by the VA.

CERTIFICATION REQUIRED ON CONSTRUCTION UNDER FHA SUPERVISION (Strike out inappropriate phrases in parentheses)

I hereby certify that plans and specifications and related exhibits, including acceptable FHA Change Orders, if any, supplied to VA in this case, are identical to those (submitted to) (to be submitted to) (approved by) FHA, and that FHA inspections (have been) (will be) made pursuant to FHA approval for mortgage insurance on the basis of proposed construction under Sec.

31A. NAME AND ADDRESS OF PROSPECTIVE LENDER (Include ZIP Code)

Ready Funding Corporation
0000 Anywhere Drive, Alltown, USA

31B. TELEPHONE NO. OF LENDER/REQUESTER
400-4000

32. SALE PRICE OF PROPERTY
$ 41000

33. REFINANCING AMT. OF PROPOSED LOAN
$

34. SIGNATURE OF PERSON AUTHORIZING THIS REQUEST

35. TITLE
Mortgage Officer

36. DATE
9/1/-

Federal statutes provide severe penalties for any fraud, intentional misrepresentation, or criminal connivance or conspiracy purposed to influence the issuance of any guaranty or insurance or the granting of any loan by the Administrator.

37. DATE OF ASSIGNMENT

38. NAME OF APPRAISER

VA FORM 26-1805

EXISTING STOCKS OF VA FORM 26-1805 WILL BE USED.

VETERANS ADMINISTRATION
RESIDENTIAL APPRAISAL REPORT

CASE NUMBER: 0000000

1. MAJOR STRUCTURES	A. TYPICAL COND.	B. BUILT-UP	C. AGE TYPE BLDG.	D. OWN OCCUP.	E. VACANCY	F. ZONING	G. LAND USE CHGS.	2. PROPERTY IS	3. BLDG. WARRANTY IN FORCE?
NEIGHBORHOOD	GOOD	20 %	20	100 %	0 %	RES	STABLE	☐ OCCU-PIED	☐ YES ☒ NO
BLOCK	GOOD	50 %	15	100 %	0 %	RES	STABLE	☒ VACANT	☐ UNKNOWN

4. STATUS OF PROPERTY
☐ A. PROPOSED ☐ B. PREVIOUSLY OCCUPIED ☒ C. EXISTING, NOT PREVIOUSLY OCCUPIED ☐ D. ALTERATIONS, IMPROVEMENTS, OR REPAIRS

5. CONSTRUCTION COMPLETED BEFORE DATE HEREOF
☐ A. WITHIN 12 CALENDAR MOS. ☒ B. MORE THAN 12 CALENDAR MOS.

6. NAME AND ADDRESS OF FIRM OR PERSON MAKING REQUEST (Complete mailing address. Include ZIP Code.)

Ready Funding Corporation
000 Anywhere Drive
Alltown, U.S.A.

7. PROPERTY ADDRESS (Include ZIP Code)

0000 Sycamore Lane
Yourtown, Whiten County
U.S.A. 10000

8. TYPE OF PROPERTY
☒ HOME
☐ MOBILE HOME LOT

REFINANCING - VETERAN APRESENT OWNS AND OCCUPIES RESIDENCE AS HOME

9. MANDATORY HOME ASSOCIATION MEMBERSHIP? ☐ YES ☒ NO

10A. NO. BLDGS. 1
10B. NO. LIVING UNITS 1

11. LOT DIMENSIONS 100' x 150' / 15000 Sq

12. DESCRIPTION				SPLIT LEVEL	NO. ROOMS 5	DINING ROOM	CAR GARAGE	GAS	10A. CEN. AIR COND. ☒
DETACHED ☒	WOOD SIDING	CINDER BLOCK	STONE	% BASEMENT	BEDROOMS 3	KITCHEN 1	CAR CARPORT	UNDERGR'D WIRE	TYPE HEAT. & FUEL ghw
SEMI-DET.	WOOD SHINGLE	BRICK & BLOCK	SLAB		BATHS 1	FAMILY RM.	WATER (Public)	SEWER (Public)	ROOFING DESCRIP.
ROW	ALUM. SIDING ☒	STUCCO	CRAWL SPACE ☒		1/2 BATHS	UTILITY RM.	WATER (Comm.)	SEWER (Comm.)	A/S
CONDOMINIUM	ASB. SHINGLE	STORIES 1	YRS. EST. AGE 15		LIVING RM. 1	FIREPLACE 1	WATER (Ind.) ☒	SEPTIC TANK ☒	
	BRICK VENEER								

13. LEGAL DESCRIPTION

Block 1, Lot 12 of Map of
Rolling Woods filed Whiten
County Clerk

14. TITLE LIMITATIONS, INCLUDING EASEMENTS, RESTRICTIONS, ENCROACHMENTS, HOMEOWNERS ASSOCIATION AND SPECIAL ASSESSMENTS, ETC.

R.O.W to Public Highway
Utility Easements
Lake Rights

15. OFFSITE IMPROVEMENTS

A. STREET SURFACE. BT	D. ADD'L. IMPROVEMENTS	
B. STREET ACCESS	☐ STORM SEWER	
☐ PRIV. ☒ PUB.	☐ SIDEWALK	
C. STREET MAINT.	☐ CURB/GUTTER	
☒ PRIV. ☐ PUB.		

16. REPAIRS NECESSARY TO MAKE PROPERTY CONFORM TO APPLIC. MPR'S

REPAIR SMALL SECTION OF RETAINING
WALL NEAR LEFT FRONT OF DWELLING $ 300

SCRAPE PAINT BATH CEILING $ 25

TOTAL ESTIMATED COST OF REPAIRS $ 325

17. REMARKS (Complete A through F. Use supplemental sheet or reverse, if necessary.)

A. DETRIMENTAL INFLUENCES   NONE INCLUDING AIRPORTS

B. REAL ESTATE MARKET IN COMMUNITY   MODERATELY ACTIVE

C. HIGHEST AND BEST USE   RESIDENTIAL - PRESENT USE

D. FEDERAL FLOOD HAZARD MAP ISSUED? ☒ YES ☐ NO (If "Yes," complete item 17E)

E. PROP. IN SPECIAL FLOOD HAZARD AREA? ☐ YES ☒ NO

F. EXPLAIN DEPRECIATION

PHYSICAL - AGE NORMAL WEAR + TEAR - ECON PRIVATE ROAD

18. MARKET DATA

ITEM	SUBJECT PROPERTY	COMPARABLE NO. 1	COMPARABLE NO. 2	COMPARABLE NO. 3
ADDRESS	000 SYCAMORE LANE YOURTOWN	000 SYCAMORE LANE YOURTOWN	00 ELM DRIVE YOURTOWN	000 MAPLE LANE YOURTOWN
SALE PRICE		$ 43000	$ 37000	$ 40000
TYPE OF FINANCING		V.A.	CONV	CONV

DATE OF SALE	DESCRIPTION	ADJ.	DESCRIPTION	ADJ.	DESCRIPTION	ADJ.	DESCRIPTION	ADJ.
		$	9/1/-	$	8/2/-	$	4/3/-	$
LOCATION	GOOD LAKE LOCATION		SIMILAR		SIMILAR		SIMILAR	
SITE IMPROVEMENT	GOOD		SIMILAR		SIMILAR		SIMILAR	
AGE/CONDITION	15 - GOOD		20 GOOD		10 FAIR	+2000	10 GOOD	
GARAGE/CARPORT	1G		1G		1G		1G	
CONSTRUCTION	FRAME		FR		FR		FR	
PORCHES, POOL, ETC.	LAKE RIGHTS		LAKE RIGHTS		LAKE RIGHTS		LAKE RIGHTS	

ROOM COUNT/SIZE	ROOMS	BDRMS	BATH	S.F. AREA	ROOMS	BDRMS	BATH	S.F. AREA	ROOMS	BDRMS	BATH	S.F. AREA	ROOMS	BDRMS	BATH	S.F. AREA
	5	3	1	711	6	4	1	1000	6	4	1	950	5	3	1	750
NET ADJUSTMENT (Show (+) or (−) adjustment)					$			−2000	$			−2000	$			40000
INDICATED VALUE OF SUBJECT PROPERTY					$			41000	$			39000	$			40000

19. PROPERTY SHOWS EVIDENCE OF (Check): TERMITE ☐ DRY ROT ☐ DAMP-NESS ☐ SETTLE-MENT ☐ NO EVIDENCE ☒

20. ESTATE (Check): A. FEE SIMPLE ☒ B. LEASE-HOLD ☐

21. REMAINING ECONOMIC LIFE (Years) MAIN 40 OTHER

22. COST APPROACH CU. ☐ SQ. ☒ OTHER

23. DATA	DESCRIPTION	CONDITION	24. EQUIP.	DESCRIPTION	DEPR.VALUE	25. OTHER IMPROVEMENTS	DEPR.VALUE		MAIN	711	RATE PER FT.	$ 30
ROOF	A/S	E	RANGE	WEBULT	$ 0	LANDSCAPING	$ 300		REPLMT. COST	$		2 (300
FOUND.	MASONRY	G	(15 YEARS OLD)			DRIVE + WALKS	500		PHYSICAL DEP.	$		1000
BSMT.	50%	G				DET GARAGE	1200		FUNCTIONAL	$		
FLOORS	OAK	G				CONC PATIOS TERRACE	1000		ECONOMIC	$		1000
INT. WALLS	DRYWALL	G				ALUM S/S	200		TOTAL DEP.	$		2000
BATH FINISH	CERAMIC	G							DEPR. COST	$		19300
GUTTERS	ALUM	G							TOTAL DEPR. COST OF IMPR.			$ 19300

26. ANNUAL TAXES

GENERAL	SPECIAL	OTHER
$ 1400	$	$

				TOTAL	$ 3000	OTHER IMPR. AND EQUIP.	$ 3000
						LAND VALUE	$ 18000
						TOTAL DEPR. COST OF PROP.	$ 40300

27. DOES PROPERTY CONFORM TO APPLICABLE MINIMUM PROPERTY REQUIREMENTS? YES ☒ NO ☐ (If "No" explain on reverse)

28. ESTIMATE FAIR MONTHLY RENT TIMES RENT MULTIPLIER (If applicable) $ N.A.

29. RECONCILIATION

A. MARKET APPROACH	B. COST APPROACH	C. INCOME APPROACH (If applicable)
$ 40000	$ 40300	$ N.A.

30. I ESTIMATE "REASONABLE VALUE" ☐ "AS IS" ☒ "AS REPAIRED" ☐ "AS COMPLETED" $ 40000

31. ESTIMATED REASONABLE VALUE $ 40000

32. SIGNATURE OF APPRAISER Samuel T. Brown

33. DATE SIGNED 10/5/-

VA FORM 26-1803

VA FILE COPY 5

NOTE: No determination of reasonable value may be made unless a completed appraisal report is received (38 U.S.C. 1810). I HEREBY CERTIFY that (a) I have carefully viewed the property described in this report, INSIDE AND OUTSIDE, so far as it has been completed; that (b) it is the same property that is identified by description in my appraisal assignment; that (c) I HAVE NOT RECEIVED, HAVE NO AGREEMENT TO RECEIVE, NOR WILL I ACCEPT FROM ANY PARTY ANY GRATUITY OR EMOLUMENT OTHER THAN MY APPRAISAL FEE FOR MAKING THIS APPRAISAL; that (d) I have no interest, present or prospective, in the applicant, seller, property, or mortgage; that (e) in arriving at the estimated reasonable value I have not been influenced in any manner whatsoever by the race, color, religion, national origin, or sex of any person residing in the property or in the neighborhood wherein it is located. I understand that violation of this certification can result in removal from the fee appraiser's roster.

Figure 17.5

A MODEL VA APPRAISAL REPORT FORM

Step E—Verify All Other Data Items 4 Through 15—Verify in the field and correct where needed all other data typed by requester in Items 4 through 15 on the report.

Step F—Specify Repairs and Estimated Repair Costs—In Item 16, list specific repairs with individual costs itemized. (See Chapter 4 on Inspections.)

Step G—Comment on Comparables—In Item 18, compare comparables to subject with adjustments made in terms of dollars.

Step H—Complete Items 19 through 33—From your field interior and exterior inspection and data collection, complete the form for additional description and comment in Items 19 through 27, cost calculations and income rent multiplier (if applicable) in 22 and 28, reconciliation in 29 and final estimate, signature and date in Items 30, 31, 32, and 33. The Market approach is most important and should be relied on for your opinion of value.

Chapter 18

How to appraise a farm

This chapter is on farm appraising. It traces the decline of family farming and the rise of "agribusiness" and per acre prices of farms in America. The urbanization and population pressures which have mainly caused this decline are evaluated. The comparatively new methods of agriculture districts, tax deferrals and development easements being used recently to combat this decline are detailed. The importance of government subsidy programs and cooperative farm credit agencies are stressed. There is a section on how to use government agencies to collect data for farm appraisals. There are step-by-step procedures and a field checklist on farm appraisal methodology. This chapter also provides guidance on how to use soil data and maps, how to prepare a farmland use map and how to appraise farm buildings and lands. Finally, a Model Farmers Home Administration Appraisal Report From is included with specific instructions on how to complete it.

URBAN IMPACT ON FARMING; "AG" DISTRICTS, TAX DEFERRAL AND OTHER RELIEF MEASURES

Two thousand years ago, Virgil warned his countrymen that the loss of agriculture would destroy Rome. Today, as then, a nation is weakened when it can no longer produce its basic food supply. About 1.25 million acres of cropland are lost yearly to urbanization in America. A complex of economy, population and even technical appraisal and legal factors have caused this continued decline.

In 1935, one in four Americans lived on a farm. By the mid-seventies, only one in 25 did. Yet farm production has continued to meet and exceed increased demand because of mechanization and because of farm industrialization by big agribusiness firms. Many small farmers could not meet the increasing costs of this mechanization and of irrigation costs, particularly in arid western areas. Pressures from developers on farmers to sell their farms near metropolitan areas have decimated family farming. Land speculators buy farms, sell off the homesteads and barns with a few acres to lower taxes and then await the tide of development for capital depreciation. An analysis by the Federal Land Bank Association Farm Credit Service in one county 75 miles from a Northeastern city showed that 15 of the total farms sold that year went to investors and developers.

The Census Bureau defines a farm as a place of 10 acres or more generally selling more than $250 a year in agricultural products. This definition has become mostly historic since the small farm has mainly disappeared. The total value of U.S. farm real estate as of the mid-seventies was about $420 billion. The average value of an operating farm was $165,000.

There are countervailing forces. New federal agencies like the Environmental Protection Agency are tightening up on water and sewer grants to communities to minimize these pressures of urbanization. The EPA is aware that farms once subdivided and improved with houses, shopping centers and blacktop will never be retrieved. Farmland, the EPA reasons, is open space. It protects watersheds, is a compatible use for wetlands and flood plains. In a total environment sense, farmland maintains the quality of life. Also, the Department of Interior in the late seventies, through its Bureau of Reclamation and through its control of irrigation projects, began to try to break up the large agribusiness landholdings which have been engulfing traditional smaller family farms.

This background and data is of more than historic interest to the farm appraiser. For example, in property tax assessment, the appraisal practice of estimating the value of land at its highest and best use has undoubtedly been one of the main factors driving farmers off their land. Appraisers have testified and courts have ruled time and again that the value of land must be established on its highest and best use for, say a residential subdivision rather than on its current use as a farm. In metropolitan regions, this has put unbearable property tax pressures on farmers since their assessments kept increasing because of this legal-appraisal approach. Agricultural districts, property tax deferrals, limited tax exemptions and tax payments have been instituted by many communities to give tax relief. An innovative development easement program in Suffolk County, N.Y. in the late seventies featured buying up forever the rights of development from farmers. This is done by paying the farm owner the difference of two appraisals, one assuming the land is used for real estate subdivision and the other assuming continued farm production. These measures are being undertaken in many areas to preserve viable farmland by offering these limited tax exemptions and development easement purchases.

These various conflicting pressures driving the number of smaller farms down, the big farms up and diminishing cropland, have also resulted in a steady increase of per acre prices of farms. The following table published by the U.S. Department of Agriculture (Publication CD-81), shows this dramatic recent price surge (Figure 18.1).

HOW TO USE GOVERNMENT AND COOPERATIVE
CREDIT PROGRAMS AND DATA

At best, farming is a hazardous occupation, being dependent on many factors beyond human control such as weather, drought, erosion, fluctuation, markets, over-production, etc. Government subsidy programs including farm crop supports or FmHA loan programs, or technical service programs like the Department of Agriculture (ASCS) County Offices, are all there to sustain the economic well-being of the farmer engaged in this economically hazardous industry. There are also cooperative farm credit agencies like the Farm Credit Service of the Federal Land Bank Association which help farmers financially.

Credit is the life blood of farming, not only for operating funds in this seasonal industry but also for farmland sales. Many farms are sold through seller contracts or ''purchase money'' mortgages from seller. However, the majority of farm transfers are made possible through first and secondary mortgages from Federal Land Banks, from insurance companies, commercial banks and other lenders. The following recent USDA illustration (Figure 18.2) charts this distribution of loan funds:

Supportive government, quasi-government and other federal and state agencies are also among the best sources for data collection for appraisals. Systematic data collection and analysis are always fundamental to the appraisal process; they are particularly important in farm appraising which is so sensitive to government policies and support. The overall step-by-step procedure for farm appraising is as follows:

Step 1—Define the Problem—As in all types of appraising, the problem posed in the farm appraisal assignment is first defined.

Step 2—Accumulate Data—Through personal inspection of the property and field investigation, data is accumulated.

Step 3—Write the Appraisal Report—Analyze the collected data and write the report to include the following:

(a) A physical description of the property, noting all land features.

(b) An estimate of the productive capacity of the property, the type of farm operation, the kind of crops and livestock, the typical yields per acre and the typical dollar return.

(c) An opinion of market value developed from the personal inspection data collection and analysis.

Table 1—Farm real estate: Indexes of average value per acre, by State, grouped by farm production region, March 1, 1965 and 1970-75 and Feb. 1, 1976[1]

(1967=100)

State	1965	1970	1971	1972	1973	1974	1975	1976
Northeast								
Maine	89	128	146					
New Hampshire	86	149	178					
Vermont	83	155	177					
Massachusetts	89	126	139	174	198	231[2]	257[2]	278
Rhode Island	89	132	145					
Connecticut	87	134	149					
New York	90	123	132	155	176	233	275	296
New Jersey	82	144	155	180	211	278	340	377
Pennsylvania	88	145	154	167	201	262	315	350
Delaware	92	116	131	134	155	199	242	288
Maryland	85	138	150	162	191	227	248	299
Lake States								
Michigan	84	113	115	127	150	174	184	201
Wisconsin	85	124	137	148	179	214	240	271
Minnesota	90	118	121	127	144	186	242	294
Corn Belt								
Ohio	86	115	120	127	147	184	208	252
Indiana	80	104	109	113	131	161	200	244
Illinois	84	107	108	116	129	173	209	260
Iowa	79	114	114	122	141	189	234	294
Missouri	82	124	130	143	160	207	214[2]	241
Northern Plains								
North Dakota	87	120	122	127	142	193	265	310
South Dakota	86	112	114	118	130	172	214	241
Nebraska	86	115	117	127	145	183	215	271
Kansas	88	107	109	118	137	178	211	235
Appalachian								
Virginia	85	121	132	149	171	223	250	278
West Virginia	93	137	153	177	211	275	317	398
North Carolina	91	113	128	138	164	200	216	232
Kentucky	93	116	123	137	153	182	203	239
Tennessee	88	123	128	142	167	206	236	251
Southeast								
South Carolina	88	124	135	162	179	238	273	284
Georgia	80	138	152	175	201	264	298	299
Florida[3]	100	121	128	136	155	200	224	237
Alabama	85	121	139	146	167	211	233	258
Delta States								
Mississippi	81	125	127	129	144	182	204	205
Arkansas	84	129	127	143	159	186	191	213
Louisiana	80	116	127	139	148	174	191	201
Southern Plains								
Oklahoma	87	115	122	131	150	183	212	234
Texas	89	119	125	138	156	191	193	213
Mountain								
Montana	89	124	131	142	159	203	237[2]	278
Idaho	91	120	128	141	159	203	243	264
Wyoming	88	116	119	134	153	191	218	254
Colorado	88	105	114	128	152	194	209	244
New Mexico	88	120	127	136	151	186	197	206
Arizona	85	127	139	159	170	208	211	217
Utah	89	137	154	173	186	216	232	261
Nevada	83	155	181	213	251	299	299	307
Pacific								
Washington	88	124	124	130	145	160	178	213
Oregon	91	137	152	170	187	213	228	242
California	91	110	109	112	115	131	150[2]	156
48 States	86	117	122	132	150	187	214	244

[1] Includes improvements. (See figure 5 for map of farm production regions.) [2] Revised. [3] Indexes for 1973-76 are estimated by the average of the percentage change in Georgia and Alabama index values.

Figure 18.1

DEPARTMENT OF AGRICULTURE
FARM REAL ESTATE ACREAGE VALUE TABLE

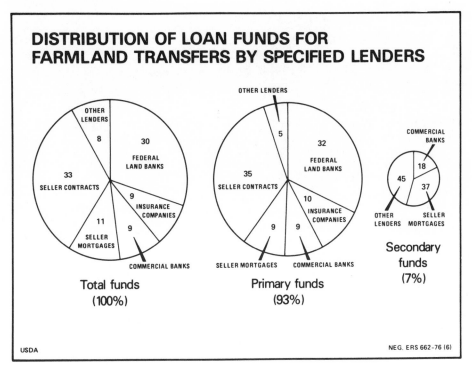

DISTRIBUTION OF LOAN FUNDS FOR FARMLAND TRANSFERS BY SPECIFIED LENDERS

Total funds (100%)

Primary funds (93%)

Secondary funds (7%)

USDA

NEG. ERS 662-76 (6)

Figure 18.2

FARM MORTGAGE LOAN FUNDS CHART

Later sections in this chapter give guidance and a field checklist on farm appraisal data collection from all sources. Because of its importance to farm appraisals, the following "government" guide deals specifically with important government and quasi-government data sources:

Department of Agriculture (USDA)—The mission of this department is farm support. The USDA also issues regular reports on market development, farm real estate transfers, farm financing and non-farm influences on farm real estate markets. Farm appraisers should be on the USDA regular mailing list for its publication CD81, "Farm Real Estate Market Developments." In addition, the USDA operates a nationwide system of county offices which are an invaluable source for local farm conditions, soils data, land use maps and appraisal sales data.

Farmers Home Administration (FmHA)—This arm of the Department of Agriculture has important responsibilities besides housing. Money is an indication of its impact on farming. It recently pumped $5½ billion in one year at interest rates of 1% and up into farm loans. In addition to home loans, the FmHA makes loans on non-farm enterprises to supplement farm income, project loans to youths aged 10 to 21, farm operating loans, new construction and rehabilitation farm loan commitments, emergency loans, guaranteed lender loans and grants or loans for rural community facilities. Its local offices are an excellent appraisal source for rural statistical data and farm sale comparables.

Department of Census—This is an important source for vital statistics and other demographic studies. For example, recent studies report on the decreasing fertility of women on the farm, contributing to less farming population and less farms. These census reports enable the appraiser to keep up with national and local farm trends.

Department of Commerce—Monthly reviews of national and area economic trends are available here.

Environmental Protection Agency—This agency is comparatively new on the farm scene. The EPA has a vital interest in preserving farmland and keeping it in food production. It is the major source for data on pesticide pollution and publishes technical reports on the application of new, proven pollution techniques. The EPA's stress on solar research has resulted in such innovations as inexpensive metal roofs combined with fans which reduce heating costs 50% in hog houses and grain drying buildings. Such data are available from the EPA, and they are most useful in appraising modern farm building improvements.

U.S. Superintendent of Documents—Farm appraisers should get on the Superintendent of Documents mailing list. The Superintendent sends mailings which list all recent publications by all U.S. agencies including farm agencies.

State Agencies—State farm agencies maintain field offices and publish regular farm reports. These offices are also important appraisal data sources for local market conditions, sales comparables, soil data and maps.

County and Municipal Offices—These offices maintain and have available data on local economics, population, land use, recreation and zoning. Assessor's offices have information on assessment, taxes, equalization (true value to assessment) and often have verified comparable market sales data. Engineer-building inspector offices, town clerks and planning boards can furnish area trends, maps and other important local data on farms.

HOW TO USE SOIL MAPS, PREPARE LAND USE MAPS AND APPRAISE FARM BUILDINGS AND LAND

Farm appraising, like farming itself, is a specialized field. For example, a home appraisal normally finds its major value in the building which improves the plot. In farm appraising, however, the objective is to arrive at that value for the buildings which their function adds to the land value. Farm buildings have value only in terms of their degree of usefulness to the farm operation.

The farm appraiser analyzes soil and land uses. On each farm appraisal assignment, one of the first data collection steps is to contact the County Office of the USDA Agricultural Stabilization and Conservation Service for soil maps, soil bulletins, soil type sheets and soil rating sheets covering the particular location. From this data and from personal inspection of the property, a land use map is then drawn for analysis and later attachment to the appraisal report. If there is no survey of the farm available, the legal description should be plotted to make a farm sketch or map, including boundary lines and important farm features. Whenever possible, an accurate base map of the farm should be obtained from the ASCS County office or from some other source. This base map normally shows boundary lines, fields, swales, location of buildings, cropland, woodland and other features. From inspection, other features should be added such as direction and per cent of slope, kinds of soil, erosion, fences, recommended land use and weed areas.

These basic collection and analysis procedures, including full contact with local businessmen, lenders and other farmers, are important parts of the following "Field Checklist for Farm Appraisals":

FARM APPRAISAL FIELD CHECKLIST

Owner _____ Acres _____ Date _____

Location _____ Appraiser _____

THE COMMUNITY

Rural? _____
Suburban? _____
Development Pressures _____
Off-Farm Employment _____
Local Financing Available? ____
Typical Area Farm _____
Typical Farm Rents _____
Farm Sales Activity _____
Farm Products Activity _____

THE FARM

Size, Shape _____
Type of Soils _____
Percent Pasture _____
Percent Cropland _____
Percent Timber _____
Bldgs. Value Effect _____

SALES DATA SOURCES

Public Deed Records _____
Brokers _____
Sellers _____
Assessor _____
Lawyers _____
Lenders _____
Others _____
_____

SALES DATA INVESTIGATION

Type of Operation _____
Price of Pastureland _____
Price of Timberland _____
Price of Cropland _____
Crop Yields _____
Rotation Used in Area _____

Land Uses _____
Fencing _____
Drainage _____
Erosion _____
Location re Market _____
Roads Paved, Accessible? _____
Terms of Sale, Cash? _____
Contract, % Interest _____
Aerials Available _____
Legal Description _____
Map of Property _____
Topography _____
Water Resources _____
Other _____
_____

Lease Terms _____
Cash Rents _____
Crop Shares _____
Taxes _____
Insurance _____
Cost of Seed, Fertilizer
   Herbicide, Pesticide _____
Management Fees _____
Bldg. Values _____
No. of Acres _____
Location _____
Time of Sale _____
Other _____
_____

List 5 Comparable Farm Sales—

1. _____
2. _____
3. _____
4. _____
5. _____

REMARKS (Use other side if needed)

_____
_____
_____

The three-approach system of Cost, Income and Market is still required on farm appraisals by most government agencies and lenders. Like the FmHA does in its appraisal guide, however, most agencies and lenders stress the Market approach. However, this traditional correlated three-approach valuation system must still be used in the written farm appraisal report.

For the *Income Approach* on farms, derive net income by deducting the following expenses. Then divide the capitalization rate into your net profit for the property valuation.

1. Taxes and special district assessments.

2. Seed, herbicide, pesticides, fertilizer, lime, harvesting, and marketing costs.

3. Insurance.

4. Operating and maintenance costs on buildings, fences and irrigation.

5. Management fees.

Capitalization rates for owner-operated farms generally reflect the following and usually approximate mortgage rates in most areas.

1. Capital investment of the farmer's capital.

2. A home for the farmer.

3. An occupation for the farmer.

Capitalization rates for absentee management farms are usually higher to almost double going mortgage rates in many areas because no amenities nor occupations are involved, only return on invested capital. Band of Investment techniques can be used to develop this capitalization rate. (See prior commercial chapter.) If enough data can be secured on the net income of comparable sales in the area, then a more accurate capitalization rate can be determined.

For the *Cost Approach* on farms, working from your data collection and interviews with informed persons in the area (see field questionnaire), Put a price on each classification of land on the property being appraised. Enter so much per acre for say the 90 acres of rolling cropland, so much for the 50 acres of fenced pasture, the 5 acres of farmstead around the buildings. Do the arithmetic to derive the land value; add the depreciated value of the buildings to arrive at the total property valuation.

For the *Market Approach* on the farms, the following items are the major subject to sales comparison critera. (FHA Form 422-10 at the end of this section is a good comparable analysis worksheet.) Opinion of value from the Market approach is then derived by comparing each selected close comparable on a plus or minus adjustment basis to the subject.

(1) *Location*—Accessibility; closeness to market, to town.

(2) *Size and Shape*—Topography, water resources typical to farms in area? Regular shape? Irregular shape causing point rows and cropland waste?

(3) *Soils and Land Use*—Compare subject to sales for type, productivity, grade, use of soils and land, proportion of cropland to total land.

(4) *Buildings and Improvements*—Farmhouse, barns, other buildings, their quality, their functional utility value to the farm operation, the type and yield of water supply.

(5) *Time*—Unlike residential appraising, farm sales are not as numerous in most areas. Older sales of similar properties often have to be used, sometimes even up to four years, in areas of slow sales. Adjustments for time have to be

analyzed and culled carefully for annual percentage trend from the collected sales data and from government reported per acre prices for the region.

(6) *Terms of sale*—Percentage interest on the mortgage? Did sales contract have unusually favorable terms? Unusually low or typical to area down payment amounts? Sale to a relative? Sale for tax purposes?

In *correlation* of the three-approach system on farms, the Income approach is usually not as reliable because the influential capitalization rate is so subjective and minute changes in the cap rate cause such large changes in the valuation. The Cost approach is even more subjective in terms of allocation of prices and depreciation of buildings. (In condemnation appraisals of farms, however, the Cost approach is usually the best way to show damages to the property.) As ever, the Market approach is the most reliable indicator of farm value in most appraisals.

A MODEL FmHA APPRAISAL REPORT

The following completed Appraisal Report Form FHA 422-1 (including Form 422-10) is a good, inclusive, model format for farm appraisals. It also demonstrates the correlated three-approach method of appraising farm properties.

Instructions for completion of this form are as follows:

Part 1 A —*Location*—Locate farm as to trading center, schools, etc.

   B —*Roads and Community*—Grade roads as to type and condition. Identify type of farming in community.

   C —*Farm Services*—Check available services and number of miles to market.

   D —*Community Factors*—Compare subject to other farms in community.

   E —*Condition of Land*—Comment on fertility factors.

   F —*Natural Resources*—Check any natural resources. Mention if leases of minerals or other resources are involved.

   G —*Water*—Enter type and yield data for both household and livestock water supply.

   H —*Farming Hazards*—List any flooding or other hazards.

   I —*Ownership History*—Review last sale of farm.

   J —*Rental Terms*—Enter typical cash or share rents.

   K —*Taxes*—Enter all property and special assessment taxes.

Part 2—*Summation Value*—Enter detailed information on all the building improvements. Standard cost handbooks are used for replacement costs. Take depreciation.

Part 3—*Sales Data*—Select similar arm's-length, bona fide comparables which need minimum adjustment. (Use prior illustration, "Appraisers Worksheet for Comparable Properties," to rate the sales on a plus or minus quality point basis.)

Part 4—*Land and Buildings*—Comment on general appearance, utility, structural aspects in relation to how facilities would contribute to a successful farming operation. Discuss favorable and unfavorable building features. Enter needed land improvements and describe any deficiencies affecting the value of the farm.

Part 5—*Use of Land Resources and Improvements*—Select crops based on a typical operation for the farm being appraised in its community. Show a crop rotation followed by a typical farmer to protect soil productivity. Government allotments of controlled crops must be considered for this selection. Insert acreage of each typical crop. Insert yield per acre of crops, including forest crops, representative of yields a typical operator would expect. Insert total amount of production for each crop and price per unit for each commodity, as well as the total value of each commodity produced. Complete the rent and deduction entries, derive the net income and enter capitalization rate based on the money market, physical and economic risks and marketability. Divide the net farm income by the Capitalization Rate to get the capitalization value.

Part 6—*Summation Value of Farm*—List major soil types and land classes, compute the acreage of each class and describe as indicated by column headings. Add the summation value of buildings to the total market value of the acreage to find the Summation Value of the farm through this Cost approach method.

Part 7—*Recommended Market Value of Farm*—This represents the final determination of value and is a judgment determination after analysis of all factors and approaches with major reliance on the Market approach.

Part 8—*Comments*—Include any other favorable or unfavorable comments, off-farm employment opportunities for farmers off-season, community factors, etc. Sign and date the report; attach the completed farm map.

USDA–FHA

Form FHA 422–1   APPRAISAL REPORT – FARM TRACT   FORM APPROVED
OMB NO. 40-R3769

Applicant's Name _____ State _____

Address of Property __LONGVIEW FARM, ANYWHERE, USA__ County _____

PART 1. GENERAL INFORMATION

A. LOCATION OF FARM

NAME OF NEAR. TOWN __ANYWHERE__
DIRECTION FROM TOWN __NORTH__
MILES FROM TOWN __6__
MILES FROM NEAR. SCHOOL __5__
MILES FROM NEAR. CHURCH __6__

B. ROADS AND COMMUNITY

CONDITION OF ROADS ☐E ☐G ☒F ☐P
KIND OF FARM ROAD __DIRT__
MILES TO NEAR. PUBLIC GRAVEL OR H–S ROAD __1/4__
RIGHT-OF-WAY TO FARM ☒YES ☐NO
FARM. DIST. CONDITION ☐E ☐G ☒F ☐P
TYPE OF FARM. IN COMMUNITY __CASH GRAIN__

C. FARM SERVICES

☒R.F.D. ☒PHONE ☒POWER LINE ☐MILK ROUTE
MILES FROM: ELEV____ GINS____ MKTG. FACIL. __6__

D. COMMUNITY FACTORS

FARM COMPARED WITH AVERAGE IN COMMUNITY:
LOCATION ☒AVG. ☐BETTER ☐POORER
DESIRABILITY ☒AVG. ☐BETTER ☐POORER
SALABILITY ☒AVG. ☐BETTER ☐POORER
RENTABILITY ☒AVG. ☐BETTER ☐POORER

E. CONDITION OF LAND

GENERAL FERTILITY ☐E ☒G ☐F ☐P
NOXIOUS __NONE__ ____%
WEEDS: ____%
LAND NEEDS:
DRAIN __10__ AC LEVEL ____ AC CONTOUR ____AC
OTHER (SPECIFY) _____ AC
IRRIGATED* ____ AC, NAME OF IRRIGATION DIST.

* ATTACH SUPPLEMENTAL REPORT FHA 422–2

F. NATURAL RESOURCES *

☐ MINERALS * ☐ OIL OR GAS
☒ TIMBER ☒ GRAVEL
☐ OTHER (SPECIFY) _____

G. WATER *

| | FARMSTEAD | | PASTURE AND |
	FAMILY USE	LIVESTOCK	CROPLAND
SOURCE	DRILLED WELL	DRILLED WELL	—
WELL DEPTH	180'- 6 GPM	240'- 20 GPM	—
CONVENIENT	☒Y ☐N	☒Y ☐N	☐Y ☐N
ADEQUATE	☒Y ☐N	☒Y ☐N	☐Y ☐N
DEPENDABLE	☒Y ☐N	☒Y ☐N	☐Y ☐N
QUALITY			
ACCEPTABLE	☒Y ☐N	☒Y ☐N	☐Y ☐N

H. FARMING HAZARDS AND DETRIMENTS

☐OVERFLOW ☐HAIL ☐UNTIMELY FREEZES ☐CROP DISEASE
☐HARDPAN ☐ALKALI ☐WIND EROS. ☐DROUGHT
☐WATER EROS. ☐INSECTS ☐GRAVEL (DROUGHTY) SUBSOIL
☒OTHER (SPECIFY) __SEASONAL FLOODING ON 10 ACRES__
COMMENTS __OF MEADOW IN SOUTHWEST CORNER__

I. OWNERSHIP HISTORY

DATE BOUGHT __1950__ ACRES __180__ PRICE $ __44,000__
CHANGES: DATE   COST
__REPLACED BURNED BARN 1965 $ 18000__

COMMENTS _____

J. TYPICAL RENTAL TERMS

ANNUAL RENT $ __7200__ CASH $ ____
SHARE ____% PROD. QTY. ____

K. TAXES

ASSESSED VALUE $ __50000__ REAL EST. TAXES 19 ____
ASSESS. RATE $ __16 PER M__ % $ __800__ (AG. DISTRICT)
MILL LEVY ____ SPEC. IMPROVE. DIST.
TAXES* $ ____

PART 2 – SUMMATION VALUATION OF BUILDINGS AS IMPROVED

KIND OF BUILDING	YEAR BUILT	CON-STRUC-TION	KIND OF ROOF	KIND OF FOUN-DA-TION	SIZE DIMENSION OR AREA OF GROUND FLOOR	STOR-IES	COND-TION OF BUILD-ING	REPLAC-MENT COST	USEFUL LIFE REMAIN-ING	SUMMA-TION VALUE	DEPRECIATED REPLACEMENT VALUE (INSURANCE COVERAGE)
(1)	(2)	(3)	(4)	(5)	(6)	(7)	(8)	(9)	(10)	(11)	(12)
A. DWELLING	1910	FR	METAL	RUBBLE	1050	2	F	$35000	30 %	$14000	$
B.	1955	FR	COMP	P.C.	1400	BARN	G	25000	60	15000	
C.											
D.											
E.											
F.											
TOTALS										29000	

(ADD AN ATTACHMENT IF ADDITIONAL SPACE IS NEEDED TO DESCRIBE BUILDINGS)

Figure 18.3

USDA-FHA COMPLETED MODEL FARM APPRAISAL REPORT

PART 3. SALE DATA FOR COMPARABLE PROPERTIES

DATE OF SALE	IDENTIFICATION OF PROPERTY	TOTAL ACREAGE	SALE PRICE TOTAL	PER ACRE	LOCA-TION	LAND	BUILD-INGS	TIME	OTHER	ADJUSTED VALUE PER ACRE	TOTAL
(1)	(2)	(3)	(4)	(5)	(6)	(7)	(8)	(9)	(10)	(11)	(12)
A. 1/19/-	A. FORT TO MEADE	106	$ 39000	$368	$ 0	$ 0	$ -50	1/2 YR $ 0	$ 0	$318	$ 33700
B. 3/14/-	B. EMERY TO WALTON FARMS	176	45000	255	0	+75	0	1 YR 0	0	330	58100
C. 8/16/-	C. SWART TO MARTIN	196	55000	280	0	0	0	3 YRS +50	0	331	64700
D. 2/15/-	D. SCOVIL TO CANON	215	64300	300	0	0	0	1 YR 0	0	300	64500
E. 9-/10/-	E. SHAW TO REEVES	230	77500	337	0	0	0	1½ YR 0	0	337	77500

* ADJUSTMENT FACTORS

* INDICATE (+) OR (-) ADJUSTMENT IN DOLLAR AMOUNTS

INDICATE (0) OR (≈) IF NO SIGNIFICANT DIFFERENCE

(ROUNDED) MARKET VALUE $ 330 $ 59500

COMMENTS:

ALL COMPARABLES IN SAME TOWNSHIP IN SIMILAR RURAL LOCATIONS.

Figure 18.3 (Cont'd.)

Form FHA 422-10

UNITED STATES DEPARTMENT OF AGRICULTURE
FARMERS HOME ADMINISTRATION

**APPRAISER'S WORKSHEET
FOR STUDY OF COMPARABLE PROPERTIES**

SUBJECT PROPERTY: LONGVIEW FARM, ANYWHERE, USA

QUALITY POINTS	A. FORT TO MEADE *	B. EMERY TO WALTON FARMS *	C. SWART TO MARTIN *	D. SCOVIL TO CANON *	E. SHAW TO REEVES *
Location	EQUAL	EQUAL	EQUAL	EQUAL	EQUAL
Soil And Topography	EQUAL	POORER	EQUAL	EQUAL	EQUAL
Water Resources	EQUAL	EQUAL	EQUAL	EQUAL	EQUAL
Dwelling	BETTER	EQUAL	EQUAL	EQUAL	EQUAL
Other Essential Buildings	BETTER	EQUAL	EQUAL	EQUAL	EQUAL
Allotments	EQUAL	EQUAL	EQUAL	EQUAL	EQUAL
Proportion Of Cropland To Total Land	EQUAL	BETTER	EQUAL	EQUAL	EQUAL
Farm Layout And Arrangement	EQUAL	POORER	BETTER	EQUAL	EQUAL
General Appearance	EQUAL	POORER	BETTER	EQUAL	EQUAL
Accessibility To Services And Facilities	EQUAL	EQUAL	EQUAL	EQUAL	EQUAL
State of Cultivation	EQUAL	EQUAL	EQUAL	EQUAL	EQUAL
Woodland	BETTER	EQUAL	EQUAL	EQUAL	EQUAL
Pasture	EQUAL	EQUAL	EQUAL	EQUAL	EQUAL
Urban Or Rural Orientation	EQUAL	EQUAL	EQUAL	EQUAL	EQUAL
Alternative Uses	EQUAL	EQUAL	EQUAL	EQUAL	EQUAL

* Poorer   Equal   Better   ☆U. S. GOVERNMENT PRINTING OFFICE:___   665603/1851 REGION NO. 6

Position 8

Figure 18.3 (Cont'd.)

PART 4. LAND AND BUILDINGS

COMMENTS ON ADEQUACY AND APPROPRIATESS OF BUILDINGS TAKING INTO CONSIDERATION PLANS FOR BUILDING CONSTRUCTION OR REPAIR AS SHOWN ON FORM FHA 424-1:

BUILDINGS IN FAIR, ADEQUATE CONDITION

COMMENTS ON CONDITION OF LAND TAKING INTO CONSIDERATION PLANS FOR LAND IMPROVEMENTS AS SHOWN ON FORM FHA 424-1.

LAND CONDUCIVE FOR ITS AGRICULTURAL USE — NEEDS DRAINAGE ON 10 ACRES OF SEASONALLY FLOODED MEADOW.

PART 5. USE OF LAND RESOURCES AND IMPROVEMENTS

CROPS (1)	ACRES (2)	YIELD PER ACRE (3)	TOTAL PRODUCTION			CASH AND/OR RENTAL SHARE	
			AMOUNT (4)	PRICE PER UNIT (5)	GROSS VALUE (6)	RATE OR PERCENT (7)	VALUE (8)
POTATOES	70	225 CWT	15750	3.60	$56,700		$ 7200
WHEAT	27	32 BU	864	3.30	2850		
OATS	4	34 BU	136	3.30	448		
SOYBEANS	9	34 BU	306	4.00	1224		
RYE	10	20 BU	200	COVER CROP	SOIL IMPROVEMENT		
PERMANENT PASTURE		ANIMAL UNITS					
WOODLAND							
FARMSTEAD, ROADS, ETC.							
CASH RENT							$ 7200
TOTALS					$ 61222		$ 7200

DEDUCTIONS

REAL ESTATE TAXES AND ASSESSMENTS	$ 800
INSURANCE COSTS ON BUILDINGS,	400
MAINTENANCE COSTS BUILDINGS, FENCES, WATER SUPPLY, TILE	
OPERATING AND MAINTENANCE COSTS FOR IRRIGATION AND DRAINAGE	
ANNUAL PAYMENTS ON BONDED DEBTS	
OTHER DEDUCTIONS (SEEDS, CROP INSURANCE, WATER CHARGES, FERTILIZER, LIME, SPRAY MATERIAL, HAULING, HARVESTING, GINNING, AND MARKETING EXPENSES).	
	$ 1200
TOTAL DEDUCTIONS	$ 1200

NET FARM INCOME .... $ 6000

CAPITALIZATION RATE FOR AREA ___10___ %   CAPITALIZATION VALUE (PER. ACRE $ 333) $ 60000

Position 8

Figure 18.3 (Cont'd.)

PART 6. SUMMATION VALUE OF FARM

USE OF LAND (1)	ACRES (2)	SOIL DESCRIPTION (3)	DEPTH OF TOPSOIL (4)	KIND OF SUBSOIL (5)	TOPOGRAPHY (6)	VALUE PER ACRE (7)	VALUE TOTAL (8)
CROPLAND	70	GOOD CULTIVATABLE	8	GRAVELLY LOAM	ROLLING	$ 300	$ 21,000
	40	FAIR CULTIVATABLE	4	GRAVELLY LOAM	STEEP	170	6800
	10	POOR CULTIVATABLE	4	CLAYEY LOAM	LEVEL	70	700
TOTAL CROPLAND	120						
PERM. PASTURE							
WOODLAND	60					40	2400
FARMSTEAD ROADS. ETC.							
TOTALS	180				MARKET VALUE OF LAND	$ 30900	

SUMMATION VALUE OF BUILDINGS AS IMPROVED (OBTAIN TOTAL FROM PART 2, COLUMN 11) .... $ 29000

SUMMATION VALUE OF FARM .... (PER ACRE $___332___) $ 59900

PART 7. RECOMMENDED MARKET VALUE OF FARM .... $ 59,500

PART 8. COMMENTS

DISCUSS THE POSSIBILITIES OF RENTING OTHER LAND, FACILITIES, OFF-FARM EMPLOYMENT, FAVORABLE AND UNFAVORABLE FACTORS OF THIS PROPERTY.

PART 1-B - 1/4 MILE DIRT R.O.W. TO FARM IS A 15' WIDE DEEDED EASEMENT

PART 1-F - 60 ACRES TIMBER, NO LEASES — ONE (1) OPENED GRAVEL "BORROW" PIT.

PART 1-K - FARM IS IN AN AGRICULTURAL TAX DISTRICT WITH TAXES REDUCED BECAUSE OF AGRICULTURAL USAGE

MISCELLANEOUS — (1.) OFF-FARM EMPLOYMENT OPPORTUNITIES IN ____ CITY, 13 MI. NORTH

(2.) THERE IS ADJACENT TILLABLE LAND WHICH CAN BE RENTED

(3) THE FARMSTEAD LOCATION IS CONVENIENT FOR OPERATION OF THE FARM.

PRESENT MARKET VALUE (COMPLETE WHEN APPLICABLE) $ ___

DATE: ...... DATED ......, 19 ......   (SIGNED) ...... JOHN SMITH ......

...... APPRAISER ...... (TITLE)

Figure 18.3 (Cont'd.)

Chapter 19

How to get and handle appraisal assignments and ethics

This chapter covers appraisal fees and appraisal ethics. The constant need for a wide variety of real property appraisals is surveyed first. Then there is the ever-important matter of how much to charge for appraisal reports and analyses. The different ways to get into appraisal work and the various sources of appraisal assignments for independent fee appraisals are listed fully. There is important information here on how to improve qualifications and appraisal fees through continuing appraisal education. A Model Appraisal Bid and Authorization Letter are also included. The chapter concludes with ethics sections on the do's and don't's of appraisal conduct.

Appraisal clients will beat a path to your door if you are a real estate broker involved in and familiar with real property sales in your area. The major wealth of Americans is in real estate. Listing appraisals for sale purposes is not the only need. Clients require and will pay for written real property appraisals on such diverse matters as estates, assessment appeals, land tracts, lots, divorce assets dissolution, condemnation, residential, commercial, industrial, recreational existing and proposed improvements. Appraisal clients seek out not only brokers but also land developers, real estate investors, property managers and builders operating in and familiar with real property in their areas. Although there are probably less than 25,000 real estate appraisers in this country, there are hundreds of thousands of real estate people experienced in the real estate marketplace and capable of appraising real property.

Of the many staff appraisers who worked for me in government appraising, many were hired originally with construction backgrounds. With training and continued education, they did both inspections and appraisals. Some of the best appraisers were former builders. Most of my outside independent fee appraisers were local knowledgeable real estate brokers.

Real estate wealth in this country is vast and the need for appraisals broad. Pay is good. In the late seventies, appraisers with five years experience started in government appraisal jobs as journeymen staff appraisers for over $18,000 per year. An independent fee appraiser with 10 years of experience usually earns $50,000 and more.

HOW TO SET, BID AND COLLECT FEES

Every appraisal, like every property, is unique. There is no way that "standard" appraisal fees for "standard" reports can be established. I've charged as low as $50 for a simple appraisal letter and thousands for a complex appraisal report. There are so many variables. Not only do properties and the time needed to appraise them differ, but so do the backgrounds and experience of each appraiser.

In the past, associations have tried to provide guidance to their appraiser members on fees, at least on minimum fees. In the past, groups and individual appraisers have sometimes tried to bill based on a percentage of the value of the property. These attempts to make uniform standards were never successful and were usually illegal.

Like any service, an appraisal fee must be worthy of hire. Individual contracts are negotiated with each client based on time involved and ability and experience of the appraiser. This is done on a bid and authorization basis and should be completed in written form before doing the appraisal. The model appraisal bid and authorization letter at the end of this chapter should be helpful in this regard.

Clients who require many appraisals on a regular basis do establish specific fees. It is then up to the individual fee appraiser as to whether he will accept these established fees. There is no negotiation. In general, these fees are less than customary but make up for their discounted nature by their volume assignment. These appraisals are usually done on the clients' forms rather than by individual narrative report. For example, the VA Loan Guaranty appraisal fee in New York in the late seventies was $60 for a one-family dwelling appraisal done on a one-page VA form. A major employee relocation company pays $175 for one-family dwelling appraisals, done on multiple-page, FNMA-type forms.

There are various criteria for setting of fees:

1. Analyze the assignment in terms of the time it will take to complete.
2. Know your approximate hourly or daily rate whether it be $40 an hour or $350 per day, or more or less.
3. Relate your fees to your background and experience. Fees should be adjusted as you become more experienced.
4. If market value must be set as of a prior date rather than current market value, the fee will usually have to be higher because of the additional historical value investigation.
5. Analysis and feasibility studies should be billed on the same basis as valuation reports. The complexity of the assignment, the time needed, the anticipated travel costs, expense of any needed consultant services, cost of preparation of exhibits, photographs and artwork all have to be covered in the appraisal fee bid total.
6. If the appraisal report will involve later testimony, then the cost of the report will have to reflect its required greater detail. The bid letter should also advise the prospective client as to the daily per diem or any portion charge which is not included in the original appraisal fee.

Your bill for appraisal services in writing should accompany your completed report. Most clients pay by return mail or within a reasonable period. Collection of any overdue bills from property owners can be done by filing "mechanic" type liens by summons through local courts.

VARIOUS APPRAISAL ASSIGNMENT SOURCES

Besides individual clients with their diverse appraisal needs, government service has been a major source of appraisal work and appraiser experience. (See Chapter 17 for the many government agencies which train and employ staff appraisers and also contract and assign appraisal work to independent fee appraisers.)

There are major national appraisal organizations which do mass appraisals of communities, usually for revaluation assessment purposes.

Many local banks have appraisal committees who regularly appraise properties for bank loan committees. Many banks and insurance companies which make land and building development loans to builders often secure independent fee appraisals.

There are large employee relocation companies which hire staff appraisers and order many independent fee appraisals in connection with corporate transfers.

Appraisal societies like the Society of Real Estate Appraisers, Association of Federal Appraisers, American Society of Appraisers, National Association of Review Appraisers, Appraisal Institute and the National Association of Independent Fee Appraisers all publish directories of designated appraisal members. These directories are often used by appraisal clients looking for appraisers in different localities.

Whether real estate broker, builder, real estate investor or land developer, whether in government, bank mortgage department, employee relocation or national mass appraisal office, there are many salaried appraisal jobs available and plenty of appraisal assignments for independent fee appraisers in our massive real estate marketplace.

HOW TO CONTINUE APPRAISAL EDUCATION

Many appraisers have worked towards professionalism through appraisal society indoctrination rather than college-level programs. In fact, up to the late seventies, there was not one college-level degree program in appraisal.

The American Society of Appraisers started an innovative program recently at Hofstra College, Long Island, N.Y. which offers a Masters degree in Interdisciplinary Studies, Valuation Sciences Emphasis. There are also Baccalaureate programs planned in Real Property, Personal Property, Government Appraising, Ad Valorem Appraising, Machinery and Equipment. Under the same ASA auspices, Southwest Texas State University is currently offering a Bachelors Degree in Real Property. Pepperdine, Loretto Heights and Skidmore Colleges are working out details of their Valuation Sciences Degree programs.

Many community colleges are also offering real estate appraisal courses. Government agencies and major appraisal companies have in-house training manuals and appraisal job training programs. Related organizations like the International Association of Assessing Officers sponsor training programs. Numerous appraisal articles are published regularly in such appraisal journals as the A.S.A "Valuation." (See Bibliography.)

Learning is a continuing experience. Whether using this handbook for its appraisal precepts or keeping up to date on international, national and local events and trends, you don't stand still. To be your best, you must continue to learn, to value and to record clearly our dynamic real estate marketplace.

A MODEL APPRAISAL BID AND AUTHORIZATION LETTER

When you bid on an appraisal job, the letter should give the client the following information:

1. Identify the property.
2. State the purpose of the appraisal.
3. State the "as of" date for the valuation.
4. Notify the client when you can deliver the complete report. If a preliminary report is needed, give such date also.
5. Provide second copy of letter with space for client's signature and date signed to signify approval. Request return of this countersigned copy.

The following model appraisal bid and authorization letter is an actual recent bid which has had all identifying information deleted:

Samuel T. Barash

Residential	**REAL ESTATE APPRAISER**	Estates
Commercial	**R D 1 - P. O. Box 130**	Condemnation
Industrial	**Lakes Road - Monroe, N.Y. 10950**	Assessment Appeals
Testimony	**914-783-4240**	V A Appraiser - Inspector

September 10, _____

Mr. _____   Re: _____ Lands and Buildings
_____ Street   _____ Rd. and _____ St.
_____, U.S.A.   _____, _____

I have reviewed the appraisal assignment on the subject property which we discussed recently.

I can deliver you a written appraisal report on market value for this property as of _____, in 15 days from date of authorization.

My appraisal fee is $750, payable upon delivery of the report.

If pre-trial consultation with your attorney and/or court attendance is needed, my additional fee is $300 per day or any portion thereof.

Thank you for considering me for this assignment. Please sign, date and return one copy of this letter to signify your authorization and agreement.

Accepted:

Sincerely,

_____   _____   _____
Signature   Date   Samuel T. Barash

THE ETHICAL APPRAISER WALKS ALONE

No matter whether affiliated with an appraisal society or government-employed or independent, you alone are responsible for your appraisal opinions. Special interests have no bearing on these opinions. An objective appraisal report does not "go along" with countervailing upward value trends merely because of easy government financing on a declining urban block. An objective report contributes to no value skyrocket in suburbs where speculators are involved. An objective report is worthy of its fair hire, but not a dollar more for influenced value judgment.

These are not generalities. The major wealth of this country is in its real property. Pressures on appraisers are always intense because so much money is involved. Corrupt, improper appraisal, underwriting, foreclosure and property management practices have destroyed many city neighborhoods. In the mid-seventies, the U.S. Department of Justice filed suit against several national appraisal and lender organizations for overtly racial, ethnic and minority discriminatory standards. Many HUD-FHA government and independent fee appraisers in Detroit and other cities have been arrested at their desks. Many were convicted of corrupt appraisal practices which helped cause hundreds of thousands of FHA foreclosures in the sixties and seventies. The racket was simple. A speculator would buy an aging house for practically nothing and invest about $1,000 in cosmetic repairs. A HUD-FHA appraiser would then be bribed to write an appraisal for say $15,000. Inevitable foreclosure would be followed by a repeat of the same corrupt process until whole neighborhoods were wiped out. In the suburbs, banks lost billions because many improper, "kited" appraisals helped developers and builders "mortgage out" by receiving excessively high loans during the sixties and seventies. Such appraisal scandals have caused some states to require licensing of appraisers. Unfortunately, such governmental regulation too often is dominated by the special interests they were set up to control.

There is no substitute for individual honesty. In my decades of government work in the scandal-free Veterans Administration and in my private appraisal work, I found that appraisal skills can be acquired. Morality and honesty come from within. Real property appraisal is a subjective, highly sensitive art. Needed skills are developed through continuous learning experiences in schools, from trade association courses, from appraisal manuals and from doing appraisals. Appraisal ethics are no more nor less than personal morality translated into standards of valuation conduct. The following item-by-item breakdown of appraisal ethics summarizes most conduct standards and ethical principles enunciated by appraisal trade associations, government and quasi-government appraisal agencies:

1. *Contingent fees*—It is unethical to do an appraisal where the appraisal fee is contingent upon say, the size of the award in a law suit involving the subject property or on the amount of sale of the subject property or on the amount of the subject tax deduction claim. It is unethical for the fee to be contingent on reaching any finding or value conclusion specified by the client.

2. *Split-fees, finder's fees and rebates*—It is unethical to agree to or receive appraisal fees paid by splitting part of the broker's commission. It is unethical to pay finder's or referral fees or rebates for appraisal assignments. It is unethical to agree to or receive any payment or gratuity other than an appraisal fee.

3. *Conflicts of interest*—It is unethical to do an appraisal if a present or future interest in the subject property is involved, such as having an agency to manage, buy or sell the property.

4. *Personal responsibility*—The person signing the report must have done the appraisal report. Assistance or "leg men" may have helped gather data but the signer of the report must have done the interior and exterior inspections and report personally.

5. *Unbiased reports*—An appraisal report must be unbiased and free of race, color, creed, ethnic and minority prejudice.

6. *No advocacy*—Written appraisal reports and expert testimony in court, particularly, must be objective, complete and properly prepared or presented. There must be no withholding or stressing of information in attempts to advocate a client's goal.

7. *Offhand opinions*—It is unethical to give valuation, cost or earning power opinions without full consideration of all the facts. Preliminary written opinions can be given if conditioned as preliminary, subject to change in final report based on full data consideration.

8. *Solicitation*—It is unethical to claim appraisal qualifications which the appraiser does not possess. It is unethical to advertise unwarranted, inaccurate or misleading promises. It is unethical to under-bid to try to get the job where another appraiser has already been hired.

9. *Confidentiality*—The contents of an appraisal report, even the very fact of appraisal employment, are confidential for the client only, and cannot be disclosed to anyone except with the client's expressed permission.

The following American Society of Appraisers and the National Association of Review Appraisers Codes are representative of association standards on unethical and unprofessional appraisal practices. (See Figures 19.1 and 19.2.)

CODE OF PROFESSIONAL ETHICS

The purpose of this code is to establish clear and ethical guidelines for the Professional Review Appraiser.

1. Members of the National Association of Review Appraisers must conduct themselves in a professional manner at all times.

2. A member should always strive to maintain and improve professional standards in the appraisal review field and be willing to assist the National Association of Review Appraisers to that end.

3. A member should help to build and sustain a public image and awareness that the profession is treating all parties fairly and equally.

4. A member should recognize his or her responsibilities to the public, the profession, all parties having an interest in the case under consideration and his or her employer.

5. A member should have access to all pertinent facts relative to a case before arriving at a decision as to fair market value.

6. A member should be unwilling to accept less than a proper appraisal report.

7. A member should be unwilling to assign a fair market value until all appraisal problems relating to a case have been resolved.

8. A member should attempt to reconcile all substantive discrepencies in appraisal reports under review on a particular case.

9. A member should be aware of any conflicts of interest which may be involved in a case and report same.

10. A member should be cognizant of all state and federal laws which may be applicable to the case which he or she is considering.

11. A member should be willing and, when necessary, able to testify and support his or her conclusion of fair market value in a court of law.

12. A member should maintain his or her professional compentency in the appraisal review field through continuous educational study.

Figure 19.1

NARA CODE OF ETHICS

7 UNETHICAL AND UNPROFESSIONAL APPRAISAL PRACTICES

7.1 Contingent Fees

If an appraiser were to accept an engagement for which the amount of his compensation is contingent upon the amount of an award in a property settlement or a court action where his services are employed; or is contingent upon the amount of a tax reduction obtained by a client where his services are used; or is contingent upon the consummation of the sale or financing of a property in connection with which his services are utilized; or is contingent upon his reaching any finding or conclusion specified by his client; then, anyone considering using the results of the appraiser's undertaking might well suspect that these results were biased and self-serving and, therefore, invalid. Such suspicion would militate against the establishment and maintenance of trust and confidence in the results of appraisal work, generally; therefore the Society declares that the contracting for or acceptance of any such contingent fee is unethical and unprofessional.

As a corollary to the above principle relative to contingent fees, the Society declares that it is unethical and unprofessional for an appraiser (a) to contract for or accept compensation for appraisal services in the form of a commission, rebate, division of brokerage commissions, or any similar forms; (b) to receive or pay finder's or referral fees; (c) to compete for an appraisal engagement on the basis of bids when the amount of the fee is the sole basis for awarding the assignment, but this is not to be construed as precluding the submission of a proposal for services.

7.2 Disinterested Appraisals

Anyone using an appraisal made by an appraiser who has an interest or a contemplated future interest in the property appraised, might well suspect that the report was biased and self-serving and, therefore, that the findings were invalid. Such suspicion tends to break down trust and confidence in the results of appraisal work, generally.

Interests which an appraiser may have in a property which is to be appraised, include ownership of the subject property; acting, or having some expectation of acting, as agent in the purchase, sale, or financing of the subject property; and managing, or having some expection of managing, the subject property. Such interests are particularly apt to exist if the appraiser, while engaged in professional appraisal practice, is also engaged in a related retail business (real estate, jewelry, furs, antiques, fine arts, etc.).

The Society declares that, subject to the provision for disclosure given in the following paragraph, it is unethical and unprofessional for an appraiser to accept an assignment to appraise a property in which he has an interest or a contemplated future interest.

However, if a prospective client, after full disclosure by the appraiser of his present or contemplated future interest in the subject property, still desires to have that appraiser do the work, the latter may properly accept the engagement provided he discloses the nature and extent of his interest in his appraisal report.

7.3 Responsibility Connected with Signatures to Appraisal Reports

The user of an appraisal report, before placing reliance on its conclusions, is entitled to assume that the party signing the report is responsible for the findings, either because he did the work himself or because the work was done under his supervision.

In cases where two or more appraisers are employed to prepare a joint report, the user thereof is entitled to assume that, if all of them sign it, they are jointly and severally responsible for the validity of all of the findings therein; and, if all do not sign, he has a right to know what the dissenting opinions are.

In cases where two or more appraisers have been engaged by a single client to make independent appraisals of the same property, the client has the right to expect that he will receive opinions which have been reached independently and that he may use them as checks against each other and/or have evidence of the range within which the numerical results lie.

To implement these principles, the Society declares that it is unethical (a) to misrepresent who made an appraisal by appending the signature of any person who neither did the work himself nor had the work done under his supervision, (b) in the case of a joint report to omit any signatures or any dissenting opinions, (c) in case two or more appraisers have collaborated in an appraisal undertaking, for them, or any of them, to issue separate appraisal reports, and (d) in case two or more appraisers have been engaged by a single client to make independent appraisals of the same property, for them to collaborate or consult with one another or make use of each other's findings or figures.

An appraisal firm or corporation may properly use a corporate signature with the signature of a responsible officer thereof. But the person who actually did the appraisal for the corporation must sign the corporate appraisal report or the report must acknowledge the person who actually made the appraisal.

7.4 Advocacy

If an appraiser, in the writing of a report or in giving an exposition of it before third parties or in giving testimony in a court action, suppresses or minimizes any facts, data, or opinions which, if fully stated, might militate against the accomplishment of his client's objective or, if he adds any irrelevant data or unwarranted favorable opinions or places an improper emphasis on any relevant facts for the purpose of aiding his client in accomplishing his objective, he is, in the opinion of the Society, an advocate. Advocacy, as here described, affects adversely the establishment and maintenance of trust and confidence in the results of professional appraisal practice and the Society declares that it is unethical and unprofessional. (Also, see Sec. 4.3)

7.5 Unconsidered Opinions and Preliminary Reports

If an appraiser gives an opinion as to the value, earning power, or estimate cost of a property without having ascertained and weighed all of the pertinent facts, such opinion, except by an extraordinary coincidence, will be inaccurate. The giving of such off-hand opinions tends to belittle the importance of inspection, investigation, and analysis in appraisal procedure and lessens the confidence with which the results of good appraisal practice are received, and therefore the Society declares the giving of hasty and unconsidered opinions to be unprofessional.

If an appraiser makes a preliminary report without including a statement to the effect that it is preliminary and that the figures given are subject to refinement or change when the final report is completed, there is the possibility that some user of the report, being under the impression that it is a final and completed report, will accord the figures a degree of accuracy and reliability they do not possess. The results of such misplaced confidence could be damaging to the reputation of professional appraisers, generally, as well as of the appraiser concerned. To obviate this possibility, the Society declares it to be unprofessional appraisal practice to omit a proper limiting and qualifying statement in a preliminary report.

7.6 Advertising and Solicitation

Self-laudatory advertising and/or solicitation of appraisal engagements, using unwarranted, inaccurate, or misleading claims or promises are practices which the Society considers to be detrimental to the establishment and maintenance of public confidence in the results of appraisal work. The Society declares that such practices on the part of an appraiser constitute unethical and unprofessional conduct. (Also, see By-Laws Art. B-26)

7.7 Misuse of Membership Designations

The Constitution and By-Laws of the Society establish three professional grades of membership, namely, Member, Senior Member, and Fellow.

Figure 19.2

ASA UNETHICAL AND UNPROFESSIONAL APPRAISAL PRACTICES

(An Associate does not hold a professional grade of membership in the Society.) Members may use the designation "Members of the American Society of Appraisers." Only Senior Members may use the designation "A.S.A." Only Fellows may use the designation "F.A.S.A." The Society declares that it is unethical for a member to claim or imply that he holds a higher degree of membership than he has attained. (Also, see By-Laws Art. B-26)

7.8   Causes for Disciplinary Action by the Society

Disciplinary action against the members of the Society is taken in the event of violations of specific provisions of the Society's Constitution and By-Laws or of its Principles of Appraisal Practice and the Code of Ethics incorporated therein. Such actions are under the jurisdiction of the International President, the International Ethics Committee, and the Board of Governors. Violations may fall under four categories:

    (1) Deviations from good appraisal practice
    (2) Failure to fulfill obligations and responsibilities
    (3) Unprofessional conduct
    (4) Unethical conduct

After due investigation, the Society may take action in the form of suggestion, censure, suspension, or expulsion, in which last event the member will be required to surrender his Certificate, membership pin, and other evidences of his membership, and to desist from all reference to such membership after its termination.

Figure 19.2 (Cont'd.)

Most government and quasi-government appraisal standards on ethics are usually concise. The Federal National Mortgage Association (FNMA) standards simply require appraisers to conform to their society code of ethics. The Federal Housing Administration (FHA) underwriting appraisal report form warns, ''All persons by signing this report certify that they have no interest, present or future, in the property, application or mortgage.''

The Veterans Administration in its appraisal report VA Form 26-1803, requires the following certification:

> *''I HEREBY CERTIFY that (a) I have carefully viewed the property described in this report, INSIDE AND OUTSIDE, so far as it has been completed; that (b) it is the same property that is identified by description in my appraisal assignment; that (c) I HAVE NOT RE-CEIVED, HAVE NO AGREEMENT TO RECEIVE, NOR WILL I ACCEPT FROM ANY PARTY ANY GRATUITY OR EMOLUMENT OTHER THAN MY APPRAISAL FEE FOR MAKING THIS AP-PRAISAL; that (d) I have no interest, present or prospective, in the application, seller, property, or mortgage; that (e) in arriving at the estimated reasonable value I have not been influenced in any manner whatsoever by the race, religion, or national origin of any person residing in the property or in the neighborhood wherein it is located. I understand that violation of this certification can result in removal from the fee appraisers' roster.''*

Chapter 20

Appraisal tools
and techniques

This is a ''nuts and bolts'' chapter on appraisal tools and how to use them. The first section is on assembling and maintaining your own zoning and subdivision library. There are other sections on photo techniques, topographic map procurement and map reading. There is also a complete ''kit bag'' listing of appraisal tools and instructions on their use. Current land measurements are illustrated with helpful tables, contrasted with the metric system. There is also a step-by-step appraisal procedure on building measurement including a Model Field Inspection and Computation Sketch.

YOUR LIBRARY OF CODES

The appraisal battle is half won if zoning, building and subdivision codes are readily available. Value depends largely on what can be done legally with a property. Zoning maps accompany zoning ordinances. They make a very useful map file for appraisal location and exhibit purposes as well as for determining zoning status along with the zoning ordinance. Building and subdivision codes are especially important to the appraisal of new construction or consideration of land development feasibility.

It is critical to daily appraisal work to have up-to-date information in your own files on these local requirements. You can write or visit the town or village clerk in each municipality you work in for copies of these codes. You should also get on their mailing lists for future changes or follow up regularly if they don't mail changes automatically.

HOW TO TAKE APPRAISAL PHOTOGRAPHS

Photographs are probably the most important element in presentation of the appraisal report. Most clients require a minimum of two photos, front and rear, on most improved properties. Some clients also want a street scene photograph. Front and rear photos should be taken from opposite three-quarter diagonal directions. Wherever this "quartering" technique is possible, the two front and rear photos will show the four sides of the building.

Appraisals must be done on time. To meet deadlines, cameras like Polaroid or Kodak which develop on the spot should be used. In cold weather, warm your cameras and film. Grainy, dark or washed-out photos should be discarded. Only properly exposed photos showing clear detail should be submitted. Duplicate photos should be kept for your own records. When photographing improved properties, don't show sweeping lawns and a small dot of a structure in the distance. Fill the frame of the picture mainly with the building. Always identify the photo margin with date taken, location, client's case number and your initials.

If aerials are needed because of the scope of the appraisal assignment, they can be ordered from aerial photographers. However, you can often secure aerial copies for nominal fees from County Planning Offices, County Farm Agents or U.S. Army District Corps of Engineers Offices. These aerials should always be checked in the field for changes and additions after date of photograph.

YOUR TOPOGRAPHIC MAP FILE

A "topo" map file library is simple to assemble, inexpensive to purchase and is one of the more important appraisal tools. These government geodetic quadrangle contour maps are made, edited and published by the Geological Survey, Washington, D.C. They are in color and mainly show 20-foot contour elevations. They give the contours or three-dimensional shape of every piece of land in these United States. They also show all land features, mountains, lakes, streams, woods, cleared areas, fences, municipality lines, roads and all buildings (as of the time of the aerial photo). They are indispensable for appraisal location, analysis and illustration.

You can get an index map and copies of all the topographic maps you will need in your area of work by writing to the U.S. Geological Survey, Washington, D.C. You can also request a folder describing topographic maps and symbols from the same service. In rural areas you can also get them from sporting goods stores which often have these maps available for sale to hunters and fishermen.

APPRAISAL TOOLS AND THEIR USE

An appraisal tool kit is individual to the user. For some appraisers, pencils, a clipboard, a tape and a camera are enough. However, appraisal data collection is a systematic field process. It is a safer bet to have a good, complete appraisal kit with you always at hand or in your car. This may save you the inconvenience of coming back to the property a second time because of no flashlight for a dark basement or no probe tool for some suspected dry rot. The following is a basic appraisal tool kit:

1. Ample flat-bottom briefcase, identified against loss.
2. Covered clipboard.
3. Dictating equipment, if you prefer to work this way.
4. Long screwdriver or long awl type probe (with sharp end protected) for termite and dry rot inspections.
5. Graph paper for sketching floor plans.
6. Lined pads for miscellaneous notes.
7. Flashlight for dark interiors.
8. Pocket calculator.
9. 100-foot measuring tape with folding hook on end to measure building exteriors.
10. 6-foot folding wood rule, for interior dimensions if needed.
11. Pencils, pens.
12. Triangles for sketching building plans.
13. Rolling measurement device, if you prefer to measure buildings this way.
14. Street maps to locate property.
15. Topo maps to analyze grades, drainage, location.
16. Line level and twine for checking levels.
17. Developing camera and extra film.
18. Client's appraisal worksheet forms.
19. Your worksheet form if not provided by client.
20. Construction checklists to help you inspect. However, don't miss the forest for the trees by say, walking through a sinking structure while checking off checklist items.
21. Comparable worksheets to gather sales data.

22. Current multiple listing sales data booklets, for comparable field data checking.

23. Copy of this book for its field guides.

LAND SURVEYS AND MEASUREMENT

"My stride measures exactly 20 inches," one of my rural appraisers once told me in explaining why he used no measuring tapes. He was in excellent health from all the pacing he had done. His appraisal reports unfortunately suffered from chronic error. Land surveys and measuring tapes are more exact than paces.

Land measurement or surveying is an historic art. George Washington surveyed land in many of the areas where he slept. Land surveying establishes the exact location of a piece of property on the ground from information based on deed descriptions. The survey map which results also shows existing buildings and easements as well as computed acreage. Only a licensed surveyor can certify a survey. Property in the Eastern United States is legally described usually by metes and bounds; in most other states by ranges, townships and sections. In subdivisions and cities, blocks and lots are usually used. Metes are measurements. Bounds are natural or artificial boundaries like streams, roads or fences. Certified surveys are required by most banks and government agencies in their mortgage commitments. Read together with legal descriptions, these survey maps are invaluable appraisal aids. The following table of land measurements is helpful for reading of surveys. For computation, there is also an inches-decimal equivalents table:

LAND MEASUREMENTS TABLE

1 in.	=	.0833 ft.	144 sq. in.	=	1 sq. ft.
7.92 in.	=	1 link	9 sq. ft.	=	1 sq. yd.
12 in.	=	1 ft.	30¼ sq. yds.	=	1 sq. rod
3 ft.	=	1 yd.	16 sq. rods	=	1 sq. chain
25 links	=	16½ ft.	1 sq. rod	=	272¼ sq. ft.
100 links	=	1 chain	10 sq. chains	=	1 acre
16½ ft.	=	1 rod	160 sq. rods	=	1 acre
4 rods	=	100 links	4,840 sq. yds.	=	1 acre
66 ft.	=	1 chain	43,560 sq. ft.	=	1 acre
80 chains	=	1 mile	640 acres	=	1 sq. mile
320 rods	=	1 mile	1 section	=	1 sq. mile
5,280 ft.	=	1 mile	1 township	=	36 sq. miles
1,760 yds	=	1 mile	1 township	=	6 miles square

DECIMAL EQUIVALENTS OF FEET
(Inch/Foot Equivalents)

INCH		DECIMAL
1″	=	.08
2″	=	.17
3″	=	.25
4″	=	.33
5″	=	.42
6″	=	.50
7″	=	.58
8″	=	.67
9″	=	.75
10″	=	.83
11″	=	.92
12″	=	1.00

In the mid-seventies, a Federal law was enacted calling for voluntary conversion to metric measures in about 10 years. The metric system is the general name for the international system of measures based upon the meter. (A meter is one 10-millionth of the distance along a meridian from the North Pole to the Equator.) Ultimately, Americans will probably join the many other nations which use the meter, the gram and the liter. The meter, which equals 39.37 inches, is the basic unit in a measurement system based on decimals. For example, a kilometer, about five-eighths of a mile, is 1,000 meters. A centimeter is 0.01 meters. The traditional English measures of inches, feet, etc., will probably continue to be used along with these measurements in the metric system shown in the following English-metric equivalents table:

LENGTH:	1 inch	= 2.54 centimeters
	1 foot	= 12 in. = 0.3048 meter
	1 yard	= 3 ft. = 0.9144 meter
	1 mile	= 5,280 ft. = 1.61 kilometers
AREA:	1 sq. in.	= 6.45 square centimeters
	1 sq. ft.	= 144 sq. in. = 0.09 square meter
	1 sq. yd.	= 9 sq. ft. = 0.84 square meter
	1 acre	= 43,560 sq. ft. = 4,047 square meters

HOW TO MEASURE BUILDINGS

The following step-by-step procedure can be used for field measurement of most small to medium-size buildings. Measurements on complex structures are normally "taken off" from building plans. Even in such cases field inspection should verify whether there have been any changes or additions from plans:

STEP 1—Notify occupant—If the building is occupied, notify the occupant in advance and upon arrival. Do not trespass. Also, if you work without an assistant, the occupant often is happy to assist by holding one end of the measuring tape.

STEP 2—Measure all exterior dimensions—Use a good, clearly marked metal or fabric 100-foot tape with a folding hook on the end. (See prior section in this chapter on appraisal tool bag.)

> (2a) If the occupant or an assistant helps, he holds the tape end at one corner of the building while you roll out the tape to the next corner. Pull it tight against the building, read and write down the number of feet to the nearest inch. Work your way around the entire structure, measuring all walls, as well as porches, patios, garages and other buildings.
>
> (2b) If working alone, unfold and insert the tape hook into the edge of the building corner board or shingle joint and proceed to roll out the tape, measure and record as in (2a).
>
> (2c) If a masonry exterior or extensive shrubbery interferes with placing the tape against the building, use your screwdriver, probe tool or even a pencil to anchor one end of the tape in the lawn in line with building corners.
>
> (2d) If a building has more than one level, floor measurements on 1½-story, sloping roof, finished-attic type buildings range from 50% to 75% of the lower level area. This can be checked by interior measurements.

STEP 3—Measure interior rooms, all levels for those clients who require an interior floor plan.

> (3a) If an occupant or assistant helps, use the tape, measure and record all room measurements.
>
> (3b) If alone, use your 6-foot folding wood rule laid on the floor. There will be much bending but appraisal is an active art.

STEP 4—Complete the field sketch—It is most important that the field sketch of the building be completed while on the premises. The recorded measurements can then be easily compared and checked while being sketched. All measurements are taken in feet and inches. For sketch computation purposes, convert the inches to decimals using the decimal equivalents table in the prior section.

A model field measurement and computations sketch follows:

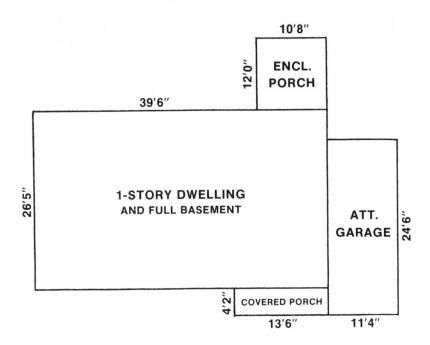

COMPUTATIONS

DWELLING -	26.42 x 50.18 =	1326 SQ. FT.
BASEMENT -	26.42 x 50.18 =	1326 SQ. FT.
FIN. BASEMENT -	20.00 x 30.00 =	600 SQ. FT.
COV. PORCH -	4.18 x 13.50 =	56 SQ. FT.
ENCL. PORCH -	12.00 x 10.66 =	128 SQ. FT.
ATT. GARAGE -	11.33 x 24.50 =	278 SQ. FT.

Figure 20.1

FIELD MEASUREMENT AND COMPUTATIONS SKETCH

Chapter 21

How to testify in court

This chapter deals with the special problems of testifying in court as an expert witness. First, the unique role of the expert witness in court is defined. Then there are chapter sections on working with attorneys, and preparing for trial. There are also item-by-item details on how to go on the stand and testify. Finally there are informative excerpted courtroom minutes from actual recent testimony by the author.

THE EXPERT WITNESS DEFINED

An expert witness is a unique exception in court. Lay people can testify only regarding facts, not opinions. Yet an expert witness who possesses particular knowledge or experience not common to laymen, say on appraisal, is permitted by law to give his expert opinion to help jurors arrive at correct conclusions themselves.

The judge qualifies the expert witness. He is the one who says whether the witness is an expert and whether his opinions can be admitted in evidence. In jury trials, the jurors determine the credibility of witnesses' testimony. Jurors are the sole judges of the facts and base decisions only on the evidence received from the witnesses as well as on any exhibits received in evidence. Jurors can disregard the opinion of any expert unless they accept as true the facts upon which the expert's opinion is based. The jurors may also conclude that an honest opinion is unsound even though they accept the facts as true. Or if the jurors reject as untrue the facts upon which the opinion is based, then they can reject the opinion.

Who is an expert witness on valuation matters? Judges have qualified witnesses based on the following:

1. Full time, trained, experienced appraisers.
2. Brokers acting as agents in buying, selling and managing real estate in the locality involved.
3. Investors, speculators, developers operating and familiar with values in the locality involved.
4. Neighbors of the property in question who have lived in the locality long enough to be familiar with real estate values.
5. Witnesses who possess a combination of the above qualifications.

A trial is an adversary procedure. The tremendous divergencies of courtroom opinions from several appraisers testifying on the identical property usually result from differing consideration of the highest and best use of the property. Too often in testimony, every highway location becomes a prime commercial site, every farm a residential subdivision. The expert who is believed by the jury is the one who backs up his determination of highest and best use with actual sales data and zoning activity proving this use.

The type of assignments which most often are followed by courtroom or hearing testimony are appraisals in condemnation or on property assessment appeals. (See Chapters 15 and 16.)

HOW TO WORK WITH ATTORNEYS

Close relations with the employing attorney are crucial to proper appraisal testimony. For example, in aforementioned condemnation trials, legal advice must be secured from the lawyer as to the "date of taking" because value is established as of that date in most localities.

The lawyer and appraiser working on a case must explain and understand each other's functions. The expert appraisal witness testifies through direct and cross-examination questions. In direct examination, the lawyer can decide to draw out the appraisal witness' opinions by a series of questions. Alternatively, the lawyer can ask the witness to narrate his opinions. Since the witness can only give his evidence and opinions in response to questions put to him, lack of understanding of each other's functions in the legal process can hamper both lawyer and appraiser. It is important that there be a pre-trial attorney-appraiser conference where the appraiser report is reviewed and legal procedure explained.

In many states, there are "discovery" procedures where attorneys can secure opposing appraisal reports for review before trial. It is important at this point that the opposing report be analyzed. The comparable data in the opposing report should also be checked in the field and valuation guidance be given by appraiser to lawyer for later court examination of the report and cross-examination of the witness.

It is also very important that an appraiser biography with complete, detailed, factual education and appraisal experience be given to the attorney at the pre-trial conference. Careful questions from this experience record during qualification testimony will not only help qualify the witness before the judge but will also impress the jury if done properly from a complete record. (See excerpted minutes of testimony in last section of this chapter.) This biographical record should include:

1. Education.
2. Experience.
3. List of representative clients.
4. Membership in appraisal societies.
5. Stress on local experience, if pertinent.
6. Real Estate Brokerage experience, if pertinent.
7. Building, developing, real estate background, if any.
8. Stress on length of time lived and worked in local area, if pertinent.

HOW TO PREPARE TO TESTIFY

Preparation for trial starts months or years before taking the stand. If the appraisal assignment is on condemnation or assessment appeal matters or on other matters which will probably involve future litigation, the appraisal report should be comprehensive. Appropriately higher appraisal fees should be charged for the additional investigation and analysis required. Guidance should be secured initially from the attorney as to "date of taking," etc.

Detailed pre-trial preparation usually involves the following:

1. Review appraisal report completely.

2. Visit appraised site and all comparable sites again just before or on the day of testimony.

3. Re-check all arithmetic in report.

4. At pre-trial conference with attorney, become familiar with real estate law in the courtroom where you will testify.

5. Prepare a list of questions for the attorney which he can consider asking you in direct examination so that you can later get your opinions into the record completely.

6. If the Cost approach must be used in court, it is advisable that a qualified cost estimator be hired to also testify. It's usually best not to go into court with figures from a cost data handbook. In fact, it's usually best not to

use the Cost approach in court at all. If the Income approach is involved in the opinion of value, preparation should include visual aid charts detailing all expenses, gross income, net income, capitalization rate and all the arithmetic of the capitalization process. Preparation for testimony in most litigation should stress the Market approach.

7. Prepare carefully all charts, maps and other visual aids to be used in testifying.

8. Not only the written appraisal report but all notes, memorandums, maps and charts used in testimony by the witness can be used in cross-examination. It is therefore most important that all such written data or visual aids be triple-checked for accuracy.

HOW TO TESTIFY

The judge is the boss in the courtroom. One of my government appraisers was once sent as custodian of government appraisal records to testify in a civil suit involving damages suffered by a homeowner allegedly caused by the homebuilder. My appraiser had been instructed by our government attorney to testify from the government records but not to surrender the files to anyone. Later that day, the appraiser telephoned me. The conversation went like this:

"The judge gave me this one phone call before he sends me to jail for contempt of court."

"What did you do, man?"

"I told the judge I couldn't let him see the records."

We made sure the judge saw the files that day and our appraiser stayed out of jail, a wiser man and a more experienced witness. It is first and most important that legal instructions from the judge be followed when you testify. Other guidance on how to testify follows:

1. Be civilized and respectful to all court officers including the attorney who cross-examines you. Dress carefully, conservatively. Be properly groomed.

2. Be informed, unruffled, unhurried when on the witness stand.

3. Avoid reflex answers.

4. Think first, then speak.

5. Wit has no place on the witness stand.

6. Don't ham it up with voice gestures and inflections trying to impress the jury.

7. Laughter sounds insincere. Smile if appropriate.

8. Speak carefully, clearly. Avoid nervous speech habits like, "You know."

9. Avoid appearance of being an advocate. Be unbiased. Your credibility as an expert witness depends on your objectivity. Try to please everyone, especially your client, and you wind up displeasing judge, jury and your client.

10. Answer questions completely, concisely. Don't rattle on.

11. Don't lose your temper or raise your voice in anger, particularly during cross-examination.

12. Take your time if you have to do calculations on the stand. Double-check all such work.

13. Don't give quick off-hand opinions.

14. Admit lack of knowledge or experience honestly. Don't get backed into a corner by attempting to be all and know all.

15. The manner in which you state your appraisal qualifications is important—modestly but not too modestly, capably but not boastfully. If you have local experience or live or work in the area, stress this local background.

16. Avoid appraiser jargon. Yet don't talk down to the jury when you explain the appraisal process.

17. Always define market value and state on what factors you based your opinion of value.

18. Don't hang around the courtroom unnecessarily before or after you testify. Talk only to the attorney who retains you. Avoid any socializing with opposing attorney even if you know him. Have no contact with any juror. Take notes on valuation testimony if you are present during opposing appraiser's testimony. It may help your testimony. Don't smile or comment during any other testimony.

19. In cross-examination, the attorney will try to discredit you as an expert and your work by questions regarding any statements made or omitted in testimony. There are always questions on approaches to value. The intricacies of Cost and Income approaches may be seriously questioned, as to mathematics and appropriateness. Again and again, safety in court testimony and credible value opinions are usually found in the Market approach.

SOME RECENT TESTIMONY BY THE AUTHOR

The following excerpted minutes of the author's testimony in a recent case illustrate some of the guidance given in this chapter on testimony. Note particularly the questions and answers qualifying the witness and defining appraisal elements:

SAMUEL T. BARASH, first having been duly sworn by a Notary Public, was examined and testified as follows:

EXAMINATION BY

Mr. _____

Q   Where do you live?

A   I live on Lakes Road in Monroe, New York.

Q   Occupation?

A   I'm a licensed real estate broker and appraiser and I also buy and sell for my own account and develop my own lots in Orange County.

Q   Are you familiar with the subject property known as _____?

A   I am familiar with the property which is approximately a mile from where I reside, and also it's in the town of Chester where I have my office. . . .

Q   You bought and sold properties in the vicinity recently?

A   I have bought and sold properties in the vicinity of _____, both in its immediate vicinity and within a 3-mile radius.

Q   Sir, will you state your background and qualifications as an appraiser?

A   I have been in the appraiser business, construction business, development business since approximately 1947. I have a B.S.S. degree from the College of the City of New York and have done graduate work at N.Y.U. and Columbia in real estate and similar courses. I was the Chief of Construction for approximately five years for the Veterans Administration of the New York office covering all of New York State except the Buffalo region. I was the Assistant Chief Appraiser for some 10 years for the . . . same New York . . . office and Chief Appraiser at Newark for the Veterans Administration for the State of New Jersey for some seven years. In that capacity I supervised some 300 appraisers who were engaged in reviewing, making and reviewing appraisals both on individual and large residential development tracts throughout both states. I recently retired as Chief Appraiser in 1972 from U.S. Government service and I'm now engaged in appraising, real estate and development in Orange County, New York, the location previously described.

Q   Sir, have you also lectured on appraisals at colleges and government seminars?

A   Yes, various colleges in New York, New Jersey and Washington.

Q   Have you also given evidence in Court as an appraiser?

A   Yes, I've been qualified as an expert in both states and in Washington.

Q   Sir, did you at my request make an appraisal to ascertain the fair market value of the subject property?

A   Yes, I completed an appraisal and delivered it to you, on October 18, _____.

Q   Sir, will you tell me what elements went into your appraisal, if you would?

A   The . . . main element . . . was determination of highest and best use . . .

Q   Sir, did you actually go and walk the property?

A   I personally walked the entire property.

Q   What else went into your evaluation?

A   It was based not only on the personal inspection but also upon an analysis of sales of this and comparable properties and a consideration of all other factors which affect value.

Q   What are they?

A   Well, zoning, utility, location, topography, amenities, depreciating influences, and present and potential uses.

Q   How about assessed valuation, does that go into your evaluation?

A   As background information, I researched the existing assessed evaluation.

Q   Now, sir, will you tell the commissioners where the location of this land is. . . .

Chapter 22

How to prepare reports and use terminology correctly

The preceding chapters have given you theories, practice, tools and examples of the appraisal process. In this final chapter, you will find various suggestions to help you actually write your appraisal report in plain English, using your individual style and avoiding look-alike formats. There are sections on how to use technical words correctly, how to be certain you spell correctly and how to train your secretaries and typists to complete your reports in a "clean" and efficient manner. There is also a handy glossary here, listing commonly used real estate and construction words to help you with proper usage and spelling. Last, but of mounting importance, is a glossary and definition guide of environmental terms which have come into common as well as appraisal usage.

AVOID "LOOK-ALIKE" FORMATS

You have seen in prior chapters, particularly on government and corporate transfer appraisal forms, examples of many reports which require mainly fill-in rather than narrative information. A client certainly won't object if you have columns of careful descriptive listings in your report making it easy for him to quickly read the specifications of the building you are appraising. However, he may certainly be warranted in believing that you did not give his appraisal assignment your best individual attention if he finds the same narrative, mass-printed, ''boiler-plate'' paragraphs describing say, the area, the neighborhood, yes, even your appraisal process, on each appraisal report you give him. He may decide to seek another appraiser to give him the individually analyzed and prepared written report for which he pays.

USE PLAIN ENGLISH

There are enough unusual and sometimes difficult words needed to exactly describe real estate matters and structures without complicating your reports with anything else but good, plain English prose. You may have to use words like ''mansard roof,'' ''gypsum drywall,'' ''riparian rights,'' ''condominium master deed'' to give specific meaning, but you don't have to use words of many syllables and many clauses just to sound impressive. Plain, simple words in your narrative are best for your client and reputation. Also, don't complicate your sentence structures. Say it straight out. Don't say, ''Crawling on the wall, is a cockroach.'' It's better to say, ''A cockroach is crawling on the wall.'' Try not to leave your sentences and client dangling.

PROPER USAGE, STRUCTURE AND SPELLING

The timeworn story of the rural preacher who ''tells 'em first what he'll tell 'em, then tells 'em, then tells 'em what he told 'em,'' is appropriate to the appraisal report. Your client wants to quickly get the gist and result of your report, ''up front.'' So, if you use a transmittal letter on lengthy reports, ''tell 'em'' right away in your transmittal letter about your conclusions and final value. The prior chapters with their appraisal models have stressed this structuring; don't lose your client in a mass of report data in his initial search for conclusions. Also, always summarize your conclusions in your closing. Throughout your report writing, keep your technical glossaries and standard unabridged dictionary handy. Never assume correct spelling. Always look up that doubtful word.

SECRETARIES AND TYPISTS

They are critical to your appraisal success. Clerical help does not write the report for you, but the quality of their work enhances the quality of your presentation. Better an old-fashioned, handwritten, legible report than a careless, error- and erasure-filled, typed presentation. Your pride in your craft must be matched in the typed report. For instance, train your typists to proofread each page when it is finished before it is rolled out of the machine. If you dictate your reports, train your secretary to use all your appraisal and construction glossaries to avoid misspellings and use of incorrect words. Proofread the final report yourself before you sign it.

A HANDY GLOSSARY GUIDE
OF REAL ESTATE AND CONSTRUCTION TERMS

Purpose of This Glossary—This glossary should assist you and your typists in the preparation of properly spelled, technically correct appraisal reports and letters. Add to it when you come across new and pertinent words.

ABSTRACT	APRON	BASEMENTLESS SPACE
ACCESS	ARABLE LAND	BATHROOM
ACCESSORY BUILDING	AREA	BATHTUB
ACRE	AREA DRAIN	BATTEN
ACREAGE	ASBESTOS	BAY
ACTUAL AGE	ASBESTOS SHINGLES	BAY WINDOW
ADDITION	ASHLAR MASONRY	BEAM
AD VALOREM TAX	ASPHALT	BEARING WALL
ADVERSE	ASPHALT SHINGLE	BEDROOM
AERIAL	ASPHALT TILE	BERM
AIR CONDITIONING	ASPHALTIC CONCRETE	BETTER
AIR RIGHTS	ASSESSMENT	BETWEEN
ALCOVE	ASSESSMENT ROLL	BEVELED
ALLEY	ATTIC	BI-LEVEL
ALUMINUM	ATTACHED	BITUMINOUS
AMENITIES	AUTOMATIC	CONCRETE
AMOUNT	AUTOMATIC WASHING	BITUMINOUS
AMPERE	MACHINE	PENETRATED
ANCHOR BOLT	AVENUE	BLACKTOP PAVING
ANGLE	AVERAGE	BLIND NAIL
APARTMENT	BALUSTER	BLOCK
APPRAISAL	BALLOON FRAMING	BLOCKING
APPRAISED VALUE	BASEBOARD	BLOWER
APPRAISER	BASEMENT	BLOW-OFF

BLUEPRINT

BLUESTONE

BOARD

BOARD FOOT

BOARD MEASURE

BOILER

BONDING

BOOK SHELVES

BORROWED LIGHT

BOTTLED

BOTTOM

BOULEVARD

BOUNDARY

BOWSTRING TRUSS

BRACING

BRASS

BRANCH CIRCUIT

BREADTH

BRICK

BRICK VENEER
 ON FRAME

BRICK VENEER
 ON MASONRY

BRIDGING

BRITISH THERMAL
 UNITS B.T.U.'s

BROOM CLOSET

BUILDING

BUILDING LINE

BUILT-IN

BUILT-UP ROOFING

BULKHEAD

BUNGALOW

BUTT

BUTTRESS

BX WIRING

CABINET

CAULKING

CARPENTER ANT

CARPORT

CASEMENT

CASING

CAST IRON

CAST IRON PIPE

CATCH BASIN

CAULKING

CAVITY WALLS

CEILING

CELLAR

CEMENT

CEMENT ASBESTOS

CEMENT MORTAR

CEMENT PLASTER

CENTER

CENTER LINE

CENTERS ON

CENTER TO CENTER

CERAMIC

CESSPOOL

CHANNEL

CHASES

CHEEK WALLS

CHIMNEY

CINDER BLOCK

CIRCLE

CIRCUIT

CIRCUIT BREAKER

CIRCUMFERENCE

CLAPBOARD SIDING

CLAY TILE

CLEANOUT

CLEAR

CLEARANCE

CLOSET

COAL BIN

COAT CLOSET

COATED

COLD WATER

COLONIAL

COLUMN

COMBINATION

COMMON INTEREST

COMMON WALL

COMMUNITY SEWAGE
 PLANT

COMPARABLE

COMPOSITION

CONCRETE SLAB

CONCRETE

CONCRETE BLOCK

CONCRETE FLOOR

CONDENSATION

CONDITION

CONDOMINIUM
 (HORIZONTAL)

CONDOMINIUM

CONDUIT

CONNECTION

CONSTRUCTION

CONTOURS

CONTRACT

CONTRACTOR

CONVECTOR

CONVENTIONAL

CONVERTED

CONVEY

COOPERATING

COPING

COPPER

CORBEL

CORNER BRACING

CORNICE

CORROSION

COUNTER

COUNTER FLASHING

COURSE

COURT

COVENANTS

CROSS BRIDGING

CROSS SECTION

CUBIC

CUBIC FOOT

CUBIC INCH

CUBIC YARD

CURRENT

CURTAIN WALL

DAMPER

DAMPPROOFING

DEBRIS

DECK

DECKING

DEED

DEGREE

DEGREE CENTIGRADE

DEGREE FAHRENHEIT

DEPRECIATION

DEPTH

DESIRABILITY

DIAMETER

DIMENSION

DINETTE

DINING ALCOVE

DINING-KITCHEN
   COMBINATION

DINING ROOM

DISHWASHER

DISTANCE

DISTRICT

DORMER

DOUBLE

DOUBLE ACTING

DOUBLE GLASS

DOUBLE HUNG
   WINDOW

DOWNSPOUT

DRAIN

DRIP CAP

DRY ROT

DRIVEWAY

DRYWALL

DRYWELL

DUPLEX

DWELLING

DWELLING UNIT

EASEMENT

EAVE

ECONOMIC

ECONOMIC LIFE

EFFECTIVE AGE

EFFLORESCENCE

ELECTRIC

ELECTRIC HEAT

ELEVATION

ENCLOSED PORCH

ENCLOSURE

ENCROACHMENT

END ROW

ENGINEER

ENHANCEMENT

ENTRANCE

EQUALIZATION

EQUIPMENT

EQUITY

ESCROW

ESTIMATE

EXCAVATE

EXISTING

EXPANSION JOINT

EXTERIOR

FACTORY-BUILT

FALLOUT SHELTER

FAMILY

FAMILY ROOM

FACADE

FAIR RENT

FASCIA

FEE APPRAISAL

FEE SIMPLE

FERROUS

FEET

FIBERGLASS

FILL

FINISH

FINISHED FLOOR

FIREBRICK

FIREDOOR

FIRE HYDRANT

FIREPROOF

FIREWALL

FIXTURE

FLASHING

FLAT

FLOOD HAZARD

FLOOR

FLOOR DRAIN

FLOORING

FLUE

FLUE LINING

FLUORESCENT

FOOT

FOOTING

FOUNDATION

FRAME

FRAMEWORK

FRAMING

FRESH AIR INTAKE

FRONT FOOT

FRONTAGE

FUNCTIONAL

FURNACE

FURRING

GABLE

GALLON

GALVANIZED

GALVANIZED IRON

GAMBREL

GARAGE

GAS RANGE

GAUGE

GIRDER

GLASS

GLAZING

GRADE

GRADEMARKING

GRANTEE

GRANTOR

GRAVITY WARM
   AIR HEAT

GRAVITY HOT
   WATER HEAT

GROSS INCOME

GROSS RENT
   MULTIPLIER

GROUND COVER

GROUND LEASE

GROUND RENT

GROUND STORY

GROUND WATER

GROUT GYPSUM

H-COLUMN

HABITABLE SPACE

HARDWARE

HARDWOOD

HEADER

HEAD WALLS

HEAT PUMP

HEATER

HEATER, WATER

HEIGHT

HIP

HOLLOW TILE

HORIZONTAL

HORSE POWER

HOSE BIB

HOT WATER

HOUSE CONNECTION

I-BEAM

IMPROVEMENTS

INCH

INCOME APPROACH

INCOME PROPERTY

INDIVIDUAL SEWAGE
   SYSTEM

INDUSTRIAL PARK

INEQUITY

INSTANTANEOUS

INSTALLMENT
   CONTRACT

INSULATION

INTERIOR

INTERIOR FINISH

INTERMEDIATE

INVERT

JAMB

JOINT
   REINFORCEMENT

JOIST

JOIST HANGER

JUNCTION BOX

KITCHEN

KITCHEN SINK

KNOB AND TUBE

LAND RESIDUAL
   TECHNIQUE

LANDSCAPE(ING)

LARGER

LATH	MARKET DATA	NET LEASE
LATH AND PLASTER	APPROACH	NET SALES
LATTICE	MARQUEE	NEW TOWN
LAUNDRY	MASONRY	NEWEL POST
LAUNDRY TRAYS	MATERIAL	NOMINAL
LAVATORY	MEASUREMENT	NON-CONFORMING
LEADERS	MECHANICAL	USE
LEAD AND OIL	MEDICINE CABINET	NON-FERROUS
LEAD PAN	METAL	NOT IN CONTRACT
LEAN-TO	MEZZANINE	OAK
LEASE	MILL TYPE	OBSOLETE
LENGTH	CONSTRUCTION	OBSOLESCENCE
LESSEE	MIINERAL RIGHTS	ON CENTER
LESSOR	MISCELLANEOUS	ONE STORY
LEASE HOLD	MILLWORK	ONE AND ONE-HALF
LEASEHOLD VALUE	MODEL	STORY
LIFE ESTATE	MONITOR ROOF	OPENING
LIGHT	MONOLITHIC	OPEN PORCH
LINEAL FEET	CONCRETE	OPERATING EXPENSES
LINEN CLOSET	MONUMENT	ORDINANCES
LINOLEUM	MORTGAGE	OUTLET
LINTEL	MORTGAGEE	OVERHANG
LIVE LOAD	MORTGAGOR	OVERHEAD
LIVING-DINING	MORTAR	OVER-ASSESSMENT
COMBINATION	MORTICE	OVER-IMPROVEMENT
LIVING ROOM	MOULDING	PAINTED
LOFT	MOVABLE PARTITION	PANEL
LONG	MUD ROOM	PARAPET
LOUVER	MUD SILL	PARALLEL
LOUVERED DOOR	FOUNDATION	PARCEL
LUMBER	MULTI-FAMILY	PARGE
MANHOLE	MULLION	PARKING
MANSARD	NEIGHBORHOOD	PARKING BAYS
MAP	NET INCOME	PARQUET FLOOR

PARTICLE BOARD

PARTITION

PARTY WALL

PATIO

PAVING

PENETRATION
  MACADAM

PERSONAL PROPERTY

PERCENTAGE LEASE

PERIMETER

PHYSICAL
  DEPRECIATION

PIER

PILE

PILASTER

PITCH

PLACE

PLAN

PLANIMETER

PLANNED UNIT
  DEVELOPMENT

PLANK

PLASTER

PLASTIC

PLASTIC WALL TILE

PLAT

PLATE

PLATE GLASS

PLATFORM FRAMING

PLINTH

PLUMB

PLUMBER'S HELPER

PLUMBING

POINTING

POINT UP

POLE BUILDING

POLYETHYLENE

PORCH

PORTLAND CEMENT
  CONCRETE

PORTICO

POWDER ROOM

PREFABRICATED

PREFERENTIAL
  ASSESSMENT

PROPERTY

PROPERTY OWNER
  ASSOCIATION

PROPERTY RECORD
  CARD

PROPOSED

PUBLIC

PUBLIC UTILITY

PULL CHAIN

PURLIN

PYRAMID ROOF

QUANTITY SURVEY
  METHOD

QUOIN

RABBETED

RADIATION

RADIATOR

RAFTER

RAKE

RAMP

RECEPTACLE

RECREATION ROOM

REFRIGERATOR

REGISTER

REINFORCED

REINFORCED
  CONCRETE

REPAIR

REPLACE

REPLACEMENT COST

REPRODUCTION COST

RESERVE FOR
  REPLACEMENT

RESIDENTIAL

RESILIENT

RESTRICTIONS

RETAINING WALL

REVALUATION

RIDGE

RIGHT-OF-WAY

RIPARIAN RIGHTS

RISE

RISER

ROMEX WIRING

ROOF LOAD

ROOF OVERHANG

ROOF SLOPE

ROW DWELLING

RUN

SADDLE (ROOF, DOOR)

SIGHT DISTANCE
  (SAFE)

SALVAGE VALUE

SASH

SASH CORD

SATURATED FELT

SAW-TOOTH ROOF

SCHEDULE

SCREED

SCREEN

SCUTTLE SEALANT

SEMI-DETACHED

SERVICE

SEWER

SHAKES

SHEATHING

SHED ROOF

SHEETROCK

SHIM

SHOE

SHORING

SHOWER

SHUTOFF VALVE

SIDING

SILL

SINK

SITE DEVELOPMENT
    COSTS

SLAB

SLEEPER

SLOP SINK

SLATE

SOFFIT

SOIL PIPE

SOIL POISONING

SOIL PRODUCTIVITY

SOLAR HOME

SPACE HEATER

SPACKLE

SPANDREL BEAM

SPECIFICATIONS

SPRINKLER

SPLIT LEVEL

SQUARE FOOT

STAINLESS STEEL

STAPLE

STEPPED RAMPS

STILE

STONE VENEER ON
    FRAME

STONE VENEER ON
    MASONRY

STOOL (WINDOW)

STORM DOOR

STORM SASH

STORAGE

STORY

STREET

STRETCHER

STRUCTURAL

STRUT

STUCCO

STUD

SUBDIVISION
    REGULATIONS

SUBFLOOR

SUBLEASE

SUPPLY

SUSPENDED CEILING

SWALES

TAPE AND SPACKLE

TAX DISTRICT

TAX EXEMPTION

TAX LEVY

TAX MAP

TAX NOTICE

TAX RATE

TAX ROLL

TENON

TERMITE

TERNE PLATE

TERRACE

TERRAZZO

TERRA COTTA

THERMAL INSULATION

THERMOSTAT

THRESHOLD

THROUGH LOT

TIE

TILLABLE

TILT-UP
    CONSTRUCTION

TIMBER

TITLE

TOPOGRAPHY

TONGUE AND GROOVE

TOWNSHIP

TOILET

TOWNHOUSE

TRACT

TRANSIT

TRANSOM

TREAD

TREATED LUMBER

TRIM

TRIMMED OPENING

TRUSS

TWO STORY

TWO AND ONE-HALF
    STORY

TYPICAL

UNDER-ASSESSED

UNDER-IMPROVEMENT

UNDEVELOPED

UNDIVIDED INTEREST

UNIMPROVED LAND

UNIT-IN-PLACE
  METHOD

UNFINISHED

UTILITY ROOM

VACANCY

VALLEY

VALUATION

VAPOR BARRIER

VARNISH

VENEER

VENTILATE

VESTIBULE

VINYL

VISQUEEN

VITRIFIED TILE

WAINSCOT

WALL

WALLBOARD

WARM AIR

WASHING MACHINE

WATER CLOSET

WATERPROOF(ING)

WATER-SUPPLY,
  INDIVIDUAL

WEATHERSTRIPPING

WIDE FLANGE

WIND LOAD

WINDMILL POWER

WINDOW

WING

WOOD

WOOD FRAME

WROUGHT IRON

YARD

ZONING REGULATION

COMMON ENVIRONMENTAL TERMS—
A GLOSSARY AND GUIDE

Purpose of This Environmental Glossary—This glossary and definition guide of modern environmental terms should help you and your clerical people cope with the mounting number of environmental concerns and terms.

ABATEMENT: The method of reducing the degree or intensity of pollution, also the use of such a method.

ACTIVATED CARBON: A highly absorbent form of carbon, used to remove odors and toxic substances from gaseous emissions. In advanced waste treatment, activated carbon is used to remove dissolved organic matter from waste water.

ACTIVATED SLUDGE: Sludge that has been aerated and subjected to bacterial action, used to remove organic matter from sewage.

ADAPTATION: A change in structure or habit of an organism that produces better adjustment to the environment.

ADSORPTION: The adhesion of a substance to the surface of a solid or liquid. Hydrophobic, or water-repulsing absorbents, are used to extract oil from waterways in oil spills.

ADVANCED WASTE TREATMENT: Waste water treatment beyond the secondary or biological stage that includes removal of nutrients such as phosphorus and nitrogen and a high percentage of suspended solids. "Tertiary treatment" is the "polishing stage" of waste water treatment and produces a high quality effluent.

AEROBIC: This refers to life or processes that can occur only in the presence of oxygen.

AGRICULTURAL POLLUTION: The liquid and solid wastes from all types of farming.

AIR POLLUTION: The presence of contaminants in the air in concentrations that prevent the normal dispersive ability of the air and that interfere directly or indirectly with man's health or with the full use and enjoyment of his property.

AIR QUALITY CRITERIA: The levels of pollution and lengths of exposure at which adverse effects on health and welfare occur.

AIR QUALITY STANDARDS: The prescribed level of pollutants in the outside air that cannot be exceeded legally during a specified time.

ALGAL BLOOM: A proliferation of living algae on the surface of lakes, streams or ponds. Algal blooms are stimulated by phosphates.

ANAEROBIC: Refers to life or processes that occur in the absence of oxygen.

ANTI-DEGRADATION CLAUSE: A provision in air quality and water quality laws that prohibits deterioration of air or water quality in areas where the pollution levels are presently below those allowed.

AQUIFER: An underground bed or stratum of earth, gravel or porous stone that contains water.

AQUATIC PLANTS: Plants that grow in water either floating on the surface, growing up from the bottom of the body of water or growing under the surface of the water.

ASBESTOS: A mineral fiber with countless industrial uses; a hazardous air pollutant when inhaled; its effects as a water pollutant are under scrutiny.

ASSIMILATION: Conversion or incorporation of absorbed nutrients into protoplasm. Also refers to the ability of a body of water to purify itself of organic pollution.

ATMOSPHERE: The layer of air surrounding the earth.

BACKFILL: The material used to refill a ditch or other excavation, or the process of doing so.

BACKGROUND LEVEL: With respect to air pollution, amounts of pollutants present in the ambient air due to natural sources.

BAFFLE: Any deflector device used to change the direction of flow or the velocity of water, sewage or products of combustion such as fly ash or coarse particulate matter. Also used in deadening sound.

BALING: A means of reducing the volume of solid waste by compaction.

BIODEGRADABLE: The process of decomposing quickly as a result of the action of micro-organisms.

BIOSPHERE: The portion of the earth and its atmosphere capable of supporting life.

BLOOM: A proliferation of living algae and/or other acquatic plants on the surface of lakes or ponds.

BOG: Wet, spongy land usually poorly drained, highly acid and rich in plant residue.

BRACKISH WATER: A mixture of fresh and salt water.

CARCINOGENIC: Cancer producing.

CFS: Cubic feet per second of water passing a given point.

CHANNELIZATION: The straightening and deepening of streams to permit water to move faster, to reduce flooding or to drain marshy acreage.

CHLORINATOR: A device for adding chlorine to drinking or waste water.

COASTAL ZONE: Coastal waters and lands that exert influence on the uses of the sea and its ecology.

COLIFORM INDEX: An index of the purity of water based on a count of its coliform bacteria.

COMPOST: Relatively stable decomposed organic material.

DESALINIZATION: Salt removal from sea or brackish water.

DETERGENT: Synthetic washing agent. Most contain large amounts of phosphorus compounds that eutrophy waterways.

DIATOMACEOUS EARTH (DIATOMITE): A fine siliceous material resembling chalk used in waste water treatment plants to filter sewage effluent.

DREDGING: A method for deepening streams, swamps or coastal waters by scraping and removing solids from the bottom. The resulting mud is usually deposited in marshes, disturbing ecological systems.

DUMP: A land site where solid waste is disposed of without protecting the environment.

DYSTROPHIC LAKES: Lakes between eutrophic and swamp stages of aging.

ECOLOGICAL IMPACT: The total effect of an environmental change, either natural or man-made, on the ecology of the area.

ECOLOGY: The interrelationships of living things to one another and to their environment or the study of such interrelationships.

ECOSYSTEM: The interacting system of a biological community and its non-living environment.

EFFLUENT: A discharge of pollutants into the environment, partially or completely treated or in their natural state.

ENVIRONMENT: The sum of all external conditions and influences affecting the life development and the survival of an organism.

ENVIRONMENTAL IMPACT STATEMENT: A document prepared by a Federal Agency required by the National Environmental Policy Act.

EROSION: The wearing away of the land surface by wind or water or by man's land clearing practices.

ESTUARIES: Areas where fresh water meets salt water.

EUTROPHIC LAKES: Shallow, weed-choked lakes, rich in nutrients.

EVAPORATION PONDS: Shallow, artificial ponds where sewage sludge is pumped, dried and removed or buried by more sludge.

FEEDLOT: A small confined land area for raising and fattening beef which also concentrates large amounts of animal waste in a small area.

FILLING: The process of depositing dirt and mud in marshy areas to create more land for real estate development.

GARBAGE GRINDING: Grinding food waste and washing into the sewer.

GREEN BELTS: Certain areas restricted from being used for buildings to serve as buffers between pollution sources and population centers.

GROUND COVER: Grasses or other plants grown to keep soil from eroding.

GROUNDWATER: Freshwater underground in an aquifer or soil that forms the natural reservoir.

GROUNDWATER RUNOFF: Groundwater that is discharged into a stream channel as spring or seepage water.

HABITAT: The sum total of environmental conditions of a specific place that is occupied by an organism, a population or a community.

HARD WATER: Water containing dissolved minerals such as calcium, iron and magnesium; usually unable to lather soap.

HUMUS: Decomposed organic material.

IMPLEMENTATION PLAN: A document of the steps to be taken to ensure attainment of environmental quality standards by a certain deadline.

IMPOUNDMENT: A body of water confined by a dam, dike or barrier.

INCINERATOR: An engineered apparatus used to burn waste substances.

INFILTRATION/INFLOW: Total quantity of water entering a sewer system.

INTERCEPTOR SEWERS: Sewers used to collect the flows from main and trunk sewers and carry them to a central point for treatment and discharge.

LAGOON: In waste water treatment, a shallow pond usually man-made where sunlight, bacterial action and oxygen interact to restore waste water to a reasonable state of purity.

LATERAL SEWERS: Pipes running underneath city streets that collect sewage from homes or businesses.

LEACHING: The process by which soluble materials in the soil, such as nutrients, pesticide chemicals or contaminants, are washed into a lower layer of soil.

LEAD: A heavy metal that may be hazardous to human health if breathed or ingested.

LIFT: In a sanitary landfill, a compacted layer of solid waste.

MARSH: A low-lying tract of soft, wet land that provides an important ecosystem for a variety of plant and animal life.

MGD: Millions of gallons per day. Mgd is commonly used to express rate of flow.

MOBILE SOURCE: A moving source of air pollution such as an automobile.

MULCH: A layer of wood chips, dry leaves, straw, hay, plastic strips or other material placed on the soil around plants to retain moisture, to prevent weeds from growing and to enrich soil.

NOISE: Any undesired audible signal. Thus, in acoustics, noise is any undesired sound.

OPEN BURNING: Uncontrolled burning of wastes in an open dump.

ORGANISM: Any living human, plant or animal.

OUTFALL: The mouth of a sewer, drain or conduit where an effluent is discharged into the receiving waters.

OXIDATION POND: A man-made lake or pond in which organic wastes are reduced by bacterial action. Often oxygen is bubbled through the pond to speed the process.

OZONE (O$_3$): A pungent, colorless, toxic gas. Ozone is one component of photochemical smog and is considered a major air pollutant.

PACKAGE PLANT: A prefabricated or prebuilt waste water treatment plant.

PCBs: Polychlorinated biphenyls, a group of organic compounds used in the manufacture of plastics. In the environment, PCBs exhibit many of the same characteristics as DDT.

PEAT: Partially decomposed organic material.

PERCOLATION: Downward flow of water through rock or soil.

POLLUTION: The presence of matter or energy whose nature, location or quantity produces undesired environmental effects.

PPM: Parts per million.

PRIMARY TREATMENT: The first stage in waste water treatment.

PUMPING STATION: A station at which sewage is pumped to a higher level.

RAW SEWAGE: Untreated domestic or commercial waste water.

RESERVOIR: A pond, lake, tank or basin, natural or man-made.

RIPARIAN RIGHTS: Rights of a landowner to the water on or bordering his property.

RIVER BASIN: The total area drained by a river and its tributaries.

RUBBISH: A general term for solid waste.

RUNOFF: The portion of rainfall, melted snow or irrigation water that flows across ground surface and eventually is returned to streams.

SALINITY: The degree of salt in water.

SALT WATER INTRUSION: The invasion of salt water into fresh water.

SANITARY LANDFILL: A site for solid waste disposal using sanitary landfilling techniques.

SANITARY SEWERS: Sewers that carry only sewage, not storm runoff.

SCRAP: Discarded or rejected materials.

SEEPAGE: Water that flows through the soil.

SEPTIC TANK: An underground tank for deposit of domestic wastes.

SEWAGE: Total of organic waste and water out of domestic-commercial uses.

SILT: Fine particles of soil or rock.

SLUDGE: Solids removed from sewage during waste water treatment.

SOLID WASTE: Useless, unwanted material, not enough liquid to flow.

SOLID WASTE DISPOSAL: Ultimate deposition of waste.

SONIC BOOM: Tremendous boom of a supersonic jet plane exceeding sound.

SPOIL: Dirt or rock removed from original location.

STORM SEWER: Carries only storm runoff, not sewage.

STRIP MINING: Surface mining of minerals.

SUMP: A depression or tank for receiving liquids.

TAILINGS: Waste material derived when raw material is processed.

TERTIARY TREATMENT: Waste water treatment beyond the secondary stage.

THERMAL POLLUTION: Degradation of water quality by the introduction of a heated effluent.

TOPOGRAPHY: The configuration of a surface area including its relief, or relative elevations, and the position of its natural and man-made features.

URBAN RUNOFF: Storm water from city streets and gutters that usually contains a great deal of litter and organic and bacterial wastes.

VARIANCE: Sanction granted by a governing body for delay or exception in the application of a given law, ordinance or regulation.

WASTE WATER: Water carrying wastes from homes, businesses and industries that is a mixture of water and dissolved or suspended solids.

WATER POLLUTION: The addition of sewage, industrial wastes or other harmful or objectionable material to water in concentrations or in sufficient quantities to result in measurable degradation of water quality.

WATER QUALITY CRITERIA: The levels of pollutants that affect the suitability of water for a given use.

WATERSHED: The area drained by a given stream.

WATER SUPPLY SYSTEM: The system for the collection, treatment, storage and distribution of portable water from the sources of supply to the consumer.

WATER TABLE: The upper level of ground water.

WETLANDS: Swamps or marshes, especially as areas preserved for wildlife.

Bibliography

AMERICAN INSTITUTE CORPORATION, "The Appraisal of Real Estate," American Institute, 155 E. Superior St., Chicago, Ill.

AMERICAN NATIONAL STANDARDS INSTITUTE, "Installation of Mobile Homes Including Mobile Home Park Requirements," ANSI A119.3, Mobile Home Manufacturers Association, 14650 Lee Road, Chantilly, Va. Development standards for mobile home parks.

AMERICAN NATIONAL STANDARDS INSTITUTE, "Standard for Mobile Homes," ANSI A119.1, MHMA, Fire and Safety Standards for Mobile Homes.

BABCOCK, Frederick M., "The Valuation of Real Estate," McGraw Hill Book Co., Inc., New York, N.Y., 1932. Classic appraisal book.

BABCOCK, Henry A., "Appraisal Principals and Procedures," Irwin Company, Homewood, Ill., 1968. Pioneered one-approach theory.

BAKER, Geoffrey B. and BRUNO, Funaro, "Motels," Reinhold, New York, N.Y.

BOECKH, Everhard H., "Manual of Appraisals," E. H. Boeckh & Assoc., Chicago, Ill.

"BUILDING CONSTRUCTION COST DATA," Robert Snow Means Co., Buxbury, Mass.

CORNWALL, Richard E., "The Mini-Warehouse," Institute Real Estate Management, 155 E. Superior St., Chicago, Ill.

DANIELS, G., "Solar Homes and Sun Heating," Harper and Row, Inc., New York, N.Y., 1976. Practical solar heating guide.

"BUILDING CONSTRUCTION ESTIMATING," McGraw Hill, New York, N.Y.

351

DILMORE, Gene, "The New Approach to Real Estate Appraising," Prentice-Hall, Inc., Englewood Cliffs, N.J., 1971.

F.W. DODGE CORP., "DOW BUILDING COST CALCULATION AND VALUATION GUIDE," F.W. Dodge Corp., New York, N.Y. Cost handbook.

ELLWOOD, L.W., "Ellwood Tables for Real Estate Appraisal and Financing," L.W. Ellwood, Ridgewood, N.J. Capitalization tables.

FREIDMAN, E.J., "Encyclopedia of Real Estate Appraising, Third edition" Revised and Enlarged. Prentice-Hall, Inc., 1978.

HUBBARD, CHARLES L., "Theory of Valuation," International Textbook Company, Scranton, Pa., 1969.

IAAO, "Real Estate Valuation in Court." Good book on assessors' testimony.

IAAO, "Property Tax Incentives for Preservation of Farmland, Open Space and Historic Sites."

INTERNATIONAL ASSOCIATION OF ASSESSING OFFICERS, "Assessing and the Appraisal Process," IAAO, 1313 E. 60 St., Chicago, Ill. Good book on assessing.

MARSHALL & SWIFT, "Residential Cost Handbook." Residential cost handbook.

"MARSHALL VALUATION SERVICE," Marshall and Swift Publication Company, 1617 Beverly Blvd., L.A., Ca. Cost handbook.

NATIONAL FIRE PROTECTION ASSOCIATION, "Life Safety Code, NFPA No. 101," NFPA, 470 Atlantic Av., Boston, Mass.

RING, Alfred A., "The Valuation of Real Estate," Prentice-Hall, Inc., Englewood Cliffs, N.J., 1970.

ROBINSON, Peter C., "Complete Guide to Appraising Commercial and Industrial Property," Prentice-Hall, Inc., 1977.

ROBINSON, Peter C., "How to Appraise Commercial Properties," Prentice-Hall, Inc., 1971. Specific for commercial property appraisals.

SCHMUTZ, George L. "The Appraisal Process," G.L. Schmutz, Manhattan Beach, Ca., 1959. Basic book on appraisal theory.

SCHMUTZ, George L., "Condemnation Appraisal Handbook," Prentice-Hall, Inc., 1963. Specific for condemnation appraisals.

STEADMAN, P. "Energy, Environment and Building," Cambridge University Press, New York, N.Y., 1976. Environmental impact on building.

TAX REFORM RESEARCH GROUP, "Tax Politics," TRRG, 133 C St., Wash., D.C. Good review of property tax system.

"UNIFORM APPRAISAL STANDARDS FOR FEDERAL LAND ACQUISITION," Stock 5259-0002, Supt. of Documents, Government Printing Office, Wash., D.C. Excellent appraisal booklet on government land acquisition and appraisal.

URBAN LAND INSTITUTE, "Homes Association Handbook, Technical Bulletin No. 50," ULI, 1200 18th St., Washington, D.C. Good handbook on Homes Associations.

U.S. ARMY CORPS OF ENGINEERS, "Real Property Appraisers Handbook," Corps of Engineers, Washington, D.C. Government appraisal manual.

U.S. DEPT. OF AGRICULTURE, "Wood Frame House Construction, Handbook No. 73," USDA, Forest Service, Wash., D.C. Excellent wood frame construction guide.

U.S. DEPT. OF HEALTH, EDUCATION AND WELFARE, "Nursing Home Care," H.E.W., Washington, D.C.

U.S. DEPT. OF HOUSING URBAN DEVELOPMENT, "Underwriting Manual," HUD-FHA, Wash., D.C., FHA Appraisal Underwriting Manual.

U.S. HUD, "FHA Minimum Property Standards for One- and Two-Family Dwellings," HUD, Wash., D.C. Excellent national building code.

U.S. HUD, "Minimum Property Standards for Multifamily Housing," HUD, Wash., D.C. Building Code for multifamily.

U.S. HUD, "Solar Heating and Domestic Hot Water Systems." Code for solar heating and hot water systems.

U.S. HUD, "FHA Techniques of Housing Market Analysis."

U.S. HUD, "Condominiums, Their Development and Management," Excellent review of condominiums.

VETERANS ADMINISTRATION, "Required Exhibits, VA 26A-3," V.A., Washington, D.C.. V.A. requirements for appraisal of proposed construction.

WHYTE, William H., "Cluster Development," American Conservation Association, 30 Rockefeller Plaza, New York, N.Y., 1964.

WINSTEAD, Robert W., "Real Estate Appraisal Desk Book," Prentice-Hall, 1968.

YOUNG, Louis B., "Power Over People," Oxford University Press, New York, N.Y., 1974. Good book on high-voltage power easements.

PERIODICALS AND OTHER SOURCES:

APPRAISAL DIGEST, New York State Society of Real Estate Appraisers, Western Ave. at Fuller Rd., Albany, New York. Quarterly.

ASSESSORS JOURNAL, International Association of Assessing Officers, 1313 E. 60 St., Chicago, Ill. Quarterly articles on assessment problems.

BUSINESS TRENDS IN LODGING INDUSTRY, Laventhal & Horwath, 1845 Walnut St., Phila., Pa.

FAIR HOUSING CIVIL RIGHTS ACT OF 1968, Public Law 90-284, Title VIII, 4-11-68, Supt. of Documents, Wash., D.C. Federal law affecting "redlining."

FINANCING THE HOME, Al.3, Small Homes Council, University of Illinois, Urbana, Ill. Good booklet on financing.

FARM REAL ESTATE MARKET DEVELOPMENTS, CD 81, Economic Research Services, USDA, Monthly. Excellent farm market data publication.

GUIDE TO FANNIE MAY, Federal National Mortgage Association, Washington, D.C. Good guide to FNMA.

GUIDE TO NEW YORK CITY BROWNSTONE NEIGHBORHOODS, Brownstone Revival Committee, 230 Park Av., New York, N.Y.

HOUSE AND HOME, McGraw-Hill, New York, N.Y. Monthly housing publication.

JOURNAL, The American Society of Farm Managers and Rural Appraisers, 470 South Colorado Blvd., Denver, Colo. Annually.

KITCHEN PLANNING STANDARDS, C5.32, Small Homes Council, University of Illinois, Urbana. Excellent criteria for evaluating well-designed kitchens.

MOBILE HOME APPRAISAL GUIDE, Mobile Home Appraisal Company, P.O. Box 428, 1318 Chorro St., San Luis Obispo, Ca.

MOBILE HOME PARK MARKET ANALYSIS AND ECONOMIC FEASIBILITY STUDY, Mobile Home Manufacturers Association, Box 201, Chantilly, Va. Good monograph on mobile home park feasibility.

MOBILE HOMES, MHMA. Annually.

MONOGRAPHS, ASA. Good monographs on various types of appraisals.

MONTHLY ECONOMIC REVIEW, U.S. Dept. of Commerce. Economic trends.

NATIONAL SOLAR HEATING INFORMATION CENTER, P.O. Box 1607, Rockville, Md. Clearing house for solar information.

REDLINING AND APPRAISERS, Valutape No. 37, ASA.

RIGHT OF WAY, American Right of Way Association, L.A., Ca. Bi-monthly.

SALES DATA, SREA Market Data Center, 150 So. Los Robles Av., Pasadena, Ca. Monthly. Single family sales data comparables.

TOWARD A NEW ENVIRONMENT ETHIC, U.S. Environmental Protection Agency, Washington, D.C. Booklet reviewing EPA programs.

THE REAL ESTATE APPRAISER, SREA, Bi-monthly.

THE FEDERAL GIFT TAX, PUBL. 592, Internal Revenue Service, Wash., D.C. IRS booklet on appraisal of gifts.

VALUATION, American Society of Appraisers, Bi-monthly.

VALUATION OF DONATED PROPERTY, PUBL. 61, IRS. On donated property.

VALUTAPES, ASA. Good series of tapes on multi-discipline appraisal problems.

Index

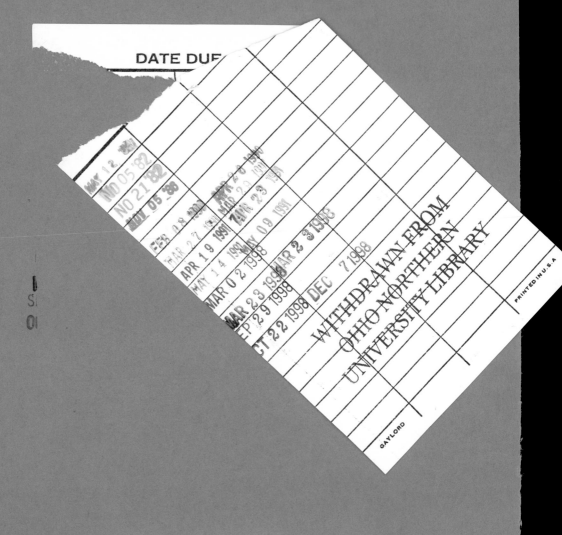